DATE DUE

DEC 0 6 1999		
OCT 0 2 2000		
APR 2 3 2001		
NOV 30 2001		
JAN 2 3 2003		
JUN 2 5 2003		
NOV 1 4 2003		
APR 2 0 2004		
NOV 3 0 2004		
JUL 0 5 2005		

≈　Public Education: An Autopsy

≈ Public Education
An Autopsy

Myron Lieberman

HARVARD UNIVERSITY PRESS
Cambridge, Massachusetts
London, England
1993

Library of Congress Cataloging-in-Publication Data

Lieberman, Myron, 1919–
      Public education : an autopsy / Myron Lieberman.
            p.   cm.
      Includes bibliographical references and index.
      ISBN 0-674-72232-9
      1. Public schools—United States.   2. Education—Economic aspects—United
States.   3. Privatization—United States.   4. Vouchers in education—United States.
5. School, Choice of—United States.   6. School improvement programs—United
States.   I. Title.
LA217.2.L54   1993
371'.01'0973—dc20   92-46732
                                      CIP

For Masayo

≈ Preface

From my first day in the first grade in McKinley Elementary School in St. Paul, Minnesota, I attended public schools exclusively. My experience in them was extremely positive. I admired and respected my teachers and maintained cordial relationships with them after graduation from high school, even after college in some cases. My classmates and teammates are still among my friends, and our school experiences are among our most treasured memories. The fact that I later became a teacher in the St. Paul public schools reflects my optimistic attitude toward public education until the 1980s.

This book would not have been written if I thought that public education could function for most young people today as it did for me more than sixty years ago. I deeply regret that this cannot happen and that public education cannot fulfill the high hopes of so many besides myself: My immigrant parents and the millions like them, so many dedicated public school teachers, principals, and board members, and countless others in all walks of life in every state. I am saddened by the anguish and the sense of loss that will eventually emerge—not necessarily or primarily or even at all from this book but from the inescapable truth of the matter.

The decline of public education does not negate the fact that many individuals associated with it perform invaluable services that deserve our respect and gratitude. My analysis concerns the strengths and deficiencies of educational systems, not of the persons associated with them. Although these things are sometimes related, conclusions about a system are not automatically applicable to the individuals associated with it, or vice versa. I hope that readers will bear this crucial point in mind, as I have tried to do.

≈ Acknowledgments

For about sixteen months, six on a resident basis as a Visiting Scholar, I received the assistance of the Social Philosophy and Policy Center, Bowling Green State University, Bowling Green, Ohio. Not only was the Center's assistance essential, but it was provided in the most pleasant and straightforward way. If this book makes any contribution to educational policy, the Center and its staff deserve the credit for making it possible. I am solely responsible for the content of the book and hope that it justifies the generous assistance provided by the Center.

I would also like to express my appreciation to the following individuals for providing valuable suggestions or assistance on earlier versions of the manuscript:

Joseph Alibrandi, Whittaker Corporation; Reene A. Alley, University of Akron; Joseph Bast, Heartland Institute; David D. Boaz, Cato Institute; Frederick H. Brigham, Jr., National Catholic Education Association; James M. Buchanan, George Mason University; James S. Coleman, University of Chicago; John E. Coons, University of California; Edward Crane, Cato Institute; Anthony Downs, Brookings Institution; Antony Flew, University of Reading; Mike Ford, Excellence Through Choice in Education League (EXCEL); William J. Fowler, Jr., U.S. Department of Education; Gene Geisert, St. John's University; Susan Gonzalez-Baker, University of Arizona; Richard M. Huber, Washington, D.C.; David Imig, American Association of Colleges for Teacher Education; Irene Impellizzeri, New York City Board of Education; Gregg B. Jackson, National Research Council; Henry M. Levin, Stanford University; Stephen Macedo, Harvard

University; John M. McLaughlin, St. Cloud State University; Charles J. O'Malley, Charles O'Malley Associates; Aaron M. Pallas, Michigan State University; Ellen Frankel Paul, Social Philosophy and Policy Center, Bowling Green State University; James L. Payne, Sandpoint, Idaho; Lewis J. Perelman, Washington, D.C.; Glen E. Robinson, Educational Research Service; Alexander T. Smith, University of Tennessee; Martha Turnage, Annapolis, Maryland; Richard E. Wagner, George Mason University; Max Weiner, Fordham University; Amy Stuart Wells, University of California, Los Angeles.

Needless to say, several persons who provided assistance disagree strongly with my views. No one except me has seen the final draft; even persons who expressed agreement with previous drafts or portions of it may disagree with subsequent changes they have not read. To all, and to anyone who may have been inadvertently omitted, I wish to express my deep appreciation for their assistance.

≈ Contents

≈   Public Education: An Autopsy

1
≈ Why an Autopsy?

Like individuals, social institutions die, and their death forces us to face an uncertain future. Sometimes heroic measures can delay the end, and the exact time of death may be an arbitrary or controversial judgment. Regardless, we cannot always wait until rigor mortis sets in to consider what should be done to meet the new situation. Avoidance or denial of the unpleasant reality is often the first problem that has to be addressed.

These thoughts underlie the title of this book. To be sure, an autopsy implies that the subject is dead, and I intend that implication. What has died is the rationale for public education. According to this rationale, public education effectively fosters basic skills, scientific and cultural literacy, civic virtues, and desirable habits and attitudes toward our society and its institutions. When public education does not produce these outcomes, the rationale assumes that "educational reform" will remedy the situation. This rationale is beyond life-sustaining measures. The practical consequences of its demise are not always evident, but they are accumulating and cannot be evaded for very long.

Perhaps the best analogy is to *perestroika*, the effort to restructure the economy and governance of the Soviet Union. Clearly, perestroika is based on the demise of socialism as a political, social, and economic doctrine. Physical and institutional manifestations of socialism survive and will do so for a long time to come. Nevertheless, socialism is a lost cause intellectually. Individuals and interest groups with a stake in its preservation may act as if socialism can be saved by reform, but in fact it is an intellectual relic.

1

Events in the former Soviet bloc illustrate another critical aspect of reform that is fully applicable to public education. Just as the changes required to restructure the Soviet economy upset the distribution of political power, so will the changes required to reform education in the United States: the changes that are needed threaten powerful political and educational interest groups. These groups block fundamental change but realize that they must be perceived as supporting it. Consequently, educational nostrums are a growth industry; attention is focused upon cosmetic changes that pose no threat to the status quo. Choice within public schools, cooperative learning, teacher empowerment, school-based management, parental involvement, peer review, open education, nongraded classrooms, differentiated staffing, higher graduation requirements, textbook reform, career ladders, merit pay, charter schools, and accelerated learning are examples. Some of these changes will make matters worse, some could lead to marginal improvement but only under circumstances that do not prevail, and some are nostrums that can be safely recycled because their past futility has been obscured by the passage of time. None will make a significant difference in the power structure of education, the way education is carried on, or student achievement.

The collapse of socialism in the Soviet Union and Eastern Europe also reflects the worldwide recognition that government provision of goods and services is usually less efficient and less equitable than provision through a market system. As I shall show, the point is as applicable to public education as to housing, transportation, health care, whatever. The point is not widely understood in the United States, precisely because a smaller proportion of goods and services are provided by government here than in many other countries. Where government provides most goods and services, the deficiencies of government provision cannot be concealed. For this reason, it is not widely recognized that the United States has been prosperous and democratic not because of government provision of education but in spite of it.

In terms of the numbers of students and teachers, and of the extent of public funding, public education may function as it does now for several years to come. Nevertheless, despite institutional inertia and the power of vested interests to preserve the status quo, public education as we know it is a lost cause. In the future, our nation will rely less and less on its public schools to foster basic skills, civic virtues, and competencies required for work or advanced education. Claims of school effectiveness will be met with increased skepticism and even outright opposition. The public education establishment will decline both on the producer side (fewer teachers and administrators) and in the loss of consumer support—not always and not necessarily in every situation, but the overall tendency will be in this direction.

Three kinds of factors explain the demise of public education. One kind consists of social and demographic changes that weaken public education regardless of the desirability of the changes. The aging of the population is an example. Nothing the public schools can do will change such developments.

A second set of factors is the policies governing or regulating or implementing public education that contribute to its loss of public support. Policies on certain issues, such as sex education, antagonize important constituencies. The very fact that some issues cannot be resolved without antagonizing important constituencies is a strong reason to question the viability of public education. Other policies avoid immediate social conflict but weaken public education because of their long-range consequences. Policies on student grades that do not require candor about low achievement fall into this category. Although usually adopted without controversy, such policies undermine the long-range credibility of public schools.

The third set of factors consists of the reasons why a market system would be preferable to the existing system of public education. Government-provided education is not going to go away merely because a market system would be more efficient and more equitable. Socially undesirable policies and institutions often endure long after their deficiencies are recognized. Nonetheless, as information about the superiority of a market approach to education becomes more widespread, it will be an important factor in the shift to a market system.

A Market Approach to Education

Technically, a market is a group of buyers and sellers who exchange goods that are highly substitutable. The extent to which one kind of education is substitutable for another (for example religious for nonreligious education) is an important issue to be discussed; at this stage, I wish only to acknowledge its importance.

Economists distinguish market economies from "command economies." In the latter, governments decide what is to be produced, by whom, in what quantities, and according to what schedules. Both theoretical and practical efforts have been made to combine market and command economies; "market socialism" was an effort by some socialist economists to combine them in one economic system. Public school choice can be regarded as an effort to do so with respect to education. As we shall see, its prospects are about as bleak as those of market socialism.

Although the United States and Western European nations are said to have market economies, there are substantial differences among them. For instance, health care is provided through a market system in some, through government in others. Even in the same country, some health services are provided through the market while others are provided by government.

Market structures also differ widely. Strictly speaking, it takes only one buyer and one seller to make up a market. Markets vary according to the number of buyers and sellers, their geographical area, the extent of competition, and in other ways. When I use the term "market system" or "market processes," I am referring to competitive markets. Ideally, such markets have the following characteristics:

1. New suppliers must be able to enter the market to meet increased demand. To the extent that this is not possible because of prohibitive starting costs, statutory prohibitions, predatory pricing, or other obstacles, competition is limited.
2. Capital and labor must flow into and out of production in response to changes in demand. For example, a market system does not exist if teachers can keep their jobs regardless of declining demand for their services.
3. Inefficient producers must become efficient or go out of business.
4. Buyers and sellers must have accurate information about the service.
5. No buyer and no seller must control enough of the market to set prices or quantities.

In the real world, these conditions rarely exist without some qualifications or limitations. The existence of competition and a market system is a matter of degree, not an either-or dichotomy. Even imperfect competition, however, can and often does lead to improved service and lower costs.

Similarly, my references to "the public school monopoly" do not denote a total monopoly without any exceptions; the existence of private schools demonstrates that the current situation should not be characterized in this way. For now, let me put it this way. A phrase or term is needed to characterize the level of competition in the existing situation. Whatever phraseology is used will require modification and qualification to be fully accurate. Among all the possibilities, "public school monopoly" most accurately characterizes a situation that cannot be fully encapsulated in a few words. Many distinguished analysts use the same phrase for the same reason.[1]

A Three-Sector Industry

Let me summarize the educational arrangements that will emerge in place of the present system if my analysis is substantially correct. I believe that public schools, nonprofit private schools, and schools for profit will all have roles to play. (Because home schooling raises so many unique issues, it is not discussed in this book.)

As I shall explain, schools for profit are essential to the existence of a market system of education. Many analysts assume that vouchers and / or tuition tax credits for nonprofit schools will create a market system. This is a major fallacy, accepted in the media as well as in most discussions of educational policy. Because the fallacy is so pervasive, let me lay it to rest at the outset.

Imagine competition between two hospitals. Hospital A is required to accept all patients, no matter how hopeless their condition. Hospital B exercises a right of refusal and does not serve terminally ill patients. Obviously, the death rate in hospital A will be higher than that in hospital B. Understandably, persons aware of the death rates but not aware of the difference in admissions policies may erroneously believe that hospital A is not as good as hospital B. In fact, scholars who study hospital efficiency try to avoid "selection bias." That is, they try to avoid drawing conclusions about hospital efficiency that do not take patient mix into account.

Similarly, private schools can refuse to admit certain students. In addition, private schools can expel students for reasons that are not applicable in public schools. Consequently, private schools may appear to be superior for reasons that have nothing to do with the effectiveness of their teaching. According to the public school establishment, these considerations would give rise to unfair competition if voucher plans included private schools. Thus the proponents of public education argue that private schools should be excluded from voucher plans or be required to compete under the same rules and regulations as public schools.

Other things being equal, the private school right to exclude pupils is a competitive advantage. Its importance varies, but is not necessarily diminished if the distinguishing characteristic of private schools is not superior teaching but superior students. From an educational point of view, better students may be more influential than better teachers. Even if the public schools employed better teachers, parents might be justified in enrolling their children in private schools on educational grounds.

To achieve fair competition, should voucher plans that include private schools require them to admit anyone who applies? Such a requirement would create several problems. If private schools were not prepared to educate a certain type of student, forcing them to do so could lead to prohibitive costs. The good faith of the school would be suspect when students dropped out: the schools would have incentives to discourage instead of encourage the unwanted students. To the extent that private schools were required to enroll unwanted pupils, market principles would be violated, and the benefits of a market system would be correspondingly weakened.

Let us assume, therefore, that subject to civil rights legislation, private schools are not required to enroll unwanted applicants for admission. As private schools view the situation, however, "unfair competition" already exists, but favors the public schools. At present, the latter enjoy an overwhelming competitive advantage: students do not have to pay. Conceivably, this advantage could be eliminated or reduced under a voucher system, depending on the amount of the vouchers and the conditions of eligibility. This brings us to a critical point. Conceptually, we could achieve "fair competition" in one of two ways: (1) by subjecting both public and private schools to the same set of rules, or (2) by offsetting the advantages of one sector by granting other advantages to the competing sector. The question is, What set of advantages and disadvantages would be fair? What rules would govern the competition? If the rules were the ones now applied to public education, their adoption would spell the end of private schools. If the rules were those now applied to private schools, they would bring an end to public education as we know it.

Is some sort of compromise possible? Public school leaders oppose any change that strengthens private education. Thus they oppose educational vouchers that would be redeemable by private schools. Their fallback position is the demand that to be eligible for vouchers private schools be prohibited from teaching religion or excluding any pupils who apply. Such demands are tantamount to requiring private schools give up their reason for existence. Note that one way to equalize the competition would be to offset the financial advantage of public schools by providing more financial assistance to parents seeking a private school education for their children. This is anathema to the public school establishment for two reasons. First, the establishment opposes any erosion of its competitive advantage. Second, this solution illustrates the possibility of fair competition that accepts the differences between public and private schools. The public schools have been very successful in avoiding debate on the amount of a voucher, which is an issue on which private schools are willing to negotiate. Instead, the debate has focused on whether private schools are willing to give up the characteristics that lead many parents to prefer them in the first place.

At present, the financial advantages of public education overshadow its disadvantages vis-à-vis private schools. If more financial assistance is provided to parents who prefer private schools, the competitive advantage of public education will decline. Where on the continuum should we set the level of financial assistance to those who prefer a private school? Will it be high enough to achieve fair competition? How will we know whether it is fair? Private schools assert that the current level of assistance is unfair to parents who prefer private schooling. Any increase would be unfair according to the public school establishment. In practice, the parties accept political compromises that do not change their underlying views about what is fair. Stability is unlikely, since the contending forces are constantly seeking to change the rules in their own favor. Even with their overwhelming financial advantage, the public school forces constantly try to impose additional regulatory and financial burdens on private schools.

Note how this situation differs from competition within the for-profit sector. In that sector, the rules of competition are ideally the same for all competitors. The companies that want the rules changed in their own favor (by tax breaks, tariffs, government subsidies, regulations on their competition, and so on) are viewed as special pleaders, which they usually are. The burden of proof is on the companies or industries seeking to change the rules in their own favor. Dozens of automobile companies that could not sell enough cars have gone out of business. When the federal government helped Chrysler Corporation stay in business in 1978, there was much concern over the deviation from the rule that if you can't supply profitably you must eventually go out of business.

Competition between public and private schools is very different. Public schools operate under one set of rules, private schools under another. In this situation, losing market share is not a result of failure to compete effectively under a common set of rules; the rules themselves determine the outcome. Although public and private schools are subject to some common rules, such as compliance with fire and safety regulations, the differences are critical.

Public and private schools do compete to some degree, but the competition bears little resemblance to competition in a market system. For instance, automobile manufacturers compete by constantly offering improvements: increased fuel efficiency, better warranties, greater safety, more comfortable interiors, easier handling, lower price, and so on. The less successful carmakers incorporate the features of the more successful ones as soon as possible. There is constant monitoring of competing companies and of consumer preferences. None of these things applies to competition between public and private schools. Parents seldom choose public or private schools on the basis of innovations or improvements in the services. They choose between relatively static systems whose services are not changed by loss of market share. The reasons why parents enroll their children in public or private schools are much the same as they were decades or generations ago. Enabling more parents to choose private nonprofit schools may be a good thing, but it does not lead to improvements in either sector. The children who transfer from one sector to the other may be better off, but the sectors do not react to their losses in market share as would a company selling a service for profit.

To summarize, there is no commonly agreed upon criterion or principle that tells us when competition between public and private schools is fair. The sector that holds the advantage characterizes the rules as fair. Politicians satisfied with existing arrangements say they are fair; politicians who seek to change them assert that the rules are unfair. Fairness is assessed in terms of who wins the competition, not in terms of the rules under which the competition takes place.

Second, the concept of fair competition between the sectors is largely a controversy between public and nonprofit producers. Neither has shown any interest in fairness toward schools for profit, even though such schools are more disadvantaged by the rules than nonprofit schools. Because public policies are so disadvantageous to them, schools for profit constitute only a minuscule proportion of K–12 schools, and they have been a negligible factor in the politics of education. The argument of this book, however, is that we cannot obtain the benefits of competition if the competition is limited to public and nonprofit schools. I shall also argue that the rules that limit or prohibit schools for profit exist for the benefit of public and nonprofit producers, not for the benefit of educational consumers. Enhancement of the ability of schools for profit to compete is essential but will be very difficult to achieve; the necessary changes will probably face opposition from nonprofit as well as public schools.

If the rules allow all three sectors to compete, several factors will affect the sectoral mix. Sparsely settled areas may be able to support schools in only two or even one sector. Where there is a large population that supports religious schools, the nonprofit sector will be correspondingly larger.

Total enrollment in nonprofit schools may increase in the short run, but these schools will also lose some students to schools for profit. They may or may not gain more students from the public schools than they lose to schools for profit. For reasons to be discussed, schools for profit may eventually make heavy inroads into the market shares of both public and nonprofit private schools. As long as the rules do not exclude or unreasonably restrict any sector, its absence in a given geographical area need not concern us; however, requests to prop up an inefficient sector may be difficult to distinguish from legitimate claims that the sector is being unreasonably restricted vis-à-vis the other sectors.

Despite my emphasis on a three-sector industry, I shall not try to predict market shares or market structures. One reason is that the desirability of a market approach cannot be fully appreciated apart from a clear understanding of the *inherent* difficulties of public education. I stress "inherent" because the widespread failure to understand this point underlies the futile efforts to reform the existing system. Thousands of publications discuss the weaknesses of public education; what distinguishes this book is the effort to show why certain basic weaknesses cannot be remedied within the framework of public and nonprofit education.

Furthermore, it is much too early to predict the market structure of a three-sector industry. As increased reliance on market processes develops, there will be a period of trial and error before the dominant modes emerge—and even then, there can be no guarantee that particular modes will remain dominant indefinitely. For this reason, arguments for a market system of education should not be based on any particular market structure. A market approach might lead to franchised schools that leave relatively little discretion at the school level. It might also lead to freestanding schools in which all decisions are made at the school level. Furthermore, new technologies may lead to drastically different market opportunities and market structures at any time. In short, one can confidently predict the advent of a market approach even though the specific ways to implement it are not clear.

From a public policy standpoint, the existence of schools for profit is not as important as the absence of unreasonable obstacles to their existence: the mere possibility that schools for profit could emerge would have some salutary effects on public schools. In any case, if schools for profit do not face unreasonable barriers to entry, they will appear in the market within a short period of time. Even under the unfavorable conditions that now exist, several companies are exploring ways to provide K–12 educational services for profit.[2] Without question, more companies will do so when the statutory environment becomes more hospitable.

The term "market system of education" can also be applied to situations in which school boards are intermediate consumers instead of producers of educational services. For example, instead of hiring teachers as employees, school districts might employ instructional companies to provide educational services. That is, instead of "making" education with their own employees, school districts might buy educational services from independent contractors.[3] This would constitute increased reliance on market processes. My concern here, however, is on the consumer role of families, not of school boards as buyers of goods and services used in producing education.

Educational Vouchers

Educational vouchers (sometimes labeled "scholarships") are widely advocated as a way to give families more educational options. A massive body of literature on voucher plans already exists, and its bearing on this book should be clarified.

Voters support voucher plans for various reasons, some of which are not consistent, or might not be in practice. For instance, one argument offered for vouchers is that they are necessary to protect religious freedom. The rationale is that if education is compulsory, and if the public school curriculum is antireligious, parents who cannot afford private schools are being forced to educate their children in an antireligious environment. At the same time, many supporters argue that vouchers are the most efficient way to provide educational services. Theoretically, however, a voucher system that protected religious freedom might be less efficient economically and educationally than the system we have now. If that should be the case, we would be forced to choose between religious freedom on the one hand and economic and educational efficiency on the other.

Some voucher supporters simply assume that a voucher system that included private schools would be a competitive market system. Others are aghast at the idea that education should be a commercial service, subject to market forces. We might draw an analogy here between education and sex. Many people oppose allowing sex to be treated as a commercial service. As a matter of fact, one prominent critic of a voucher initiative has explicitly equated it with prostitution.[4]

The assumption that a voucher plan that includes private schools is ipso facto a competitive market plan is a fallacy that has confused both proponents and opponents of vouchers. The Milwaukee voucher plan, which has been widely praised (and condemned) for applying market principles to education, illustrates this widespread confusion.

The Wisconsin legislature enacted the Milwaukee plan in March 1989. Political, legal, and administrative opposition delayed implementation until September 1990; this opposition continues, although it has been unsuccessful in blocking the plan entirely. As finally implemented, the legislation includes the following provisions:

1. Participation in the voucher plan is restricted to one percent of the enrollment in the Milwaukee public schools. Accordingly, maximum potential participation in 1990–91 was 936 pupils in grades K–12.
2. Pupils who participate must be from families whose income does not exceed 175 percent of the poverty level.
3. Voucher students must not exceed 49 percent of the students in any school that accepts voucher students.

4. Schools for profit and schools affiliated with religious denominations are ineligible to participate.
5. Voucher schools must accept all voucher-carrying students as long as space is available.
6. If voucher students exceed the spaces available, applicants must be selected by lot.
7. The Milwaukee school district is required to provide transportation as it would for public school students.
8. The amount of the voucher was set at 53 percent of the average amount spent per pupil in the Milwaukee public schools in 1990–91 (approximately $2,500).
9. Participating schools do not receive additional funds for learning-disabled or emotionally disturbed pupils, as do the public schools.
10. Schools that redeem vouchers cannot charge students more than the amount of the voucher.

In the following ways, these limitations preclude the emergence of a competitive market in education:

1. The scale is too small to justify investment in new facilities or in R&D. In addition, the small scale renders it impossible to achieve economies of scale in employment, purchasing, promotion, and other basic operations. The critical point is that the absence of any economies of scale is inherent in the basic structure of the plan.
2. The requirement that voucher students not exceed 49 percent of the enrollment in a participating school precludes expansion above a minimum level. New schools can't be established primarily to serve voucher students, and the capacity of existing schools to serve them is severely restricted.
3. Since schools for profit are excluded, educational entrepreneurs have no incentive to participate. This restriction alone would disqualify the plan as a test of a competitive market system of education.
4. The fact that schools cannot charge voucher students more than the voucher is a major deficiency. Even if the schools and the parents agree that certain changes are worth the additional charges, the changes cannot be made. The automobile industry would hardly be competitive if manufacturers

could not add improvements, no matter how much customers were willing to pay for them.

5. Because the number of voucher-redeeming pupils cannot exceed one percent of public school enrollments, the public schools need not be concerned about competition from voucher-redeeming schools. Not surprisingly, there is no evidence that the Milwaukee public schools have changed since the voucher plan became operative. Paradoxically, the major effect of the plan may have been to divert attention away from the need for fundamental improvement in the Milwaukee public schools.

In addition to the antimarket provisions in the plan itself, the uncertainties regarding its continuation adversely affect its usefulness as a test of a market system of education. For example, it is more difficult to recruit and keep good teachers when their funding may be discontinued by the legislature at any time. Needless to say, critics allege that poor teaching is the inevitable result of a market system rather than a result of the uncertainties regarding continuation of the Milwaukee plan. In any case, the plan does not and cannot result in meaningful competition, except in the conservative editorials endorsing it for applying market principles to education.

Let me emphasize that I am not opposed to the Milwaukee plan. What I am opposed to is the idea that it constitutes a test of a market system of education. The Milwaukee plan is likely to turn out poorly precisely because it is *not* a competitive market system of education. If, however, it is characterized as one, its negative outcomes will be cited as evidence that market approaches are not effective. Because virtually all of the voucher proposals in recent years are subject to this criticism, I will not discuss them here in detail. Regardless of their merits on other grounds, they cannot be considered valid experiments with a competitive market system of education.

In this book I assume that government will continue to support K–12 education, at least for a considerable period of time. Nevertheless, government does not necessarily have to provide the services that it funds; food stamps and Medicare illustrate this point. To illustrate how a market system might function, I shall assume a system of educational vouchers redeemable by schools for profit as well as nonprofit schools. Nevertheless, my objective in this book is not to propose or promote a voucher plan. Instead, it is to use such a plan to contrast public education with a competitive market system of education. A system of tax credits or a combination of tax credits and vouchers might also be used for this purpose and may well be the most feasible way to implement a market system in certain situations.[5]

Regardless of how a market system can best be achieved, certain issues to be discussed will be relevant. Why are the major deficiencies of public education inherent in government operation of schools? Why is it impossible to solve these problems by means of private but nonprofit schools? Why is the futility of efforts to improve public education becoming more evident? How would a market system address these issues? Why have recent efforts to achieve a market system failed, and how might such efforts be more successful in the future? These are some of the issues addressed in this book. Despite the absence of a timetable, my intention is to set forth an educational reform agenda that will be immediately helpful.

A Historical Note

Contemporary rhetoric asserts that public education is essential to democratic representative government and economic growth. The reality, however, is that public education was a result, not a cause, of these things. In both Great Britain and the United States, a democratic system of government was firmly established long before public education was widely adopted. In both countries, massive economic growth preceded public education. Great Britain experienced its most impressive economic growth in the late eighteenth and early nineteenth centuries despite the absence of government-supported education; compulsory education to age 11 was not established there until 1893. Indeed, in the early nineteenth century the fear was that literacy was spreading too rapidly, and until 1833 the British government tried to limit it.[6] Similarly, in the United States, public schools did not emerge on a large scale until the mid-1800s, and then only at lower grade levels. The United States experienced huge economic growth while public education was nonexistent or very limited. Education as a three-sector industry would be a basic change from a two-sector industry overwhelmingly dominated by public schools, but it would not be an unprecedented development in American education. On the contrary, education was a three-sector industry for much of the nineteenth century: schools for profit as well as denominational schools served large segments of the population until the advent of widespread public education.[7]

What changed the situation? If a three-sector industry is a good idea, why was it abandoned in the nineteenth century? Basically, the reason was that religious schools and schools for profit could no longer compete with "free public education." The conditions of competition across sectors became overwhelmingly stacked in favor of public education. Still, this explanation seems only to beg the question: Why did the American people decide to stack the competition in its favor?

During the early 1800s every state provided assistance to private schools, including denominational schools.[8] By the mid-1800s most white children, including those from the lower and middle classes, received an elementary education. This was true even though parents were expected to share some of the costs from their own pockets. It appears also that schools for profit were fairly common and that their legitimacy was not seriously challenged.

What changed this situation was the influx of Catholic immigrants in the 1840s. The number of Catholic residents in the United States tripled as more than 700,000 Catholic immigrants entered the country during this decade.[9] States that had provided aid to Protestant denominational schools on a nonpreferential basis balked at providing such aid to Catholic schools. Their solution was to discontinue nonpreferential aid to private schools and to establish public schools with a pronounced Protestant bias.

In short, public education was not established in response to the failure of private schools, including schools for profit, to meet educational needs. On the contrary, public education resulted primarily from Protestant dissatisfaction with nonpreferential assistance to Catholic schools. Its raison d'être was religious prejudice, not the need to educate all children.[10]

Of course, the shift to public education was not always justified publicly by explicit assertions of anti-Catholic bias. Furthermore, once public education was firmly established, the initial rationale for it disappeared from public and even professional awareness. This is a very common sequence of events. For example, the Army Post Exchange (PX) system was established in the early 1800s to serve army officers in isolated frontier outposts. Today retail sales in the PX system are in the billions annually, and PXs are located in such isolated frontier outposts as San Francisco, Honolulu, and New York City. Few, if any, of their customers are aware of the initial reason for establishing the PX system.

And so it is with the way most people think about public education. Insofar as they think about its origins at all, they tend to do so in terms of a comment by Jefferson: "If a nation expects to be ignorant and free, in a state of civilization, it expects what never was and never will be." Professional educators and political leaders frequently cite this sentence as the rationale for public education. The citation is a gross historical error. Jefferson wrote the sentence at a time when the vast majority of young people either did not attend school at all or did so for only a few primary grades and for a few months of the year. The notion that our founding fathers viewed public education as the way to educate citizens about the great issues of the day is preposterous.

These observations do not justify a market system of education. Their purpose is simply to emphasize that the contemporary rationale for public education had little to do with its beginnings. I do not advocate a market system on the grounds that it preceded public education in the United States; I seek only to dispel the notion that it would be an unprecedented deviation from our educational history and traditions.

2

≈ The Future Context of Public Education

In the future, public education in the United States will face an increasingly hostile environment. Its demographic and cultural foundations are being undermined by developments over which it has no control and very little influence. Educational reforms that fail to take these developments into account are tantamount to rearranging the deck chairs on the Titanic as the ship goes down.

Low Birth Rates

Let us first consider how changing birth rates will affect public education. As Table 2.1 shows, birth rates in the U.S. have fallen since 1960. The decline has been precipitous, so much so that "the birth dearth" has become a topic of public debate.[1] Birth rates are expected to continue to decline slightly in the 1990s.

Generally speaking, the birth rate required to maintain a stable population is 2.1 births per woman of childbearing age. It is slightly larger than 2.0 because not all children live long enough to have children of their own, and because the ratio of male to female babies is about 1.05 to 1.0. Thus in Table 2.1, which gives births per 1,000 women, a birth rate of 2,100 would result in a stable population, exclusive of immigration and other factors that affect the size of the total population. The U.S. birth rate has been lower than this since 1972. Although immigrants are disproportionally of reproductive age and tend to have larger families than the resident population, immigration is not likely to offset the impact of lower birth rates on public education.

17

Table 2.1. U.S. total fertility rates by race, 1960–2010 (rates per 1,000 women)

Year	Total	White	Black	Other races
Estimates:				
1960	3,606	3,510	4,238[a]	—
1970	2,432	2,338	2,949	—
1980	1,849	1,754	2,211	—
Projections:				
1990	1,850	1,781	2,170	2,175
2000	1,846	1,780	2,095	2,110
2010	1,849	1,791	2,040	2,059

a. Black and other races.

Source: National Center for Health Statistics, *Vital Statistics of the United States, 1985,* vol. 1, *Natality* (1988); tables A-4 to A-6; and unpublished data, Bureau of the Census, U.S. Department of Commerce.

The major impact of birth rates on public schools is on the number of children enrolled in them. In absolute terms, the numbers are remarkably stable: enrollments in the year 2000 are predicted to be very close to the number in 1975. Notwithstanding, the proportion of school-age children in the total population will drop considerably. Children aged 5–17 made up 24.4 percent of the population in 1975 but only 20.4 percent in 1988, and the percentage is expected to drop to about 16.2 by 2010.[2]

The present and anticipated age composition of the U.S. population reflects a demographic change of startling proportions. In 1790 there were 780 adults for each 1,000 persons under age 16. By 1900 there were 1,580 adults for each 1,000 persons under 16. Today there are about three times as many persons over as under 16. The change is due mainly to declining birth rates and increased longevity. As we shall see, the decline in the proportion of children is accompanied by a weakening of their ties to adults.

A declining proportion of school-age children in the population affects education in several ways. Fewer children require fewer teachers, and fewer teachers have less political influence. When there are fewer children, fewer parents are activists for public education. Declining birth rates also weaken the economic prospects and political influence of companies that sell in the education market.

The declining proportion of school-age children is only part of the negative demographic outlook for public education. The decline in birth rates is not uniform throughout the population. Birth rates among the lower socioeconomic groups have remained relatively stable. At the same time, birth rates among middle-class women, especially among the kind of upper-middle-class women who have led efforts to improve public education, have dropped substantially. Indeed, the most precipitous decline has been among Jewish women.[3] Inasmuch as Jewish families in the United States tend to be strong supporters of public education, the decline in the Jewish population weakens one of its major constituencies.

Within the Jewish population the birth rate varies widely by religious affiliation. Steep declines have taken place among reform and conservative but not orthodox Jews. This too is bad news for public education: orthodox Jews are strong supporters of private schools. Although orthodox Jews make up only about 4.8 percent of the total Jewish population, they enrolled over 99,000 children in their denominational schools in 1988–89; whereas fewer than 16,000 were enrolled in conservative and reform denominational schools.[4]

Similarly, among Protestants, the birth rates are highest among the evangelical denominations that are most likely to enroll their children in private schools. Evangelical Protestants are responsible for remarkable increases in denominational schools in recent years. Their denominational school enrollments increased from 110,000 in 1965–66 to 985,000 in 1988–89. For the most part, these enrollments were from families who would previously have been supporters of public schools. During the same time, enrollments in nondenominational private schools increased from 199,000 to 915,000.[5] This tremendous increase suggests the growing importance of nonreligious reasons for sending children to private schools. When 80 to 90 percent of private school enrollments were in Catholic schools, aid to parents seeking assistance for private schooling was perceived as a Catholic issue. The perception is bound to change as more non-Catholics seek assistance for private schooling.

As private school enrollments climb, the proportions of the public school population from middle- and upper-class families are dwindling and the proportion from low-income families is increasing. The adults in low-income families are less active politically and have less influence than their numbers alone would suggest.

The effects of low birth rates on higher education also have an impact on the public schools. As the pool of college-bound students decreases, colleges will resort to earlier admission to make up for the shortfall.

Some states have recently allowed high school students to enroll in higher education courses, with a pro rata share of state aid going to the institutions of higher education.[6] This option makes good sense, and more states are likely to adopt it. One result, however, will be to reduce high school enrollments. In general, the better students are most likely to take advantage of this option, thereby lowering high school enrollments qualitatively as well as quantitatively.

Low birth rates also generate pressures from private business to reduce the time devoted to formal schooling. Private business is already experiencing a shortage of teenage workers and is likely to support lowering the age of compulsory education and of entry into the labor market.[7] With both higher education and business seeking to shorten the time spent in school, the public education lobby will be hard-pressed to maintain the status quo in this regard. In addition, if organizations representing blacks and Hispanics conclude (as have many economists) that their constituents are hurt by minimum wage laws, high age levels for school leaving, and restrictions on early entry into the labor force, public school enrollments could drop significantly within a short period of time.[8] During the 1980s states showed more interest in raising than in lowering the school-leaving age, but lowering it is more likely in the future.

The discussion so far has assumed that U.S. birth rates will not rise for a long time to come. Although birth rates have fluctuated widely over time, it appears they are more likely to drop even further in the near future than to rise. As a result of more effective contraceptive measures, birth rates have been declining in all industrialized nations, often even more than in the United States. For example, West Germany before reunification had a birth rate of only 1.3 children per woman—a rate that would reduce its population by almost 17 percent by the year 2000.[9] According to a recent United Nations report, the 1989 Japanese birth rate was 10.2 babies per 1,000 population, 3.1 percent lower than the U.S. rate and far below the rate required to maintain population stability.[10] Births are not always wanted, hence more effective contraceptive measures will tend to reduce future birth rates.

This tendency is not likely to be fully offset by decreases in infant mortality and/or more effective measures to reduce infertility. U.S. infant mortality can be reduced, but the reductions cannot increase the overall size of the population very much. Although as many as one million persons are being treated for infertility, the birth dearth is not due to inability to have children but to deliberate decisions not to have them. In fact, legal and regulatory obstacles have blocked the utilization of the most effective contraceptive technologies in the United States. In any case, birth rates are not likely to rise very much, if at all.

The Aging of the Population

While the proportion of school-age children in the total population is declining, the proportion of senior citizens is increasing. As shown in Table 2.2, the increase will continue to be rapid in the 1990s and beyond. The educational significance of this trend depends on the political objectives and degree of political unity among senior citizens.

Except on a few issues, the elderly do not think and vote differently from the rest of the population.[11] After all, older people are influenced by their values, life experiences, religious organizations, unions, ethnicity, income, geographical location, and other factors that affect political attitudes and behavior. Consequently, on most issues their views do not differ very much from those of the American people as a whole.

Understandably, health care for the elderly is one of the few issues on which senior citizens show much greater cohesion than the rest of the population. Another is public education: they are less willing than younger citizens to support it financially. For instance, in 1984, when the American National Election Studies unit at the University of Michigan asked for reactions to federal spending on public education, social security, Medicare, science, the environment, crime, national defense, jobs, blacks, and food stamps, education was the only area in which replies

Table 2.2.   Percentage of senior citizens in the total population, 1960–2010

Year	Age group		
	45–64	65+	45+
1960	20.0%	9.2%	29.2%
1970	20.4	9.8	30.2
1980	19.6	11.3	30.9
1990	18.8	12.6	31.4
2000	22.9	13.0	35.9
2010	27.9	14.0	41.9

Source: Bureau of the Census, U.S. Department of Commerce, *Statistical Abstract of the United States, 1990* (Washington: Government Printing Office, 1990), p. 13.

showed substantial age differences. Whereas 94 percent of those aged 18–35 and 49 percent of those 36–64 supported increased spending for public education, only 43 percent of those 65 and over did so. Other polling data as well as anecdotal evidence also support the conclusion that the elderly are much less inclined than the public at large to support public education.[12]

At least one reason for this lack of support will be very difficult to overcome. Older people are less likely to benefit from increased spending for public schools. The 85-year-old senior citizen with a life expectancy of six years is not likely to benefit from spending for education. Of course, the elderly are not motivated solely by their own economic welfare. It would, however, be as unrealistic to ignore self-interest as to regard it as the sole influence on voting patterns.

The increase in the proportion of senior citizens in the population will affect every aspect of education; in particular, it will affect funding for public education, for the following reasons:

1. Expenditures for the elderly are much greater than those for school-age children. Richard D. Lamm, a former governor of Colorado, is one of the handful of political leaders (mostly ex-leaders!) who have discussed the situation candidly. In 1990 Lamm pointed out that 1987 federal expenditures were about $10,000 per senior citizen, $854 per child. Altogether, 60 percent of federal social spending went to citizens over 65, who made up only 12 percent of the population. The federal government pays for health costs for millionaires (such as heart transplants) while 20 percent of the nation's children do not receive vaccinations.[13] Elaborating on this point would only belabor the obvious. As the number and proportion of senior citizens increase, government expenditures for their welfare, especially for health benefits, exert tremendous pressure on spending for other public services. The 40 percent of state and local spending that is allocated to public education is likely to be reduced by spending for senior citizens.
2. Working people already spend more to take care of their parents than they spend to take care of their children. This generates pressure for government assistance to the elderly, especially since all adults expect to be the beneficiaries of such assistance eventually.
3. Senior citizens and their organizations will not want to

oppose expenditures for public education simply on the grounds that such expenditures compete with those for senior citizen welfare. Instead, they will seek public interest reasons to justify their opposition. The result will be a political environment more critical of public education than any it has faced in the past.

4. The aging of the population will also have several indirect effects that will not favor public education. In higher education, the resources devoted to the elderly will undoubtedly continue to increase. The funds devoted to other fields, such as health care and social work, will increasingly be oriented to older people, not to young children. An economics professor can shift easily from the economics of raising children to the economics of supporting parents (and grandparents); professors of child development or of elementary school teaching methods cannot shift their professional focus so easily.

Another way in which the aging of the population will weaken public education is through the severe financial pressure it will exert on the social security system. This financial pressure will lead to the adoption of policies that will shorten the duration of compulsory education. To fully appreciate this, it is essential to reject the popular but erroneous view that recipients of social security benefits are merely getting back what they have paid in over the years. In fact whatever "earnings" exist are psychological, not legal or financial. Essentially, social security taxes pay for the benefits of current recipients. The expectation is that when the current taxpayers are eligible for social security, their benefits will be paid from taxes paid by taxpayers at that time. In other words, the social security system does not function as a savings institution, in which one invests personal funds and receives back the investment plus any returns on it. Instead, the system depends on the ability of taxpayers to cover the costs for current beneficiaries.

Table 2.3 shows the drastic changes, actual and anticipated, in the ratio of social security contributors to beneficiaries. In 1950, social security taxpayers outnumbered beneficiaries by 16 to 1; in 1990, by only 3 to 1. Also, since the life expectancy of beneficiaries was less when the social security system was devised than it is today, the anticipated payouts were substantially underestimated. Recipients who live until age 85 take much more out of the system than those who live only to age 70.

Clearly, the aging of the population poses major financial problems

Table 2.3.   Ratio of social security contributors to social security beneficiaries, 1950–2010

Year	Ratio
1950	16.5 : 1
1960	5.1 : 1
1970	3.7 : 1
1980	3.2 : 1
1990	3.4 : 1
2000	3.2 : 1
2010	2.9 : 1

Source: Letter to author from Social Security Administration, Department of Health and Human Services, August 13, 1992.

for the social security system. Instead of a large number of taxpayers supporting a relatively small number of beneficiaries, a much smaller proportion of taxpayers has to support a much larger and more expensive group of beneficiaries. Political leaders are understandably reluctant to reduce the benefits; the elderly make up a large, politically potent constituency that believes that it has "earned" its benefits and that would be outraged by their diminution.

If benefits are not reduced, social security revenues must be increased to cover the increasingly unfavorable ratios of taxpayers to beneficiaries, the longer payout periods, and the huge medical costs associated with old age. Unfortunately, social security taxes are characterized by the most undesirable features a tax can have: they are already high, they are visible, and they are extremely regressive. Minor changes aside, the solutions on the revenue side are limited to adding new contributors and increasing the period of time during which contributions are made. In other words, if large numbers of persons began full-time employment at age 14 or 16 instead of 18, their additional contributions would help to maintain the solvency of the system.

We can, therefore, anticipate strong pressures to lower the age at which students are allowed to leave school. These pressures will lead to intense scrutiny of the efforts to persuade high school students to stay in school to earn a high school diploma. It will become more evident that such efforts are based on the interests of producers of education, not on the interests of the students. As the producer interests prevail, we unnecessarily delay entry into both the labor force and higher education; this is a view that will gain support from the pressures on the social security system that lie ahead.[14]

All in all, it seems unlikely that the elderly will ever become strong supporter of K–12 education. Again, I do not contend that senior citizens base their actions solely on cold-blooded calculations of their own economic self-interest. Nevertheless, the fact that many older people cannot benefit from the alleged long-range benefits of K–12 education means that they have less reason to support spending for it. As their numbers increase, this lack of support, along with other direct and indirect effects of the aging of the population, is certain to weaken public education.

The Decline in Children's Social Capital

As important as it is, the growing imbalance between children and senior citizens will not be the most harmful development affecting children in the 1990s. That dubious distinction will go to the continuing decline in children's social capital.[15] Social capital consists of the social relationships that foster children's growth and development. It can be contrasted with physical capital, such as tools and equipment and facilities used to produce goods or services. It also differs from human capital, that is, the skills, knowledge, habits, and attitudes of individuals. Frequently, social capital is a means whereby one person's human capital is made available to others.

Children are not the only beneficiaries of social capital. On the contrary, any age group may benefit from it, or may suffer from its absence. Our concern here, however, is primarily with the social capital available to children. On this issue, the major trends can be summarized as follows:

1. *The avoidance of parental responsibility by biological fathers and the increase in the number and proportion of single-parent families headed by women.* In 1987 approximately 9.4 million women were living with children under 21 whose father was absent. In about 53.3 percent of these families, the father did not contribute any support. In 12.8 percent, the mother received only partial payment of court-ordered child support.[16] Partly as the result of improved contraceptive technology and of the feminist and abortion rights movements, decisions on whether to bear children are increasingly viewed as solely the woman's prerogative. In this situation men are less likely to accept responsibility for their children. Even if efforts to require biological fathers to contribute to child support are successful—and it does not appear that they will be—they will not add to children's social capital, since social capital depends on social, not economic factors.

2. *The increase in the number and proportion of mothers who work outside the household and delegate child care to others.* With the industrial revolution, men left the home to work for wages. Today, women are leaving also, and the trend in this direction is still on the rise. The employment rate for married women with husband present and children under age 6 rose from 11.9 percent in 1950 to 58.9 percent in 1990; the rate for those with children aged 6–17 increased from 28.3 percent in 1950 to 73.6 percent in 1990.[17]

As the birth rate drops, being a homemaker is less and less of a full-time job, and more women seek long-range security in careers outside the home. When men left the home to go to work, women remained to provide care and build social capital. As women also leave to work outside the home, it becomes more difficult to provide children with social capital.[18]

3. *The weakening of ties between children and parents who are living together.* This weakening is partly due to changes in our economic system and partly to other causes, but the economic factors seem paramount.

When the United States was predominantly an agrarian society, children were usually an economic asset—milking cows, taking animals to and from pasture, sowing and harvesting crops, and so on. At a very early age, children were productive members of the family, and they accepted the responsibilities, habits, and attitudes associated with that role. Eventually agricultural employment declined in importance and children began to be employed in factories. In the earlier stages of the industrial revolution, children continued to be economic assets. Even at low wages, they could earn more than their costs to the family, at least in the short run.

Since the enactment of compulsory education and restrictions on child labor, the income-producing role of children has largely disappeared. Entrance into the labor market is delayed, often until after higher education. In brief, the economic value of children to their parents has declined; today, especially in urban areas, children constitute a net cost instead of an income-producing asset. The major exceptions are children of parents at the lowest income levels: government payments for their welfare constitute a major source of parental as well as child support. Above this level, however, children are usually an economic liability. Using 1989 data, the U.S. Department of Agriculture has estimated the cost of raising a child from birth to age 18 in a Midwestern urban area to be $105,000.[19]

Because emphasis on long-range considerations was inherent in the agrarian environment, children learned to accept a long-range point of view as a matter of course. This changed when children grew up in cities with no productive responsibilities until after graduation from high school or college. Children are expected to attend school for twelve years at least, and to benefit from such attendance many years after leaving school. Inasmuch as they frequently lack the experience that teaches the importance of long-range considerations, the absence of strong incentives to study is not surprising. Instead, children are supposed to be free to find themselves—a process that often ends up as prolonged childhood and adolescence without focus or important responsibility.

Of course, many teenagers are employed, often in part-time or seasonal employment. For the most part, however, their participation in the labor force is based on a desire for discretionary funds. The teenage consumer market is a large one but is oriented largely to immediate consumption: snack foods, automobile expenses, rock concerts, and other items of this nature. Employment for such needs is not likely to foster the same levels of maturity and discipline that are associated with full-time employment to meet basic human needs.

4. *The decline in the economic interdependence of children and parents.* In the past, families served important welfare functions, such as care of the very young and the elderly. Today, however, social security and public and private pension plans provide income security for more and more parents. As a result, parents have less incentive to invest in the productivity of their children. Other things being equal, fewer children should result in larger expenditures per child, but this does not appear to be happening.

Parents not only have less incentive to invest in their children's productivity; they have fewer means at their disposal to enforce their priorities. This is illustrated by the declining importance of inheritance. In earlier times, many persons received significant amounts of income from this source. Parents today are more likely to invest in pensions and annuities that terminate when the parents die. Thus, children are less likely to be concerned about disinheritance or about parental wishes generally.[20]

5. *Divorce.* Divorce clearly weakens social capital. Of course this is not true in every instance, but the overall effect on social capital is clearly negative. Parents who live away from their children tend to lose contact

with them, and the step-parents, if any, tend not to be as caring and as supportive as the natural parents.

Compared to Western European nations and Japan, the United States has by far the highest divorce rate. The number of divorces per 1,000 married women in the United States increased from 10.3 in 1950 to 20.8 in 1987; almost half of contemporary marriages eventually are terminated.[21] More than one million children under 18 are directly involved in a divorce every year. Obviously the high divorce rates adversely affect the social capital of large numbers of children over time.[22]

In fact, from the standpoint of children's welfare, the negative effects of our high divorce rates are widely underestimated. Popular opinion shows widespread concern about unmarried teenage mothers. As Christopher Jencks points out, however, if our concern is with the absence of the father, divorce rates are also crucial. Children whose parents are divorced are almost as vulnerable as children whose parents were never married to begin with. Divorced fathers do tend to be more supportive than never-married ones, but the similarities are more important than the differences. Furthermore, the divorce rate is spread more evenly throughout society than the rate of children born out of wedlock; the single-parent family and the social capital problems associated with it are not confined to any race or economic stratum. Poor families are less able to cope with the problems of single parenthood, but its negative effects are evident at all socioeconomic levels.[23]

6. *Residential mobility and urbanization.* Increased residential mobility and urbanization also weaken social capital. Again, this statement does not apply to every instance but to the overall effects of the trend. Children who move lose the social capital built up in their previous place of residence. The more frequent the moves, the less social capital children are likely to have. Urbanization also tends to result in a loss of social capital. In smaller communities children and families tend to know their neighbors well, but this is less likely in urban areas. The physical obstacles to interaction are greater, and there is less community support for activities with children.

7. *The decline in religious activities.* Declining participation in religious activities also lessens social capital. Religious organizations are concerned about the long-range welfare of children; unless children become mature, productive citizens with strong ties to the religious organizations, the organizations will decline over time. Furthermore, religion itself

emphasizes long-range considerations; hence a decline in religious belief and activity is likely to decrease the social capital available to children.

8. *The influence of television.* Outside of school, children spend more time watching television than in any other activity. The producers of television shows for children do not intend to hurt their viewers. For the most part, they are simply trying to get children's attention in order to sell something—chewing gum, breakfast cereals, candy, whatever. As James S. Coleman comments, their interest is in what they can get from children, not in what is in children's best interests.

Young people are not generally prudent or wise consumers. Advertising that emphasizes immediate gratification is even more likely to succeed with them than with adults. In this respect at least, television exacerbates the decline in social capital; it provides an environment in which immediate gratification takes precedence over long-range welfare. It is also an environment that trivializes acts of violence by sheer repetition of them. It has been estimated that a typical American child will have seen 200,000 acts of violence on television by age 16.[24] It would be surprising if these frequent displays of violence did not desensitize children to its exercise.

9. *The peer culture.* Because of the decline in the extended family, teenagers interact less with other family members than they did in the past. Because of compulsory education and restrictions on teenage employment, they interact less with adults outside of their families. Inevitably, teenagers spend more time among themselves, and their values and attitudes are increasingly shaped by other teenagers in similar circumstances. The social capital that is created in this way is not as helpful as the social capital fostered by extended families and productive employment.

Prospects for the Restoration of Social Capital

Overall, it seems indisputable that the sources of social capital for children are declining. Granted, there are trends and efforts to counteract the adverse consequences to children, but it is difficult to see how they can succeed. By comparison, the decision to land astronauts on the moon was easily reached and implemented. Landing on the moon was a visible, discrete objective; the obstacles were largely financial; the technological problems were readily identifiable and subject to nonideological resolution. Social capital, however, involves several ideological and policy issues and a host of powerful interest groups seeking essentially incompatible solutions. Under the circumstances, matters will probably get worse before they get better, if, indeed, they do get better.

Coleman has aptly stated the basic dilemmas raised by the decline in social capital. Should we try to reestablish the conditions under which parents had more authority and responsibility for their children, and also had a larger long-range stake in their development? Or should we try to develop more effective government mechanisms to deal with children who come under government control or influence, for whatever reasons?[25] Neither alternative seems very promising. Whichever is adopted, a wide array of political, economic, social, and cultural forces are moving in the opposite direction. As more housing excludes children, or is built for small families, or is segregated by age, housing for extended families becomes more difficult to find.[26] As gay and lesbian organizations are successful in legitimizing gay and lesbian marriages, the impact will be to increase them. As more persons with no family ties or weak ones rise to positions of power in the media and politics, we can expect a tilt in that direction. And so on. Simply stated, efforts to encourage family structures that foster children's social capital face several obstacles that will be difficult to overcome.

As Coleman points out, no other social institution has successfully fulfilled the nurturing and social-capital-providing functions of the family. To overcome the failures of the past, Coleman has proposed policies that would provide foster parents or other providers of child care with a stake in the long-range development of the children entrusted to their care.[27] For example, foster parents might be entitled to a certain share of the future earnings of their foster children. Obviously, Coleman's proposal would require a great deal of study and refinement before being implemented; however, in the absence of basic changes of this kind, children's social capital will probably decline even more in the future.

Less dramatic proposals have been made to provide more social capital to children; for example, day care regulations that require infants be "held, played with, and talked to" have been introduced in Maryland.[28] The practical impossibility of monitoring the requirement should be obvious; an army of state officials could not enforce it. In any case, the proposal illustrates the tendency to deal with the symptoms, not the causes of the decline in children's social capital. In some respects, the efforts to alleviate the symptoms exacerbate the decline, or are likely to do so. If, for example, government provides day care for all preschoolers, more parents will choose that option.

As matters stand, economic incentives do not affect family size among the wealthiest families. They can afford as many children as they wish. At the lowest income levels, government support for children is also support for the adults, hence the latter have economic incentives to have children. Contrary to conservative assumptions, very few welfare mothers get by solely on government assistance, but the assistance is a factor in decisions to apply for or remain on welfare. Welfare mothers have authority over children but not responsibility for them; government has the responsibility for supporting the children but not the authority over them. Thus one issue is whether to reestablish family responsibility for children, or to reduce family authority over them since the responsibility is not present. Public school organizations supported government funding for day care in public schools but opposed it for day care provided by religious organizations. Arguably their position is more oriented to their own needs than to the social capital needs of children.

Political rhetoric aside, we face protracted conflict over family issues. On the one hand, various groups support measures to strengthen the "traditional" family structure: children conceived by and living with married parents and perhaps some other members of a biological family. Another coalition contends that "family" should be defined as any two or more adults who choose to live together, or any single adult who chooses to bear and/or raise a child. The latter group tends to regard different family structures as equally deserving of legitimacy and government support. Of course, both positions include several variations, but they reflect the major division on family issues.

For reasons to be discussed shortly, I expect that higher proportions of children will be born into and raised in nontraditional families. One empirical issue is whether such families are as beneficial to children as the traditional one. Although I cannot assess the research here, it seems implausible that every family arrangement agreeable to adults is as beneficial to children as the traditional family structure. If this is a valid assumption (or conclusion), schools will be faced with a continuing decline in the social capital of students. As a result, educational achievement is likely to continue to decline also. This would weaken public education, regardless of the fact that factors other than school would be responsible for the decline. Theoretically, the decline could continue even though public schools were performing admirably; even the best doctors will have the highest patient death rates if they serve higher proportions of difficult-to-cure patients.

Feminism

Perhaps no sociocultural factor is having a greater impact on children and schools than feminism. Although feminism affects children and schools in several ways, my comments here will focus on its implications for the future of public schools.

First, what is feminism? One well-known critique devotes an entire chapter to this question and concludes that even feminist leaders do not agree among themselves on the answer.[29] In what follows, I shall treat "feminism" or "the feminist movement" as a social movement based on the following ideas:

1. At birth, boys and girls have the same abilities to develop skills and motives and would develop similarly if raised in the same way.
2. Men dominate societies because socialization of the sexes fosters aggressive behavior in males, submissive behavior in females. Were it not for this "sexist" socialization, leadership positions would be distributed evenly between the sexes.
3. Our socialization processes, not sex or gender per se, are responsible for the limitations society assumes for or applies to women.
4. Drastic social change is required to eliminate sexism and achieve a social order that treats women as equals instead of as subordinates.

With some trepidation, therefore, I will define feminism as the movement to eliminate gender differences that arise from discriminatory treatment of women. There is controversy over the extent of gender differences, what is discriminatory treatment, the extent and effects of discriminatory practices, and the policies that should be adopted to eliminate them. Obviously, given these differences among feminists, my references to them do not necessarily apply to every individual who is (or is labeled) a "feminist."

To a considerable degree, feminism results from the interaction of basic demographic and social changes. As a result of technological progress, physical strength and stamina are declining as occupational requirements. Consequently, women have a much wider range of work opportunities than they had in the past. This fundamental change has been obscured by controversies over whether women are physically equal to men. On the average, they are not, but the issue is becoming less and less important in the workplace.

Technology has also expanded the maternity options open to women. Contraceptive technology has made it possible for women to engage in sexual activity without becoming pregnant. Reproductive technology now makes it possible for women to become pregnant in the absence of sexual activity. Women can choose to become pregnant and with whose sperm, insofar as men allow their sperm to be used in this way. Under these circumstances, women have an enormous range of choices that were not available to them in previous generations.[30]

Increased longevity also plays a major role in the growth of feminism. More and more women live most of their lives after they have (or would have) raised their children. The instability of marriage and the declining role of children as a life-support system for parents add to the attractiveness if not the necessity of a career outside the home. Estimates of the cost of raising children typically understate the costs to mothers or potential mothers. The reason is that the estimates do not take into account the loss of earnings and career opportunities associated with bearing and raising children. Significantly, the losses to women of high earnings outside the home are greater, hence lower birth rates among such women are only to be expected.

In increasing numbers, therefore, women will have the option of bearing and raising children or forgoing a maternal role for career opportunities outside the home. Of course, these decisions will not and should not be made solely on economic grounds, and a substantial number of women, with varying degrees of success and personal satisfaction, will combine the maternal role with a producer role outside the home. In all of this, the extent to which women will be compensated for bearing and rearing children will be of paramount importance. Unless the maternal roles receive larger economic rewards, we may experience precipitous declines in birth rates. In my view such declines would be highly undesirable, but restricting work options for women would not be justified even if it were possible—which it is not. Government allowances or tax benefits for raising children are one possibility; different contractual arrangements governing marriage, cohabitation agreements, and childbearing outside of marriage are others. I do not advocate or oppose any specific changes along these lines but simply wish to empha-size that although feminism is irreversible, its effects are not necessarily beyond our control. My speculation is that a significant number of women will choose or emphasize the career option over the maternal one even if government assistance and new contractual arrangements between mothers and fathers reduce the economic disadvantages of bearing and raising children. Although we will not see the end of the traditional family, we will see a higher proportion of nontraditional ones.

To grasp the implications of feminism for the future of public educa-tion, it is essential to understand how it plays out in school operations. A brief list of feminist issues followed by a few of their educational manifestations may suffice for this purpose.

1. *Opposition to policies that treat gender differences as relevant to educational or occupational status.* Educational application: Pregnant unmarried fe-male teachers must not be treated differently from unmarried male teachers who have fathered children out of wedlock. School districts should not take pregnancy into account in employing or even inter-viewing candidates for positions. Tests of academic achievement or for occupational eligibility are attacked legally if they show disparate sexual outcomes. School districts and educational organizations routinely adopt affirmative action policies intended to redress past discrimination against women.

2. *Greater female reliance on jobs and careers instead of marriage and homemak-ing as the way to personal fulfillment.* Educational applications: Student textbooks emphasize women in occupations formerly considered male domains. Being a wife and mother is deemphasized, even ignored in some textbooks that discuss career choices. Teacher unions bargain more aggressively for benefits that enable mothers to return to teaching promptly without loss of seniority or other benefits.

3. *Support for day care to accommodate mothers who wish to continue or resume employment after the birth of their children.* Educational applications: Public school organizations support legislation that would give public schools a leading role as providers of day care. Day care is becoming a teacher benefit, and some school districts are providing day care for student mothers.

4. *Insistence upon abortion as a woman's prerogative, not a matter of legislative policy.* Educational applications: Public school organizations overwhelm-ingly oppose legislation that restricts abortion, requires students to get

parental consent for abortions, prevents school personnel from recommending abortions, or mandates school opposition to abortion in any way.

5. *Treatment of traditional gender differences in the role of parents as social and cultural facts without physical or anatomical justification.* Educational applications: More and more school curricula show males in nurturing roles with their children and women in occupational roles formerly considered male domains.

6. *An emphasis on "non-sexist" education, that is, education that minimizes sexually defined roles in socialization.* Educational applications: A mini-industry has emerged to research the various ways that schools treat boys differently from girls. Teacher education typically emphasizes the undesirability of such differences.

For present purposes, the issue is whether feminism strengthens public education, weakens it, or has no significant effect on its viability. In my opinion, feminism weakens public education in these ways:

1. Feminist issues constitute a major source of educational conflict. This conflict adds to the pressures for educational options that are not provided by public schools. As the following section points out, educational conflict tends to weaken public education regardless of the merits of the issues giving rise to the conflict.
2. Feminism is one of the causes of the demographic trends previously discussed that weaken public education.
3. A dominant thrust of feminism is to give a higher priority to individual interests than to family interests that formerly served to keep families intact. As a result feminism is a significant factor in the decline of children's social capital.

Most emphatically, the above assessment is not a judgment about the merits of feminism, nor does it imply any criticism of feminists. To avoid any misunderstanding on this important point, let me elaborate on it briefly. Partly as a result of feminism, women are entering several occupations that were formerly male domains. Presumably, this weakens the talent pool entering the teaching profession, which formerly attracted many women who were excluded from these occupations. On these assumptions, however, we could not sensibly criticize feminism for "weakening public education." The effects of feminism on public education are important, but they are the result of a movement whose merits must be assessed on other grounds.

Heterogeneity

By virtually any criterion—income, religion, language, ethnicity, value orientation, family type—the United States is becoming a more heterogeneous society. This trend, especially in social, cultural, and lifestyle matters, is generating more conflict than public education can constructively absorb. Its resources are increasingly devoted to conflict management instead of to education, and its ability to provide high-quality education is correspondingly weakened.

Although the nation as a whole included a variety of ethnic, religious, and cultural groups in the nineteenth century, communities were much more homogeneous than they are today. Inasmuch as education was a local function (where it was a governmental function at all), there was relatively little social conflict over educational issues. The one major exception was Protestant-Catholic conflict over nonpreferential aid to denominational schools. The Protestants were victorious on this issue, and no serious political threat to public education emerged for almost 150 years.

For various reasons, the American people are becoming increasingly heterogeneous, not only nationally but at the state and local levels as well. No one doubts that we have tremendous disparities in wealth and income. No matter what the foreign policy issue, ethnic groups on all sides of it are usually active. Scores of religious denominations as well as large numbers of the nonreligious and the irreligious are found within most communities. Differences in language, culture, and lifestyle are commonplace: federal appropriations support language instruction in 146 languages in order to provide equal opportunity to students not proficient in English.

The more heterogeneous people are, the more difficult it is for them to agree on educational issues. The more difficult it is to agree on educational issues, the stronger the pressures to move away from a system of majoritarian control of education. Consider, for example, the 1990 proposal by the chancellor of the New York City school system to make condoms available in the city's high schools, free of charge and without requiring parental consent. The proposal was advocated as a way of reducing the high incidence of AIDS in New York City.

The list of speakers at a public hearing on the "Chancellor's Plan for Expanded HIV/AIDS Education Including Condom Availability" can be broken down as follows:

- 77 no organization listed
- 31 students
- 28 religious organizations
     12 Catholic
      9 Protestant
      5 Jewish
      1 Muslim
      1 interdenominational
- 27 community organizations
- 22 elected officials
     12 city
      9 state
      1 federal
- 21 health organizations
- 17 AIDS-related organizations
- 14 teachers
- 14 parents
- 8 gay/lesbian organizations
- 5 higher education institutions or organizations
- 1 research organization.[31]

Many individuals and organizations who felt strongly about the issues did not submit statements or participate in the hearings. Dozens of different positions were advocated in one or more submissions. Leaving aside the question of whether public opinion should resolve the issue, it was impossible for the New York City Board of Education to assess public opinion accurately or to stay abreast of changing public attitudes on the issue.

.A recent news article discussed the school problems of children of homosexual parents. One youngster was reportedly asked to identify someone who often picked him up at school. The matter-of-fact response was "That's my father's husband." The article did not state the number of children growing up in these circumstances but did report that the number was increasing.[32] The fact that the avowed homosexuality of adults is no longer a barrier to their efforts to adopt children suggests that we are institutionalizing new kinds of families.

The incident described in the article suggests the difficulties of coping with increasing heterogeneity in public schools. What kind of curriculum in "home economics" or "family living" or "civil rights" (to cite just a few problematic areas) should schools provide? No curriculum will satisfy the different groups with diametrically opposed views on family issues. And even if such a curriculum were developed, how many teachers would be knowledgeable and unbiased enough to teach it objectively? How many school districts would buy the necessary instructional materials? Avoidance of the issues is perhaps the only feasible outcome, but avoidance dissatisfies many groups that want schools to support their religious or family values.

To be sure, our heterogeneity is often regarded as a strong reason to strengthen public education and to limit resort to private schools as much as possible. It is contended that the nation's diversity increases the importance of a common set of experiences among our young people. Regardless of one's position on this issue, it seems clear that increasing heterogeneity renders it more difficult to achieve a workable consensus on educational issues, and that the rising social and economic costs of reaching agreement on educational issues increase the pressure to shift from public education to a less confrontational system. In the words of Nathan Glazer, a leading scholar of ethnic and religious conflict:

> I am convinced the conflicts of values in this country today, between the religious and the secular, the permissive and the traditional, those seeking experience and those seeking security and stability, between the culture of the coasts and the culture of the heartland, between the cosmopolitans of Los Angeles and New York and the staid inhabitants of smaller towns and cities (as well as of most of the inhabitants of Los Angeles and New York), are so great that the vision of a truly common school, in which all are educated together, simply will not work . . . a decent opportunity for withdrawal to a more homogeneous and educationally effective environment is necessary and can be provided without destroying our democracy and or our multiethnic society.[33]

Juvenile Crime and School Authority

In recent years, crimes committed by young people have reached unprecedented levels. The number of arrests per 1,000 persons aged 14–17 increased from 4 in 1950 to 117 in 1989. In 1989, about 15 percent of all offenders were under 18 and another 30 percent were aged 18–24. About 56 percent of arrests for murder, nonnegligent manslaughter, and forcible rape were from these two age groups. A 1992 FBI report showed that the juvenile arrest rate for violent crime had increased by 27 percent since 1982; all races and social classes showed an increase, although not to the same extent. In fact, some authorities have identified the growing frequency of violent crime by teenagers and subteenagers as the most ominous trend in the criminal justice system.[34] The rate of juvenile arrests for weapons violations reached an all-time high in 1990, while arrests for drug use or sale increased by 713 percent from 1982 to 1992.[35]

These trends have had a significant impact on public education. For instance, the fifteen largest school districts recently reported that their three major problems were weapons on campus, gangs, and drugs. According to a government estimate, 500,000 violent incidents occurred every month in public secondary schools in 1988.[36] Obviously, safety and security problems of this magnitude are bound to have adverse effects on many aspects of education.

Under such conditions a larger proportion of scarce resources must be spent on measures to improve safety and security. Despite such increases, however, a growing number of parents are concerned about the safety of their children in public schools. Private schools are becoming a more attractive option, especially since they are not as restricted as public schools in coping with crime and delinquency. Also, justified or not, many citizens regard public schools as partially responsible for crime and delinquency among young people.

While juvenile crime and delinquency have been increasing, school authority to cope with them have been eroded in various ways. Recent Supreme Court decisions have made it more difficult for public schools to expel or suspend students, search their lockers, regulate their dress, or regulate their publications, to cite some restrictions that render it more difficult for public schools to cope with undesirable student conduct. In effect, school authority over pupils has declined just when the need for it has greatly increased.

If pupils, especially teenagers, were still accountable to their families, the loss of school authority might not be such a negative development. As it is, however, students do not suffer sanctions or penalties for failure to take schoolwork seriously. An adolescent who is frequently absent from work is likely to be fired; if frequently absent from school, the adolescent is implored to return on the grounds that staying in school is in his or her long-range interests.

One cause of the decline in school authority is the frequent resort to litigation, in and out of education, to establish group rights of one sort or another. In Chapter 12 I shall argue that a great deal of this litigation could be avoided by reliance on private contracts instead of government regulation to govern the relationships between the parties to the educational process. In this connection, it might be noted that larger proportions of students in Catholic schools than in public schools feel that they are being treated fairly. This is true even though, because they are not governmental agencies, Catholic schools are not required to provide certain due process rights that are legally available to public school students.[37] It may be that the limitations on public school authority have contributed more to academic decline than to fair treatment of pupils.

International Economic Competition

Along with the collapse of the command economies, a major economic development of our time is the growing importance of international competition. Producers in one nation have to be concerned about competition from producers in others. More and more, efforts to restrict competition within a country fail because producers outside of it cannot be restricted. Over time, an increasing number of industries will have to compete effectively in an international market or decline. Our automobile and electronics industries are prominent examples of the results of failure to compete successfully.

This trend raises the educational stakes considerably. As long as economic competition was within national borders, the failure of one company was offset by the growth of others. Under international competition, however, the successful or surviving companies will not necessarily be located in the United States. If U.S. companies have to teach their employees how to read and write and use simple arithmetic, they will be at a severe disadvantage in international competition. Competitive pressures are already forcing them to shift production to countries where they can avoid training costs that weaken their ability to compete.

It is often asserted that unless education prepares a higher proportion of workers with "high tech" skills, our economy will be dominated by Pacific Rim and Western European nations with better educated labor forces. Actually, the skill requirements of the labor force are not likely

39. Cyert + Mowery, Tech + Employ, 1987, Natl Acad Press

to change dramatically in the near future. The problem is that the United States is unable to meet relatively stable demands for educated personnel.[38] The problem of being competitive is intensified by the quantity and rapidity of technological diffusion; innovations originating in foreign countries must be adopted promptly in the United States to avoid competitive gaps. Unless our labor force has the capacity to adopt innovations promptly, its markets will decline, often irreversibly. The flexibility required consists of habits, attitudes, and organizational factors as well as technical skills. It is difficult to see how the anticompetitive environment of public education can meet the needs of a competitive economy.

Schooling in the United States first emerged for religious objectives. When our nation was overwhelmingly based on an agricultural economy, formal schooling did not play a leading economic role. Subsequently, formal education was justified on political grounds, such as the importance of "Americanizing the immigrants" or of developing an informed citizenry supposedly essential to democratic representative government.

In the future, however, economic considerations will be paramount. This is not to say that religious or political or sociocultural factors will no longer play a role, or that economic considerations were absent from educational policymaking in the past. The point is that economic considerations will overshadow others, just as religious and political considerations overshadowed economic ones in the past. The economic considerations will affect the pace as well as the substance of educational change. Issues pertaining to separation of church and state may be debated for centuries; survival in a competitive international economy does not allow for such a leisurely pace of resolution.

The 1991 trade negotiations between the United States and Japan provided a striking example of economic pressures on educational policy. The U.S. negotiators alleged that Japan was unfairly excluding U.S. products from Japanese markets. The Japanese rebuttal was that U.S. educational deficiencies, not Japanese policies, were the reason U.S. companies could not compete successfully in Japan. In the course of the discussions, the U.S. negotiators promised to improve the quality of American education.[39] Just how they intended to deliver on this promise was not explained, but the scenario would have been unthinkable in the past. When the United States sent an educational mission to Japan in 1946, its purpose was not to learn from the Japanese but to advise them on how to rebuild their educational system. In the future, as U.S.

NY Times, Jun 13/91 p. 5.

companies in high-tech fields unsuccessfully compete against foreign companies whose governments spend less for formal education, the huge U.S. investment in public education will lose economic credibility. As we shall see, efforts to justify it on the basis of noneconomic outcomes will be even less persuasive.

Income Levels

Economists generally agree that income levels will rise in the 1990s. As income levels rise, so does discretionary income; as discretionary income rises, fewer consumers are satisfied with what everyone else has. Consequently, rising incomes are likely to lead to increasing demands for private schooling.

Indisputably, the private sector is inherently more effective than the public sector in responding to variations in consumer preferences. This is clearly true in education. For example, more than half the enrollments in private schools are in denominational schools, but public schools cannot offer the option of religious education. Nor can they offer several others, because of legal or political restrictions or problems of scale that do not apply to private schools.[40]

I do not assume that all income levels will share, or share equitably, in increases in personal income.[41] Nevertheless, rising income levels among a substantial proportion of citizens will increase defections from the public schools. Obviously, the extent of government funding will also affect enrollment levels in private schools, perhaps even more than the future levels of personal income.

Theoretically, rising income levels can coexist with a rising proportion of low-income families. The probability is, however, that for the first time in our history the affluent will outnumber or at least equal the poor. The consequences will not be limited to an increase in the number and proportion of families seeking private education. The political influence of more affluent families will be increasingly supportive of private instead of public schools. The public schools cannot afford to lose many of these families, but sizable defections are inevitable as long as a single expenditure standard applies to all family income levels. After all, no such standard applies, or is even proposed, for food, shelter, transportation, or any other service.

If rising incomes encourage private schooling, why was the proportion of pupils in private schools virtually the same in 1989 as in 1955, when incomes were much lower? The answer is to be found in the characteristics of private school enrollments. In the mid-1950s approximately 80 percent of private school enrollments were in Catholic schools. These schools were staffed largely by members of religious orders who were paid far less than market rates for their services. As a result, tuition in Catholic schools was extremely low, and few parents were unable to afford them.

As explained in Chapter 6, the proportion of such teachers in Catholic schools has declined drastically; hence Catholic schools are more expensive than in the past. Currently only about half of all private school enrollments are in Catholic schools; meanwhile, enrollments in private schools as a proportion of total enrollments have remained stable because more parents, Catholic and non-Catholic alike, have been able and willing to pay for private education. In other words, the proportion of pupils in private schools reflects a much greater ability and willingness to pay for private education now than it did in the mid-1950s.

Of course, considered in isolation, rising income levels render it easier to allocate funds to elementary and secondary education. Unfortunately for public education, questions of how much to spend for education will not be resolved in isolation from other issues, such as health care for the elderly. Nor will they be resolved without closer scrutiny of claims about the benefits of public education. As we shall see, scrutiny of these claims will often lead to their rejection.

The Resurgence of Promarket Ideologies

Changes in the intellectual environment will also have important implications for the future of public education. Market-oriented views are more influential today than at any time since the 1920s. The economic and political distress in the former Soviet Union and the Eastern European economies has eliminated socialism, at least explicitly and for the time being, as a worthwhile policy target. At the same time, market-oriented organizations and policy centers have expanded in recent years. In other words, the resources available to advocate promarket policies have increased while the targets of opportunity have decreased.

Chapter 12 explains why the market-oriented policy centers have had little impact on public education thus far. Even the ones that formally support a market approach to education lack a viable program or strategy to achieve it. Nonetheless, the financial and intellectual resources to do so are potentially available. Given the importance of education from several standpoints, and the nation's enormous expenditures on it, it is only a matter of time before market-oriented policy organizations pay serious attention to public education. Although some will merely add to the confusion—as they do now—the overall result will be the most hostile intellectual environment for public education since its origins in the nineteenth century.

3

≈ Producer-Consumer Conflict

An "industry" is a group of people who make highly substitutable goods or services. The term has no ideological implications; "the education industry" exists whether education is provided by public or private schools. Education, like any other industry, involves both producers and consumers, and the interests of the two groups are often in conflict. The producers are the teachers, principals, administrators, school board members, and support personnel, plus the organizations representing these groups and the state and federal education bureaucracies. The consumers are all the beneficiaries and/or clients of public education: students, parents, and local, state, and federal publics. Conflict between producers and consumers exists with respect to all of these groups. My concern here is not to prove the existence of such conflict, but to explain why public education is an undesirable way to resolve it.

Let us begin by reviewing why producer-consumer conflicts of interest are important and how they are resolved in the private sector. First of all, everyone is a consumer. Not everyone is a producer, but most adults are. In most societies, being an adult is supposed to mean that you carry your weight as a producer. That is, your productive activities provide the compensation required to meet your consumer needs. In other words, most of us are both producers and consumers.

As consumers of goods and services, we welcome and expect improvements: automatic transmissions over manual shifts, low-cholesterol over high-cholesterol foods, pharmaceuticals without harmful side effects, painless drilling over painful drilling by dentists, jet over propeller-driven aircraft, color over black-and-white television, and so on. Our interests as consumers are served by constant improvement in price, quality, and accessibility of goods and services.

Improvements in what we buy, however, are based on competition among producers. Without such competition, few such improvements would materialize. Unfortunately, competition may be disastrous for us as producers. Cheaper air travel has led to lower employment in intercity bus companies. Fax machines have weakened the courier business and telegraph companies. Fuel-efficient cars have led to unemployment among the manufacturers of fuel-inefficient cars. And so on.

As producers, we try to protect ourselves from changes that would threaten us. Thus industries threatened by foreign competition try to protect themselves by imposing tariffs on imported goods. Unions try to negotiate prohibitions against layoffs; if an outright prohibition cannot be achieved, unions try to negotiate severance pay, bumping rights, relocation allowances, lengthy advance notice of dismissal, and retraining allowances. The 1990 negotiations in the U.S. automobile industry focused on just this type of worker security.

From an individual standpoint, the ideal solution is to have monopoly status as a producer, while receiving the benefits of competition as a consumer. Obviously, this solution cannot be made widely available. The more producers who are protected from competition, the fewer the consumers who benefit from it.

Before focusing on producer-consumer conflict in education, let us see how the conflict plays out in other fields. General Motors produces and sells automobiles. It tries to persuade consumers that GM automobiles are their best buy. The company and its dealers advertise heavily. In doing so, they do not highlight the deficiencies of GM cars. In fact, GM tried unsuccessfully to discredit Ralph Nader's efforts to publicize the poor safety features of GM cars.

Government provision of a service does not eliminate producer-consumer conflict. The Iran-Contra situation leading to the trial of Colonel Oliver North illustrates this point. The federal government produces national defense. In doing so, it may act in ways that citizens find objectionable. When this happens, government officials often try to conceal the objectionable activities. Generally speaking, government officials do not invite attention to deficiencies in public service except in (1) situations in which the deficiencies are likely to become public information regardless of government opposition or concealment; (2) cases in which one political party stands to benefit by publicizing the alleged poor performance of another party; and (3) situations in which the alleged deficiency justifies appropriations to eliminate the deficiency.

Producer-consumer conflict cuts across national and geographical boundaries. The Soviet Union has had a long history to trying to conceal its failures as a producer from its people and from other nations; ultimately, the failures became so pervasive and so overwhelming that government admissions of failure added little to what its citizens did not already know.

The reader may object that in the United States government does play a vital role in representing consumer interests. For example, the Food and Drug Administration (FDA) protects consumers from harmful foods and drugs. As a matter of fact, some analysts contend that the FDA insists upon unreasonably high standards of safety and purity with the result that pharmaceutical companies face excessive delays and costs in bringing new products to market.[1]

The activities of the FDA illustrate the important point. The federal government does not manufacture and sell pharmaceuticals. For this reason, its protection of consumers is not in conflict with its role as a producer. In areas in which government is a producer, however, the needs of its consumers become subordinate to government's need to protect its producer activities from criticism. Negative information about a government service may help consumer-voters, but it is usually politically damaging to the government producers.

Of course, some producer-consumer conflict exists within government even when government is the regulator and not the producer. In such cases, the producers try to guide government in one direction; consumer organizations try to guide it in a different one. These conflicts may threaten either producer or consumer interests or both. Despite some similarities, however, these situations are fundamentally different from those in which government is both the producer of the service and the representative of consumers with respect to it. In such cases both producer and consumer functions are ultimately responsible to the same political leadership, which often resolves conflict in favor of the producer over the consumer bureaucracy.

Teacher Unions as Producer Representatives

Because the teacher unions are the most powerful producer organizations, I shall begin by discussing their policies on consumer complaints. The following proposal on parent complaints is taken from a model contract disseminated by the California Teachers Association (CTA), the nation's largest state teacher union. Union proposals in most other states do not differ significantly from this one.

Article XII

1. Any citizen or parent complaint about a teacher shall be reported immediately to the teacher by the administrator or Board member receiving the complaint.
2. Should the involved teacher or the complainant believe that the allegations in the complaint are sufficiently serious to warrant a meeting, the teacher shall schedule a meeting with the complainant. An Association representative shall be present at said meeting, if so requested by the teacher.
3. If the matter is not resolved at the meeting to the satisfaction of the complainant, he/she shall put his/her complaint into writing and submit the original to the teacher with a copy to the teacher's immediate supervisor. The teacher shall be given compensated released time for the purpose of initialing and dating the written complaint and preparing a written response to such complaint. If no written complaint is received, the matter shall be dropped.
4. The written complaint and the attached response shall be placed in the teacher's personnel file. If the teacher challenges the truth of the allegations contained in the complaint, he/she may file a grievance on that basis, and finding to the effect that such allegations are untrue shall result in the immediate destruction of the written complaint. The failure by the teacher to file a grievance shall not be construed as an admission by the teacher that the allegations contained in the complaint are true.
5. The Board shall not dismiss or refuse to reemploy a teacher on the basis of allegations in a citizen or parent complaint.[2]

Because the CTA and the National Education Association (NEA) constantly assert their concern for minorities and the disadvantaged, let us consider the CTA proposal briefly in this context.[3] Assume that a migrant farm worker has a complaint concerning a teacher. The CTA proposal gives the teacher the right to schedule a meeting but says nothing about parental rights to do so. The teacher but not the parent is entitled to representation at such a meeting. If not satisfied with the outcome of the meeting, the parent must put the complaint in writing—an onerous task for an illiterate farm worker. Because farm workers usually work long hours for a few days before moving to other employment, the parent will probably have to lose pay to follow up on a complaint. In contrast, the teacher will be paid for preparing a defense against the charges, and the proposal sets no limit on released time for this purpose. The matter is dropped if no written complaint is received. Thus if the farm worker family has to move before the matter is resolved, the school administration cannot pursue the matter independently.

The complaint is also subject to the grievance procedure. If the farm workers and their children have moved, no one will be available to challenge the teacher's version of events in the grievance procedure. The proposal to destroy the record is also producer oriented. In many situations, it is not clear whether an incident is an isolated case or is part of a pattern. Destroying the record might result in destroying evidence that subsequently would help to demonstrate a pattern of conduct.

Of course, union proposals are not always accepted. It may be that few school districts have accepted proposals like these in their entirety. The important point, however, is that the proposals show what policies the unions try to have adopted. Clearly, these policies do not demonstrate much concern for consumer interests.

Consumer policies like those proposed by teacher unions would be unthinkable in the private sector. Imagine trying to express a complaint to the management of a department store, only to be told that you must put it in writing and confront the employee and the employee's union representative. In practice, private-sector management usually tries to facilitate the expression of consumer complaints; this is the best way to avoid dissatisfied customers who might take their business elsewhere.

Note that facilitating the expression of parental complaints in no way implies that management would act unfairly toward its employees. Respect for consumer interests requires information about consumer views; what should be done about those views, especially as they affect employees, is another matter. The union proposals, however, protect teachers by making it difficult for parents to pursue their complaints.

The teacher unions constantly express their support for parental involvement. The CTA proposal suggests that these expressions are merely pro forma. Upper-middle-class parents, accustomed to dealing with various agencies and institutions, may occasionally submit their complaints in writing and confront teachers and their union representatives with them. Migrant workers, illiterate parents, and inner-city single parents rarely do so.

In general, legislation sponsored by teacher unions disadvantages consumers as much as union bargaining proposals. Legislation limiting class size illustrates this point. According to the California Education Code, "It is the intent and purpose of the Legislature to encourage, by every means possible, the reduction of class sizes and the ratio of pupils to teachers in all grade levels in the public schools and to urge every effort to this end be undertaken by the local school administrative authorities." The next section of the Code penalizes school districts if their class size exceeds thirty in grades one to eight or thirty-one or thirty-three in kindergarten.[4]

These limits have no credible relationship to educational achievement or productivity. Let us assume, however, that adding a pupil to a class of thirty adversely affects educational achievement. Would this justify a decision not to assign more than thirty pupils to a class? The costs of splitting a class in California would be over $50,000 (average California teacher salary of $40,000 in 1990–91 plus 25 percent fringe benefits for an additional teacher). The underlying issue, however, is whether spending $50,000 this way is the optimal use of district funds. This judgment requires an understanding of the district's needs and resources. In the overwhelming majority of cases, the harm done, if any, by adding a pupil to a class of thirty would be negligible. Splitting the class, however, would cost the district a substantial amount that could be used on other needs, such as laboratory equipment, or teachers of other subjects, or instructional supplies. In effect, these sections of the Education Code penalize California districts for making the most cost-effective use of their funds; teachers benefit from the legislation, regardless of its impact on pupils.

The statutory limits on class size were allegedly enacted to protect pupils. If new educational technology enabled teachers to teach fifty pupils as effectively as they now teach thirty, who would benefit? While the statute is in effect, no one. In fact, the statute discourages research and development that would increase educational productivity.

Legislation that serves producer interests is invariably justified as a consumer benefit. For instance, according to the California Education Code a specified minimum percentage of school district operating budgets must be spent for teacher salaries. The minimum is 60 percent for elementary districts, 55 percent for K–12 districts, and 50 percent for high school districts.[5] Most restrictions on school districts are of this nature, and most were initiated by the teacher unions. Putting this aside, however, let us consider the California salary statute on its merits.

The avowed rationale for the statute is the imperative need to reduce school bureaucracy. What better way to do it than to require that a certain percentage of school operating funds be spent for teacher salaries? Perhaps, but we could hardly envisage such a requirement in the private sector. Would a private company agree that no matter what, a certain percentage of its income would be allocated to labor costs? It is impossible to be certain of the future costs of any factor of production. Unpredictably, any cost may go up or down. Since the goal is to operate as efficiently as possible, it would be foolish to insist that a minimum percentage of revenues must be spent for any specific factor of production.

Companies try to reduce costs. The larger the cost of any specific factor as a percentage of total costs, the more effort goes into reducing it. If insurance is one percent of costs, and labor is 50 percent, the focus will be on reducing labor costs. Not in education, however. Education is a labor-intensive industry, perhaps the most labor intensive of all major industries. According to some estimates, 85 percent of the costs of public schools are spent for salaries and fringe benefits of school district personnel. Teacher costs are usually 50 percent or more of total school costs. If we are serious about increasing public school efficiency, we should be searching for ways to reduce its labor costs. There are several ways to do this without reducing output, by whatever means output is measured.[6] Even if this were not possible, the California statute does not make sense. It discourages research and innovation on ways to reduce teacher costs. Why try to find a way to reduce labor costs if school districts are not allowed to adopt it?

Hundreds of statutes like these underscore the futility of educational reform in the United States. The same producer political clout that leads to their enactment stands in the way of their repeal. California alone has enacted scores of such producer-oriented statutes. Educational reformers who ignore their existence can themselves be safely ignored.

Most teacher union proposals cannot plausibly be presented as consumer benefits. For instance, teacher unions consistently propose that teachers be released from duty at the end of the pupil day. If such proposals were accepted, teachers would have no contractual obligation to be available to help pupils who need assistance. The unions typically try to restrict the number of evening meetings, making it more difficult for parents to talk to teachers. When the Philadelphia school system tried to require its most experienced teachers to teach in the inner-city schools, the outcome was the longest and most acrimonious strike in the history of the district. Proposals to pay teachers more for accepting assignments to difficult schools are ridiculed as "combat pay"; although paying more for less desirable assignments is a widely accepted practice in our economy, teacher unions adamantly oppose it. The reason is that the practice would create internal problems for the unions. For instance, the problem of negotiating salary differentials based on teachers' aversion to certain schools could split the union.

Teacher unions exist to provide benefits for teachers; whether they achieve benefits for pupils, parents, or communities is secondary. These are not pejorative statements; people are entitled to form organizations to look out for their interests. It is not necessarily wrong for teachers to oppose a policy that is in the interests of students. It might be in the students' interests to have teachers stay in school until 5:00 P.M. every day to help students. On the other hand, it would be unreasonable to expect teachers to agree to the policy for this reason. Teachers have legitimate interests in their terms and conditions of employment. At some point, it becomes unreasonable to expect them to absorb the costs of a policy that is in the interests of students. Patients might be better off if physicians routinely made free house calls, but we don't expect physicians to make them for this reason. Therefore, the fact that teacher unions frequently propose unreasonable benefits for teachers is irrelevant. When teacher unions propose high salaries for teachers, they do so in terms of pupil welfare: salaries must be high enough to attract and keep good teachers. Still, the appeal to pupil welfare is largely pro forma; the underlying issue is the welfare of teachers, not that of pupils.

I do not mean to imply that teachers consciously resolve every issue on the basis of what is best for themselves. This would be a caricature of their behavior, probably of the behavior of any group. Like most people, teachers believe in the importance of their work and the enterprise in which it is carried on. Like others, teachers are critical of any suggestion or implication to the contrary. In other words, teachers manifest the very human tendency to defend their contribution to society. This reaction is independent of economic self-interest. Thus if teachers believe they are being criticized for acting selfishly when they have no sense of doing so, they will resent the criticisms and dismiss them out of hand. I do not make these comments to gain teacher support, which is unlikely in any case. My intention is to avoid the banal controversies over whether teachers are more self-serving or more idealistic than other occupational groups; on the whole, they are neither.

By the same token, I do not assume that market processes (including incentives) provide a comprehensive account of how people do or should behave. In trying to show how the neglect of market forces has led to undesirable policies, I do not wish to deny the preeminence of nonmarket processes in many important areas of concern. Not all human action can or should be subject to market forces.

Producer Domination

Public education is an industry in which the producers are dominant. This does not mean that the producers prevail on every issue. Instead, "producer domination" denotes the undue influence of the producers over a broad range of policies, practices, operating structures, and discussions of educational reform. It is reflected in what issues are discussed and which ones are not. None of this is necessarily explicit; producer domination is often reflected in what is taken for granted, not what is articulated.

To assess producer domination of public education, let us first examine issues on which the economic interests of teachers should not be a factor, at least if the issue is to be resolved on the basis of pupil welfare. There is no significant disagreement between the teacher unions on the issues I shall discuss. None of the issues is a subject of teacher bargaining; that is, none is a term or condition of teacher employment. For this reason, they provide a useful vantage point from which to assess the relationships between teacher interests and pupil interests.

1. *Minimum wage laws.* Economists overwhelmingly believe that minimum wage laws adversely affect minority youth.[7] By making unskilled labor more expensive, the laws discourage employment of it, thereby increasing the already high unemployment rates among young people, especially minority youth. Lack of employment adversely affects development of skills, habits, and attitudes essential for career development.

The NEA and the American Federation of Teachers (AFT) support increases in the minimum wage.[8] They also oppose enactment of a subminimum wage for young people. Several nations have enacted such legislation, and it appears to be a useful mechanism for assisting young people to enter the labor force. If, however, youth are in school and not in the labor force, the demand for teachers is stronger, hence teacher compensation is greater. Also, the teacher unions gain additional members, dues revenues, and political influence.

2. *The duration of compulsory education.* This is a highly controversial issue. High absentee rates, sometimes 25 percent or higher in inner-city areas, indicate that inner-city youth have little faith that they will improve their life prospects by remaining in school. Employment would be a more productive long-range activity for many. It would also reduce the disruptions and substantial costs that result from forcing youth to attend school when they have no genuine interest in doing so.[9]

Compulsory education of mid-teenagers is justified on the grounds that they are not mature enough to decide for themselves whether to remain in school. It is instructive to compare this point of view with other restrictions on teenage decisionmaking. For example, suppose it is necessary to decide whether to expose a seriously ill teenager to a risky operation. At what age should the decision be made by the teenager, not the parents or persons in loco parentis?

In a very interesting study, Allen E. Buchanan and Dan W. Brock reached the conclusion "that children by age fourteen or fifteen usually have developed the various capacities necessary for competence in health care decision making to a level roughly comparable to that obtained by most adults."[10] Buchanan and Brock point out that there may be conflicts of interest between parents and child in this type of situation; the other family members may have a financial stake in the outcome that conflicts with the best interests of the child.

This is also true of another critical teenage decision, whether or not to marry. At what age should this be the teenager's prerogative? The age limits on this issue vary, but one point stands out: with parental consent, the age limit for marriage is usually as low or lower than the age limit for compulsory education. In short, we allow some teenagers and their parents to make decisions about marriage—but not about whether to stay in school. Perhaps the reason is that there is no producer lobby trying to prevent 15-year-olds from deciding whether to marry. Granted, parents will sometimes make critical decisions in their own interests rather than their children's. By the same token, decisions about children made by legislators, teachers, and bureaucrats are not always in the best interests of children. Although no system can avoid some decisions contrary to children's interests, surely most children would be better served if parents instead of others decided when they could leave school. Nonetheless, the NEA and the AFT oppose lowering the age at which education is no longer compulsory.

3. *Child labor laws.* The history of these laws provides a classic example of producer influence disguised as consumer protection. In the early 1900s, labor unions attempted to prohibit child labor to protect their members from competition. To achieve this objective, the unions sought legislation that prohibited the interstate sale of goods made with child labor. Such legislation said nothing about education, compulsory or otherwise. When the legislation was declared unconstitutional by the Supreme Court, the unions were forced to find a different way to prohibit child labor. Compulsory education was (and still is) this way. Understandably, the labor movement found eager allies among the public school forces seeking to expand public education. In state after state, compulsory education was tied to child labor legislation; the age at which youth could go to work was the age at which they no longer had to attend school. Both the labor unions and the education lobby had a strong interest in high age limits for compulsory education and for eligibility for full-time employment. To this day, these interest groups oppose any change in the child labor laws that would facilitate earlier entry into the labor force. As a matter of fact, the NEA and the AFT are members of the Child Labor Coalition, a group of organizations seeking both a U.S. exclusion of goods made in whole or in part by children under age 15 and a worldwide ban on trade in such goods.[11]

4. *Aid to parents of children in private schools.* The weight of research evidence indicates that denominational schools are more successful than public schools in developing basic skills and reducing dropout rates. The NEA and the AFT oppose government assistance to parents for the purpose of enrolling their children in private schools, denominational or nondenominational. The president of the California Teachers Association has even characterized such support as "evil" and equated it with "legalized child prostitution."[12]

5. *Day care.* Federal support for day care has been a major policy issue in recent years. Some groups oppose federally funded day care, asserting

that it encourages the separation of mothers from children. It is also alleged to be another step in government's usurping, and thus weakening, family functions and relationships. According to this view, if day care is supported from public funds, parents should be allowed to choose the providers, including denominational organizations.

The NEA and the AFT supported federal funding for day care, but they proposed that it be provided primarily in public schools. Of course, if it were, the unions would be able to organize the day care workers. The teacher unions also tried to exclude denominational organizations from government-funded day care.[13]

There are two critical points about the policy positions summarized above. First, in every case the teacher union position turns out to be the one that advances the welfare of teachers and/or their unions. The union positions would increase the demand for public school teachers, avoid any weakening of demand, and/or prevent any competition between public and private schools. Some positions, such as those relating to day care, serve all of these objectives. Policies that increase the demand for public school teachers and also shield them from competition from private schools obviously benefit public school teachers.

The second point is that in no case do teachers cite their interests as a reason for their position. Instead, they justify their positions on the basis of student or national welfare, even when the preponderance of expert opinion clearly supports an opposing view.

Among economists, there is widespread agreement that consumers are better served by competitive than by monopolistic markets. Most also agree that the undesirable effects of monopoly are likely to emerge regardless of whether the producer is a government or a private enterprise. Indeed, it is anomalous that our public policies seek to break up private-sector but not public-sector monopolies in industries that could be competitive.

The NEA and the AFT are opposed to competition to public schools. In recent years they have begun to represent support-service employees, such as bus drivers and cafeteria workers. Not surprisingly, they are now opposed to competition among vendors of support services to school districts. Interestingly enough, the teacher unions do not oppose competition to provide school buses or food products for school cafeterias. Competition is bad only when it threatens their role as producers; otherwise they have no problem with it. To reiterate, I do not regard teachers or their unions as acting on a lower ethical level than other producers in our society. On the contrary, my objective is to show their similarities to other producers, most of whom would operate monopolistically if they were permitted to do so.

We have seen how producer interests dominate union policies that are allegedly based on the welfare of pupils. My claim, however, is that producer interests dominate even the ways nonproducers think about educational issues. To illustrate this point, let me briefly discuss policy on teacher salaries.

According to the conventional wisdom, the basic problem in education is that the average level of teacher compensation is too low. Many if not most economists would argue that the lack of high rewards for outstanding technological innovators and entrepreneurs is a more serious problem. The absence of such rewards results in the absence of the kinds of persons who can raise the level of productivity of the entire enterprise. In public education, however, asserting this point of view would be the kiss of death; what candidate for political office or school board would assert that the absence of opportunities to earn millions is a serious educational problem? None have up to now, and parrot-like repetition of the alleged need to raise teacher salaries is the most likely future scenario.

Most educational reformers emphasize the importance of increasing teacher salaries. The reason is that school districts are unable to recruit qualified teachers in certain subject areas, especially mathematics and science. The people best qualified to teach these subjects can earn much more in other fields that require competency in mathematics or science. Ergo, teacher salaries must be raised to attract more qualified candidates into the schools.

Unfortunately, this solution creates more problems than it solves. The overwhelming majority of teachers are paid on the basis of the amount of their formal training (degrees and course credits) and their years of teaching experience. The grade levels and subjects taught are usually irrelevant in salary placement. Likewise, very few teachers are paid, even in small part, on the basis of the quality of their teaching or the results achieved by their pupils. Regardless of other factors, a high school mathematics teacher with a master's degree in mathematics and ten years of teaching experience is paid the same as a kindergarten teacher with ten years of experience and a master's degree in early childhood education.

The upshot is an oversupply of teachers in some subjects and a simultaneous shortage in others. The only way to raise the salaries of mathematics and science teachers is to raise the salaries of all teachers, including those in fields where there already is an oversupply of qualified teachers. Consequently, at any given time, large numbers of teachers are overpaid, in the sense that competent teachers could be employed to fill their positions at a much lower cost. If market conditions justify higher salaries to attract mathematics and science teachers, they also justify lower salaries in fields characterized by oversupply of qualified teachers. In fact, the two issues are closely related: the savings achieved by ending the overpayments could be used to pay higher salaries in the fields experiencing shortages.

How did it happen that virtually all K–12 public school systems adopted salary policies that ensure overpayment in some fields, underpayment in others? Earlier in this century, different patterns prevailed. For example, secondary teachers were usually paid more than elementary teachers. It was often difficult to disentangle sex discrimination from the elementary-secondary distinction because most secondary teachers were male, most elementary teachers female. Even apart from this, however, teacher compensation frequently reflected grade level or subject distinctions.

What changed this pattern? Elementary teachers contended that the change would be in the best interests of students: that the importance of early childhood required the best teachers to be in the primary grades. Interestingly enough, higher education is characterized by the opposite approach. Those who teach doctoral courses are typically paid more than those who teach freshmen. The supply and demand for people who can do the work, not the importance of the work, is the most critical factor in setting salaries. Thus although early childhood is an important period, the real explanation for the change lies elsewhere. There are twice as many elementary as secondary teachers. One could not rise to a leadership position in teacher organizations while advocating higher salaries for secondary teachers. Not surprisingly, school boards (which often depend on teacher organizations for campaign support) were easily persuaded to accept the elementary teachers' argument for single salary schedules. On the administrative side, single salary schedules were easier to administer and avoided the continuing hassle over the differentials. Furthermore, internal unity in teacher organizations would have been impossible if various subgroups of teachers had insisted on higher salaries for themselves. In short, the structure of teacher salaries is based on producer convenience, not on the welfare of young children. The inefficiencies resulting from this situation are absorbed by the taxpayers, most of whom have never considered the underlying issues.[14]

Merit Pay

The professional and media discussions of merit pay provide dramatic examples of producer domination. I base this conclusion on many years of familiarity with the discussion. In 1956 I published my first book, *Education as a Profession*,[15] which included an extensive discussion of merit pay. As it happened, after studying everything I could find on the subject, I was undecided on whether it was or was not a good idea. Thus the book listed the arguments for and against merit pay, and left it at that.

About ten years later I began to moonlight as a labor negotiator for school boards. I worked full or part time as a board negotiator and consultant for the next twenty-four years. In six states and dozens of school districts, I frequently had to deal with merit pay as a school board advisor or negotiator. My proposals on the subject led to the establishment in 1987 of the National Board for Professional Teaching Standards; if merit pay materializes on a broad scale in the United States, it will probably do so by this vehicle.[16]

Over the years school boards often requested that I negotiate some merit pay arrangement. Without fail, the unions were adamantly opposed to it. I am not critical of the unions for this. Usually I tried to persuade the school boards to drop the proposal; my view was that the costs of negotiating and implementing the merit pay proposals were not worth the benefits they might bring about. Of course, my obligation was to make a good faith effort to negotiate merit pay if the school board still wanted it.

Newspaper and television reporters often covered teacher bargaining, especially in impasse or strike situations. The reporters frequently asked the union negotiators why they were so opposed to merit pay. Without exception, the union negotiators offered three reasons. First, merit pay would be used to reward bootlickers, but would be withheld from outstanding teachers who did not get along with the administration. Second, even if implemented in good faith, merit pay would open the way to subjective judgments that could not be substantiated. Third, merit pay could be used to discriminate on ethnic or religious grounds, or to reward anti-union elements among the faculty. Without exception, the reporters accepted these explanations. I do not mean the reporters always agreed with them. My point is that the reporters always accepted the union objections as the actual reasons for union opposition to merit pay. Such acceptance illustrates the pervasive consequences of producer domination.

To see why, note that unions are political organizations. That is, control is exercised through a voting system, in which each member has one vote. Furthermore, unions are devoted to economic goals. In working to achieve them, union leadership tries to avoid situations in which one constituency appears to be getting more than others. This is a pervasive problem in politics. Presidents try to avoid the appearance of favoring one area of the country over another. Mayors try to avoid appearing to provide better services to some neighborhoods at the expense of others. Teacher unions have the same problem; the main difference is that their different constituencies are occupational, not geographic. High school teachers must not be perceived as getting more benefits than elementary teachers. If teachers of academic subjects but not vocational teachers get a duty-free preparation period, the latter will resent their "second-class citizenship."

In short, equality of benefits is a union imperative. Merit pay directly conflicts with this imperative. In order for merit pay to be meaningful, the pay differentials must be substantial. The more substantial the differentials, the fewer teachers will receive them. The fewer teachers who receive large differentials not available to the rank and file, the more dissatisfaction among the latter. The more dissatisfaction among the rank and file, the more precarious the position of union leaders. Ergo, they nip the process in the bud by opposing merit pay.

No matter how fair and objective the plan for merit pay, some teachers will be upset by not receiving it. They will sincerely believe that they deserve merit pay as much or more than the teachers who receive it. How will union leaders respond to these complaints? Will they respond by saying, "The procedures were fair and objective, and the teachers awarded merit pay deserve it more than you do"? No such response will be forthcoming—ever. The union leaders can count. They will not accept a large number of disgruntled teachers for the sake of large rewards for a few teachers. Furthermore, suppose those who did not receive merit pay filed a grievance alleging that they deserved merit pay more than the recipients of it. Such grievances would force the union to support some union members at the expense of others. From the standpoint of union leadership, this would be a no-win situation. Union leaders naturally want no part of merit pay.

The reality thus turns out to be precisely the opposite of the rationale universally accepted in the media. Union leaders have more to fear from a fair and objective system of merit pay than from an unfair, subjective one; an ideal plan of merit pay, not vulnerable to valid criticism, would be a union disaster. Teachers would still feel aggrieved by not being awarded merit pay, no matter how fair the procedures. In my forty-five years in education, I have never encountered media coverage that recognizes the problems merit pay would create for unions. Likewise, most teachers accept the union explanation without question. This is not the only instance in which most of the producers regard their own propaganda as the truth of the matter.

School Boards

Most school board members serve in an unpaid capacity. Typically, they are paid expenses but only a small stipend or none at all for time devoted to board business. It might seem, therefore, that producer interests would not dominate school boards, at least to the same degree that they dominate the policies of their full-time employees.

Board members are more likely to represent consumer interests in smaller school districts. For one thing, board members are known to parents in small districts; parents often call them to express complaints. This is less likely to happen in large districts, where most parents do not know any board members and where board members would be overwhelmed if they considered parental complaints individually.

As district size increases, board members are more likely to subordinate consumer interests to producer interests. Whether elected or appointed, board members are damaged politically by negative publicity about school district operations or effectiveness. Furthermore, and especially in larger districts, board members rely on support from teacher unions to be elected or appointed. This reliance renders them less likely to support pupil and parent interests over those of teachers. In addition, membership on a school board is a mark of recognition and prestige; it is difficult to be publicly critical of a service that provides these satisfactions.

For the most part, school boards and their organizations oppose any form of competition with public schools. Their opposition to competition would be inexplicable if pupil and parent interests were their highest priorities. In that case, school boards would view public schools as a means to an end; the end would be better served by competition than by a monopoly of service providers. In practice, however, school boards are almost as eager as teacher unions to preserve the public school monopoly. Their reasons are political rather than economic, but the outcome is the same. Likewise, when it comes to education, states are not intelligent buyers: they buy only from monopolies (local school boards) they have created themselves. Intelligent consumers prefer competition among their vendors.

It thus turns out that cooperation between unions and school boards to prevent competition is similar to labor-management cooperation to prevent competition in other fields. American automobile manufacturers and the United Auto Workers have conflicting interests at the bargaining table. Nevertheless, they work together to restrict imports of Japanese cars. Such restrictions shield both manufacturers and employees from competition—and in the process, force American consumers to pay billions more for automobiles. As in education, the argument is that competition might be desirable in principle, but not in this particular situation.

Besides teachers and school boards, the producers of education include principals and central office administrators, who also stand to gain from the public school monopoly. Furthermore, administrators are not likely to support policies opposed by boards that hire, promote, and fire them. Such opposition is especially unlikely in view of the fact that administrator organizations lack the power of teacher unions to protect their members. The bottom line is that school administrators, like teachers, would be threatened by competition. Their opposition to competition is a rational policy that protects their interests.

Implications of Producer Domination

One of the major themes in public administration is the tendency for producers to gain control over the agencies that are supposed to regulate them on behalf of consumers. Utility commissions are "captured" by the electric power companies. Health care agencies are dominated by the American Medical Association. The Federal Aviation Administration was controlled by the airlines. And so on. A large body of literature is devoted to "regulatory capture" and its undesirable consequences.[17]

A question arises: If even agencies that regulate producers tend to become controlled by the producers, what can we expect when the producing agency itself is accorded the role of consumer protection? The answer is clear: We can expect producer interests to prevail over consumer interests. Anticompetitive policies will win out over policies that foster competition. To the extent that producers are able to avoid competition, consumers suffer from the absence of innovation. Clearly, this is what has happened in public education. Teacher tenure, excessive licensing requirements, protection against layoffs, limitations on contracting out, limitations on assignments, on teaching load, on transfers—a panoply of statutory and contractual provisions protect school district personnel, but only at an enormous cost to consumers.

To be blunt about it, the largest cost of producer domination is the impossibility of fundamental improvement. The past few decades have witnessed significant improvements in health care, transportation, financial services, telecommunications—virtually every major service except education. Meanwhile, education is carried on as it has been for generations. In no field is there more rhetoric about change, and in no field is there less actual change reflecting real improvement in the quality or cost of the service. Cosmetic changes, which are the only kind possible, are frequently adopted and quickly discarded; they give the appearance that something is being done to improve matters. As with public services generally, political and educational leaders have a larger stake in the appearance of improvement than in its actual existence. Reelection or tenure in office depends on the public perception that education has improved or that promising efforts to improve it are under way. Actual improvement, however, usually requires more time than is available in the short run. The "short run" is the next election or the period of time before reappointment.

Despite official rhetoric espousing "parental choice," producer control of public education increased during the Reagan and Bush administrations. During that time, teacher unions have intensified their efforts to organize support personnel: bus drivers, secretaries, custodians, paraprofessionals, and so on. In the past, these employees were more concerned than teachers about the possibility that school boards would contract out their work to private companies. In order to organize them, the teacher unions pledged to work for statutory or bargaining prohibitions on contracting out.[18] These efforts were often successful. Obviously, if a school board cannot contract out a service, the employees who provide it have achieved monopoly status.

Unquestionably, if schools were owned and operated privately in a competitive environment, school owner-operators would be adamantly opposed to restrictions on their right to contract out instruction, food service, transportation, or anything else. Such restrictions would put them at a competitive disadvantage vis-à-vis schools that enjoyed competition among their vendors. Because schools are a public monopoly, taxpayers and parents suffer the losses resulting from the prohibitions against contracting out by school boards.

Producer control has also been augmented by the "teacher empowerment" movement. Tales of the classroom teacher struggling against a mindless, insensitive bureaucracy are a staple at teacher conventions. Political candidates seeking support from teachers must pledge to empower the creative spirits who are frustrated by educational bureaucrats. When teachers identify bureaucratic interference as the major obstacle to reform, educational media publicize this self-serving conclusion as if it were the discovery of cold fusion. Astonishingly, the most obvious questions are not even asked, let alone answered plausibly. What is it that teachers are not empowered to do? What would they do if empowered and why would it result in large educational gains? After forty-five years in public education, I have yet to encounter plausible answers to these questions.

In short, "teacher empowerment" is a producer buzzword; it is achieved by turning over more control to the producers, not by fulfilling the wishes of parents or communities. Teacher empowerment would make sense in a market system. In public education, it is a declaration of intellectual bankruptcy. Supervisors and administrators are seldom present in classrooms or otherwise in a position to observe teachers at work. Teachers, and teachers only, have the right to negotiate on a wide range of educational policies. They are present at department, school, and district meetings where policies are discussed and adopted. Typically, teacher organizations and only teacher organizations have contractual rights to consultation and/or negotiation before school management can act on various issues. In some states, teachers have the legal right to strike; thus they are the only interest group with the legal right to stop delivery of educational services unless and until their demands are met. The problem of educational reform is not how to empower teachers; it is how to empower educational consumers to overcome the monopoly power of educational producers.

As discussed earlier, when government produces a service, government officials try to avoid exposure of producer deficiencies. Such avoidance compromises government's role as representative and watchdog for consumer interests. In education as in other government services, the political process does not remedy the problem for several reasons:

1. In order to be elected, incumbents and candidates of the party in power tend to avoid exposure of producer deficiencies; exposure would usually help the opposition candidates. School board members running for reelection do so on the basis of what they have achieved, not what has gone wrong.
2. Elections often hinge on noneducational issues, hence candidates most knowledgeable about educational deficiencies may not be elected.
3. No matter who wins an election, a large number of teachers, administrators, board members, and regulators have a stake in the status quo. Their opposition, even just their inertia, may be an insurmountable obstacle to change.
4. As will be explained in the next chapter, media treatment of education rarely clarifies important educational issues. This renders it difficult for political leadership to act constructively on these issues.

Nevertheless, governments do change occasionally from government to private delivery of services, or vice versa. Separation of church and state is an example: where it took place, governments shed their role as producers of religion and allowed the private sector to produce religious services.

In recent years many governments in all areas of the world have "privatized" various public services. The decline of government ownership and control in Eastern Europe and the Soviet Union has been most highly publicized, but privatization has emerged on every continent, in all types of governments.[19] The tremendous variety of what has been privatized strongly suggests that the inefficiencies giving rise to privatization are due to government operation per se; no other common factor explains why so many different services have been shifted to the private sector.

For the most part, however, the privatization movement has not affected education, even in the nations that have privatized many other services. One exception is the United Kingdom, where the government is aggressively trying to shift more of its educational system to the private sector. The absence of privatization of education elsewhere, however, is not necessarily due to reasons favorable to public education. In some nations, a large proportion of school-age children are already enrolled in private schools. Privatization of education may also raise unique political problems that are independent of its merits. Producer opposition to privatization tends to be ineffective if the service being privatized employs a small fraction of the labor force. In democratic nations, privatization is politically more difficult if a large number of employees would lose the benefits of government employment. As will be pointed out in Chapter 12, public education in the United States is especially subject to this difficulty.

Producer-consumer conflict is a strong reason to support market over government delivery of educational services. The market approach will allow government to play a consumer-protection role, free from pressure to protect government itself as producer. Of course, private producers will try to control government information and regulatory roles, but such efforts will be less likely to succeed if government is not the service producer.

Conflict between producers and consumers is an extremely pervasive issue; the discussion of it thus far has been introductory, not comprehensive. The avoidance of competition from private schools, excessive job security for teachers, resistance to educational technology, indefensible teacher licensing requirements, research and development oriented to the needs of producers instead of consumers, overemphasis on degrees and diplomas, opposition to labor market alternatives—the manifestations of producer domination show up in every aspect of public education. Perhaps none is more important than its impact on the information system associated with public education. I turn next to this neglected but critically important problem.

4

≈ The Information System of Public Education

Information needs vary among users. The needs of voters, parents, school board members, legislators, and others overlap on some issues, diverge on others. As a government service, however, public education is subject to all the caveats concerning good government generally. An informed citizenry is presumably necessary to set appropriate objectives, monitor public school efforts to achieve them, and modify the objectives and the means as circumstances warrant.

A common assumption is that elected officials will respond to citizens who are adequately informed about the issues. The assumption raises the question of what citizens need to know about education in order to carry out their civic roles effectively. Clearly, unless we are willing to give legislators and public school personnel a free hand without accountability, citizens have a huge informational burden. Educational policy is made at local, state, and federal levels. At each level, different officials or agencies may influence policy. For instance, at the state level, governors are usually the most influential figures. State boards of education and state superintendents of instruction also play important roles. At the local level, school boards and mayors are usually major actors, as are several elected officials at the federal level. Citizens normally have the opportunity to vote for a number of officials who exercise major educational responsibilities:

Local
  School board members (Most school boards have five, seven, or nine members; I shall assume seven-member boards in the following discussion.)
State
  Governor
  State superintendent of public instruction
  State senator
  State representative
Federal
  President (and vice-president)
  Senator (2)
  Representative in Congress

This gives a total of sixteen elected officials with significant educational responsibilities. Eight of the sixteen also have major responsibilities outside the field of education.

Even many citizens who regard education as important consider other issues to be more important. For example, in *Washington Post*/ABC News polls conducted from 1984 to 1989, voters were asked: "What do you think is the most important problem facing the country today?" The quality of education was seldom mentioned by more than one percent of the respondents.[1] Presumably even citizens who care deeply about education often cast their votes on the basis of noneducational issues. Naturally voters are less likely to seek out educational information if it plays a secondary role or none at all in their voting patterns.

For the sake of discussion, let us assume that voters consider only the issues affecting education. With sixteen different offices and several candidates for each office (do not overlook primaries) citizens presumably need to study the educational views of fifty to one hundred candidates. They also need to become knowledgeable about the issues. Surely this is unrealistic. One reason is the enormous quantity of educational legislation at all levels of government. Each year about fifteen hundred bills affecting education are introduced in California, and about five hundred in New York and Ohio.[2] Many of the most important do not specifically refer to education. For example, proposed legislation on tax exemptions can affect school revenues. Legislation on health insurance can have significant effects on school finance and personnel policies.

Legislation addressing the health hazards of video display terminals may affect school districts in several ways. Even the educational producer organizations are sometimes unable to track all the bills that affect education; the overwhelming majority of voters are completely unaware of them. It is hardly surprising that educational producers are frequently able to enact legislation that benefits themselves at the expense of educational consumers.

In addition to legislation, many states provide for voter initiatives or referenda to be submitted directly to the electorate. For instance, in the 1988 California elections, voters were asked to vote directly on a large number of bond acts, constitutional amendments, and statutory initiatives. The California attorney general is required to disseminate a publication explaining these measures. The 1988 explanations ran to 159 pages, much of it in small print. Several California communities also listed similar measures on their ballots.[3]

These exercises in direct democracy often involve important educational issues. In California an initiative to limit property taxes was enacted in 1978; its passage led to drastic changes in school finance.[4] A 1988 initiative directed that a certain proportion of state revenues be allocated to public education. California leads the nation in the number of initiatives presented to voters, and the number is increasing. It is increasing despite ample evidence showing that (1) many voters do not read the initiatives; (2) many voters vote for precisely the opposite of the outcome they prefer; (3) reading levels required to understand many initiatives disenfranchise a substantial proportion of the electorate; and (4) advertising campaigns play a major role in the success or failure of initiatives.[5]

The discussion so far has emphasized information problems at the state level. I have not mentioned the plethora of municipal, federal, and school board policies that affect education. Even if citizens ignored every other type of public policy, they could not possibly be well informed on all of these educational policies. In short, if it is essential that citizens be well informed on educational policies, public education faces some immense information problems.

It might be argued that most of the educational measures introduced at the local, state, and federal levels are not very important, and I could readily agree. Still, how can one know which bills are not important without analyzing them? After all, seemingly innocuous legislation often has far-reaching consequences. Furthermore, the legislative categories voters deem safe to ignore are inevitably used to shield important legislation from public scrutiny.

Of course, citizens need not know all the ramifications of all local, state, and federal policies affecting education. We should not assume, however, that the time citizens devote to educational matters enables them to be adequately informed on the matters that do require citizen guidance or exercise of oversight responsibilities. The educational matters citizens consider are limited by the time they make available for them much more than the time they make available is adjusted to the importance of the issues. Furthermore, there is no feasible way for citizens to distinguish essential from nonessential issues. In the absence of any practical way to draw the line, citizens inevitably devote too much time to trivial issues but not enough to important ones. The supporters of public education do not discuss these time and information problems, perhaps because they recognize a Pandora's box when they see one.

Probably most citizens would agree that changing social, economic, demographic, and technological conditions may require changes at any time. For this reason, our concern must be with the information system and its adequacy on a continuous basis. By "information system," I mean the answers to the following questions:

1. Who produces information about education? What is the competence of the producers, and what are their biases?
2. What information is produced? What is not produced that should be?
3. Who uses the information, and for what purposes?
4. How is information about education disseminated, stored, and retrieved?
5. To what extent does the information meet system needs relating to topics, timeliness, accessibility, clarity, and cost?
6. Who pays to produce information, and who pays for information about education as a consumption item?

It is not feasible to answer all of these questions here. They are raised only to point up the complexity of the important information problems of public education.

Let me now anticipate a potential objection. Most of my criticisms of the information system associated with public education apply to other public services as well. Consequently, it may appear as if my argument is really an attack on the ability of citizens to govern themselves.

I do not agree with the criticism, but it merits discussion. At any given time, citizens can be knowledgeable about only a limited number of public policies. Voters may be capable of understanding each of a thousand different policies individually, but not all of them collectively. They have insufficient time, resources, or incentives to do so.

The Absence of Prices

Some of the information problems of public education result from the absence of prices for educational services. Of course, school districts rely on prices when they purchase teacher services, management, textbooks, supplies, equipment, and so on. Nevertheless, individual parents do not buy public education as they buy houses or automobiles or groceries. The costs of education are defrayed from federal, state, and local tax revenues. Taxpayers may think they know how much education costs, but they do not know how much they pay personally for public education. There is not much reason to know, since most taxpayers can do little or nothing about it.

The fact is that public education lacks the critical information provided by prices. Prices tell us how much consumers are willing to pay for goods and services and whether producers are willing to produce them for various returns. Significantly, prices can take account of intensity of preferences in ways that are not available to public services. The absence of meaningful prices was a major weakness in command economies such as those in Eastern Europe and the Soviet Union. Governments produced goods and services consumers did not want, and/or failed to produce goods and services they did want. These failures occurred on a massive scale because prices were not established by the free interactions of producers and consumers.

School boards can only guess at consumer preferences. For example, suppose some parents want computer education in elementary schools. If parents who enrolled their children in computer education were charged for its costs, we would know how strongly parents wanted it. When school boards decide the issue, they have no comparable mechanism to assess parental preferences on a continuous basis. School boards rely on prices in buying factors of production, but these prices do not function as signals about the educational preferences of consumers. By and large, such preferences are divined through political processes which cannot isolate preferences or measure their intensity.

The Media

Information about education comes from several sources. As far as broad educational policy is concerned, the media provide most of it. The media include television and radio broadcasting, book and magazine publishing, and newspapers, to mention only the more obvious categories. Significant differences affecting education exist within each of these categories. For instance, national newspapers, such as the New York Times, employ reporters who specialize in education news and analysis, but the education reporters on most newspapers report on several other subjects as well.

Criticism of television and press treatment of news is a mini-industry. The extent of such criticism should give us pause. If the criticism is valid and has been publicized for a long time, why hasn't there been some corrective action? The answer to this question highlights an obstacle to public school reform.

Perhaps the most misunderstood fact about the media is the identity of their customers. The customers are advertisers, not television viewers or newspaper readers. Advertisers buy access to viewers and readers, the more the better. News or information is not the objective of either the media companies or the companies that advertise in the media. "News" is simply one means of increasing the number of viewers and subscribers.

This basic point underscores the futility of educational appeals for improved media treatment of education. For instance, teachers are usually portrayed in television sitcoms in an unfavorable or unrealistic way. In addition, teachers are rarely shown actually teaching a subject. Doctors and lawyers and police officers are typically shown carrying out their work; teachers are not. Pleas to the media to portray teachers in a favorable light miss the point. Television producers are not out to criticize teachers. They are out to sell advertising on successful television shows. The impact of these shows on the group portrayed is a secondary concern at best. The media's point of departure is not what citizens should know about education. It is what news and analysis will increase the number of viewers or readers.[6]

What news is most conducive to meeting this objective? According to those who earn their living by answering this question, news about conflict ranks high, as evidenced by media attention to wars, strikes, presidential elections, and the availability of condoms in public schools. News about prominent personalities, the unique, the close to home—all of these and more overshadow policy significance as criteria for what is shown or published. To put it bluntly, news about education doesn't attract many viewers or readers. Educators lament the fact, but there is very little they can do about it. The media's modus operandi is not likely to change merely because the public is uninformed about education.

The following discussion is devoted primarily to network television and newspapers because they are the most important sources of information for most people.[7] Throughout, readers should bear in mind the system issues: What are the educational information needs of citizens under public education, and what are the prospects that their information needs will or even can be met by the media?

Television

Television, especially network television, appears to be the major source of information in this country. Indisputably, education is a low-priority topic in network news and policy analysis. None of the three major networks has employed a full-time education specialist in its news division. Ordinarily, they do not employ even part-time education specialists. Not surprisingly, a very low proportion of network news is devoted to education. A ten-year study (1973–1982) of network news found that 2 percent of the time was devoted to education news.[8] This estimate is in line with others covering different years. The study also concluded that the time devoted to education was largely about unimportant topics. Although network time devoted to education increased after publication of *A Nation at Risk* in 1983, the study concluded that the networks paid no attention to the causes of low achievement.

A 1986 NBC documentary narrated by Tom Brokaw illustrates the level of network analysis of educational issues. The documentary featured a high school teacher moonlighting as a liquor store salesman. Predictably, the teacher asserted, "I wanted to be a teacher—and this is what I have to do." An NEA news release about the program stated that the teacher "faces the same dilemma confronted by thousands of his colleagues across the country . . . turning to moonlighting to make ends meet or keep from falling into debt."[9]

Unquestionably, this explanation of teacher moonlighting is a media staple. Who has not seen or read about the underpaid teacher struggling to earn enough to continue teaching? Interestingly enough, moonlighting is a common practice in higher education, despite salaries being higher there than in the public schools. The vast majority (80–90 percent) of professors have outside employment. One study showed that over 60 percent engaged in some type of consulting activity.[10] Two-thirds of the nation's research universities have adopted some restrictions on outside employment (usually limiting it to one day a week).[11] In practice, however, many universities have no restrictions, and the restrictions that exist are usually quite liberal and not vigorously enforced. In all probability, the higher-paid professors at the higher-paid institutions moonlight more than faculty elsewhere. In short, moonlighting is hardly synonymous with scraping to make ends meet.

In fact, recent studies demonstrate that the NBC documentary was very misleading. In one, some teachers said they moonlighted because of their financial needs. "Need," however, was defined subjectively, so that a teacher making $40,000 a year might have expressed a need while one making considerably less might not have. Regardless, over half of the moonlighting teachers said they would continue to moonlight even if the amounts they were earning by moonlighting were added to their teaching salaries. Furthermore, the moonlighters devoted more time than nonmoonlighters to tutoring their regular pupils. Paradoxically, moonlighting showed no correlation to teachers' salaries, household income, or age and experience.[12]

The NBC documentary illustrates a common weakness in network programs on education. Since the networks (CBS, NBC, ABC) do not employ persons knowledgeable about education on a full-time basis, they seek "expert" advice on programs devoted to education. In most cases, they turn to individuals and organizations that are only too happy to promote their own agendas when the opportunity arises. The network producers may not even be aware of the agendas, or may be sympathetic to them; for all I know, NBC officials believed they were performing a public service by calling public attention to teacher moonlighting. It probably never occurred to them that overpayment of teachers in certain grades and subjects (in which there is a teacher surplus) may be as serious a problem as underpayment of teachers in fields unable to attract qualified teachers.[13]

Newspapers

Education is a low-priority area of newspaper coverage as well. Amy Stuart Wells pointed out in 1986 that fewer than 250 of 1,730 U.S. daily newspapers listed an education reporter or editor. Most of those listed had other responsibilities in addition to education. These responsibilities were often in fields unrelated to education, such as gardening, entertainment, real estate, and automobiles. In addition, the education assignment was characterized by low prestige and high turnover. It was seldom a stepping-stone to high-level management or editorial positions: relatively few editors were promoted from the ranks of education reporters.[14]

Press neglect of education was not a concern within the field of journalism; according to Wells, the leading magazines devoted to the press and the media did not publish a single article on the subject prior to 1985.[15] Wells's summary of the space devoted to education news from 1956 to 1985 in the *New York Times,* the *Chicago Tribune,* and the *Los Angeles Times* showed that only 7.7 percent of the education articles were carried on the front page, whereas 43.7 percent were found in the back sections or after page 50 in the papers.[16]

The basic deficiencies in media coverage of education are not due to liberal or conservative bias. The assumption that a good reporter can report on anything is a much more important factor. The assumption is not always explicit, and occasionally one encounters exceptions to it. Nonetheless, the predominant practice of the media is consistent with the assumption. For instance, the most influential newspapers, such as the *New York Times* and the *Washington Post,* do not require any formal training in education to report on it.[17] Edward Fiske, the education editor of the *New York Times* from 1974 to 1991, started as a clerk assigned to the religion editor in 1964. He later became a religion reporter and then the religion editor before being assigned as education editor in 1974. In Fiske's view, this was as it should be; he told Wells, "I was very good at dealing with dogma, so they kicked me over to education," and "There are no education courses worth taking, probably. Education isn't significantly different from covering any other beat—you learn what you have to know."[18]

Parenthetically, some of the nation's leading scholars, such as James S. Coleman, past president of the American Sociological Association, and Lee J. Cronbach, past president of the American Psychological Association, teach or have taught education courses. The underlying significance of Fiske's comments, however, is their confirmation that the *New York Times* did not employ someone knowledgeable about education to serve as its education editor. Although the holder of this position exercises unparalleled influence over public information about education, the person employed to fill it was expected to learn about education through on-the-job experience. We are not told how much time Fiske needed to "learn what you have to know," but his comments suggest cavalier treatment of education in the nation's leading newspaper.

Wells sent a questionnaire to 120 education reporters employed by newspapers ranging in circulation from 3,000 to 1 million. The responses indicated that few newspapers considered the formal study of education to be essential to report on it. Although 94 percent of the reporters had bachelor's degrees, only one was in education. About two-thirds had not taken any coursework in education, such as educational policy, school finance, education law, or educational testing.[19]

Of course, education is not the only field that is subject to the media assumption that reporters need not be knowledgeable about a field to report on it. If the assumption is a problem, it is unlikely to be resolved apart from a basic change in the media. The fact is that except for national or large regional or local organizations, the media cannot afford to employ specialists in several different fields. Furthermore, reporters can't hope to climb the ladder to more prestigious assignments if knowledge of the field is a prerequisite to the assignment. Absent basic changes in the media's modus operandi, then, media coverage of education will continue to be covered by reporters who do not know very much about it.

Educational News: The System in Operation

Ultimately, we must go beyond background factors to examine what is actually presented as education news. I shall do so here by discussing media treatment of three educational topics. Their importance and the prestige of the media involved should leave no doubt about their representative character.

A Nation at Risk

By all accounts, *A Nation at Risk* was the most widely publicized and most influential educational publication of the 1980s.[20] The publication was sponsored by the National Commission on Excellence in Education, an eighteen-member commission appointed by the Secretary of Education. It was released in April 1983, and hundreds of thousands of copies were distributed by the federal government. Major portions of it were reprinted in the *New York Times* and other leading print media. *A Nation at Risk* was the main topic of discussion at thousands of education conventions and conferences, and virtually every journal in the field published one or more commentaries on it.

Despite this massive coverage, the media ignored the fact that *A Nation at Risk* was a unanimous report. It was unanimous because the commission members agreed that it should be. Inasmuch as the commission included representatives of every major educational interest group, the unanimity policy precluded any recommendation that posed a threat to any of these groups.

Surely there is a world of difference between saying "This is what we believe should be done to improve American education" and saying "This is what we believe should be done to improve American education, excluding all issues on which we do not have unanimous agreement among commission members." The requirement of unanimity limited *A Nation at Risk* to cosmetic issues, or to pie-in-the-sky proposals on important ones. Predictably, the report did not lead to any significant changes despite the enormous media attention it received. How could it? How could any recommendations based on the premise of unanimity among interest groups lead to changes in the roles, rights, responsibilities, and powers of those groups? The reason for the unanimity approach was not stated but was hardly a mystery—the report was intended to generate political support, and you do not do that by antagonizing influential interest groups. Had even a handful of education reporters—perhaps only one in a major national newspaper or news magazine—expressed interest in the unanimity issue, our nation might have been spared years of irrelevant discussion and debate that diverted attention from the real problems that must be faced if we are to improve education.

Teacher Salaries and Benefits

According to a 1990 publication of the U.S. Department of Education, the average teacher salary for the 1989–90 school year was $31,304. The publication says that "this represents an increase of 5.9 percent, in current dollars, over the revised figure of $29,547 in 1988–89."[21] Five months earlier, the NEA had issued a news release that began with the following sentence: "Salaries of classroom teachers across the country are estimated to increase to an average of $31,304 for the 1989–90 school year, a hike of 5.9 percent over last year, a new report by the National Education Association disclosed today."[22] In other words, the department did not conduct the research on teacher salaries; instead it relied on the estimates and interpretive comments of the nation's largest teacher union. Such reliance was neither new nor secret; the department has followed this practice for several decades. Likewise, the media rely almost exclusively on the NEA for salary data. By doing so, they misinform the American people about teacher compensation.

Generally speaking, a school district has a certain amount of money to spend for teacher welfare. Quite often, teachers prefer that a substantial portion of it be applied to fringe benefits instead of salaries. One reason is the tax advantage of doing so: the fringe benefits are not taxed, whereas the same money applied to teachers' salaries would be taxable income. Also, by having district funds applied to fringe benefits instead of salaries, teachers benefit from the perception that they are underpaid. Sometimes school boards also prefer this course of action to protect themselves against criticism for overpaying teachers. At any rate, the salary figures disseminated by the Department of Education and the media omit the dollar value of teacher's fringe benefits. A partial list includes contributions to teacher pensions, health and dental insurance, a wide variety of leave benefits (sick, sabbatical, parental, adoption, military, union business, and so on), extra duty pay (coaching, band, school paper, student clubs, and so on), and workmen's compensation. These fringe benefits greatly exceed those paid to private school teachers. In some states, their dollar value is more than one-third of straight salary.

Let us now trace the path of public information about teacher salaries. The NEA generates annual salary figures that substantially understate teacher compensation. The U.S. Department of Education releases the NEA figures as its own. Newspapers, magazines, government reports, educational reform proposals, and television networks use and rely upon these "official" figures. Quite often, the media compare teacher salaries to those in other professions. The comparisons seldom mention the fact that teachers work only 180 days a year on the average, and that their workday is shorter than those in most full-time positions. They also overlook several benefits, such as teacher tenure and layoff and reemployment rights, that are not available to most private-sector employees. These benefits often impose direct and indirect costs on school districts, but they are not included in the summaries of teacher compensation.

When all of these factors are taken into account, teacher compensation appears in a much more favorable light.[23]

What reasons does the NEA give for omitting data on fringe benefits from its annual survey of teacher salaries? One is that it would be too expensive to get the data. The other is that private-sector employees also receive fringe benefits, so the comparisons aren't really misleading. Neither reason survives examination. Private-sector employees do receive fringe benefits, but the benefits are usually substantially less than for public employees. This is especially true of teachers: both salaries and fringe benefits are much higher in public than in private schools.

In 1989–90 the unrestricted income of the NEA and the AFT combined was well over $200 million. The revenues of their state and local affiliates probably exceed $750 million, perhaps by a large amount.[24] The claim that these unions cannot afford research on fringe benefits is preposterous. The fact is that they already have the data. If you negotiate for a school board, the union representative will quickly point out that your fringe benefits lag behind those in neighboring districts. Within seconds, the representative can bring up the data on a computer. After deleting the districts that provide less in fringe benefits, the NEA representative will show you the districts that provide more health insurance, sick leave, sabbatical leave, paid holidays, personal business leave, longer duty-free lunch periods, shorter school days, and so on. Salaries and benefits are the raison d'être of teacher unions; the notion that the unions cannot afford to find out their dollar value is for education reporters. If comparisons of fringe benefits showed teachers to be at a disadvantage, the media would be inundated by them. Unfortunately, the media and the U.S. Department of Education ignore the fact that the figures are prepared by an organization with a huge stake in how they are interpreted.

The I.Q. Controversy

Controversies about I.Q. tests have played a major role in education, especially since 1969. The discussion that follows is based on a remarkable book by Mark Snyderman and Stanley Rothman devoted to media treatment of such controversies.[25] The authors carefully compare what 231 experts believe about I.Q. issues with the treatment of these issues in the media from January 1, 1969, to December 31, 1984. The members of the media studied were the *New York Times,* the *Washington Post,* and the *Wall*

Street Journal; Time, Newsweek, and *U.S. News and World Report;* and the television networks ABC, CBS, and NBC. Careful safeguards were employed to ensure objective evaluation of the articles and broadcasts.

Some of the conclusions reached by Snyderman and Rothman are as follows:

1. The inability of media personnel to interpret technical reports led to egregious errors in reporting.
2. Media deadlines led to errors on matters that required more time to study.
3. The private views of journalists played an important role of the aspects emphasized. The aspects most antithetical to their views were most likely to be treated pejoratively.
4. Consultants quoted tended to be the extremists who would be most controversial, not the most informative.
5. On several issues, the consultants quoted followed neither the moderate views nor the consensus of expert opinion.
6. The media constantly distorted the views of prominent scholars whose views were contrary to mainstream media views.[26]

Table 4.1 summarizes the number of media presentations supporting various conclusions about the abuse of intelligence tests. On every issue included in the table, the emphasis in media treatment was contrary to the consensus of expert opinion on the issue. Snyderman and Rothman comment:

> It is obvious from these data just how uncritical the *Times* and *Post,* and the elite media in general, have been in reporting test misuse. Comparing these data to the relevant survey responses [of the experts] . . . is particularly distressing, especially since experts are often used as sources for claims of test abuse . . .
>
> Newspaper authors, particularly in the *New York Times,* apparently feel more comfortable asserting or implying various test misuses than test usefulness.[27]

Because its focus is on the most influential members of the media, Snyderman and Rothman's study provides impressive evidence that the American people are misinformed about basic educational issues.

The preceding examples underscore a paradoxical feature of the media's approach to educational news. It is de rigueur for education reporters and editorial writers to decry the training and employment of

Table 4.1.   Media presentations concerning misuse of intelligence tests, 1969–1984

1. Students are often misclassified, mislabeled, or stigmatized on the basis of their intelligence test scores.

	NYT	WP	WSJ	Newsmags	TV
			Number of Articles or Broadcasts		
Positive	21	6	1	7	4
Negative	0	0	0	0	0
Both	2	2	0	0	0

2. A student's knowledge of his or her intelligence test score often results in negative self-concepts and expectations (acts as a self-fulfilling prophecy).

	NYT	WP	WSJ	Newsmags	TV
Positve	3	3	1	1	0
Negative	0	0	0	0	0
Both	0	0	0	0	0

3. A teacher's knowledge of a student's intelligence test score has a significant effect on student performance.

	NYT	WP	WSJ	Newsmags	TV
Positve	6	1	1	1	0
Negative	0	0	0	0	0
Both	0	0	0	0	0

4. Tests are or have been used to promote racist or other inegalitarian ends.

	NYT	WP	WSJ	Newsmags	TV
Positive	15	6	1	1	3
Negative	0	0	0	0	0
Both	1	0	0	1	0

5. Test scores are over-relied upon (are too important in people's lives).

	NYT	WP	WSJ	Newsmags	TV
Positive	11	7	0	5	1
Negative	1	0	0	0	0
Both	0	1	0	0	0

Source: Mark Snyderman and Stanley Rothman, *The I.Q. Controversy* (New Brunswick, N.J.: Transaction Publishers, 1988), p. 212.

teachers who lack a thorough knowledge of their subject. This deficiency certainly deserves criticism, but as the examples suggest, lack of knowledge of a subject is just as harmful in the media as it is in classrooms.

Information about Educational Achievement

Virtually everyone agrees that U.S. students are not learning as much as students in other industrial nations. This achievement gap exists at every grade level and at every socioeconomic level. Nevertheless, parents do not appear to be correspondingly dissatisfied with their schools. Although they often believe that public schools in general are inadequate, parents tend to be satisfied with the schools attended by their own children. Obviously, something is wrong here. If schools generally are ineffective, parental dissatisfaction should be widespread also.

The same discrepancy is evident in student perceptions of their own achievement. For instance, students who are poor in mathematics often rate their proficiency higher than students who have achieved at much higher levels. Thus students in the Virgin Islands, who ranked last in mathematics achievement, were second highest in student assessments of mathematics proficiency. At the other extreme, students in North Dakota ranked first in mathematics achievement, but only 11 percent deemed themselves proficient in mathematics.[28] Such data suggest the need for a closer look at information about educational achievement.

Government is the main source of information about educational achievement. State departments of education and school districts provide such information on an aggregated basis. School districts also provide information to students (and their parents) about educational achievement on an individual basis. Let us consider first the information provided on an aggregated basis.

John J. Cannell, a West Virginia physician, reported in 1987 that he had "surveyed all fifty states and discovered that no state is below average at the elementary level on any of the six major nationally normed, commercially available tests." In addition, Cannell asserted that 90 percent of local school districts claim that their averages exceed the national average and that "more than 70 percent of the students tested nationwide are told they are performing above the national average."[29] After considerable controversy, it turned out that Cannell's charges were substantially accurate. Indisputably, state education departments and school districts all over the United States were misinforming their constituents about the educational achievement of their students.

Investigation of Cannell's charges made it clear that average test scores had been inflated in the following ways:

1. Poor students were excluded or discouraged from taking the tests.
2. Teachers assigned tests as homework or taught test items in class.
3. Test security was minimal or even nonexistent.
4. Students were allowed more time than prescribed by test regulations.
5. Unrealistic, highly improbable improvements from test to test were not audited or investigated.
6. Teachers and administrators were not punished for flagrant violations of test prodedures.
7. Test results were reported in ways that exaggerated achievement levels.

After efforts to disprove Cannell's charges failed, the companies that produced and sold the tests were criticized for selling deficient tests. Actually, they were selling precisely what the states and school districts wanted to buy, to wit, tests that would help them appear to be efficient producers.

Grades and Report Cards

Parents need information about the educational progress and problems of their children. Grades and report cards are supposed to meet these needs. In this context, grades and report cards are the major producer communications to consumers that are not filtered through any third parties. Other kinds of direct communications to parents, such as parent-teacher conferences, telephone calls, letters, and newsletters, are less significant and will be omitted from this discussion.

Conceptually, grades and report cards inform parents of pupil progress, suggest actions parents should take, and help third parties (future teachers, guidance counselors, college admissions officers, and employers) make informed judgments about students as the need arises. (Because grades are included on report cards, references to report cards should be understood to refer to grades also, unless the context makes it clear that the inclusion is not appropriate.)

Report cards have been the subject of thousands of books and articles, and they raise several issues not discussed in this book. My concern here is with their informational dimensions. What information do report cards communicate? How helpful is this information to students and parents? To what extent, if any, is the information provided (or not provided) affected by producer-consumer conflicts of interest? How would or how might these issues be affected by a change to a market system of education?

Let me clarify the terminology to be used. A "grade" is a communication about the results of an assessment. The assessment may be of academic achievement or student behavior. "Assessment" involves some type of measurement of an activity and evaluation of the results of the measurement. When assessment takes place, the results are assigned a mark, letter, percentage, or other symbol that refers to a certain level of achievement. The symbol—that is, the grade—is then communicated via the report card.[30]

Student Achievement on Report Cards

Report cards presumably provide information about educational achievement. The way they do so varies a great deal from district to district; often there is variation within districts or even among teachers in the same school. Approximately 80 percent of school districts use letter grades in grades 4–12. Although a sizeable number use percentage grades, either solely or as a supplement to letter grades, I shall confine the discussion to letter grades. Also, I shall confine it to practice in grades 4–12, since there is relatively little variation below grade 4.

A critical issue is whether grades should be based on relative standing in a group or on performance criteria. Suppose a student correctly answers five out of ten questions in an arithmetic examination. If graded on the basis of specific criteria, the student may receive a low or even a failing grade. Suppose, however, that five is the highest number of correct answers in the class. If the grade is based on relative standing in the class, it will be the highest one possible. In technical terms, grading based on relative standing within a group is "normative"; grading based on standards of performance without regard to the performance of others is "criterion referenced."

As consumers, parents might wish to be informed about achievement according to both of these criteria. From time to time, each kind of information might be helpful; given the available technology, it would not be difficult to provide both kinds. In practice, this is rarely done. According to the Educational Research Service (ERS) survey cited in note 30, almost 60 percent of the districts reported that grades for achievement were based on specific standards for all students. That is, it was assumed that all students should achieve specified levels of proficiency; the grades were based on students' progress toward achieving these levels. Unfortunately, the survey did not provide any data on the standards used or how they were established. Another 17 to 25 percent of the districts reported that grades were based on progress toward learning objectives for each individual student. The survey did not explore the question of how teachers arrived at the objectives for each student. In addition, 11 to 17 percent of the districts reported that grades were based on student achievement relative to overall performance of the class. Under this approach, students who learned a great deal but ranked low in their class would receive low grades; students who learned very little but who ranked high in their class would receive high grades.

In 5 to 7 percent of the districts, grades at one or more grade levels were based on the individual ability of pupils. Presumably, low-ability students who did not learn very much would receive higher grades than high-ability students who learned more but not as much as their ability would suggest. There would be nothing wrong with this if the report cards also included grades based on achievement. The report cards would be informing parents about their children's performance according to different criteria. The fact that a grade according to one criterion was much more favorable than a grade based on other criteria would not be a valid criticism of the report card. Interestingly enough, only about one percent of the districts based their grades on student performance in standardized tests. This practice was much more common in the early 1900s, but was largely abandoned by 1930.

To summarize, districts vary widely in how they grade educational achievement: a given level of achievement leads to very different grades, depending on the standard used to evaluate achievement. Unless parents understand this, they do not get accurate information from report cards. Furthermore, the likelihood of parent confusion is even greater than would appear from the discussion thus far. Over 90 percent of the nation's school districts grade effort in one way or another. About one-fourth to one-third have no uniform policy on how this is done. District policies on the issue differ, sometimes even for different grade levels in the same district. For example, about two in five school districts grade effort separately from academic grades in the primary grades; about one in four include effort in the academic course grade. At the secondary level, about one-third of the districts include effort within the course grade, while one-fourth grade effort separately.

Note the added confusion when effort is included as a factor in grading. Does a grade of "B" reflect average achievement but outstanding effort? Outstanding achievement but average effort? Above-average achievement and above-average effort? Without such a breakdown, the grade does not convey much information. If the grade is based on average performance but outstanding effort, parents should praise the effort; if the grade reflects outstanding achievement but average effort, a different parental response will be appropriate.

To add to the confusion, effort is not the only additional criterion that is sometimes factored into a single letter grade. Although most districts do not grade attendance or note it separately, 15 to 26 percent of the districts either include attendance in course grades or have no uniform policy on the issue. Needless to say, the informational value of grades is weakened if attendance is included with other factors in a single letter grade.

The number of distinctions used in grading also affects their informational value. The most widely used pattern consists of a five-point scale: A, B, C, D, and F. These letter grades typically symbolize the following assessments:

A = Excellent, or outstanding
B = Good, or above average
C = Fair, or average
D = Poor, or below average
F = Failing, or no credit allowed.

Most criticisms of grading practices focus on this scale, alleging various negative outcomes from its use. Regardless of their merits, the criticisms have led to the adoption of grading scales with four, three, or only two distinctions. As the number of distinctions is reduced, each grade reflects a wider range of achievement, hence is less informative. This is particularly evident when two-point scales (Pass/Fail or Credit/No Credit) are used. The "Pass" category might range from performance barely above failure to the most outstanding levels of achievement. In this connection, the ERS survey showed that two-point scales were used more frequently in higher grade levels: whereas only 3.8 percent of the districts used them in grades 4–6, 30 percent did so in grades 10–12.

Several other factors also affect the informational value of report cards. According to the ERS survey, school districts varied widely on the following criteria:

1. The uses of student grades.
2. Whether checklists were used and their contents.
3. The use of anecdotal comments by teachers.
4. The grade levels at which attendance policies affected academic grades.
5. How grade point averages were computed and their uses.
6. The use of minimum competency tests.
7. The extent to which grading criteria differed across curriculum paths, such as college preparatory, vocational, or business programs.
8. The frequency of reporting.

In practice, the variability in grading practices and report cards is much greater than indicated by this summary. District policies must be interpreted and applied. Identical policies may be interpreted and applied differently, not only from district to district but even within districts and schools. Some districts do not have uniform policies on many issues. In some, policies on grades and report cards may be established by principals, whereas in others teachers may operate autonomously with respect to grades.

Theoretically, these differences may not be particularly important. As long as report cards are clearly understood by the users, the fact that they differ from report cards in other districts may not be significant. What is theoretically possible, however, is often practically unrealistic; the belief that parents will understand report cards that differ so much is a case in point. Many of the differences cited are significant but are not easily explained or understood. In many cases, the teachers themselves would be hard-pressed to justify their practices. For example, where grades are awarded on the basis of the relationship between achievement and ability, how do teachers assess the ability of each pupil? Do teachers of different subjects follow the same procedure in assessing ability? If grades are based on relative standing among the student's classmates, how can parents tell if the classmates are diligent or indolent scholars?

Teacher mobility is another factor to be considered. Teachers may be subject to different grading policies as they change from district to district, school to school, subject to subject, or grade level to grade level. Teachers subject to a new grading policy often need training to implement it properly. They need to know how to deal with large variations in class size, with students who come into the class during the semester, with wide variations in group achievement, and so on. Nevertheless, such training is rare; the ERS survey did not even inquire into it.

Do other communications to parents change the conclusions reached on the basis of grades? Although many districts use parent conferences for at least some grade levels, such conferences do not appear to be a major source of information for parents. Generally speaking, they are arranged either in conjunction with the dissemination of report cards or to deal with severe disciplinary matters. At the secondary level, the sheer number of students per teacher discourages extended conferences with parents. Utilization of parent conferences declines as grade level rises: whereas 82 percent of districts use parent conferences in grades 1–3, only 51 percent do so in grades 10–12.

Producer-Consumer Conflict in Grades and Report Cards

Do report cards "tell it like it is"—or do they avoid unpleasant truths about educational achievement? In light of the previous discussion, we should anticipate an absence of candor, and candor is indeed absent. Let us consider the producer interests in the matter. One such interest is the avoidance of consumer dissatisfaction. Obviously, low or failing grades generate more consumer dissatisfaction than favorable or average grades. Teachers realize that they are held at least partly accountable for their pupils' performance. Justly or unjustly, poor grades are perceived to be a sign of failure on the part of teachers as well as—if not instead of—pupils.

Understandably, many educators advocate the elimination of failing grades. Thus in 1971 the National Council of Teachers of English adopted a policy statement that read in part as follows: "After the early years, at all educational levels only passing grades . . . should be recorded on a student's permanent record."[31]

Similar recommendations have often been made by various educational leaders and organizations. As noted earlier, criticisms of the traditional five-point scale have led to grading scales with fewer distinctions. Elimination of failing grades is often the outcome when the number of distinctions is reduced. In addition, many teachers and administrators are sympathetic to a "no fail" policy in practice, even if they say nothing about it publicly. Such persons are likely to avoid or minimize negative grades. Of course, not every authority on the subject or every teacher supports a "no fail" policy, but many do. Their main rationale is that failing grades weaken children's self-esteem and discourage effort on their part. Presumably, low grades as well as failing ones do so. That "no fail" policies shield public school personnel from criticism is undoubtedly an incidental or absent factor in many cases. Still, even if we attribute the most benign motives to "no fail" policies, they have undoubtedly contributed to parental complacency in spite of low educational achievement.

In my view, we should separate assessment agencies from instructional ones. This separation is essential, regardless of the kind of educational system that is adopted. Of course, teachers have to assess pupils for instructional purposes; nothing said here questions that premise. On the other hand, assessments should not be hostage to producer interests not related to improving instruction or disseminating useful information to parents. This requires that certain assessments not be controlled by producers, public or private.

My criticisms of producer control of assessment are not based on a lack of concern for children's self-esteem. First, it is fallacious to assume that honesty in grading necessarily shatters the self-esteem of poor achievers. How results are communicated is critical. The focus must be on performance and what must be done to improve it. If this focus is maintained, candid evaluation need not be psychologically destructive. The efforts of teachers and administrators to avoid the immediate unpleasant consequences of low grades results in much more harmful long-range consequences. Students acquire an unwarranted perception of their skills and abilities; when these turn out to be inadequate for continued education or employment, the students naturally reject any responsibility for the situation.

Several incidents illustrate the self-defeating outcomes of liberal grading policies. In the District of Columbia, senior high school valedictorians have been denied admission to local colleges because of their failure to meet the academic standards for admission.[32] Florida enacted legislation in 1976 requiring students to pass a test of "functional literacy" in order to receive a high school diploma. In this case, the test was simply an additional hurdle to overcome after students had met all other requirements for a diploma. Students who passed all the required courses but did not pass the literacy test were to receive a "certificate of completion." Students were given three chances to pass the test. In the class of 1979 (the first to be subject to the test), 20 percent of the black seniors but only 1.9 percent of the white seniors failed to pass after three opportunities to do so. In October 1979, ten black seniors initiated a class action lawsuit challenging the test and its administration on several grounds, including racial bias in the test itself. Another of the grounds was the large discrepancies between the results of the Florida Literacy Test and student grade point averages.

An earlier lawsuit in California also suggests that report cards are least informative when candor is essential. The California case involved a high school graduate who was nonetheless illiterate. The student sued the San Francisco school district for malpractice.[33] Although the case was dismissed before trial, the student was prepared to show that his report cards over the years indicated normal progress toward graduation. There is no reason to believe this student's situation was exceptional. Such cases have even emerged in higher education as student-athletes have come forward with lawsuits or public charges after receiving passing grades for several years (even their degrees in some cases) despite being illiterate. In some cases, the student plaintiffs have received substantial out-of-court settlements. In my own experience, large urban districts have been visibly reluctant to investigate the distribution of grades, especially among student populations characterized by low achievement.

Another producer interest is to minimize the time devoted to grades and report cards. One way to further this interest is to restrict the frequency of reporting. In recent years, more and more districts have reduced the amount of teacher time required for preparing report cards by adopting computerized grading and reporting. Teachers simply fill in the grades and the computers are programmed to print out a letter to parents and a report card. Teachers can even buy books that provide a menu of possible comments; they need only check the comments they wish to include, and the parents receive a letter that appears to be individualized.[34] I see nothing wrong in using technology to facilitate reporting on pupil progress, but the savings in teacher time do not appear to benefit students in any way. For instance, it does not appear that any of the time saved is devoted to providing more informative report cards.

Another neglected problem related to grades is the denial of due process to students. Generally speaking, teachers enjoy enormous discretion in grading pupils. As a result, it is easy for teachers to rationalize unfair decisions. Needless to say, racial or religious or gender bias crops up among teachers, just as it does among other large groups in our society. Teachers may fail to devote sufficient time to grades or may lack the skills to grade properly. For all sorts of reasons, some teachers will grade some students unfairly from time to time. It is, therefore, incumbent upon school districts to provide some measure of due process for students who wish to challenge a grade. Incumbent or not, the teacher unions typically propose that there be no appeal from grades given by teachers. For example, a model contract disseminated by the New Jersey Education Association includes the provision that "No grade or evaluation shall be changed without approval of the teacher."[35] In some districts, the contracts explicitly state that the teacher has the final decision on grades.[36]

To all this criticism, the school establishment has a ready, plausible response: Parents prefer letter grades and the report card system used in their districts. The basic issue, however, is not whether they prefer it but the basis for the preference, if indeed it exists. Have the parents been fully informed about the informational deficiencies of letter grades and report cards? Have they been exposed to alternatives that would better meet their real needs? Should parental silence or acquiescence in the grading system be treated as approval of it? The answers to these questions justify the conclusion that producer interests dominate grades and report cards, just as they do other aspects of the information system of public education.

In addition to the lack of candor in report cards, college admission requirements—or their absence—reinforce the complacency of students and their families about educational achievement. Half of our high school graduates go on to college. Most colleges do not have any admission requirements that require diligent study in precollege education; only a few hundred of approximately 3,400 institutions of higher education are academically selective. The upshot is that high school graduates admitted to college (and their parents) naturally assume that their precollege education was adequate. Thus the deficiencies in the information provided by grades and report cards are not an isolated phenomenon;

they are part of a disinformation process that is all the more insidious because much of it results from benign motives.

A recent study by the Committee for Economic Development confirms the gravity of the problem. The study found a substantial "reality gap" between the way students and parents view preparedness and the way employers and college officials view it: "To put it succinctly, the current crop of students and their parents are deluding themselves. This points up the real necessity of enlisting and informing American parents about what employers and higher education institutions expect . . . Until this gap is closed, little progress can be made in ensuring that America has a truly educated workforce."[37] It is astonishing that the CED study does not unequivocally identify grades and report cards, which are controlled by schools, as the major source of the "reality gap."

Conclusion

The inescapable reality is that the information problems of public education are inherent in government operation of schools. As long as education is provided by government, every aspect of it is a public policy, to be resolved by a legislative body (including school boards) or by public officials. Unless we are willing to accept their actions without public accountability, the information system must inform the public about student achievement, the costs of education, the terms and conditions of educational employment, school board policies and practices on dozens of controversial social issues, school purchasing policies, parent and student grievance procedures, and so on ad infinitum. No existing institution can present this mass of changing information in usable form, and citizens could not absorb and act upon the information even if it were somehow made available to them.

In practice, the information that becomes available is usually prepared by the producers of education and serves their interests and objectives. The basic lesson to be learned from the Cannell report is about information, not testing or educational achievement. Cannell was not an educator or a test expert. Educationally speaking, he was an intelligent layman. His report, however, raises hard questions about the experts, such as the tens of thousands of professors of education. Clearly, in the face of massive educational deception over a long period of time, they did not contribute to public awareness of the issues he raised. Similarly, Cannell's charges demonstrated the inability of education reporters to assess claims about education by government officials.

The effort to focus responsibility for false information on the testing companies diverts attention from media failure and from the fact that the testing debacle is only one example of a much larger problem. Cannell's charges surprised many people, but hard-nosed candor about educational achievement would have been the real surprise. Parties who generate and disseminate information do so in ways that put themselves in the best possible light. This is the general rule, regardless of whether the parties are in the public or the private sector. Partly for this reason, the proposal by John E. Chubb and Terry M. Moe that government establish Parent Information Centers to help parents choose schools wisely is highly unrealistic.[38] The issue that remains is whether a market system of education would provide a superior educational information system.

5
$\approx$ Educational Information
under a Market System

I nasmuch as a market system of education does not exist, we cannot be certain what kind of information system would emerge from it. Nevertheless, we know a great deal about information systems associated with private-sector services; in the absence of reasons to anticipate different outcomes, we can expect similar information systems to emerge in a market system of education.

It is essential to avoid comparing the imperfect information system associated with public education to an ideal but nonexistent information system under a market approach. To avoid such a misleading comparison, we must take into account the positive and negative features of both systems. Essentially, we will be comparing the information problems of markets to the information problems of politics. Such a comparison reveals several striking differences even though reliable information is essential in both systems.

In a market system, prices instead of votes provide the information consumers and producers use to make decisions. When we buy goods or services, prices tell us what we have to give up. If a car costs $10,000, you have a good idea of the goods and services you must forgo to own the car. This information enables you to decide whether or not to buy it. Now contrast this situation with the costs of public education—the costs to ourselves, not to government. The funds for public education are derived from local, state, and federal taxes. The federal government and the states especially draw upon several different taxes to raise the revenues for education. Most of these taxes, such as income and sales taxes,

94

are spent for several government services, and the amounts for each service are not disaggregated, taxpayer by taxpayer. Consequently, taxpayers do not have the vaguest idea of how much they are paying from their own funds for public education. Inevitably, the thinking is that "the government pays"—and for "free public education" at that!

It would be difficult to overestimate the implications of this situation. Since taxpayers do not know how much they are paying from their own pockets for public education (or collectively, as pointed out in Chapter 6), they lack information about the desirability of alternatives to it. As Thomas Hobbes, England's most renowned political philosopher, once commented, "It is easy to see the benefit of such darkness, and to whom it accrueth."

Information needs in politics and markets differ drastically. This distinction is clearly applicable to education. Under a market system, parents would compare schools within their attendance area. Essentially, they would have to decide whether their children would be better served by school A, B, C, or D. Under public education, children are assigned to schools on a geographical basis; hence parents have no need to compare schools unless they are considering a change of residence. This situation is not significantly affected by legislation or school district policies that purport to provide parents with a choice of public schools.[1]

To illustrate the differences, let us try to visualize how a highly controversial issue in public schools would be resolved under a market system. My example is the New York City Board of Education policy, adopted February 27, 1991, making condoms available, free of charge and without requiring parental consent, in New York City high schools. One reason for choosing this example is the intensity of feeling about it. Clearly, many opponents of condoms in the schools would enroll their children in schools that did not offer condoms, if such schools were available and affordable.

The decision to provide condoms in the New York City high schools was preceded by a lengthy internal study. In 1987 the school district established an advisory committee on health education. At that time and subsequently, the incidence of AIDS was rising dramatically in New York. This was not the main reason why the committee was established, but it assumed increasing importance with the passage of time. The committee heard from several experts and interest groups before submitting its report. The proposal to make condoms available was only one of its several recommendations; however, when the chancellor of the New

York City schools expressed support for it, the proposal attracted national attention. Even before the proposal was on the board's agenda, reporters for the *New York Times* called the seven board members to elicit their views on the issue. The *Times* subsequently published several articles that revealed the deep divisions on the issue among board members and in the city generally. Articles on the issue were published in the national media as well.

The board held a public hearing on the proposal on February 6, 1991. As noted in Chapter 2, hundreds of persons sought to address the board at the hearing. Those who did, and many others who did not speak at the board meeting, expressed a multitude of conflicting positions. The board adopted condom availability by a 4–3 vote in February, but controversy over the policy erupted again in July. At that time, a majority of the board expressed support for a policy of allowing parents to opt out of the program. In turn school chancellor Joseph Fernandez charged that the board was undermining the policy it had previously agreed upon.[2] The controversy has continued since then and is frequently cited as a reason to change the structure and membership of the board.

Suppose an educational market system existed in New York City. Schools that wished to do so could make condoms available on whatever basis they deemed appropriate. Such action might be noted as a news item, just as the availability of any unusual product or service might be regarded as news. Parents could put as much or as little importance on it as they wished, without imposing their views on others. There would be no need to wait until the next election—or the next two or three elections—to assess public reaction. This example points up an important advantage of a market system over public education: in a market system mistakes are likely to be corrected more promptly. Suppose condom availability prevailed, but unimpeachable evidence demonstrated that the policy led to increases in student sexual activity, and thus in the incidence of teenage pregnancy and AIDS. In the public schools, proponents of the policy would face political embarrassment, especially in future elections. Private schools in a market system might be embarrassed also, but they could more easily focus on the future instead of being forced to defend their past policies. Almost immediately, private schools could change their instructional materials, teacher assignments, and student programs geared to condom availability; in the public schools, these changes would face a host of procedural, regulatory, and political obstacles. One may not like this conclusion, but the underlying principle is hardly debatable. Private producers in market systems utilize and respond to new information more rapidly and more effectively than governments as producers.[3]

The Role of Advertising

The evils of advertising are often cited as a reason not to adopt a market system of education. Educational hucksters would entice parents to enroll their children in poor schools. Because the harmful consequences might not show up for several years, exposure of false advertising would be especially difficult, perhaps impossible before irreparable damage was done.

The concerns about advertising underscore the importance of avoiding a double standard of judgment. In the first place, the public school establishment advertises extensively on behalf of public education. For several years, the most prominent educational advertisement on a regular basis has been a weekly column in the Sunday *New York Times* sponsored by the American Federation of Teachers. This weekly advertisement, usually commentary by AFT President Albert Shanker, promotes public education with as little regard for objectivity as the worst examples of commercial advertising. Not to be outdone, the National Education Association also advertises extensively, extolling the benefits of public education and decrying the evils of any alternative to it. Even before these forms of advertising emerged, public school organizations used advertising to promote enrollments in public schools.[4]

In any event, it would be unrealistic to consider the role of advertising in a market system but to ignore its equally important role in politics. After all, public education is dependent on the election of public officials supportive of it, and advertising is routinely used to elect such officials. Is advertising for candidates for public office more informative and more objective than advertising for commercial products or services? Any such claim would be difficult to sustain.

In recent years, the quality of political advertising has emerged as an issue in its own right. In a 1990 address, Governor Michael S. Dukakis, the 1988 Democratic candidate for president, urged Eastern European nations "not to import a troubling new development in our democratic tradition—namely, the increasingly shallow nature of electoral campaigns that trivialize important issues in the service of image making."[5] The point made by Governor Dukakis transcends candidates or parties, or any particular political office. Political candidates at all levels of government as well as editorial writers, columnists, and academics have expressed similar concerns. Political advertising is probably less informative and less restricted by factual considerations than commercial advertising. Advertising for most commercial products or services is intended to appeal to repeat buyers who would object to tactics that are often taken for granted in political advertising. Whether or not political advertising is less informative and less scrupulous than regular commercial advertising, advertising plays a similar role in both sectors; the same producers of advertising function in both sectors and follow the same techniques in both.

The use of focus groups illustrates this point. Essentially, a focus group consists of a cross-section of a target audience. The target audience may be senior citizens, teenagers, yuppies, housewives, blacks, whatever. The group is brought together for an informal, unstructured discussion of topics of interest to the advertisers. For example, the Republican presidential election campaign in 1988 relied heavily on results gleaned from focus groups; the much discussed political advertisement featuring Governor Dukakis's parole of Willie Horton was based on focus group discussions. By the same token, many other issues and themes emphasized by both parties in the campaign were based on interviews with focus groups.

Paradoxically, the views expressed in focus groups have often resulted from information disseminated by the media. In effect, the media influence attitudes and opinions; political candidates use these attitudes and views in formulating policy objectives and campaign strategy. Education is not immune to this process. For example, GOPAC, a Republican political action committee, concluded that public school choice was a winning political issue on the basis of focus group discussions. The committee produced a video with supporting materials for Republican congressional candidates. The project was GOPAC's first effort to identify winning issues for Republican candidates. Significantly, no analyst knowledgeable about the educational issues was consulted at any stage of this project.[6] Subsequent events have confirmed that public school choice has no potential to generate significant educational improvement.[7] It would be difficult to find a more telling example of the futility of trying to achieve educational reform through conventional political processes.

Grades and Report Cards under a Market System

At first glance, it appears that grades and report cards would be less informative under a market system than under public education. Public schools need not be concerned about losing clients over low grades; private schools in a market system would presumably be much more vulnerable on this issue.

These legitimate considerations would be overshadowed by the role of competition in a market system. True, schools that are not effective would try to conceal the fact. On the other hand, effective schools would have strong incentives to expose the deficiencies of ineffective schools. Under these circumstances, schools would not be able to deceive parents over a long period of time. Even if the parents were deluded, employers and educational institutions at higher levels would not be, at least for very long. In other words, although schools in a market system would have incentives to conceal their ineffectiveness, they would also have incentives to reveal poor service by other schools. For this reason, a market system would provide a corrective force that does not exist under public education.

At the present time, most private schools are denominational ones. This limits their ability to publicize the deficiencies of public schools. Schools for profit would not be deterred for this reason. If such schools are allowed to compete, we can expect more vigorous criticism of both public and nonprofit schools.

There is one additional reason to anticipate more realistic grades and report cards under a market system. Schools in a market system would have a strong interest in dampening unrealistic expectations. Otherwise, they would be criticized for not reaching anticipated levels of achievement. To avoid such criticism, schools would have to point out the negative factors that affect student achievement. The school that promised admission to an Ivy League college would have to deliver.

As a matter of interest, the most extensive comparison of public to Catholic schools concludes that "Grades are an especially prominent determinant of dropping out of Catholic schools."[8] This conclusion raises some doubts about the allegations that a market system would exacerbate grade inflation. On the one hand, it is alleged that private schools will maintain students by grade inflation. On the other hand, private schools are criticized for pushing their failures into the public schools. The private schools would hardly do so if they were trying to maintain their enrollments by grade inflation. Significantly, Catholic schools have not introduced less rigorous courses in order to maintain enrollments. Their refusal to do so also suggests that the fear of grade inflation in a market system is probably exaggerated. As we have seen, grade inflation is an existing problem in public schools; the suggestion that it would be a more serious one in a market system seems to be based on a double standard of judgment. Furthermore, to the extent that standardized tests are used to assess student progress, competition between schools would expose grade inflation as a means of recruiting students.

The preceding discussion of grades is consistent with information theory. Such theory emphasizes the tendency of information producers to disseminate information that serves their interests, and to ignore or deemphasize information that does not. This tendency is evident at every level of government as well as in the private sector. Janet A. Weiss and Judith E. Gruber reported in 1981 that every aspect of federal education statistics was heavily influenced by political and bureaucratic considerations.[9] The U.S. Department of Education was able to get data from the states only if the states concluded that it was safe for them to release the data. Data relevant to controversial policies or to outcomes were not collected, in fact, were deliberately avoided. For instance, despite the billions spent for compensatory education, the Department of Education has very little useful data on its effectiveness. Congressional mandates that local school districts provide "appropriate objective measurements . . . for evaluation annually" are simply ignored on a large scale. The Department of Education could not enforce the requirement even if it tried, which is an unlikely event to begin with. In short, the lack of information in grades and report cards is not an aberration or the result of a plot to deceive parents; it is the normal outcome of any government-sponsored information system.

Representative Government and Information Issues

When our nation was founded, the scope of government was very narrow; as the scope has expanded, it has become more difficult for citizens to monitor any one area of public policy. Citizens are capable of understanding educational policy, but it is practically impossible for them to monitor thousands of local, state, and federal statutes and regulations. Even if media analyses were jewels of lucidity and insight, citizens' lack of time and interest would still be an insuperable obstacle to a comprehensive understanding of educational policy.

Public opinion regards the burden of persuasion to be on the advocates of a market system; insofar as information issues are relevant, the burden should be on the existing system. In England, as in the United States, democratic representative government emerged when the scope of government was much more limited than it is today. In fact, there was very little government as we think of it today in seventeenth-century England.[10] Most services considered "public" today were not carried out by government employees but by contractors who relied on user charges to defray their costs. For instance, most roads and bridges were financed this way, not by tax revenues. Of course, who received the rights and what they charged were matters of concern, but the users were in a better position to monitor providers than taxpayers were to monitor government agencies. At the same time, citizens were better able to control governments that were extremely limited in scope by contemporary standards.

My point is not to denigrate democratic representative government but to emphasize the importance of limited government if democratic representative government is to function effectively. Public education is only one of thousands of functions that have been added to government since our nation was founded; however, few if any of the others impose such a heavy informational burden on citizens or officials. If citizen control of government requires limiting government's functions, public education is a prime candidate for transfer to the private sector.

As Anthony Downs cogently explained in 1957, we earn our income in one field but spend it over a wide range of products and services.[11] Inasmuch as time is a limited resource, we cannot hope to be as well informed over each area of consumption as we are in our role as producers. Furthermore, our producer roles are usually more important to us than any single consumer role. Even while their children are attending school, most parents devote more time to information about their own producer roles than to any one of their consumer activities, such as education.

Putting aside the folklore of education, it would be irrational for most parents to devote a great deal of time to getting educational information, either for voting purposes or to influence educational policy. The information required is not just about education; it must also include information about how others think or can be persuaded to think and act on the educational issues. After all, being well informed on educational policy is futile unless many others are also well informed and motivated to act in concert.

Being informed about policies involves costs; the costs of just the time involved may be prohibitive. For this reason, most citizens have strong disincentives to be well informed about public policies. The reason helps to explain why governments continually enact policies that benefit a small group of producers at the expense of most citizens as consumers. If consumers are not aware of how they are disadvantaged by producer benefits, they will not object, and political leaders need not be concerned about consumer reactions to them. On many issues, citizens who are not well informed and who are indifferent to the issues constitute a majority of the voters; because their votes depend on irrelevant factors, political campaigns likewise emphasize these factors. As Downs points out, "Only a few citizens can rationally attempt to influence the formation of each government policy; for most, it is irrational to know anything about formulation of even those policies which affect them . . . In general, the economic decisions of a rational government are biased against consumers and in favor of producers."[12]

James L. Payne has provided some dramatic evidence that supports Downs's conclusion. Payne studied the testimony of 1,060 witnesses at fourteen congressional hearings on spending programs. The witnesses testified as follows:

    1,014   supported the spending program
        7   opposed the spending program
       39   did not favor or oppose the program
    145:1   ratio of witnesses in favor to witnesses opposed to the
            spending program.

Payne also found that 63 percent of the witnesses were government officials. Most of the others were lobbyists for interest groups; many of these were former government officials and were subsidized by federal funds in their "private" capacity.[13]

Although Payne did not focus on education, his analysis is clearly applicable to it. The Committee for Education Funding (CEF) illustrates this point. Founded in 1969, CEF is a coalition devoted primarily to federal funding of educational programs authorized by Congress. Its 1992 membership was as follows:

AFL-CIO
American Association for Counseling and Development
American Association of Classified School Employees
American Association of Colleges for Teacher Education

American Association of Community and Junior Colleges
American Association of Educational Service Agencies
American Association of School Administrators
American Association of State Colleges and Universities
American Association of University Professors
American Council on Education
American Educational Research Association
American Federation of State, County and Municipal Employees
American Federation of Teachers
American Library Association
American School Food Service Association
American Vocational Association
Association for Educational Communications and Technology
Association of American Publishers
Association of American Universities
Association of Proprietary Colleges
California Community Colleges
California State University
Career Colleges Association
City University of New York
The College Entrance Examination Board
Cooperative Education Association
Council for American Private Education
Council for Educational Development and Research
The Council for Exceptional Children
Council of Chief State School Officers
Council of Graduate Schools
The Council of the Great City Schools
Detroit Board of Education
Georgetown University
International Communications Industries Association
International Reading Association
Michigan Department of Education
Military Impacted Schools Association
National Association for Equal Opportunity in Higher Education
National Association of College Admission Counselors
National Association of Elementary School Principals
National Association of Federal Education Program
    Administrators

104 ≈ Public Education: An Autopsy

National Association of Federally Impacted Schools
National Association of Independent Colleges and Universities
National Association of School Psychologists
National Association of Secondary School Principals
National Association of State Boards of Education
National Association of State Directors of Special Education
National Association of State Directors of Vocational and Technical Education Consortium
National Association of State Scholarship and Grant Programs
National Association of State Universities and Land Grant Colleges
National Association of Student Financial Aid Administrators
National Conference of State Legislatures
National Council of Educational Opportunity Associations
National Council of Higher Education Loan Programs, Inc.
National Council of Teachers of Mathematics
National Education Association
National School Boards Association
National Vocational Agricultural Teachers' Association, Inc.
New York State Department of Education
New York University
Ohio Department of Education
Princeton University
Rochester City School District
Society of School Librarians International
Texas Education Agency
United States Student Association
University and College Labor Education Association
Graduate School of Education/University of California at Berkeley
University of Miami
University of Michigan
University of South Carolina
Washington State Education Agency.[14]

With its own full-time staff, CEF lobbies for federal appropriations for education. It maintains a constant presence in Congress through publications, briefings, seminars, awards, and other activities characteristic of efforts to influence Congress. These activities supplement those sponsored directly by CEF member organizations. Some of these organizations are private schools and companies that sell to the education market, but none represents taxpayers or educational consumers.

What resources are available in the nation's capital to represent consumer interests? The National PTA was a member of CEF until 1991–92, when it withdrew over the dues it was required to pay. Significantly, the PTA has never differed from the NEA on a major policy issue—a devastating commentary on its subordination of consumer to producer interests.[15] The other policy organizations in the Washington area that ostensibly represent consumers or taxpayers include the following:

American Enterprise Institute
American Legislative Exchange Council
Americans for Choice in Education
Cato Institute
Citizens for a Sound Economy
Free Congress Foundation
Heritage Foundation
National Taxpayers Union.

With few if any exceptions, none of these organizations employs full-time staff devoted to education; collectively, their resources devoted to it are minuscule compared to the educational producer resources devoted to media and political action. The disparity underscores Downs's point that our political system is more responsive to producers than to consumers. In market systems, however, consumers need not persuade a large number of voters to take action. Usually, cooperative action with other consumers is not necessary; producers respond to the wishes of small groups of consumers, acting spontaneously and individually. This fact gives the individual consumer in a market system leverage that is not available to voters in the political system. Partly for this reason, market systems are sometimes deemed systems of continuous representation. Consumers can express their wishes continually, instead of intermittently at long intervals that favor the organized producers.

Ascertaining "the Will of the People"

In recent years, political scientists have debated the rationale for democratic representative government. Is democratic representative government justified because it is "the will of the people"? Or is its justification that citizens have the right to change their government officials if they wish to do so? The "populist" position contends that legislative bodies can and do reveal "the will of the people" and this is the raison d'être for our system of government. The "liberal" position is that no system of voting and majority rule efficiently and fairly reflects the will of the people on policy issues. If all the different positions on issues are presented for vote, no position can achieve a majority; if the number of policy positions is reduced in order to make it possible to achieve a legislative majority, the reduction will be unfair to the adherents of the positions excluded from legislative consideration. In the liberal view the right to change our government leaders is the justification for democratic representative government.

Among political theorists, the liberal position is the most widely accepted. To understand why, consider again the controversy over condoms in the schools. Although we do not (and cannot under political determination) know the precise breakdown of opinion on the issue, let us assume it to be as follows:

% of citizens	Policy position
20	no availability under any circumstances
15	availability only with parental consent
10	availability only with sex education emphasizing abstinence
10	availability only with parental consent and sex education emphasizing abstinence
15	availability without restrictions of any kind
5	availability only after interview with guidance counselor on dangers of unprotected sex
10	availability without parental consent but with sex education emphasizing that all lifestyles deserve respect
5	availability only in senior high school
5	availability from seventh grade with restrictions
5	availability from seventh grade, no restrictions.

This list does not include all the policies that citizens might support. Note also that if their preferred policy is not adopted, citizens' fallback positions may differ as much as their first-choice positions do. Many citizens who support condom availability with certain conditions may prefer no availability if the conditions cannot be fulfilled.

In this situation, what is the will of the people on making condoms available in the schools? There is none, at least if the phrase refers to a position preferred by most citizens; despite the rhetoric of representative government, legislative outcomes often diverge widely from what most citizens would choose. In the example at hand, the optimal resolution of the educational policy issue is only one of several positions on it. To achieve a legislative majority, it is necessary to negotiate with supporters of several positions. Inevitably, the compromises reached deviate from the optimal resolution of the problem. To assume that the eventual resolution reflects the will of the people is to ignore the legislative dynamics; a majority may have agreed to a policy they detest to avoid an even worse policy, or in exchange for support on an unrelated issue.

A market system of education would avoid the futile political effort to ascertain "the will of the people" on thousands of educational issues.[16] While I am mindful of the dangers of analogy, let me suggest one that illustrates this important point. When we buy an automobile, we do not inquire into the following issues:

the terms and conditions of employment of auto workers
whether the carmaker utilizes site-based management
whether the carmaker adopts merit pay
the carmaker's management structure
the efficiency of the carmaker, as distinguished from the efficiency of its cars
the carmaker's procedures for dealing with subcontractors
the carmaker's pension plan
whether the carmaker uses "peer review"
how the carmaker finances its operations.

These are only a few of the problems we ignore in buying an automobile. We compare and choose among cars, not the policies under which they are manufactured. In contrast, because education is provided by government, hundreds of issues that are ignored in buying automobiles must be resolved by legislative bodies. If education were provided through a market system, most of these issues would also be ignored by legislators.

In addition to reducing the total amount of information required, a market system of education would render it feasible to ascertain the will of the people on the issues that are presented to them. After all, we know the will of the people as it relates to Edsels and Toyotas. Similarly, we would know the will of the people on educational services offered through a market system—not perfectly and not without qualification, but much more comprehensively and accurately than is possible under public education. The market would provide this information on a daily basis, not confused by an overwhelming mass of data and issues best left to producers. It is ludicrous to contend that parents would lack the information to choose schools wisely while assuming that they have the information to choose wisely among scores of candidates for public office and thousands of legislative proposals relating to public education.

Educational Information in the Transition Period

In many situations, political dynamics simply rule out any consideration of desirable policies. The absence of large monetary rewards in public education is an obstacle to its improvement, but the issue is not discussed in the political arena—and probably cannot be in a sensible way. To put it bluntly, it may never be in the interests of any candidate or party to raise certain basic issues. There may be no wrongdoing by anyone, yet critical policy issues are often not articulated, let alone resolved in a more satisfactory way.

As long as the debate over educational reform is limited politically to secondary issues, educators welcome increased media and political attention. Supposedly, this will lead to progress. In practice, it leads to more posturing and wheel spinning. Increased attention to education since publication of *A Nation at Risk* in 1983 demonstrates that more attention to education does not necessarily result in wiser educational policies.

As previously noted, I do not anticipate any change in media structure or dynamics. The strategy required is not to change the media; it is to articulate the problems of producer domination within the existing framework of media coverage. To do so, we must recognize that the information problems of moving to a market system of education differ structurally from the problems that would arise under such a system. To move toward a market system, consumers must be able to counter the producers in the media and in legislative proceedings. For every producer news conference, press release, or expert witness, the consumers must have an effective response. Ideally, the consumer organizations would be prepared to take the initiative, not merely respond to producer initiatives as the need arises.

As we have seen, however, the organizations that represent educational consumers lack the resources to compete with the educational producers for media and legislative attention. Basic changes in philanthropy and in educational policy organizations are essential to reduce the disparity, but this is only part of the problem. It is also necessary to minimize the progovernment bias in the policy organizations that supposedly represent consumers.

In Washington there is constant interchange between government and policy organizations. Federal officials who leave government often wish to return to it, or hope to be funded by it in some way. Frequently, these interests undermine their effectiveness as policy analysts. For instance, as an analyst employed by the Heritage Foundation, William J. Bennett is not likely to be critical of his own performance as U.S. secretary of education. Furthermore, in view of his desire to run for elective office, his analyses understandably avoid criticism of the constituencies and organizations that serve as his political and financial base. In this respect, the situation illustrates a problem that goes far beyond any individual. I cite Bennett to illustrate a pattern, not to criticize him for taking advantage of his opportunities.

Essentially, there are two problems. One is organizing and funding the consumer presence. The other is ensuring its integrity as a consumer presence. The establishment of such a presence should include safeguards against potential conflicts of interest. For instance, the compensation arrangements might include payments to a pension fund that would be forfeited if the employee returned to government service or accepted a position allied with producer interests. In other words, the employment arrangements must reflect the organization's purpose. Dozens of organizations currently claim to represent educational consumers, but none has adopted adequate safeguards against producer influence.

Significantly, the U.S. Office of Education was established in 1867 as an information agency. Proposals to improve its information services are made frequently; as recently as 1991 a prestigious commission proposed a system of educational indicators that would monitor our educational progress or lack thereof. The absence of such a system is especially remarkable in view of the governance structure of education. Inasmuch as education is primarily a state and local responsibility, one might suppose that the federal government would not be inhibited in providing critical information on a district-by-district basis. The fact that it does not do so, and never has, should give us pause. True, some of the information disseminated by the Department of Education is about programs that have congressional or presidential sponsorship, so we can expect the department to treat them gently. Even so, the nonthreatening nature of information about public education seems anomalous. The reason for it is that the same producer clout that elects state and local officials is reflected in federal politics as well. Partly for this reason, reliance on government for information is as risky as reliance on it to protect educational consumers.

Conclusion

Ultimately the information argument for public education is that parents can evaluate school quality but prefer not to invest the resources, mainly time, to the process. Instead, parents prefer to delegate the responsibility for monitoring educational quality to government. This is what we do with respect to drugs and potentially dangerous appliances and equipment. Theoretically, we could rely on market forces for protection, but reliance on government despite its imperfections may be preferable. Generally speaking, however, the argument for regulation is less applicable to schools than to drugs, to cite just one example. The average citizen is not equipped, technically or financially, to monitor the side effects of drugs. A plausible (though not necessarily decisive) argument can be made that it is more efficient to delegate such testing to government agencies that can provide the necessary resources at a low cost per taxpayer.

Clearly, this argument does not justify government provision of a service as distinguished from government regulation of it. Government does not produce drugs or automobiles or many other potentially harmful products and services. Furthermore, deficient schools are not lethal, as are deficient drugs or automobiles. The risks to educational consumer are less and can be assessed periodically long before they pose any permanent harm.

It is not feasible here to delineate all the informational problems that would disappear or emerge under a market system. Both proponents and opponents of a market system have expressed some silly arguments on these matters, but let me summarize the major points to bear in mind.

1. Most discussions of parental choice completely ignore the literature on consumer behavior. This suggests that the positions are based on interests, not on objective analysis of how parents would choose a school.

2. The more intense the competition, the more likely it is that a lack of information on the part of any particular parents would not matter one way or the other. If competition is intense, producers cannot afford any gap in quality or price between themselves and their competitors.

3. If schools are not tied to residence, parents have greater freedom to choose where to live. Any information costs associated with choosing a school may be offset by savings in choosing a residence. Under the current system, some parents choose where to live by whether the neighborhood has a good school. If they are mistaken, or if the school's quality deteriorates, the family cannot ordinarily move to avoid an undesirable school. A market system of schools would be more effective in dealing with this problem.

4. Under a market system, the children of uncritical and uncaring parents would often benefit from the school choices of parents who were deeply concerned about schools. Automobile manufacturers often incorporate safety features to attract a minority of careful buyers. As a result, all automobile buyers benefit from improvements stimulated by discriminating buyers. The same process would take place in the school situation. The children of the most indifferent parents would probably be better served by a highly competitive system of schools than by the public school monopoly.

5. Generally speaking, parents would have more opportunity to evaluate schools than any other major product or service they buy. Information about schools would be readily available from neighbors, church members, fellow employees, and other sources. We could also expect an increase in private information and advisory services not beholden to any particular school. Even in the absence of such possibilities, parents would rarely be required to enroll their children for more than a year at a time. A poor school for a year is always undesirable, but it is not an irremediable catastrophe.

6. Advertising would be more influential in publicizing the availability of schools than in retaining their pupils. Parents who have direct contact with schools are likely to rely on their experience, not on advertising, when deciding whether to keep their children in a particular school.

7. Schools would probably be more forthright in informing parents about the handicaps facing their children. Inasmuch as schools would be more likely to be held accountable for poor educational performance, they would have a bigger stake in being candid about the obstacles to achievement and the steps required to overcome them.

8. Most of the criticism of a market system on informational grounds treats parental choice of school as a one-shot, once-and-for-all decision. This is highly unrealistic. If there were real competition, schools would probably allow dissatisfied parents to transfer their children without penalty, at least for a certain period of time after enrollment. Some private schools already offer this option, even in the absence of a market system.[17]

9. A market system would drastically reduce the information burden on parents, voters, and government agencies. Because parents would be able to act on the basis of their information, they would have more incentives to be informed; they would no longer be forced to rely on protracted, expensive, and uncertain political processes for improvement or redress of grievances.

10. Public agencies, largely relieved of their responsibilities to produce education, could be more forthright in providing helpful information, especially in situations where low achievement is currently obscured out of consideration for producer interests.

The changes listed do not include the informational benefits to our political system. Under a market approach, parents as consumers instead of legislators and bureaucracies would monitor the quality and costs of education. It is hardly debatable that consumer monitoring of quality and costs is more effective than taxpayer monitoring of them. It is usually inefficient for individual taxpayers to monitor the quality and cost of government services. If inefficiencies are found and eliminated, the savings to the individual taxpayer who identifies them are minuscule compared to the costs of identifying them. In contrast, consumers can benefit immediately by monitoring the costs of services they purchase. The fact that citizens and legislators would be relieved of an informational burden would be a significant advantage of a market approach;

the fewer public services to monitor, the more effectively they can be monitored.

The information case for a market system of education seems especially persuasive in view of the levels of consumer information in other fields. For example, many consumers lack good information on doctors and hospitals. This is especially serious in life-threatening emergency situations; quite often, individuals requiring emergency treatment could not use good information on providers even if they had it. Patients get information from friends and relatives, but the availability of such sources varies, as does the quality of their advice. Despite all such informational problems in health care, consumers of health care exercise choice of provider. Consumers can buy into plans that restrict their choice, but this is itself a consumer choice. The facts underscore an important point about a market system of education: we should avoid insisting on levels of consumer information and sophistication that do not prevail in other services in which choice of producer is taken for granted.

Even under a market system, some educational issues would remain on the political agenda, and some new ones would be added to it. Overall, however, education would become less prominent as a political and social issue. In some respects at least, this would be desirable. To illustrate, the Bush administration, including President Bush himself, tried to promote "school based management." So have hundreds of governors, legislators, and federal and state education officials. The absurdity of these efforts would be evident if educational services were provided through a market process. Political leaders and public policymakers do not (or should not) run around the country telling private companies how to structure their management. That issue is resolved by the companies, not by politicians.

6
$\approx$ The Real Costs of
Public Education

Educators often believe that the concept of efficiency applies only to the production of tangible goods. This is erroneous. Efficiency refers to the relationship between resources used and outcomes produced. A system is more efficient if it produces more with the same resources, uses fewer resources to produce the same output, or some combination of the two. Granted, this approach to efficiency oversimplifies some issues and ignores others. I do not believe, however, that it leads to erroneous conclusions on the issues to be discussed.

This chapter is devoted to cost issues, the following chapter to outcomes as efficiency issues. My objective in these chapters is to compare the costs and outcomes of public education with the costs and outcomes under a market system of education. The comparisons must be interpreted tentatively for the following reasons:

1. At the present time, private schools do not constitute a market system. Even if we knew the full costs and outcomes of private schools, and we do not, the information would not enable us to compare the efficiency of public education with a market system of education.
2. Estimates of the costs of both public and private education grossly underestimate their real costs.
3. Cost comparisons are misleading unless related to all relevant outcomes. Data on several important outcomes of public and private education are not available or are subject to highly disparate interpretations. This is especially true of outcomes affecting parties other than students.

4. A market system of education could be introduced in various ways, which would have different costs and different outcomes. Comparisons of public school costs or outcomes with one version of a market system would not be applicable to different but equally plausible market systems of education.

In the following discussion, I use the term "inefficiency" to mean any larger cost required to achieve the same result, any negative difference in the results when the costs are equal, or any combination thereof. Although important, efficiency is not the only criterion for assessing public education or its alternatives. Equity and liberty are also important, as are other considerations.[1] In these chapters, however, I shall focus on the efficiency issues.

The major source of data on the costs of education is the National Center on Education Statistics (NCES), a unit of the Office of Educational Research and Improvement (OERI) in the U.S. Department of Education. Another source is the Research Division of the National Education Association (hereinafter RD-NEA or NEA). The Bureau of the Census also publishes data on school costs, but its publications are not as frequent or as useful as the NCES and NEA publications on the subject.[2]

Both NCES and NEA use current expenditure per pupil in average daily attendance as the measure of school costs. According to the NEA,

> Current expenditure per pupil in average daily attendance (ADA) is the most frequently used indicator for examinations of public school spending, appearing in studies, newspaper accounts, and so on, where states are compared with one another on school expenditures. As with other state-level measures, current expenditure per pupil in ADA suffers from the shortcomings inherent as a statewide average. Use of the figures should be supplemented by the readers' own knowledge of factors unique to their state or locality that would affect spending levels.[3]

I shall use the phrase "per-pupil costs" as shorthand for "current expenditure per pupil in average daily attendance." "Expenditures" are not always synonymous with "costs"; I will try to take account of this in the discussion.

At the present time there is widespread controversy over spending for education. Some assert that we do not spend enough for it; others disagree. Obviously, to get a handle on the issue, we should know how much is actually being spent; however, government spending for education is less than total spending for it. For example, suppose we are comparing school expenditures in states A, B, and C, and in private schools. Assume that textbooks are paid for as follows:

State A—public funds buy all textbooks in public schools.
State B—public funds pay for some but not all textbooks in public schools.
State C—public funds pay for some textbooks in both public and private schools.
Private schools—parents buy all textbooks from personal funds.

Other things being equal, state A will spend more per pupil than state B, state C, or private schools. This fact, however, does not justify the conclusion that state A is less efficient than the others. Overall, state A may be the most efficient, even though its per-pupil expenditures are higher than those of state B, state C, or private schools. From the taxpayers' point of view, it might be desirable to have more pupils enrolled in private schools, but the reason would not be their greater efficiency. Private schools might be highly inefficient, but the taxpayers would not object inasmuch as they would not bear the costs. To generalize, reliance solely on governmental expenditures might lead to highly inaccurate conclusions about the efficiency of public schools.

Comparing Costs in Public and Private Schools

To illustrate the prevailing view on efficiency issues, I shall rely mainly on the publications of Henry M. Levin, professor of economics and education at Stanford University and a leading authority on efficiency issues in education. Levin's major conclusion about cost comparisons between public and private schools is that the "evidence is too weak to be conclusive." Referring to comparisons that show lower per-pupil costs in Catholic schools, he points out differences between public and private schools in both the services provided and the methods of accounting used to calculate per-pupil costs. In his view, "much of the apparent disparity in costs is due to massive gaps in cost accounting in private school data rather than to real cost differences."[4]

Although I disagree with Levin's conclusions, I do agree that we should avoid "massive gaps in cost accounting"—in public schools as well as private schools. For example, public school costs are estimated on the basis of average daily attendance (ADA), while Catholic school costs are estimated on the basis of enrollment. Obviously, enrollment figures are higher than ADA figures. Dividing total costs by enrollment will yield lower costs per pupil than dividing costs by the number of pupils in ADA. Therefore, unless some type of adjustment is made, comparisons of per-pupil costs will be biased in favor of Catholic schools.

Arguably, cost estimates should take into account differences in student populations. Public schools enroll a higher proportion of students in vocational programs, which usually cost more than academic ones. Public schools also enroll a higher proportion of students in special education, that is, students who are mentally retarded, deaf, blind, autistic, emotionally disturbed, brain damaged, or otherwise learning-disabled. A 1991 report to Congress indicated that about four and a half million students, approximately 10 percent of all K–12 students, were receiving special education services. Of these, about 30 percent were enrolled full time in special education programs.[5]

Because of government mandates, the costs of educating these students are higher than is generally realized. My estimate is that the average cost of educating a full-time special education student in 1988 was $13,600; this is $9,160 more than the $4,440 national average for all students in 1988.[6] Since the average for all students includes those receiving special education services, the average for those not receiving such services would have been significantly less than $4,400. Consequently, per-pupil costs in public schools may be higher than in private schools because public schools enroll a higher proportion of students who are more expensive to educate. In that case, the higher average costs in public schools will not necessarily indicate less efficiency on their part. It must be emphasized, however, that not everyone agrees that we should spend more to educate the learning-disabled; the increased costs are often due to government mandates that are not based on actual needs or services.

Even when costs are known, their interpretation can affect efficiency comparisons. A 1982 study of high schools found that public schools employed one security guard for every 1,824 pupils while Catholic schools employed one guard for every 17,055 pupils.[7] On the surface, this seems to be a substantial efficiency advantage of Catholic over public schools. If, however, the differences in security guards per pupil are due to the fact that public schools are more often located in areas that require security guards, the higher expenditures for them in public schools do not indicate any inferiority in school efficiency.

"Massive Gaps in Cost Accounting"

Do "massive gaps in cost accounting" account for the allegedly lower per-pupil costs of Catholic schools? Granted, a valid comparison must take into account all the costs of Catholic schools. It so happens, however, that the statistics on public schools also omit several substantial costs. Table 6.1 lists several that are not included in government estimates of the current per-pupil costs of public education.

Several caveats apply to this table. First, it is not a comprehensive list of omissions. Second, particular costs are sometimes omitted by one or more but not all states or school districts. Consequently, the magnitude of some omissions varies according to the number and size of the jurisdictions that omit the costs from their estimates.

Another caveat relates to double counting. For instance, two of the costs omitted from estimates of per-pupil costs are faculty time in higher education devoted to public education and foundation grants to institutions of higher education for the purpose of improving public education. In some cases, however, foundation grants are used to defray the costs of faculty time. Unless either "foundation grants" or "faculty time" is reduced accordingly, there is double counting of omitted costs. Table 6.1 includes several such instances, but it was not possible to compute the amounts involved. In my opinion, however, the double counting would not invalidate the conclusions I have reached.

Some of the items in Table 6.1 are also omitted from estimates of per-pupil costs in Catholic schools. In many cases, the costs are not applicable to Catholic schools or were not obtainable. With respect to a few types of expenditures, such as parental out-of-pocket costs, per-pupil costs are undoubtedly higher in Catholic schools than in public schools.

Finally, I have not always tried to estimate the cost changes that would take place under a market system. Presumably some costs, such as those for attracting students, would increase, but by how much is not discussed. Likewise, no effort has been made to quantify all the savings that would be virtually certain to result from a market system of education. In my opinion, the gaps and uncertainties do not preclude judgment on system costs and their implications.

Table 6.1.   Costs of public education not included in U.S. Department of
Education estimates of current expenditures per pupil in average
daily attendance

Federal
   Educational R&D
   Training
   Remedial or compensatory programs (e.g., Head Start, Trio)
State
   "FOB" expenditures[a]
   Pensions[b]
   Social security[b]
   Textbooks[b]
   Administrative costs[b]
   School district labor relations[b]
   Judicial costs
   Noneducational agencies performing K–12 services
Local school district
   Capital outlay
   Interest
   Capital equipment
   Facilities already paid for
Higher education
   Remedial courses and programs
   Teacher training
   Faculty research and time
Donations, contributions, fees
   Foundation grants
   Donated time (e.g., school board time)
   Business contributions
   Fees and charges paid by parents
System costs
   Professional organizations, publications, conferences
   Rent-seeking and opposition thereto[c]

---

a. "FOB" expenditures are expenditures "for or on behalf of free public
education." This is a catch-all category intended to pick up costs carried on budgets
other than those of school districts and state departments of education.
  b. Omissions, if any, vary by state.
  c. "Rent-seeking" is the process of achieving monopoly benefits.

Capital Outlay and Equipment, Interest, Land, and Facilities

In computing per-pupil costs, federal and NEA statistics do not include capital outlay, interest, and several others lumped together in a category labeled "current expenditures for other programs." These omissions result in substantial understatements of costs. Table 6.2 brings this out very clearly. "Current expenditures, other programs" includes some expenditures that should not be charged to public education, such as funding for services provided to private schools and for state libraries, state museums, and other supplementary services that are sometimes administered by state departments of education. It also, however, includes some expenditures, such as those for summer school programs and teacher placement services, that are clearly costs of public education in whole or in part. Even if we delete the costs in line 5 of the table entirely, capital outlay and interest come to $26.7 billion—almost 13 percent of the per-pupil costs that are counted.

Significantly, the costs of equipment (items that are repaired rather than replaced, such as school buses, overhead projectors, and kitchen equipment) are considered capital outlay and therefore are not included in the estimates of per-pupil costs. NCES and NEA do publish figures for expenditures for capital outlay but do not include them in their estimates of current expenditures per pupil in ADA, the estimates that are included

Table 6.2. Public school expenditures, 1991–92 (in thousands)

Amount	Category
1. $210,966,871	Total current expenditures for public schools included in NEA estimates; excludes lines 3–6 below
2. 5,452	Expenditures per pupil in ADA, based on line 1; this is the "official" figure, used by government agencies and in the media
3. 21,581,532	Capital outlay
4. 5,119,214	Interest on school debt
5. 3,454,906	Current expenditures, other programs
6. $ 30,155,652	Total omitted from estimates of current expenditures per pupil in ADA

Source: Research Division, NEA, *Estimates of School Statistics, 1991–92,* 45.

in press releases and cited in the media. The reason most often cited for the omissions is that there is no commonly agreed upon way to convert capital outlay and interest to per-pupil costs. The reason does not withstand scrutiny. The per-pupil costs of capital outlay and interest could be estimated in several ways. If no one way commands dominant professional support, the costs could be estimated on the basis of alternative assumptions. This is a common procedure in data-gathering agencies. To illustrate, the Bureau of the Census presents different demographic projections based on different assumptions or contingencies. Similarly, it should be possible to provide estimates based on different assumptions about the per-pupil costs of capital outlay and interest.

Another way to show the costs of capital assets on a per-pupil basis would be to include depreciation in the cost figures. This would be consistent with recognized economic and accounting principles. For example, if a public school were sold to a school for profit, the latter would include depreciation immediately as a cost of operation. The same kind of problem is involved in comparisons of public and private hospitals. Nonprofit hospitals do not show depreciation as a cost; hospitals for profit do. Thus hospital comparisons that rely on accounting costs, instead of economic costs, are misleading.

As in the public sector generally, statistics on the costs of education ignore depreciation, thereby understating the real costs. The probability is that the per-pupil cost of facilities is higher in public than in Catholic education. On the one hand, costs of land acquisition and construction tend to be higher for public than for Catholic schools. The latter face greater pressure to keep costs down; their financial structure is less conducive to the purchase of larger sites and more expensive construction. On the other hand, the per-pupil costs of buildings and grounds may be higher for private independent schools than for public schools.

Federal Expenditures for Education

With some exceptions to be noted shortly, government costs of public education that do not show up as expenditures by a state department of education or a local school district are not included in estimates of per-pupil costs. Because some federal expenditures for public education are not transmitted to states or school districts, they are not counted in per-pupil costs.

For example, the Department of Education spent about $80 million in 1991 to administer the following programs: compensatory education (Chapter I, ESEA), impact aid, bilingual education, special education, Indian education, drug abuse education, vocational education, and adult education. The fifty states spent a much larger amount for these purposes.[8] These amounts are not included in the per-pupil cost figures. In addition, the 1991 appropriation for the Office of Educational Research and Improvement (OERI) was $232 million. A great deal of it went to institutions of higher education to fund research on elementary and secondary education. As a very rough estimate, I would say that $2 billion of Department of Education funds is not transmitted to states and local school districts, hence is not counted in the estimates of per-pupil costs.

We must also bear in mind that federal funds for K–12 education are often administered through federal agencies outside the Department of Education. Several hundred million dollars for educational research and development is provided by other federal agencies and is not included in the costs of public education or the per-pupil costs (see Chapter 11). Head Start funding is another example. The amount appropriated for Head Start for 1990–91 was $1.96 billion. Head Start funds are allocated to localities according to the number of children aged 3–5 classified as disadvantaged by federal standards. All recipients are supposed to use the funds for compensatory education, primarily for that age group.

In response to the upsurge in juvenile crime and delinquency, Congress established the Office of Juvenile Justice and Delinquency Prevention (OJJDP) in 1974. OJJDP sponsors a variety of educational programs and services on curriculum development, data collection, school safety, child safety, gang suppression, and drug testing, to mention just a few. Only a small proportion of OJJDP funding goes to state departments of education and school districts, hence only a small proportion is included in estimates of the per-pupil costs of public education.[9]

How much, if any, of the funding for Head Start and OJJDP (for example) should be viewed as a cost of public and/or private education? A careful answer to this question would require identifying the beneficiaries, deciding what services are "educational" and allocating costs between them, and resolving several other complex issues. Consequently, I have not tried to estimate how much of this funding should be viewed as a cost of public education. A few billion might be a reasonable estimate, but it would not loom very large in the total picture. Still, to paraphrase a comment by former Illinois senator Everett Dirksen, a billion here and a billion there and pretty soon you are talking about real money.

Remedial Instruction in Higher Education and Business

For some purposes, we wish to know how much is spent to educate elementary and secondary students. For other purposes, we wish to know how much is spent for elementary and secondary education regardless of the age level of the recipients. The estimates on the latter basis will be much larger than the estimates of expenditures for students in K–12 schools.

All over the United States, colleges and universities are spending substantial sums for "remedial education." Remedial education typically consists of teaching basic skills that should have been learned in elementary or secondary school. According to a study by the U.S. Department of Education, 30 percent of all college freshmen in 1989–90 enrolled in at least one remedial course: 21 percent of freshmen were enrolled in remedial mathematics classes; 16 percent in remedial writing, and 16 percent in remedial reading.[10] Inasmuch as about half of our high school graduates go on to college, the costs of such instruction must be enormous. The National Council of Educational Opportunity Associations is a confederation of organizations established primarily to lobby for federal funding of remedial and compensatory programs. Its members are largely college and university administrators of five federal programs serving disadvantaged students enrolled or preparing to enroll in postsecondary institutions. Federal funding for these programs increased from $2.0 million in 1966 to $219.3 million in 1989.[11] In addition, the programs receive state and private funding. A substantial share is devoted to secondary students, or to secondary-level educational activities in institutions of higher education. Inasmuch as the funds go to institutions of higher education, they are not included in the estimates of per-pupil costs for public schools.

By the same token, some school district costs should be allocated to higher education or to other public budgets. For instance, the costs of high school courses for which students receive college credit should be shown as a cost of higher education in some situations. Additional examples of this kind can undoubtedly be cited. Overall, however, realistic accounting would result in a substantial net increase in the costs of elementary and secondary education.

We must also consider elementary and secondary education provided by corporations. According to a 1990 survey of 200 major U.S. corporations, 22 percent teach reading, 41 percent teach writing, and 31 percent teach computation to their employees; one estimate is that 93 percent of the nation's largest companies will be teaching reading, writing, and arithmetic to their employees in 1993.[12] When he was CEO of the Xerox Corporation, David F. Kearns estimated that the corporate costs of teaching basic literacy and mathematics skills, and of the productivity losses while employees were learning basic skills, were $25 billion annually.[13] Most of these costs should be counted as costs of elementary and secondary education.

Teacher Education Costs on Higher Education Budgets

In the private sector, training costs are counted as a cost of doing business. Not so in public education. A large part of its training costs are carried on the budgets of institutions of higher education. These costs should be considered costs of public education.

Suppose that government continued to operate elementary and secondary schools but withdrew its support to institutions of higher education for training teachers. Suppose also that school districts provided teacher training, just as some school districts did in the past. In that situation, it would be clear that the cost of public education should include the training costs. If an institution of higher education provides the training at the teachers' expense, the cost may be reflected in higher salaries paid to teachers. Even taking these things into account, however, the pre-service and in-service costs of teacher training are not fully reflected in the estimates of the per-pupil costs of public education.

The entire cost of college programs to prepare teachers should not be viewed as a cost of elementary and secondary education. Most teachers would have gone to college even if they had not become teachers. Nevertheless, even on the most conservative assumptions, the costs of teacher education for public schools probably runs into several billion dollars annually.

Of course, Catholic schools also want to employ well-trained teachers. Interestingly enough, the average Catholic school teacher has less formal training than the average public school teacher.[14] These differences, however, are reflected in their salary schedules. For example, if the average public school teacher has an M.A. degree or equivalent and the average Catholic school teacher only a B.A., the difference in their training will be partially reflected in their salaries. Inasmuch as their salaries are included in estimates of per-pupil costs, the differences in training appear to be accounted for. In fact, they are not. Taxpayers absorb a large share of the costs of training teachers and administrators in public schools. Inasmuch as teachers and administrators in Catholic schools have less formal training than their counterparts in public schools, the costs of training are lower for Catholic schools.[15]

Educational research is still another K–12 cost carried on the budgets of institutions of higher education. Obviously, many professors conduct research that is as applicable to private as to public schools. Research on more effective teaching practices is a case in point. At the same time, other research focuses on issues that are applicable only or predominantly to one sector. Research on the effect of state tenure laws will not ordinarily be useful in private schools; research on diocesan school boards will not be very useful in public education. Although the per-pupil costs of educational research are not available, and the dollar differences are probably not large in any case, the costs are probably larger in public schools.

In Chapter 11, I estimate that the value of faculty time devoted to educational research in 1988 was $327 million. To this and the costs of graduate student time and teacher education, we must add the costs of training tens of thousands of school administrators every year. At a minimum, K–12 costs carried on higher education budgets must be several billion dollars annually.

State Agency Costs outside Education

Approximately thirty-five states have enacted laws that provide collective bargaining rights for teachers. These laws are administered by state agencies whose jurisdiction may or may not be limited to education. Either way, the costs of administering this legislation in public school districts should be counted as part of the costs of public education.

The California Public Employment Relations Board (PERB) is an example. Its 1991–92 budget was about $6,360,000. About 70 to 80 percent of its work load is devoted to employment relations in public school districts. These costs do not include the costs of the services provided by the State Mediation and Conciliation Service (SMCS).[16] PERB and SMCS costs are not applicable to private schools in California; there is no private school offset or counterpart to them.

Public education also gives rise to other legislation that would not exist in its absence, hence must be deemed a cost of it. For instance, tenure disputes involving public school teachers may be resolved by administrative agencies or quasi-judicial agencies not included in education budgets. Inasmuch as state agencies (except for the courts) do not resolve such disputes involving private schools, their costs are a gap in cost accounting that favors public education. Textbook commissions also illustrate this point. In many states, public school textbooks must be approved by a state agency, at least if the state purchases the books for local school districts. Private schools are not subject to these restrictions; generally speaking, they are free to purchase what they want and when they want it, without bureaucratic constraints. The costs involved in obtaining state approval for textbooks should also count as costs of public education.

Unreported Costs due to Accounting Procedures

In all probability, some sizeable costs of public education are omitted because of inadequate accounting procedures. For example, in twenty-three states, the state governments make social security or retirement fund contributions for school district employees. The state treasurers make the payments directly to the appropriate retirement accounts; thus the costs are not shown as expenditures on school district or state department of education budgets. Some states also follow this pattern for textbooks, transportation, and/or other expenditures for public education.

In 1986–87 these "ghost" expenditures not included in the estimates of per-pupil costs amounted to about $5.8 billion in just twenty-three states. In some states they were as high as 12 percent of total school district revenues. Needless to say, these omissions led to significant underestimates of per-pupil costs.[17] To avoid such errors in the future, NCES and NEA added an "FOB" provision to the instructions for completing their surveys of school expenditures. "FOB" stands for "For or in behalf of free public elementary and secondary education." The FOB provision requests that the following expenditures be included:

> Direct program support expenditures by the state for current operations, such as state (employer) contributions to retirement systems, pension funds, or Social Security on behalf of public school employees; state expenditures for textbooks distributed to local school districts; and all other expenditures made by the state on

behalf of free public elementary and secondary schools. Include current expenditures made for vocational/technical elementary or secondary education.[18]

One difficulty is that NCES and NEA have no way to enforce accurate reporting. Theoretically, NCES has some leverage, but federal agencies are extremely reluctant to pressure the states on reporting issues. For one thing, the states would have to change their reporting systems, and this would lead to charges of "federal intrusion." Also, state personnel would have to be trained to implement the new forms and procedures properly. In practice NCES has greatly improved its reporting of FOB expenditures in recent years, but its statistics on per-pupil expenditures still do not include several costs of public education that are carried on the budgets of noneducational agencies.[19]

As pointed out earlier, the costs of providing elementary- and secondary-level education should be considered even if the students involved are adults. State and local expenditures for adult education are not included in the estimates of the costs of public education. Nevertheless, adult education is often provided to help dropouts and immigrants become literate or earn a high school diploma. Many would agree that such costs should be considered costs of elementary and secondary education, with corresponding adjustments in the number of pupils. After all, the public education lobby is the first to take credit for an increase in literacy or in the proportion of the population with high school diplomas. Surely the state and local expenditures that contributed to the increase should also be charged in some way against elementary and secondary education.

One other unreported state cost illustrates the problems of estimating per-pupil costs for public education. Some states do not fully fund their teacher retirement obligations from current revenues. As a result, the legal obligations of the retirement system may increase without any expenditures. When there is a shortfall, it must be made up by state appropriations. At any given time, therefore, the per-pupil costs of public education may be understated for this reason, sometimes by a significant amount.[20]

At least one type of record-keeping error overstates the costs of public education. This error consists of double counting the costs of educating pupils who live in one school district but attend school in another. Frequently, the school district of residence pays tuition to the school district of attendance. This is a common practice in states that have elementary school districts and regional high schools: the elementary districts are often required to pay a tuition fee to the high school district. If the elementary district shows the tuition paid as a cost, and the high school district counts the actual costs of educating the incoming students, the costs are double counted. This type of situation also arises when pupils attend vocational or special education or other specialized public schools outside of their district of residence. The extent of double counting is not clear at this time, but it is a potentially serious problem in some states.[21]

Professional Organizations and Publications

Every year, large amounts are spent on professional organizations and publications devoted to elementary and/or secondary education. My reference here is not to teacher unions or union publications; these will be discussed later in this chapter. Instead, I am referring to organizations such as the National Science Teachers Association and the International Reading Association. Nationally, there are scores of such organizations. Many have regional or state affiliates with separate budgets. Most publish journals, usually funded by membership dues. At all levels, these organizations devote their resources to disseminating research, discussing educational policy and practice, alerting members to trends and developments, and other activities intended to improve educational services. Because these activities are funded by membership dues, their costs are not included in the estimates of per-pupil costs of either public or private education. Still, if our objective is to understand the extent of the resources being used to educate our youth, the costs of these organizational activities should be included.

I have no estimate of the costs of all such activities. My guess is that they run to at least several hundred million dollars annually, probably much more. Because of their higher salaries, public school teachers can and undoubtedly do spend more per pupil from personal resources on professional activities.

Family-Paid Services and Supplies

In some states, school districts cannot legally charge pupils or their families for any school services or supplies. Doing so has been held to violate state laws or constitutions mandating free public education. In other states, such charges are allowed. Efforts to prohibit them suggest that the amounts are significant, but comprehensive data on this issue are not available.

At any rate, payments for summer school constitute a substantial omission from estimates of per-pupil costs. In the past, summer school was primarily a remedial or catch-up program. In recent years, however, summer school students have been taking more Advanced Placement or college preparatory courses. Parents are typically required to pay all or some of the costs. Both the amounts paid by parents and those paid by school districts are excluded from cost estimates. If our objective is to estimate the total costs of public education, or the total costs per pupil, summer school costs should be included in the estimates.

Donations to Schools and School Efficiency

Despite common opinion to the contrary, private schools receive some government assistance. The nature of it and the amount vary according to the characteristics of the student bodies and the benefits provided. States sometimes provide textbooks and transportation to students in private schools, to cite just two examples. On the other hand, if a private school does not enroll any disabled students, it does not receive government assistance targeted to this group.

The amount of government assistance to denominational schools is as controversial as the desirability of it. For instance, should their tax exemptions be regarded as a government contribution to them? Whatever one's answer, the question illustrates the complexity of efficiency issues. Insofar as Catholic schools rely on church funds and support, parents who contribute to the schools through the church can deduct their contributions on their tax returns. The costs of Catholic education to the parents are correspondingly reduced. As Catholic schools increasingly rely on tuition, the parents are not able to deduct the costs of Catholic schooling. Meanwhile, affluent parents who send their children to public schools deduct their school taxes from their income tax returns. Whether or not this is an inequity vis-à-vis the Catholic school parents, it illustrates a striking inequity within the public school system. Because the poor seldom pay property taxes, they do not deduct this cost of public education from their returns; affluent parents with a mortgage are more likely to do so. In effect, the federal government absorbs a larger share of the costs of public education for the affluent than it does for the poor. Of course, the way tax codes treat the costs does not affect the question of what the costs really are.

Religious personnel teach in Catholic schools for less than the market rate of their services. Antimarket analysts such as Henry M. Levin contend that these contributed services help to foster the erroneous perception that Catholic schools are more efficient than public schools.

Let us see how this plays out. The services of teachers in religious orders constitute the largest contribution to Catholic schools. In 1989–90 Catholic schools employed approximately 137,000 teachers. Of these, about 117,000 (85.3 percent) were lay teachers and 20,000 (14.7 percent) were members of religious orders. About 20 percent of the religious were paid the same as lay teachers.[22]

Salary data are available separately for Catholic elementary and secondary teachers and for religious and lay teachers in each category. Comparisons to public school compensation involve several assumptions and uncertain factual and policy issues. One critical issue in the estimates is how to measure the value of donated time. Catholic school sources estimate the contribution as the difference between what religious teachers are paid and what they would be paid as lay teachers in Catholic schools. On the basis of this approach, the 1989–90 contribution of Catholic religious teachers was $28 per pupil for the entire Catholic school population. If the value of the contribution is based on the difference in compensation between religious personnel and public school teachers, the contribution per pupil in Catholic schools is $61. The first basis appears to be the more appropriate for these reasons:

1. There is considerable interchange between Catholic and public schools. This suggests that the nonmonetary benefits of teaching in Catholic schools are worth the lower salaries. Teachers who prefer the benefits of teaching in Catholic schools to the higher salaries paid by public schools are not donating the salary differential.
2. Many religious personnel teaching in Catholic schools would prefer to do so as lay teachers over teaching in public schools.
3. Criticisms of an efficiency advantage for Catholic schools are based on the contributions of religious teachers, not on the lower compensation of lay teachers in Catholic schools.
4. Teachers in public schools tend to have more years of teaching experience and more formal training than teachers in Catholic schools. The differences in average compensation between the two sectors are partly due to this fact.

Another consideration is that most public school teachers are union-ized, most Catholic school teachers are not. As a result, public school teachers are paid more than would be the case if market rates of pay prevailed in public as they do in Catholic schools. Parenthetically, more and more religious orders are insisting upon the full salary of lay teachers for their members, and this trend is likely to continue. For demographic reasons also, the proportion of teachers from religious orders, and there-fore the amount of donated services, will probably continue to decline in the 1990s. In any case, the services donated by teachers in religious orders probably explain only a small part of the differences in per-pupil costs between public and Catholic schools.

Since efficiency comparisons should reflect donated services, they should reflect the time donated to the public schools by 96,000 local school board members. School boards generally are required to meet at least once or twice a month, but most meet more often, especially when district budgets or teacher bargaining issues must be resolved. Of course, the vast majority of members devote additional time to board business away from formal board meetings. Assessing the dollar value of board members' time is difficult. According to my very rough estimates, the value of school board time nationwide is about $14 per pupil.[23] This estimate does not include the value of time running for school board office, campaign expenses, and election costs. None of these costs would be present in a market system of education.

What about school board costs in Catholic schools? First, many Catho-lic school systems do not have school boards. Second, Catholic school boards do not ordinarily exercise managerial or executive authority as public school boards do. Control of Catholic schools is vested in church officials, not in the laity. For this reason, Catholic school boards function more as fundraisers than as governance bodies. Furthermore, many members of Catholic school boards are religious personnel whose time has already been accounted for. Like other members of Catholic school boards, they are appointed, not elected. Despite some factors pointing in the other direction, the per-pupil value of school board time is proba-bly much lower in Catholic than in public schools.[24]

Parents also donate time to schools, and Catholic school parents undoubtedly contribute more time on the average than public school parents. Catholic elementary schools raise about 7.5 percent of their per-pupil costs from school activities such as candy sales, raffles, and carnivals. Parents are primarily responsible for these events in approximately 75 percent of Catholic schools. An NCES study showed that half the parents of eighth-grade students in private schools served as school volunteers whereas only 15 percent of the parents in public schools did so.[25]

Public schools also benefit from a variety of volunteer programs. In FY 1990 there were 799,000 volunteers in Head Start programs; the estimate for FY 1991 is 880,000.[26] Reliable data concerning the amount of time they contribute are not available. Even if such data were available, it would be difficult to say how much is devoted to education and what rate should be used to determine its value. The per-hour value of such contributed time is not very large, hence the amount may not be significant in economic terms.

Actually, the major contribution parents make is the time they devote to the education of their own children. From an economic point of view, this time can be given a value and factored into estimates of per-pupil costs. Unfortunately, there is no feasible way to do this for policymaking purposes. If less parental time constituted an "inequity" deserving government redress, parents would have incentives to devote less time to their children's education, or to underreport their time. Keeping track of such time would also pose several major problems. Another complication is that the dollar value of parental time is not necessarily correlated with its educational value. We might add $750 to average per-pupil costs in the United States by raising teacher salaries, buying more textbooks, and lowering class size, but these expenditures taken collectively might not be as effective as $100 of parental time computed on some reasonable basis.

Arguments that we should spend more for education typically overlook this crucial point. It is doubtful whether any reasonable level of expenditure can fully compensate for parental neglect or other deficiencies in social capital. A market system in itself would not eliminate all differences in achievement due to differences in social capital, but it would clarify what could be done and at what cost. In this way, a market system would be a more useful guide to educational policy than generalized appeals for larger appropriations for education.

Private Funding for Public Schools

Public schools receive substantial funds from philanthropic foundations. For example, in the fall of 1990, the MacArthur Foundation announced a $40 million grant to the Chicago school system—the largest grant below the college level in our history.[27] The National Academy of Education has estimated that twenty-eight large foundations contributed $272 million to education in 1989.[28] Although the estimate is based on the larger foundations active in education, it necessarily excludes a significant amount from foundations not in the survey. In addition, grants for alcohol-, drug-, and AIDS-related education are not included, nor are the substantial amounts earmarked for education in grants for "civil rights" or "race relations." For example, the 1990 report of the Carnegie Corporation describes a $750,000 grant to the Mexican-American Legal Defense and Educational Fund as follows:

> Since 1974 the Corporation has contributed to MALDEF's program in education. The current three-year grant is allowing MALDEF to continue its advocacy and litigation efforts on behalf of Hispanic students whose English proficiency is limited and promoting reforms in standardized testing, on which minority children tend to score lower than do their white counterparts. It also initiates litigation against state and local school systems that do not equitably distribute their resources, and it monitors the progress of school desegregation cases brought to court by others. In addition, MALDEF operates the Parent Leadership Program to help Hispanic parents become more effective advocates for their children at school.[29]

The Carnegie report also lists grants of $555,000 to the NAACP Legal Defense and Educational Fund and $450,000 to the NAACP Special Contribution Fund for similar activities, and at least twelve additional grants, ranging from $25,000 to $850,000, devoted to minority problems in public education. These grants are only those reported by one foundation in a single year.

In the past, private schools were the main beneficiaries of foundation grants for elementary and secondary education. This appears to be changing. An authoritative summary of foundation grants for 1989 asserts: "Problems related to the performance of the nation's elementary and secondary school system received concentrated attention in the philanthropic sector in 1989. This reflected a widespread perception that the schools—especially public schools—are insufficiently preparing students for competitive participation in a rapidly shrinking global economy."[30]

While philanthropic contributions to public schools have been increasing, parental contributions to Catholic schools appear to be declining. In a 1987 study, Andrew Greeley found that parishioner contributions to Catholic churches dropped to 1.1 percent of parishioner income in 1984, about half of the level in 1960. According to Greeley, the decline was partly due to resentment of church positions on birth control and premarital sex. With a smaller proportion of teachers in religious orders, the drop in parental contributions poses severe financial problems for Catholic schools.[31]

Since the issue of contributions has been raised, however, it should be noted that public school districts have begun to seek contributions from the private sector on a regular basis. In this respect, their efforts resemble those of the fundraising foundations established by various universities. Analogously, Local Education Funds (LEFs) are trying to play this role for local school districts. The Public Education Fund Network (PEFNet) is the national coordinating body of these local education funds. According to its literature, "PEFNet's mission is to improve public education particularly for low income students, through the development of local education funds."[32] Based on the principle that "public schools are the critical institutions for breaking the cycle of poverty," PEFNet helps to establish local education funds and provides assistance on fundraising and program. Some LEFs receive funds from their local school districts and/or the United Way, but all seek to raise private contributions for public education. In 1990 about sixty state, regional, and local affiliates were in operation.

Donations of time to assist disadvantaged pupils must also be considered. Not only Head Start but many other programs provide volunteer services for the disadvantaged. To illustrate, a recent study sponsored by the U.S. Department of Education states that in the 1987–88 school year 921 institutions of higher education operated 1,700 tutoring and mentoring programs, overwhelmingly for students in public schools. These programs, funded mainly by the institutions of higher education, served 198,300 students.[33] Although Catholic schools have enjoyed impressive success in educating disadvantaged youth, public schools enroll more students in this category, both absolutely and in terms of their proportion of the school population. For this reason, donations of time to serve the disadvantaged are more likely to be costs of public education.

Corporations and business foundations also provide substantial assistance that is not necessarily targeted for disadvantaged students. A recent study listed the following forms of business assistance to the public schools:

Career days
Cash awards to students
Cooperative education
Curriculum development
Dropout prevention
Equipment/supplies
Executive loans
Field trips
Gift matching
Grants for institutions
Interlibrary loans
Mentor programs
Teacher education institutes
Underwriting performance arts
Volunteer teachers
Work/study programs.

In addition, several hundred corporations, including some of the nation's's largest, participate in "Adopt-a-School" or "Join-a-School" programs.[34] These programs often include assurances of employment for qualified high school graduates. Paul O'Neill, chairman of the President's National Advisory Commission on Education, stated in April 1991 that business had contributed "billions" to elementary and secondary education.[35] O'Neill's estimate may have included some of the foundation assistance previously mentioned, but the amount is impressive, regardless. In any event, business donations should be counted as part of per-pupil costs in both public and Catholic schools. More evidence is needed on whether such donations are larger in public than in Catholic schools on a per-pupil basis.

Economists agree that nonprofit organizations, especially if supported by contributions, are less efficient than for-profit enterprise. Let us assume, contrary to what is surely the fact of the matter, that contributions to private schools from all sources are so large that their per-pupil costs are greater than for comparable pupils in public schools. This outcome would be irrelevant to the issue at hand. Charitable contributions to nonprofit schools are relevant to their efficiency but not to comparisons of the efficiency of private schools with the efficiency of a market system of education; you cannot compare the efficiency of public education with the efficiency of another nonmarket system to arrive at conclusions about the comparative efficiency of a market system of education.

Transaction Costs

According to one line of argument, public schools are more efficient than private schools because transaction costs are minimized in public schools. To get the public benefits of education, government must decide whether to "make or buy" education. The costs of finding, negotiating with, and monitoring service providers are "transaction costs." As transaction costs increase, companies are more likely to provide a needed service internally than to buy it. Analogously, in view of the difficulties of ensuring that private schools provide the public benefits, "making" education through public schools instead of buying it from private schools is allegedly consistent with mainstream economic analysis.[36] The argument supposedly applies to parents as well as government officials responsible for the quality of education.

If parents choose schools, they must devote significant amounts of time and resources to the process. Otherwise, they will be vulnerable to poor-quality and even fraudulent schools. Public education, however, supposedly enables parents to avoid these transaction costs. Because public schools are operated by public authorities under public supervision, parents need not invest their own resources in selecting schools for their children.

It is difficult to see how the appeal to transaction costs justifies or requires government operation of schools. The argument is based on an ex post facto rationalization, not on an initial justification for public education. We feel comfortable buying groceries or prescriptions anywhere in the United States; clearly, government operation of grocery stores and pharmacies is not essential to health or safety or quality of service in these areas. Most of us wish to avoid buying unsafe cars, but few if any would advocate government manufacture of automobiles for this reason.

In any event, if we are going to be concerned about transaction costs, we should be concerned about all of them, not simply those associated with monitoring private education. What about the transaction costs of electing 96,000 school board members? The costs associated with tens of thousands of bills in local, state, and federal legislative bodies? The costs of trying to express a complaint through political instead of market processes? The costs of the efforts of school district employees to elect sympathetic school board members, legislators, governors, and federal officials, and to persuade them to support particular proposals? The opponents of the employees' proposals must also devote resources to the political process. In addition, we must factor in the costs of school board and legislative hearings, and of legislative conflicts at local, state, and federal levels. These enormous costs would not be necessary under market resolution of educational issues.

So far as efficiency is concerned, we can frame the issue this way: Should we expect the highest level of efficiency from (1) a system in which 4.5 million school district employees achieve their employment objectives by electing supportive legislative bodies and persuading elected officials to meet their demands; or (2) a system in which educational personnel can achieve their employment objectives only by satisfying customers in a competitive market? In my opinion, the answer is not even a close call, but that is not the only critical point here. Another is that the proponents of the transaction-cost argument simply ignore the legislative and political transaction costs of public education.

Opportunity Costs

We have yet to consider what are perhaps the most important neglected costs of public education, to wit, the opportunity costs. These costs do not show up on budgets or balance sheets or profit-and-loss statements; they are the value of the alternative use of resources. If you could earn more during your lifetime by going to work instead of college after high school graduation, the opportunity costs of going to college would exceed the gains from it.

A simple example from socialist bloc economies may help to illustrate opportunity-cost issues in public education. In the socialist economies, governments limited investment to government banks. Citizens were not allowed in invest in stocks, bonds, real estate, or other types of investment. Consequently, the opportunity cost to individuals of investing their money in government banks was zero. Even though investing in such banks offered very little return, that return was more than any alternative available to citizens. Both individuals and society suffered from the limitations. Individuals could not invest in more productive enterprise, hence society lost the benefits of such enterprise.

Although not widely recognized, the same process is operative in public education. Compulsory education prevents teenagers from investing their time in anything but education; it is the socialist bank of our society. Because it is the only investment of time open to young people, its paltry return on investment does not threaten its customer base.

Conceptually, the real costs of education are the resources used to provide it plus the opportunity costs. When these costs are combined, we have a good idea of how productive public education must be to justify our investment in it. Currently, the opportunity costs of education to individual students are low because they are not allowed to accept full-time employment until their late teens. Here, we come back to demographic issues discussed in Chapter 2. Demographic pressures are likely to lower the school-leaving age. As we increase the work options for teenagers, the opportunity costs of secondary school will rise. As these costs rise, more students will choose employment over public education, or would if they could.

Needless to say, the school lobby will contend that greedy corporations will "exploit" young people if we lower the school-leaving age. To this observer, such "exploitation" could hardly be more harmful than the exploitation going on under the label "education." In 1990–91 about 91 percent of all 16-year-olds were in school. If students could enter the labor force at age 14, schools would have to demonstrate that the value of staying in school exceeds the value of entry into the labor force. Both public and private schools would have to compete, not just against each other but against the work option as well. It would be astonishing if such competition did not result in immediate improvement in both public and private education. Indeed, the neglect of this issue is a highly revealing feature of the debate over choice.

The private school forces urge that school choice include choice of private as well as public schools. So far, so good, but why stop at this point? Why shouldn't choice include the choice of entering the labor market? After all their arguments showing that parents can choose schools wisely, private school leaders can hardly argue that parents are unable to choose wisely between school and work for their children. If private school leaders really believe in parental choice, why their silence on this critical issue?

The answer exposes the lack of candor on both sides of the debate over school choice. The work option is never raised by private school leaders because their interest is help for private schools. To get such help, they will fight the public schools up to a point—the point being parental freedom to choose the work option. More precisely, they believe parents can decide what is in the best interests of their children as long as going to school is agreed upon as in their best interests. The situation suggests the danger of eventual collusion between public and private schools to take advantage of parents and taxpayers.

Conclusion

None of us knows the costs of public education, from our own pockets or the government's. These costs are extremely diffuse and intermingled with others beyond identification. Even with the help of a supercomputer, it is impossible to ascertain what any individual is paying for public education.

Comprehensive accounting, however, would undoubtedly show a substantial cost advantage for Catholic schools in educating comparable kinds of students. In Catholic schools, teacher salaries and fringe benefits are less, school facilities are not as expensive, school debt is lower, the governance system devotes fewer resources to conflict management, the schools are not subject to several regulatory costs such as collective bargaining and tenure laws, the reliance on self-help is greater, and there is a stronger tendency to extract maximum use from what they have. The countervailing factors such as donated services would not offset the differentials favorable to Catholic schools. Of course, some of their cost advantages might erode if their enrollments experienced a quantum increase; for example, it would become more difficult to recruit teachers willing to work for the compensation they offer. There is reason to question the magnitude of the Catholic school cost advantage, but the claim that such an advantage does not exist, or is of trivial magnitude, encounters an overwhelming body of evidence to the contrary. To reiterate, I do not believe the lower per-pupil costs of Catholic schools demonstrate the desirability of a market system of education, or are necessarily relevant to that issue, but since the cost comparisons are on the table, they should be discussed realistically.

Although some costs might increase under a market system, opposition to such a system on this basis is highly suspect. For instance, Levin points out that average costs per transported pupil were $258 in 1984–85. He goes on to assert that transportation costs would rise under a market system because more students would need transportation and more would need special routes.[37] Perhaps, but Levin does not mention the following points about a market system of education:

1. School options are less likely in rural and sparsely settled areas, the areas in which the per-pupil costs of transportation are highest. Thus the national average cited by Levin is higher than the average in districts where competing schools will be available.

2. If the number of students transported increases substantially, the per-pupil costs will decline because of economies of scale; also, competition among transportation companies will be more likely.

3. Increased transportation costs will lead to increased scrutiny of school schedules in search of changes that will reduce costs. Consider. In June of any given year, high school seniors are attending school thirty to thirty-five hours a week. In September, they are college freshmen attending class sixteen to eighteen hours a week. The students do not change that much over the summer. Clearly, the amount of time spent in high school classes could be reduced without harm, perhaps even with benefit to the students. In terms of transportation, suppose high school students in the upper grades went to school only four days a week. The transportation savings would be substantial.

4. Perhaps the most egregious omission in Levin's analysis is his failure to consider the probability that educational producers would locate near educational consumers in competitive markets. His argument relies on data from a system in which the producers dictate the locations at which services are provided. Interestingly enough, U.S. institutions of higher education have established hundreds if not thousands of branch campuses and extension centers in order to bring their services to students instead of requiring students to travel to inconvenient producer locations. To emphasize the additional costs of transportation under a market system while ignoring the tendency of market systems to reduce consumer transportation costs hardly qualifies as objective analysis.

My point is not that transportation costs would be lower under a market system; despite my caveats, they might be higher. My concern is with the bias in the discussion of cost issues by leading critics of a market system of education. This bias is especially blatant in Levin's contention that state regulatory costs would increase under a market system. Levin asks: How can the states be sure that pupils are attending school in a market system? He cites California to illustrate the problem. The state relies on 1,000 school districts to monitor attendance. Under a market system, the state itself would have to monitor the attendance of 5 million students; to do this, it would supposedly have to establish a huge centralized bureaucracy.[38]

For the sake of discussion, let us assume that private schools must comply with state regulations governing pupil time in school. State agencies are frequently ineffective in regulating other state or local government agencies. One reason is that political factors often intrude: the deficient government agency often has political power at the regulatory level. This was especially obvious in desegregation controversies, when state officials often refused to take action against local districts for flagrant violations of the law.

State regulation of local school districts is notoriously weak and ineffective. The example cited by Levin is a good illustration of the problem. Local districts frequently claim higher attendance than is actually the case. This happens because state aid is usually based on average daily attendance, hence local districts have incentives to exaggerate actual attendance. Suppose voucher payments to private schools were also based on average daily attendance. Would private schools be more likely than local school districts to falsify their reports to the state? Levin's argument fails to recognize that government regulation of other government agencies is less effective than government regulation of private enterprise. Public schools are not going out of business because they falsify attendance reports. The responsible parties (teachers, principals, attendance officers, superintendents) are virtually never punished, despite the frequency of the practice.

Private school violations would be a very different matter. The state agency could fine the private school or even put it out of business. The violators would risk severe personal and corporate penalties. Under these circumstances, we should expect a higher level of compliance by private than by public schools. Granted, state regulation of private schools is weaker in the United States than in most nations with advanced educational systems. It is also weaker than regulation of public schools in this country.[39] These facts might be interpreted as challenging the conclusions that state regulation of private schools in a market system would be more effective than state regulation of public schools. We should not forget, however, that most private schools in the United States operate under denominational auspices. Close regulation of private schools thus encounters religious objections and issues of separation of church and state that are not applicable to nondenominational private schools. Inasmuch as the proportion of denominational schools is declining and might well decline more rapidly under a market system, denominational opposition to state regulation of private schools would probably decline in any case. In addition, private schools in a market system would be more of a competitive threat to public schools than they are now. For this reason, we can anticipate much closer scrutiny of them under a market system.

Finally, we need to recognize the time dimension in any cost comparisons. Consider the services now provided through the market: transportation, communications, health care, information storage and retrieval, data processing, to cite just a few. Over the past few decades or less, all have experienced major improvements in service quality and/or reductions in service costs. We have no reason to anticipate a different outcome in a market system of education. It is, therefore, highly dubious economics to treat the existing efficiency level of private schools, whatever that may be, as their efficiency level over time in a market system.

In conclusion, it should be noted that the history of public education fully supports the preceding analysis. The founding rationale for public education was not its cost advantage over a market system, or over private schools. Instead, public education was deemed to be the only way to avoid public funding for Catholic schools; at most, its costs were a secondary consideration. By the same token, efficiency arguments for public education today are based on claims that its outcomes are superior, not that its costs are lower. As the following chapter shows, these claims cannot withstand objective scrutiny.

7

≈ Educational Outcomes as an Efficiency Issue

To be useful as measures of efficiency, cost comparisons must relate to the same objectives. If we are planning a trip from New York to Boston, the cost differences between air and rail transportation (including the value of time) are differences in efficiency. Travel from New York to San Francisco instead of Boston is not less efficient because it costs more. The cost comparisons might lead us to change our travel objectives, but such a change would not ordinarily be based on efficiency considerations. The same problem could arise in education. Public education might cost more than private schooling because its objectives are different.

Comparing the educational objectives of public and private schools is as difficult as comparing their costs. Differences between producer and consumer objectives are one source of complexity. To illustrate, the Catholic church established schools for religious reasons, but many parents enroll their children in them despite their religious orientation, not because of it. Even when parents have religious objectives, the overlap with public school objectives may be more important than the differences. The parents may send their children to Catholic schools partly for religious reasons but more because they believe Catholic schools are more effective in achieving the secular objectives that would be pursued in a public school.

Objectives tell us what schools try to accomplish. Outcomes tell us how successful they are in achieving their objectives. The main problem in assessing outcomes is distinguishing school from nonschool effects.

143

We have a good idea of whether children can read; we do not know as much about the contribution of schooling compared to the contribution of families, neighborhoods, and the media. In other words, the term "outcome" is ambiguous. What is the outcome of schooling per se and what is due to other factors? In particular, the problem of selection bias must be considered. To what extent are differences in pupil outcomes between public and private schools due to differences in their student populations rather than to differences in the effectiveness of the schools? The answers to this question, like those to questions about the costs of education, vary widely.

Another set of problems arises from the fact that educational objectives are sometimes inconsistent, even contradictory. For instance, suppose the objective is to increase proficiency in mathematics. Achieving this objective will require devoting more time to mathematics, less to other subjects. Theoretically, more time could be added to mathematics without decreasing time to other subjects, but that is very unlikely, at least on a scale likely to improve proficiency in mathematics. The problem, however, is much more intractable. Achieving greater proficiency in mathematics calls for increased enrollments and higher standards in mathematics. Other things being equal, these measures will cause more students to drop out. They will also lower the self-esteem of students who have low ability and no interest in mathematics. In other words, the conflict over objectives is not simply conflict over the allocation of resources; it is over which objectives should take precedence when the achievement of some has a negative impact on the achievement of others.

To summarize, discussion of outcomes must take into account several complicating factors:

1. Disagreement over what the objectives are and should be.
2. The absence of agreed-upon standards to measure progress toward the objectives.
3. Uncertainty over what factors contribute how much to the achievement of specified objectives.
4. Inconsistencies, even contradictions, among the objectives themselves.

As David H. Monk points out, these complexities have fostered a much criticized reliance on test scores as a measure of educational achievement.[1] The tendency is to rely on test scores as a proxy for other outcomes that are more difficult to measure. If all desired outcomes were positively and highly related to one another, this reliance would make more sense than it does. To the extent that some objectives have a negative correlation with test scores, reliance on the latter as a proxy for progress may be misleading. I am not arguing against the use of test scores as a measure of cognitive achievement or even necessarily as a proxy for other outcomes; my point is simply to underscore the complexity of outcome issues.

Academic Outcomes

For the time being, let us hold in abeyance the questions of whether the schools themselves or other factors are most responsible for particular outcomes and look at the outcomes themselves. As previously noted, large numbers of college students require elementary- or secondary-level instruction. This is only one indication that the outcomes of K–12 education are not satisfactory. The evidence to this effect is very extensive, but a few examples should be sufficient to convey the seriousness of the problem.

Mathematics and science. High levels of achievement in mathematics and science are essential if our economy is to be competitive. Persuasive evidence shows that U.S. 13-year-olds lag far behind those of most other advanced nations in these fields. The only exception is that U.S. 13-year-olds are slightly more proficient in science than 13-year-olds in Ireland. According to the U.S. Department of Education assessment of the data:

> Among students in a group of advanced and developing countries, U.S. students had a mediocre performance on an international test of science proficiency. The U.S. students scored in the middle among the 10-year-olds, near the bottom among the 14-year-olds, and last among the 18-year-olds. Although a relatively large proportion of U.S. 18-year-olds were enrolled in school, comparatively few were in the advanced science classes that qualified them to participate in the examinations.[2]

Practically, the international ratings might not be very important if the absolute differences between nations were small. Being last in a group that is closely bunched is not as serious as being last in a group that is spread out widely. Unfortunately, the differences are quite large. For instance, only 9 percent of U.S. 13-year-olds demonstrated the ability to deal with complex mathematical topics, whereas 40 percent of Korean 13-year-olds did so.

Literacy. Literacy skills are obviously important. A 1985 study revealed that:

1. Fewer than half (48.4 percent) of U.S. high school graduates could locate information in a news article or almanac.
2. Barely half (50.2 percent) could follow travel directions on a map.
3. Fewer than half (49.4 percent) knew how to enter deposits and checks and balance a checkbook.[3]

Writing proficiency. Assessments of writing skills are similarly depressing. The national assessments of these skills are based on test scores that require more explanatory detail than is feasible here, but a recent Department of Education study concludes that "average writing test scores show that students do not write well." The same conclusion with different wording applies to reading proficiency.[4]

Knowledge of history and literature. A 1986 study asked nearly 8,000 17-year-old students straightforward questions such as "When was the Civil War?" The percentage of students who chose each of the possible multiple-choice answers was as follows:

_____ Before 1750	3.7%
_____ 1750–1800	22.6
_____ 1800–1850	38.4
_X_ 1850–1900	32.2
_____ 1900–1950	2.5
_____ After 1950	0.6

(The percentages do not add up to 100 because some students did not respond to this question.) Even among the students who scored in the top quarter of the history assessment, three out of ten could not place the Civil War in the appropriate half-century. On the average, students answered correctly only 54.5 percent of all the history questions of this type, even though 97.6 percent of them had taken American history and 78 percent were taking it when they took the test. Inasmuch as a substantial amount of guessing took place, even the percentage of correct responses overestimates student knowledge of history and literature. Furthermore, some of the correct responses were undoubtedly due to television or movies or other media rather than to schooling.[5]

SAT scores. The most widely publicized evidence of educational decline is the drop in scores on the Scholastic Aptitude Test (SAT). This is the test most widely used in the college admissions process. Table 7.1 shows the decline from 1967 to 1991. The 1991 scores on the verbal part of the SAT were the lowest in its history.

Some analysts, however, reject the idea that declining SAT scores are evidence of educational decline. In their view, achievement scores were higher in the past because a more select group of students were being tested. They attribute the lower test scores in recent years to the fact that a much larger proportion of our youth are in school and are being tested. Although widely held, this point of view does not explain the falling scores. The underlying reason for the decline since the 1970s has not been the expansion of the pool of students taking the SAT but an actual decline in achievement.[6] (The reasons for this conclusion will be discussed in Chapter 10.) Furthermore, decline or not, the nation is unlikely to prosper with such a large proportion of poorly educated students. Thus even if there had been no "decline," we would still have strong reason to be concerned over our educational situation.

Nonacademic Outcomes

To learn complex skills and subject matters, students must apply themselves to demanding tasks over long periods of time, avoid distractions and interruptions, and otherwise exercise traits associated with social responsibility. As a matter of fact, some research suggests that social and emotional factors are more accurate predictors of educational achievement than intellectual factors.[7] Long before such research, leading national reports on education emphasized nonacademic as well as academic outcomes as educational objectives.[8]

Table 7.1. Average SAT scores, 1967–1990

Year	Verbal			Math		
	Men	Women	Total	Men	Women	Total
1967	463	468	466	514	467	492
1972	454	452	453	505	461	484
1977	431	427	426	497	445	470
1982	431	421	426	493	443	467
1987	435	425	430	500	453	476
1990	429	419	424	499	455	476
1991	426	418	422	497	453	474

Source: Educational Testing Service.

Assessment of nonacademic outcomes presents many of the same problems as assessment of academic outcomes. First, there is no consensus on the nonacademic outcomes to be considered. Attitudes toward political and social institutions are important. So are work habits, such as punctuality, dependability, and ability to concentrate. So is a long-range perspective on personal and social issues. Even within the field of education, vocational skills, civility, and the ability to cooperate with others are essential. Efforts to assess these and other nonacademic outcomes encounter a multitude of objections and technical problems. As we might expect, the problem of distinguishing school from nonschool effects affects nonacademic as well as academic outcomes. Let us survey a few nonacademic outcomes before trying to assess the relative influence of school and nonschool factors.

Teenage pregnancy and abortion. Despite the decline in birth rates since the 1950s, sexual activity among teenagers has increased considerably since then. Two of the consequences of this activity, pregnancies and abortions among unmarried teenagers, have increased dramatically as well. For example, the number of pregnancies per thousand unmarried women aged 15–19 was 12.6 in 1950 and 31.6 in 1985; the number of abortions per thousand women aged 15–17 was 15.7 in 1972 and 30.8 in 1985. These increases reflect adversely on teenage judgment and self-restraint. The extent to which public education contributes to these outcomes is debatable; its inability to reverse or even halt the trends is not.[9]

Alcohol and drug use. Drug use among teenagers is still quite high although it appears to have declined in recent years: the percentage of high school seniors who said they had used any illicit drug in the past 30 days changed from 30.7 for the class of 1975 to 19.7 for the class of 1989. Teenage consumption of alcohol remained rather constant during this period. The percentage of youth aged 12–17 who had consumed alcohol during the past year was 90.4 in 1975 and 90.7 in 1990; the percentage who had consumed alcohol during the past 30 days declined from 68.2 to 60.0 during this time.[10] These are remarkably high figures in view of the fact that all states prohibit the sale of alcoholic beverages to persons under age 21.

Causes of death. Deaths from motor vehicle accidents per 100,000 persons aged 15–19 increased slightly from 35.9 in 1960 to 37.3 in 1988.

Deaths from suicide in this age group more than tripled from 3.6 in 1960 to 11.3 in 1988; deaths from homicide almost tripled, from 4.0 in 1960 to 11.7 in 1988.[11]

Outcomes and School Efficiency

Comparisons of the effects of public and private schools are like most educational issues: each side can cite "research" to buttress its position. James S. Coleman, unquestionably the leading scholar on this subject, has concluded that the superior academic performance of students in Catholic schools is due partly to effects of the schools themselves; that it cannot be attributed solely to selection bias.[12]

From time to time, other analysts have criticized Coleman's research procedures and conclusions.[13] Although I regard Coleman's analysis as the more plausible, it is not necessary to resolve the issues here. Coleman's critics assert that any educational superiority of Catholic schools is practically trivial. Even if this is true, it follows that the Catholic schools are much more efficient; their outcomes for comparable groups of students are approximately equal but their per-pupil costs are much lower. Indeed, Catholic schools might be more efficient even if their pupils did not achieve as well as those in public schools. The huge additional costs of public education might not be worth the academic gains, if any, they produce.

The available data on nonacademic outcomes are also not very helpful in comparisons of public and private schools. For example, although the arrest rate has risen dramatically since 1950, there is no breakdown of persons arrested by what type of school they attended. Even if there were, it would be necessary to avoid selection bias; if one sector enrolled a higher proportion of students likely to commit crimes, the higher crime rate of its graduates would not be evidence of comparative failure to inculcate respect for law.

Coleman showed that tardiness, absence, and disruptive behavior were less prevalent in Catholic than in public schools.[14] It seems highly plausible that these factors would help to explain a Catholic advantage on nonacademic as well as academic objectives, but the public school lobby is having none of it. As they see it, the students who attend Catholic schools are more likely to be law abiding or orderly or to have good work habits to begin with. In principle, this objection must be considered. In practice, it illustrates the persistence of the public school ideology despite extensive experience that refutes it. For well over a century, supporters of public education in the United States and the United Kingdom have asserted that it would reduce crime.[15] "Open a school, close a jail"—this was a prominent mid-nineteenth-century rationale for public education. Since it was advocated before any evidence on the subject was available, it is not surprising that the rationale is unfounded. In fact, crime rates have increased along with the proportion of children educated in public schools and the duration of their education.

Theoretically, crime rates might be much higher in the absence of public schools. Unfortunately for the theory, the one serious effort to study the issue concluded that public education leads to higher crime rates.[16] In addition to the empirical evidence for the conclusion, there is a plausible rationale for it. From an economic perspective, the costs of crime include the loss of income associated with incarceration. Individuals with high incomes risk more than individuals with low or no incomes. This principle also applies to investment in human capital. Individuals who have invested more of their own funds in building up their human capital are less likely to risk loss of their investment. Investment in human capital by government is likely to be less effective than investment from personal funds in deterring crime. This would be the case even if the education received were the same in both cases. It is interesting that the scholar who investigated this issue, John R. Lott, Jr., is an economist not tied to the public school establishment; that establishment seems content to rely on assumptions instead of evidence about the beneficent effects of "free public education."

For the present, however, let us defer our inquiry into the effects of schools on nonacademic outcomes and look at how leading analysts have framed the issues. This will give us a broader perspective on the evidence.

The argument that public education is more efficient than private education, or more efficient than a market system would be, is based largely on two related ideas: externalities and the distinction between public and private goods. I shall try to present these ideas fairly before explaining why they do not support the contention that public education is superior to a market system on efficiency grounds.

Externalities

Let me first illustrate the idea of externalities in the private sector. Suppose a factory is built next to X's unimproved land. The value of X's land increases because it can now be developed for housing or for a shopping mall to serve factory employees. In this situation, locating the factory near X's land is a positive externality as far as X is concerned. A transaction to which X was not a party has nevertheless increased the value of X's property.

Externalities, however, are not always positive. Suppose that the factory pollutes the area in ways that X cannot prevent. As a result, the value of X's land goes down instead of up. In this case, locating the factory near X's land is a negative externality as far as X is concerned. A transaction might also result in both positive and negative externalities. Further, both kinds might affect the same third parties, or they might affect some in a positive way, others in a negative way.

The economics of externalities are critical. In the first situation, the factory might add to the value of several nearby properties. As a result, the total value created by the factory might be much greater than the increased value of the land on which the factory is located. In the second situation, the factory might be profitable only if it did not have to reimburse third parties for their losses due to factory pollution. If it had to do so, it might be unprofitable.

Analogously, it is argued that the value of public education is much greater than the value added to the students. In economic terms, education is said to have positive externalities. These positive externalities are often referred to as "public goods." Michael Krashinsky, who believes public education does have an efficiency advantage, puts it this way: "Education generates economic growth, alleviates poverty and increases equal educational opportunity, provides the informed and literate electorate necessary for a democratic society, and inculcates in students the common values required in a democratic society."[17] This statement seems more like a wish list than an empirical assertion, but it illustrates the concept of public goods. The concept applies to efficiency issues in several ways. For instance, if funding were based solely on the value added to students, public education would be underfunded. The level of funding should be adequate to achieve the positive externalities, that is, the public goods, as well as the added value flowing directly to students. Some analysts reject the idea that there are public goods over and above those to be found in the value added to students. For present purposes, I am willing to accept it, but we must also accept the possibility that public education may have negative externalities and market systems may have some positive ones.

Public versus Private Goods

When applied to private schools, the argument is that in private schools, especially denominational ones, private benefits tend to crowd out public ones. In an even stronger version, the private benefits are viewed as public negatives. For example, as Henry M. Levin sees it, public schools have become more egalitarian over time in the following ways:

Reduction in spending disparities
Abolition of religious practices in public schools
Financial and legal support for female, handicapped, bilingual, and disadvantaged pupils
Affirmative action
Attacks on social segregation.

In Levin's view, these egalitarian advances have occurred at the expense of private privilege, especially of groups that had been able to dominate public school programs. These groups are allegedly leading the movement to achieve public support for private schools. According to Levin, their objective is school choice, either through public school reform or by public support of private school options.[18]

How can government ensure that it is getting the public benefits that justify public support for private education? According to Levin, this might be done by personnel requirements, curriculum requirements, and/or measures of output. Inasmuch as most private schools are denominational, however, the kind of regulation required would lead to government entanglement with religious organizations. Furthermore, reasonable people could disagree on how to define or assess the public benefits of private schooling; requiring that such issues be resolved politically could be extremely divisive.

In addition, Levin argues that "some important public goals produced by education are inextricably related to the choice of educational process, and that the process itself will be affected by the fact of public or private sponsorship of schooling." To illustrate his point, Levin cites the probability that Catholic schools will not tolerate open discussion of abortion, military schools a candid discussion of disarmament, or evangelical schools a discussion of evolution. As long as only 10 percent of all students attend private schools, these antidemocratic tendencies can be held in check. If, however, a much larger proportion were enrolled in private schools, the loss of a democratic orientation could be disastrous.[19]

Levin's argument is based on a valid point that is frequently over-looked. The consequences of private schooling on a large scale might be very different from the consequences on a small one. Note, however, that some of the differences would favor private schooling. For example, if it should expand dramatically, the economies of scale would improve private school efficiency. Be that as it may, however, Levin is insinuating, if not asserting directly, that private schools have undemocratic out-comes. This is an astonishing argument; after all, since tens of millions of students have been educated in private schools, any antidemocratic effects of such schools should be evident by now. Nevertheless, Levin cites no evidence to support his views on this issue. The absence of evidence is especially remarkable in view of the fact that the public school lobby has the resources and the incentives to provide it. It has never hesitated to criticize private schools on other grounds; hence it would surely do so on antidemocratic grounds if such evidence could be found.

Actually, although more light on the subject would be useful, some evidence on the issues is available. In 1966, Andrew M. Greeley and Peter Rossi studied the differences, if any, between Catholic students educated in Catholic schools and those educated in public schools. Their study covered both religious and nonreligious outcomes.[20] The criteria they used to compare students would be widely accepted as appropriate in studies of this kind; for example, they sought to ascertain whether there are any significant differences in acceptance of racial diversity. In brief, the study found either no significant difference in civic attitudes or conduct, or a slight advantage to students who had studied in Catholic schools.

The "public goods" argument for public education ignores evidence from other nations as well. Lott has shown that "higher levels of totalitari-anism are associated with increased expenditures for schooling." His explanation is that totalitarian governments view schooling as a form of indoctrination; they spend more on schooling for the same reason they spend more to control radio and television broadcasting. He notes that "these results strongly challenge the presumed public goods relationship between schooling and democracy."[21]

Religion as a Private Good

Religious instruction is the private benefit that is most frequently cited by supporters of public education. Most private schools are denominational; of these, over half are Catholic. The argument is that religious indoctrination is a private good, and that a full-fledged system of private schools would crowd out instruction devoted to public goods.

This argument assumes that denominational (or ideological) schools would dominate a market system; I regard this assumption as highly dubious. Nonetheless, let us examine the argument in terms of the potential conflict between public and private goods in denominational schools.

As matters stand, parents who send their children to denominational schools anticipate higher levels of achievement in secular as well as religious outcomes. In their minds at least, their choice of a denominational school poses no conflict between religious training and public goods. Nevertheless, such conflict is a possibility. What is the likelihood that the private benefits would take precedence over the public goods in a market system?

If we had a market system of education, parents would have to choose between schools that emphasized religion (a private good, according to the argument) and schools that emphasized the development of human capital (a public good, according to the argument). Which would most religious parents choose? How many parents would send their children to a denominational school if they knew that the school was less likely than others to develop their children's productive capabilities?

There is persuasive evidence that only a small proportion of parents would do so. For example, about 12 percent of the students in Catholic schools are not Catholics.[22] Presumably, they are enrolled for human capital, not religious reasons. Surveys of the parents of Catholic students in Catholic schools show that a high proportion expect secular educational benefits from Catholic education. Thus while we are being warned that denominational schools will emphasize private benefits, most students are enrolling in them at least in part for human capital reasons.

Consider also that the curricula in public and denominational schools are remarkably similar; the time devoted to religion appears to be the only noticeable difference. Even on this issue, the differences are not very large. Let us suppose, however, that a denominational school devotes one period a day to instruction in religion. If the school utilizes a six-period day, should we conclude that one-sixth of its time at least is devoted to private goods? Such a conclusion would be erroneous. In educating pupils, schools are concerned with habits and attitudes as well as the acquisition of subject matter and basic skills. I refer here to such things as punctuality, dependability, and persistence on task. These are as essential to public as to private goods. A course devoted to religion can contribute just as much to these objectives as a course in science or American history; there is not the slightest reason to think otherwise.

Similarly, there is ample reason to anticipate a Catholic school superiority in educating disadvantaged pupils.[23] Just about every serious analyst of our political, social, and educational situation agrees that popular opinion and public policy are excessively oriented to short-term instead of long-term considerations.[24] Examples are a tendency to sacrifice long-term benefits for immediate consumption; an unwillingness to spend adequately for maintenance of public infrastructure; and the tendency of political officials to avoid expenditures whose benefits will not materialize until after they have left office.

Overemphasis on immediate gratification at the expense of future benefits is an acute problem among young people. Students are bombarded with advertising that encourages immediate consumption and gratification; they receive relatively little reinforcement for taking a longer view. The incidence of teenage pregnancy is merely one result of teenagers' tendency to undervalue long-range considerations.

More than any other institution, religion emphasizes long-range over short-range considerations. It is, therefore, likely that denominational schools are more effective with children who are especially lacking in such perspectives. Under these circumstances, even if private schools also turned out to be less effective in inculcating open-mindedness, the denominational schools might still produce the largest public goods: the gains associated with their development of a long-range perspective might far exceed the losses associated with less open-mindedness.

The Outcomes of Special Education

As noted in Chapter 6, the proportion of students with learning disabilities is higher in public than in Catholic schools, and the cost of educating such students in public schools is four to five times as much as for other students. There is a striking dearth of information about the educational benefits of these high expenditures for students with disabilities. It's as if it is immoral to raise the issue because the students so obviously need assistance and evoke sympathy from all of us. In my opinion, however, there is too much at stake to continue to avoid the cost-benefit issues.

The public school lobby contends that cost comparisons are misleading because public schools enroll a higher proportion of expensive-to-educate students. When outcomes are the issue, it asserts that comparisons are misleading because public schools enroll a higher proportion of students who are less likely to achieve satisfactorily. As far as they go, these are valid points. The difficulty is that they do not go far enough.

Let us assume that annual expenditures for special education students average $13,600, or $163,000 over a twelve-year period.[25] What or how much should students in special education be expected to achieve? Of course, the answer will vary from one subgroup to another. Educational expectations for brain-damaged children will be different from those for mentally retarded or emotionally disturbed children. Still, special education should not be regarded as a black hole into which we pour large amounts of money without any idea of the anticipated or actual return.

To illustrate the problem, suppose that after twelve years of schooling, brain-damaged students, on average, can speak only fifty words and have no skills that would enable them to earn a living. In that case, we have paid $163,000 for custodial care for twelve years, 180 days a year, perhaps seven hours a day. If frankly recognized as custodial, however, such care is available for much less than $163,000. On these assumptions, the public schools would be highly inefficient with respect to brain-damaged students.

I do not mean to suggest that assistance for students with learning disabilities should be terminated if they do not benefit very much from special education. The issue is whether there are better ways to assist many of these students. Would the students and their parents spend the $163,000 for special education if the decision were theirs to make? Surely, some would be better off by using the $163,000 as a lifetime nest egg to help defray the financial burdens likely to be associated with their handicaps. The fact that the $163,000 is available only as special education services suggests that the primary beneficiaries are special education teachers and administrators, not children with learning disabilities. It also suggests that taking the student mix into account does not necessarily lead to more favorable conclusions about public school efficiency.

The higher costs of students in special education suggest a lack of candor in both voucher and antivoucher positions. Many voucher proposals base the amount of the voucher on per-pupil costs in public schools. As just noted, private schools enroll a lower proportion of expensive-to-educate pupils. Consequently, the voucher proposals are based on costs that are not as applicable to private as to public schools. Not surprisingly, the same problem has emerged in comparisons of public, nonprofit, and for-profit hospitals. Cost comparisons that do not take into account their different patient mixes are very misleading. One of the benefits of competition in education would be that it would force a breakdown of costs. Large cost differences that are obscured by averages would be replaced by more accurate figures relating to different sub-groups within the student population.

Controversial Issues in the Public Schools

As we have seen, the critics of a market system allege that private schools will present a biased view of controversial issues. The implicit assumption is that public schools provide unbiased consideration of them. How realistic is this assumption?

The NEA and the AFT annually adopt scores of resolutions on highly controversial political, social, economic, and educational issues. As pointed out in Chapter 8, the NEA has explicitly accepted racial quotas in its governance structure since 1975; although it would be difficult to identify a more controversial issue in American society, the NEA's quota provisions have not been debated at an NEA convention since their adoption in 1975. I doubt whether teachers who have accepted racial quotas for years without dissent in their own organizations discuss quotas in their classrooms in an unbiased way.

As a matter of fact, a resolution adopted by the NEA's Board of Directors in May 1991 prohibited any organization that opposes NEA policies from renting space in the NEA convention exhibition area.[26] The policy even barred NEA delegates themselves from exhibiting materials opposing NEA policies if the materials were produced by outsiders. Pursuant to the policy, the exhibitors for the Boy Scouts of America were asked to leave; the reasons given were their ban on homosexuals and the fact that Boy Scouts must pledge an oath to God. In addition, an anti-abortion group was prohibited from displaying five of its eleven buttons and eight of its twenty-three pamphlets. At its 1992 convention, the NEA's Representative Assembly (RA) changed its policies to allow NEA affiliates, delegates, and caucuses to use exhibit and fundraising areas to dissemi-nate materials contrary to NEA policy. In the same resolution, however, the RA adopted the following two policies:

> Groups external to NEA will be permitted to use the exhibit area
> to distribute material or disseminate information related to NEA's

agenda, provided that such material is not contrary to or does not advocate a change in NEA policy.

Groups that do not adhere to NEA policies and resolutions on nondiscrimination will not be permitted to use the exhibit area to distribute material or disseminate information of any kind.[27]

The RA has adopted scores of policies on a wide range of subjects. The NEA's restrictions on materials critical of these positions hardly inspires confidence in the way teachers are likely to treat controversial issues.

Perhaps the teachers who exclude material contrary to NEA policies from the convention exhibition area give objective consideration to it in the classroom. Perhaps, but there is persuasive evidence to believe otherwise. One example is an instructional unit on nuclear war published by the NEA in cooperation with the Massachusetts Teachers Association and the Union of Concerned Scientists. The unit was field-tested in thirty-four states before publication in 1983. At one point, the unit asks students to consider the alternative uses of spending for nuclear weapons. Increased spending for public services like education and medical care is mentioned. Reducing taxes is not one of the options students are asked to consider. In addition, the unit urges students to collect signatures on a petition calling for a freeze on production of nuclear weapons. This unit was developed while the NEA's executive director, Terry Herndon, was president of Citizens Against Nuclear War, an organization that operated out of NEA headquarters in Washington.[28]

The instructional materials sponsored by the AFT for classrooms are as biased as those sponsored by the NEA; the only difference is in the subjects involved. For example, the AFT urges its members to use a sourcebook on labor unions published by the United Federation of Teachers for classroom use.[29] The sourcebook portrays the AFL-CIO as a long-time foe of racial discrimination, even though the AFL-CIO included racially discriminatory unions until such unions were prohibited by Supreme Court decision.[30] In discussing the reduction of racial discrimination in the building trades union, the sourcebook states, "It should be kept in mind that this progress was achieved under the union's own leadership—it was not imposed by some government agency." It is egregiously false to state or imply that government pressures, including lawsuits filed by the Equal Opportunity Commission, did not play a major role in reducing racial discrimination in the construction unions. In addition to such egregious falsehoods, the sourcebook attempts to foster support for unions by pedagogically indefensible examples. For example, in discussing "Why a Worker Joins a Union," it relies on a biographical sketch. The sketch features an employer who explains why his employees are not working as follows: "Oh, I have plenty of work all right, but I thought it would be good psychology to let the boys walk the streets a few days. It will put the fear of God into their hearts."[31] Not surprisingly, the sourcebook does not consider the possibility that workers might refuse to join unions for legitimate reasons.

The NEA and the AFT support an increase in the minimum wage. As pointed out in Chapter 3, the consensus among economists is that minimum wage laws are especially harmful to disadvantaged minorities. Such laws render unskilled labor more expensive and reduce the cost of racial discrimination to employers. Not surprisingly, facts such as these are not mentioned in the AFT unit.

Are public or private schools more likely to consider conflicting points of view on controversial issues? The answer may well be more favorable to private than to public schools. The latter are subject to a much broader range of restrictions and prohibitions. Granted, the denominational schools are often unwilling to allow criticism of their denominational dogma, but these restrictions are relatively narrow ones. Although undesirable, they do not prevent consideration of different points of view on other issues. We cannot assume, however, that discussion of controversial issues in public schools is robust and critical because no single interest group controls public education. In practice, more interest groups exercise veto power over what is taught in public schools. The extent of veto power varies from district to district, and from subject to subject, but its pervasive presence is not to be denied. For this reason, bias is not necessarily a more serious problem in private than in public schools. For every instance of bias in private schools, one can easily cite comparable instances in the public schools.

Economic Literacy

In principle, everyone agrees that it is important for students to understand our economy. According to Levin,

it is expected that all students understand the basis for a capitalist economy and their potential roles in such an economic setting. This means that they must be familiar not only with the philosophi-

cal and institutional basis for the U.S. economy, but also the requirements for participating productively in economic institutions.
They must understand the basis for modern work organizations
with their principles of hierarchy and supervision, division of labor,
labor markets, role of technology, and wages and salaries. They
must understand the functions of investment and savings as well as
consumption and both the potential and limits of government
intervention in the economy.[32]

How effective are public schools in teaching these understandings? A
recent study of citizen attitudes toward a market system in the United
States and the Soviet Union provides some interesting evidence. Identical
telephone interviews, based on thirty-six questions pertaining to free
markets, were conducted in New York City and Moscow in May 1990.
The finding was that public understanding of and attitudes toward market systems were generally the same in both countries.[33]

Americans' incomplete understanding of their own economic system
may have significant political consequences. As the economist Mancur
Olson observes:

> the politics of the United States as of other countries is influenced,
> and influenced for the worse, by the fact that the use of markets
> are imperfectly understood by a majority of the citizens. No doubt
> this popular ignorance of economics does on occasion lead to the
> gratuitous or even harmful use of government to perform certain
> social functions for which the government does not have a compara-
> tive advantage. Though there are some valid arguments that point
> in the opposite direction, it is surely a reasonable hypothesis that
> the limited understanding of economics among the laity leads to a
> somewhat bigger public sector than would be optimal.[34]

Applying Olson's analysis to education, we come to this paradoxical
conclusion: Public education has flourished because it fails to educate
effectively. Its failure to foster an understanding of market systems has
led citizens to accept a larger public education sector than a more
informed citizenry would permit.

Civic Responsibility

At the outset, it should be emphasized that neither public nor private
schools seem to have a significant impact on civic understanding and

conduct. The overwhelming majority of voters get their information on public policy issues from television and newspapers; what is learned in school has little or no relevance to voter perception of the issues.[95] As a matter of fact, the effects of formal schooling on political participation are ambiguous at best. According to the conventional wisdom, political participation increases with educational attainment. Data on voting rates are one kind of evidence cited to support this claim: for example, in the 1988 presidential election 47 percent of those with just a high school education voted, while 75 percent of college graduates did so.[36] The unstated implication seems to be that education contributes to a higher level of civic responsibility.

There is no evidence, however, of a causal relationship between increased educational attainment and higher voting participation; both may be attributable to the same factors. It is also problematic whether voting per se is a useful measure of constructive civic participation. It is not at all clear that the farmer who votes in order to maintain price supports for his crops, or the auto worker who is politically active to prevent the importation of foreign cars, is more civic minded than the citizen who does not vote at all. Furthermore, voting in national elections has declined considerably over the past century, even while the average amount of formal education per voter has increased very substantially. Between 1956 and 1980, for example, while the percentage of eligible voters who voted in presidential elections declined, the proportion of the population with college degrees doubled. In the leading study of the effects of education on political sophistication, Eric R. A. N. Smith concludes: "Formal education has an effect on political knowledge and sophistication, but a small one. The growth of education in the United States . . . may have done many things, but it did not contribute much to the public's understanding of politics. In sum, education is not the key to the public's understanding of politics."[37]

In brief, we have several reasons to be skeptical of the beneficial civic effects of either public or private schools. The more such issues are examined by scholars with no vested interest in the outcome, the less persuasive the case for the civic benefits of schooling.

Universal versus Means-Tested Benefits

Earlier I asserted that consideration of externalities would weaken the efficiency argument for public education. Thus far, the discussion has challenged the positive externalities cited by its supporters. Let me now move to identifying some negative externalities.

Whenever government provides a service, it must decide who is eligible to receive it. Should government provide the service only to those who cannot afford it? Or should government provide the service to everyone, that is, provide a universal benefit? Suppose, for example, it is deemed essential that everyone have available a minimum package of health benefits. Let us say this benefit package is worth $1,000 annually. Government could raise taxes to provide it for everyone. Or it could establish a means test, and provide it only for those unable to afford it from personal resources.

Theoretically, the alternatives need not affect most taxpayers very much. Instead of purchasing the services privately, taxpayers would pay for them through taxes. Since taxpayers must cover the costs for the indigent in one way or another, the financial impact of universal benefits might be very similar to that of means-tested benefits. At the same time, the universal approach appears to have several advantages: There is no means test, hence no recipients are stigmatized; everyone is entitled to the benefits. Bureaucratic hassling is minimized. Equality is served; there is one standard of government provision for everyone.

In recent years, however, policymakers have begun to question the advantages of universal benefits.[38] Various long-range outcomes, not anticipated when universal benefits were enacted, have drastically altered the assessments of their advantages. Universal benefits indisputably weakened the family and community relationships that had formerly supported the elderly, the very young, and the indigent. Bureaucratic hassling did not disappear. Efforts to expand the benefits began to preoccupy legislators. Tax rates began to weaken incentives to work and invest. At the same time, recipients of services provided by government lost their incentives to economize; since the government paid, why not use the entitlement to the limit?

A study of educational vouchers in British Columbia illustrates how both their proponents and opponents fail to consider all the relevant outcomes. In 1980, British Columbia enacted a voucher system. Donald A. Erickson studied its impact on parents and school officials. He found that the latter became more responsive to provincial officials, less responsive to parents, and that parental participation dropped off considerably as a result of the change from parental to provincial financing.[39]

Clearly, in comparing outcomes of public and market systems of education, it would be a mistake to focus solely on pupil achievement. The effects on parents, school personnel, and legislatures must also be considered. Inasmuch as we do not have a market system of education, the effects of such a system are necessarily speculative to a certain extent. In the example cited, supporters of education vouchers did not anticipate the effects they would have on parental involvement. We can say, however, that supporters of public education also pay little attention to its indirect long-range effects. Their attention is focused on how other parties and institutions can assist public education; the effects of public education on such things as the family, personal incentives, tax rates, or legislative processes are ignored or assumed to be beneficent. No serious thought is given to the possibility that public education could have a negative impact on nonstudents or noneducational institutions.

In my view, the broader the outcomes and the range of parties that are considered, the stronger the case for a market system of education. A wealth of evidence suggests that public education is characterized by the negative outcomes resulting from universal benefits; for example, the high absentee rates in many public schools would be unlikely if families had to pay more of the costs of education from their own resources. Of course, all things considered, it may be that the benefits of public education outweigh its negative outcomes. Still, we cannot reach a defensible conclusion on the issue unless and until we consider all the relevant outcomes.

Because the same problem arises in other fields, our approach to it in education is likely to depend on our approach to social policy generally. For instance, policymakers disagree on whether the problems of the urban underclass are due to impersonal social forces or to a lack of personal responsibility. Is the high dropout rate among black teenagers due to impersonal forces over which they have no control? Or is it the result of unwillingness to accept personal responsibility for their performance? We are just beginning to address such questions, and the answers will affect a wide range of public services.[40] Probably both ''impersonal social forces'' and ''failure to accept personal responsibility'' will be part of the answer. The mix, however, will be crucial, and will play a crucial role in the resolution of several issues raised in this book. In general, the ''impersonal social forces'' explanation will strengthen public education; the ''lack of personal responsibility'' explanation will favor a market approach. To be sure, these are oversimplifications, but

I believe they reflect an underlying reality that cannot be overlooked in the years ahead.

Multiculturalism

In recent years, "multiculturalism" has received an extraordinary amount of attention, perhaps more than any other educational topic. The rationale for multiculturalism is based on our diversity. Supposedly, if the American people are to live together harmoniously, all cultures and lifestyles must be respected and appreciated. To help achieve this objective, the curriculum must show the contributions of groups that receive inadequate attention in conventional curricula. Furthermore, the favorable but uncritical treatment of Western culture must be replaced by a more realistic, that is, critical, perspective. For example, conventional curricula glorify Columbus but ignore his harsh treatment of native Americans or the negative consequences of colonization on them.

Although definitions of multiculturalism vary, I believe these comments express its core elements. It must be emphasized that "multiculturalism" is not limited to ethnic and religious diversity. Groups that regard themselves as the victims of discrimination or as being undervalued view multiculturalism as a means of reducing the stigma associated with their status. For example, gay/lesbian/bisexual groups view multiculturalism as a vehicle for fostering respect for their constituents and acceptance of their lifestyles.

In practice, the advocates of multiculturalism are caught in a dilemma. On the one hand, they decry what they perceive to be the uncritical approval of Western culture and of "traditional" lifestyles. On the other hand, objective treatment of virtually any ethnic or religious group, or of any lifestyle, will include some facts that are not conducive to the self esteem of its members or adherents. Faced with this dilemma, multiculturalists usually are guilty of the same practice they impute to others; that is, they fail to mention important facts that would presumably weaken the self esteem of the alleged disadvantaged groups. Multicultural activists are not apt to point out that some African tribes enslaved others for sale to European slave traders or that some native Americans routinely practiced cannibalism or human sacrifices. I do not cite such omissions to defend conventional curricula, which I would gladly change on other grounds. The point is that intellectual integrity fares no better under multiculturalism than under the curricula that it is supposed to replace.

Proposals for a curriculum that will emphasize what the American people share in common instead of their differences are an understandable reaction to increasing heterogeneity. The problem is that a certain level of unity is required to achieve agreement on what students should be unified over. Unfortunately, as the controversy over condom availability illustrates, the required level of unity does not seem to be forthcoming. What is happening is poorly understood, even by the partisans in the conflict. As "diversity" increases, the public school curriculum reflects more compromises between various interest groups. These compromises result in programs and courses that lack coherence or unity of purpose. Instead, they are a mishmash reflecting the politically feasible, no matter how pointless they may be educationally.

While controversies over ethnic relations, religion, and lifestyle dominate the public school agenda, technology and the demands of a competitive economy underscore the importance of scientific and technological objectives.[41] These objectives are not served by the emphasis on multiculturalism. To be effective, the scientific and technological curriculum must begin in the primary grades and must be implemented consistently throughout the United States. Unfortunately, media and political attention are focused on multicultural conflicts.

Conceptually, a viable solution is possible. Public schools could be limited to the basic skills, civic backgrounds and processes, and the common technological/scientific education required by the economy. Instead of trying to accommodate every differentiating demand, public schools could leave such demands to the groups that promote them. Practically speaking, however, I do not see any hope for such an approach; in fact, public schools are adding to, not cutting back on, their educational and social objectives. The following courses illustrate this proliferation of objectives:

AIDS education	Health education
Alcohol education	International education
Consumer education	Multicultural education
Driver education	Parent education
Drug education	Sensitivity education
Economics education	Sex education
Environmental education	Values education

Each additional objective requires more resources, and each increases social conflict over educational ends and means. In the past, dominant groups were able to impose their curriculum on politically weak minorities and immigrant groups. Contemporary conflict, however, is between a plethora of powerful groups; there is no majority, except on a very limited range of issues. In public education, there is very little "do-power," but a tremendous amount of veto power. This was not the situation that prevailed when communities were much more homogeneous than they are today. While everyone is praising "diversity," our nation is devoting a disproportionate share of its resources to the management of conflict resulting from diversity. A market system would greatly reduce this dissipation of our spiritual as well as our material resources.

Efficiency and Political Dynamics

Public schools are inherently more bureaucratic than private schools. John Chubb and Terry Moe have pointed out why excessive reliance on bureaucracies is inevitable under public education.[42] Interest groups try to enact and implement programs they espouse. The groups realize, however, that elected officials come and go—and when they go, there is the danger that the programs they support may go also. To protect themselves against such eventualities, interest groups try to establish their programs by legislation. Inevitably, public schools are unable to terminate programs that have outlived their usefulness.[43]

As in the public sector generally, it is very difficult to budget for preventive maintenance in public education. Elected officials are under strong pressure to spend revenues for immediate benefits, especially benefits for public employees. Spending tax revenues to avert costly repairs a long time in the future requires a time horizon longer than most elected officials can accept. The upshot is that buildings and facilities tend to deteriorate in the public sector. Owners of private property have stronger incentives not to allow this to happen; the owners, not the public at large, would have to absorb the losses due to inadequate maintenance. At any rate, although systematic data on private school facilities are not available, public school maintenance is clearly underfunded according to the standards required by sound business practice.[44]

Budgeting schedules are also conducive to public-sector inefficiency. Most governments, including school boards, are under pressure not to have a budget surplus over and above a reasonable reserve at the end of their fiscal year. To do so might lead to a reduction in revenues, or teacher demands that the surplus be distributed as a salary increase. Another possibility to be avoided is taxpayer demands that taxes be lowered because revenues exceed expenditures. To avoid all such consequences, public officials tend to spend to the limit of the funds available, regardless of efficiency considerations. These anti-efficiency pressures are present only in attenuated form, if at all, in the for-profit sector.

According to the public goods argument discussed in Chapter 6, education would be underfunded if left to market processes. What about the possibility that it will be overfunded if resolved by political processes? As shown by James M. Buchanan and others, when government provides a service, it invariably creates an interest group and legislative partisans who seek to expand the services beyond their original rationale or level of support. This raises the possibility (in my opinion, the reality) that public education is overfunded. Be that as it may, the leading experts on school finance do not even mention the possibility. If objectivity is a criterion, the omission is cause for concern.

The bias in favor of public education is also in discussions of externalities. Almost without fail, the academics who emphasize educational externalities emphasize the beneficial effects of public education and the negative externalities of market systems. As Monk puts it: "The basic flaw in the market is its inability to force decision makers to internalize the full costs and benefits associated with various courses of action. The larger and more widespread these spillover effects are, both positive and negative, the less socially efficient will be the market solution."[45]

Monk goes on to partly justify public education on the basis of the negative spillover effects of the market system. Regrettably, neither he nor other pro-public education analysts consider the negative spillover effects of government policies and actions. As Yeager observes:

> The private sector is routinely made the target of regulation because of externalities, meaning cases in which the persons who decide on some activity or its scale decide wrongly because they do not themselves bear or take full account of all of its costs and benefits. How ironic, then, routinely to expect a solution from government! Government is the prototypical sector in which decision makers do not take accurate account of all the costs as well as all the benefits of each activity. The fragmentation of decisionmaking and responsibility goes part way toward explaining the condi-

tion, along with the kinds of opportunities and incentives that bureaucrats, politicians, legislative staff members, judges, and citizens have.[46]

Outcomes and Options

Other things being equal, a system that provides more options is more efficient than a system that provides fewer. First of all, most options are worth something. People frequently pay for options; in fact, there are markets for several kinds of them. With this in mind, let us consider a family moving to another state. After diligent investigation, they buy a house near an outstanding public school. Sad to say, school quality deteriorates soon thereafter. The outstanding principal accepts a superintendency elsewhere. Several good teachers who retire are replaced by poor ones. In short, things go downhill fast. What can the family do? They cannot feasibly move to another school zone. To do so would require a substantial loss of money and time—and after moving, they would still have no guarantee of continued stability and quality in the new school. Suppose, however, that a market system is in effect. Perhaps there are three or four schools within the family's attendance range. This being the case, the family can change schools without having to move.

How much are school options worth? In rural areas, perhaps nothing. In urban areas, they might be worth a great deal. Indisputably, millions of families have moved in order to avoid their designated public school. In large cities, many black and white parents alike adopt a false home address in order to avoid one school and enroll their children in another. In brief, school options would be worth a significant amount. Nevertheless, as far as I can tell, none of the critics of a market system has included the value of options in comparing the outcomes of public education with outcomes under a market system.

Conclusion

Despite its limitations, the analysis in this chapter points unambiguously to the conclusion that a market system would be much more efficient than public education. Inasmuch as the evidence on costs will clearly favor a market approach, public education will increasingly rely on claims of superiority of outcomes. As the outcomes fail to improve, the public school lobby will argue that a market system would have a negative effect on educational objectives that cannot be measured.

It is perhaps the supreme irony of the situation that the public schools are already emphasizing unmeasurable objectives while the denominational schools are citing secular ones. Presumably, the unmeasured goals of public education are such things as cooperative attitudes, patriotism, honesty, and respect for others. Personally, I believe that progress toward such goals can be assessed. If not, however, we have no reason to think public education is contributing to progress on them.

It stands to reason that a market system would be superior both in defining the goals of education and in the means of assessing progress toward those goals. Schools would try to demonstrate that they are more effective than their competitors; to do so, they would be forced to define the standards of comparison. The dynamics of the process would improve assessment, whether of academic achievement, attitudes, work and study habits, or any other nonacademic objective.   Monk - Educ. Fin.

Under the present system, school personnel have a vested interest in avoiding clear-cut criteria for evaluation. If progress cannot be assessed, there is no way to hold anyone accountable for results. Furthermore, even if academic achievement were the sole or the dominant outcome to be assessed, progress on this criterion requires desirable habits and attitudes, such as effective study habits. A company that was not sure what products it was supposed to produce and had no way of knowing how efficiently it was making them would be in poor shape. Similarly, claiming to achieve goals that cannot be measured is the last refuge of a system that cannot achieve goals that can be assessed.

In a paid advertisement in the *New York Times* in September 1991, AFT President Albert Shanker reiterated AFT opposition to government assistance to parents who prefer private schooling.[47] According to Shanker, private school students did not demonstrate any educational superiority in the latest results of the National Assessment of Education Progress (NAEP). He cited this lack of superiority despite the freedom of private schools to select their students as validating AFT opposition to government assistance for private schooling.

Even if Shanker's premise regarding NAEP scores is valid (and this is far from clear), his argument is fallacious for several reasons. For one thing, students' performance in existing private schools may be far inferior to their likely performance in a market system of education. Second, Shanker's argument totally ignores cost issues. If private schools can achieve substantially the same results but at a much lower cost, there are strong public policy reasons to assist students who prefer private schools. Third, Shanker ignores the pervasive social conflict over public education and the strong likelihood that a market system would minimize this conflict and its horrendous costs. Finally, Shanker ignores the possibility that unrestricted entry into the labor force at a lower age would be preferable to either public or private schooling. As a union president, Shanker does what interest-group leaders normally do, that is, he ignores contrary evidence or logic in efforts to gain public support.

At the outset, I pointed out that efficiency is not the only basis for evaluating the desirability of public education. Even some economists who support public education concede that it is less efficient than a market system would be. Their argument is that public education is justified by other considerations; among these, fairness is perhaps the most important, and the following two chapters will deal with it.

8

≈ The Educational
Consequences
of Racial Conflict

Since the 1950s, racial issues have been the leading source of conflict in American education: forced busing, white flight, racial balance, racial segregation, affirmative action, reverse discrimination, Afrocentrism, role models, quotas, multicultural education, diversity—each of these is the focal point of extensive controversy that shows no sign of diminishing.

These controversies tend to weaken public support for public education. Because education is provided by government, racial and ethnic groups must reach an accommodation on various issues. As the accommodations become increasingly distasteful to one or more groups, the disaffected parties become more supportive of alternatives to public education. The pattern resembles the situation when religion was the major source of conflict over education. Various religious groups that were dissatisfied with the public schools established their own schools. The same outcome is beginning to emerge when racial instead of religious conflict is involved.

My major purpose in this chapter is not to evaluate the merits of racial issues. Instead, it is to explain how and why controversies over them affect the future of public education. Although I shall express my views on various issues, my discussion of them is not as thorough as it would be if the focus were on their merits.

A great deal of racial conflict in education is over equality of educational opportunity. This concept has important nonracial dimensions as well. Because of its complexity and importance, the concept is discussed in the following chapter, where both the racial and nonracial dimensions are addressed. It must be emphasized, however, that racial conflict often involves issues that are nonracial on their face. For example, should teachers be required to achieve a certain score on standardized tests to be eligible to teach? Although the issue is not racial on its face, various racial and ethnic groups have positions on it. Similarly, some of the most important consequences of racial conflict are its effects on ostensibly nonracial issues. In many cases, the racial dimensions of a conflict are not apparent from the issue giving rise to it.

The Language of Racial Conflict

Racial conflict in education poses difficult editorial and definitional problems. In the first place, we cannot fully understand developments within education apart from developments outside of it, but a thorough discussion of those developments is beyond the scope of this book. In what follows, I shall refer to the noneducational developments briefly while citing sources that analyze them extensively. Most issues giving rise to racial conflict in education have emerged in other public services, and they are not likely to be resolved solely on their educational dimensions. Affirmative action is a case in point. It is an extremely important issue in education, but the way it is resolved will depend to some extent on developments outside of education.

Generally speaking, our political and educational systems try to avoid sharp conflict over principles and policies. Partly for this reason, they foster resort to ambiguous terms that obscure rather than clarify basic issues. To avoid this danger, let me first clarify the terms to be used in the following discussion.

Civil Rights

Few persons are comfortable opposing "civil rights." For this reason, one way to encourage a favorable attitude toward a proposal is to characterize it as a civil rights one. The result is a widespread tendency to apply the phrase to policies that may have little or nothing to do with civil rights as commonly understood. The definitional problem is compounded by good-faith disagreements over the meaning of "civil rights." These disagreements would exist regardless of efforts to use the phrase for political advantage.

Originally, the phrase "civil rights" referred to "civil capacity to contract, to own property, to make wills, to give evidence, and to sue and be sued."[1] In the following discussion, however, it also includes the right to free expression and the rights to participate in the political process, to worship or not to worship as one chooses, to travel, to be free of arbitrary or capricious government action, and to enter and/or work at a vocation or profession or business of choice. All of these rights are subject to some limitations that are not spelled out here. As used here, the term "civil rights" does not include any financial entitlements or protection against all private expressions of prejudice. It does, however, include the right not to be subject to discrimination by government. "Discrimination" refers to impermissible treatment of individuals on the basis of race, creed, color, sex, age, or national origin. What actions are impermissible, hence "discriminatory"? Here, I can only note but not resolve the large number of issues involving the meaning or application of "discrimination."

The impact of racial conflict in education does not necessarily depend on the merits of the positions in the conflict. Aggressive pursuit of a just claim may weaken public education; the triumph of an unjust position may strengthen it. Suppose black parents and students boycott the high school football team, alleging that the white coaching staff is discriminating against black players. As a result of the boycott, the team loses a coveted championship. Gate receipts decline, and racial tensions in and out of the school increase dramatically. School and community become polarized over the issue. Such conflict weakens public education regardless of the merits of the boycott.

If the protest is characterized as a racial conflict, a genuine civil rights issue may be ignored. If the protest is characterized as a civil rights conflict, a claim for preferential treatment may be treated as a civil rights issue. We must often characterize claims before we can assess their merits, but the way the claims are characterized affects public attitudes toward them. In practice, the phrase "civil rights issue" is sometimes applied to racial issues; the phrase "racial issue" is sometimes applied to genuine civil rights issues. To complicate matters even further, some controversies do raise both civil rights and racial issues. Inasmuch as I wish to discuss racial conflict without prejudging these issues, the ambiguity can only be noted but not resolved at this point.

Civil Rights Organizations

The lack of clarity over "civil rights" carries over to "civil rights organizations." Most such organizations were established to protect the civil rights of specific ethnic or religious groups, or to combat discrimination and prejudice directed against them. The National Association for the Advancement of Colored People (NAACP), the Anti-Defamation League (ADL) of B'nai B'rith, the Japanese-American Citizens League, the Puerto Rican Legal Defense and Education Fund, and the Catholic League for Religious and Civil Rights are examples. In contrast, some civil rights organizations do not have ethnic or religious sponsorship: the American Civil Liberties Union is perhaps the most prominent.

The definitional problem arises from the fact that the civil rights organizations are often active on other issues. The ADL opposes developments deemed prejudicial to Israel. Similarly, the NAACP also serves as an interest-group organization on behalf of black citizens. It is not always clear whether it is protecting their civil rights or their economic interests as perceived by the NAACP.

Furthermore, organizational claims to represent certain groups are not always valid. Although the NAACP is said to "represent" black citizens, it does not necessarily represent all or even most on specific issues. It sometimes supports policies opposed by black citizens or local affiliates in particular communities. The same point applies to other civil rights organizations.

Finally, it should be noted that the civil rights organizations are not a monolithic group. For example, the ADL position on minority scholarships is ambiguous; the NAACP supports them unreservedly.[2] Thus to say that civil rights organizations support minority scholarships would be misleading: some do and some do not.

Minority

When the term "minority" is not qualified, its use often leads to wildly inaccurate generalizations. For example, blacks and Hispanics typically oppose standardized testing for certain purposes, such as college admissions; Jews, Japanese, and Chinese do not. In general, the ethnic minorities that perform well on tests support their use; the ethnic minorities that perform poorly oppose their use. Consequently, one cannot refer to a minority position against testing unless "minority" is used as a code word for ethnic minorities that perform poorly on tests.

In this analysis, the term "disadvantaged minorities" refers to the ethnic minorities that are lagging educationally. Blacks, Hispanics, and Native Americans are the largest groups in this category. These minorities tend to adopt common positions on a wide range of educational issues. Except on bilingual education, the following discussion emphasizes the positions of black organizations, but these positions are generally supported by other disadvantaged minorities.

This chapter is not an overview of racial conflict in education. Instead, it is intended to show how racial conflict often affects a large number of students, parents, teachers, and others, many of whom are not parties to the conflict. Although I shall not pursue all the ramifications of such conflict, the discussion is intended to demonstrate its general tendencies. Examples to the contrary can be taken for granted, but they do not invalidate the conclusions about the tendencies.

Assignment to Schools

In 1954 the U.S. Supreme Court held that government could not require pupils to attend racially segregated schools. State-imposed racial segregation was held to violate the Fourteenth Amendment, which obligates the states to provide equal treatment to their citizens. From 1954 to the present, however, racial conflict over pupil assignment has emerged as a problem in every region of the country. It is not unusual for litigation over pupil assignment to continue for a decade or longer.

In the 1960s and 1970s federal courts were frequently called upon to formulate remedial orders to end racial segregation in education. Such orders were complicated by the fact that attendance zones based on proximity to schools were not always conducive to racial integration. This was especially true when residential areas within a school district were racially homogeneous. In order to eliminate the racial identification of schools, federal judges sometimes ordered that students be bused from their neighborhoods to schools elsewhere. Such orders were sometimes applied to school districts with a history of intransigent opposition to racial integration. In effect, the busing orders applied to the districts that were most determined not to carry them out. In these situations, the orders resulted in vehement white opposition to "forced busing." Eventually, the issue surfaced in national as well as state and local politics.[3]

Opposition to forced busing emerged in black as well as white communities. One reason was that black pupils were more often bused to white schools than vice versa. Also, some black parents resented the implication that black pupils had to be in predominantly white classrooms to learn effectively. Conflict on buses and hostile reactions in receiving schools also weakened black support for busing of black children. The fact that racial integration threatened the jobs of black teachers and administrators, although often overlooked, was another factor.

One early response to the 1954 Supreme Court decision was the enactment in some states of "freedom of choice" plans. Basically, these plans allowed students to enroll in private schools with state support. Because the private schools could admit or reject students as they pleased, they were envisioned as a way to maintain racially segregated schools.

In 1968 the U.S. Supreme Court ruled that freedom of choice legislation enacted to maintain racially segregated schools was unconstitutional.[4] The aftermath of this legislation, however, continues into the present. Civil rights organizations, especially those representing blacks, have been hostile to school choice legislation ever since it was enacted to maintain racially segregated schools. This hostility persists even when school choice is advocated as a way to reduce instead of increase racial segregation in education. The rationale for such advocacy is that the ethnic composition of public schools reflects neighborhood residential patterns. When these patterns are racially homogeneous, as is often the case, schools will be also. Proponents of a market system of education contend that freedom of school choice would foster schools that cut across racial lines; opponents contend that freedom of choice would increase racial segregation among schools.

White parents are often reluctant to have their children attend schools with black majorities. Although the reasons for their reluctance are matters of dispute, many white families have moved to avoid enrolling their children in such schools. This phenomenon, widely referred to as "white flight," was especially evident in the 1970s. As many white families moved to the suburbs, school districts in the large central cities enrolled higher proportions of children from disadvantaged minorities. In the twenty-five largest central cities in the United States, the percentage of school-age children who were white dropped from 84.5 in 1950 to 48.7 in 1980.[5]

These demographic changes triggered racial conflict over other issues, such as school finance. State legislatures distribute financial aid to school districts. In doing so, they must reconcile the claims of city, suburban, and rural districts. White flight exacerbated this problem by converting the city-suburban-rural split into a racial as well as a geographical division. Representatives from urban areas frequently allege that their constituents are denied a fair share of state aid because of racial prejudice or because suburban and rural legislators don't care about the poor.

In recent years, racial conflict over pupil assignment has emerged in a variety of ways. In Missouri, the courts have held that the state of Missouri shares legal responsibility for racial segregation in the Kansas City school district. Because of white flight, however, it is no longer possible to achieve racial integration within the district. Efforts to persuade or require surrounding districts to enroll black students from Kansas City have been unsuccessful. In view of these facts, several black students (the plaintiffs in the case) have requested state vouchers to cover the costs of education in private schools. Several private schools in the Kansas City area have agreed to enroll black students for half the per-pupil cost of education in the public schools. The outcome is not clear, but the voucher proposal has added another dimension to protracted racial conflict over assignment.

Another controversy over assignment involves a very different approach. Several urban school districts, including New York City, Baltimore, and Milwaukee, have announced plans to initiate, or to study, the establishment of schools for black male students. These proposals have been challenged legally and severely criticized by feminists and by leaders, black and white, who advocate racial integration in education. Despite the criticism, however, the proposals probably reflect a sizable segment of black opinion. Many black students prefer to attend predominantly black schools. White and black high school seniors taking the SAT in 1990 showed striking differences in their colleges of choice. Only three colleges (Florida State University, Syracuse University, and the University of North Carolina) were among the top fifteen colleges preferred by both white and black students. Of the fifteen top choices of black students, ten, including the top six, were predominantly black institutions.[6]

These data illustrate the dilemmas and contradictions of race relations in education. The predominantly white institutions of higher education are trying constantly to enroll more black students, but many black students prefer black colleges. This preference reflects black ambivalence about racial integration. The predominantly black institutions are less inclined to view integration as a major goal.

Racial issues also play an important role in controversies over public school choice. More than half the states have enacted or are considering legislation allowing parents to send their children to public schools of their choice. In addition, many school districts have adopted some form of choice within the district. Virtually everywhere public school choice is an active issue, the possibility that it would foster racial segregation is a major concern. Its supporters assert that public school choice enables inner-city black and Hispanic students to transfer to presumably better upper-middle-class or suburban schools. In practice, only a small number of such transfers have occurred.[7]

The legislation providing for public school choice often includes stringent safeguards against an increase in racially segregated schools. These safeguards allow only transfers that do not upset some predetermined racial balance in the schools. For instance, a school district may decide that white students shall not exceed 65 percent of enrollment in any school. Such plans are often referred to as "controlled choice." Suppose that school X is at the 65 percent limit, and two students, one black and the other white, apply from school Y. Under the conditions specified, the white student will be denied admission while the black student will be admitted.

In short, by limiting choice to fit "racial balance," the choice plans frequently deprive large numbers of students, usually white ones, of the choices they really prefer. Black students usually end up with more choices than white ones, but both groups may be limited to choices that do not include the schools they prefer.

Tracking

Black and white students who are assigned to the same school often enroll in different programs within the school. Although not based on race, such enrollment may nevertheless follow racial lines to a considerable extent. This situation underlies current controversies over "tracking."

For present purposes, tracking is defined as the assignment of pupils to courses and/or programs on the basis of ability or career plans. For example, a high school may have four tracks as follows:

Academic:	Students going on to higher education.
Vocational:	Students preparing for local employment in a trade or vocation.
General:	Students not sure of what they plan to do after graduation.

Commercial:	Students (mostly female) planning to work in office occupations.

Legally, students may be free to sign up for any track, but counselor guidance plays an influential role in student choices. As the counselors often view the situation, the lower standardized test scores of black students indicate that they are less likely to succeed in the academic track. In addition, black students often show less interest in going to college and have smaller resources to finance this option. Consequently, a relatively low proportion of black students enroll in the college preparatory track.

Organizations of blacks and Hispanics see it differently. A recent policy statement by the Committee on Policy for Racial Justice, a group predominantly composed of leading black professors, asserts that:

> because research findings consistently indicate that inflexible track placements and rigid ability grouping segregate, stigmatize, and deny those in the bottom tracks the same access to quality education those in the upper tracks receive, we believe that these practices should be ended. It is well known that black and other low-income minority students are over-represented in the lower-ability tracks in our nation's school systems, yet it is frequently overlooked that the differences in the kind of instruction across tracks make it increasingly difficult for these students ever to climb up the academic hierarchy. In this way, low expectations and mindless bureaucracy crush the potential of thousands of black youth each year and limit their future opportunities. Staff development programs in multicultural education are an example of a readily available avenue that must be seized upon to address issues of diversity within regular classroom settings.[8]

Hispanic organizations share this view. Responding to a memorandum disseminated internally by the Department of Education's Office of Civil Rights (OCR), Suzanne Ramos, an attorney for the Mexican-American Legal Defense Fund, commented, "We object, basically, to any kind of grouping at all."[9] The memorandum itself outlined five types of situations in which ability grouping having segregative effects would violate Title VI of the Civil Rights Act of 1964. These are situations in which recipients of federal funds:

1. Cannot offer an educational justification for their grouping policy.
2. Use practices that do not substantially serve their educational objectives.
3. Employ ability criteria that do not adequately measure student ability.
4. Apply criteria inconsistently, thereby increasing segregation.
5. Use subjective measures (including teacher recommendations) that have segregative effects but are not based on clear-cut standards.

This list illustrates how the civil rights bureaucracies expand the scope of their activities. Policies governing assignment to schools are failing to bring about significant improvement in the educational achievement of disadvantaged minorities. Tracking is being perceived as the reason, hence it is also viewed as a civil rights issue. The result is that we can expect more conflict over assignment within schools. Such conflict is already widespread, but its growth potential is virtually unlimited.

Let me illustrate the rationale that underlies the opposition to tracking. Suppose pupils A and B are of equal ability. Pupil A is placed in the college preparatory track. In this track, pupils are regularly expected to do homework. Pupil B is placed in the general track, in which little homework is assigned. Inasmuch as expectations for B are lower, less is demanded of B, hence B's achievement is correspondingly lower. The expectation of low performance leads to low performance—this is the antitracking argument.

In my opinion, the argument is not persuasive. Of course, schools sometimes underestimate students and assign them to programs on the basis of erroneous assessments. Unfortunately, no system or policy on pupil assignment is free from error. If opposition to tracking means that all students should be enrolled in the same programs, regardless of ability, achievement, or interest, it is unrealistic. Opposition to tracking is not helpful as long as it fails to distinguish acceptable from unacceptable criteria for grouping students for instruction.

Tracking takes place in all-white schools, integrated schools, and all-black schools. Inasmuch as all have "tracks," it is difficult to accept racial explanations for their origins or outcomes. Even if a higher proportion of black students are assigned to the college preparatory track in all-black schools, we do not know whether such students achieve more than comparable black students assigned to other tracks in other schools.

Furthermore, we cannot assume that the "college preparatory track," or any track, requires the same level of academic competence in all schools offering the track.

Tracking is virtually always criticized for underestimating, not overestimating, students' ability to handle difficult courses. Since the personal and social losses due to overestimation can be as harmful as those due to underestimation, the preoccupation with the latter suggests that the underlying issue should not be conceptualized as whether to have more or less tracking. It is how to achieve a better match between students' preparation and needs and the courses they take.

As a matter of fact, tracking is often the result of factors that are ignored in the criticisms of it. For example, students are often assigned to remedial classes because the school districts receive more state or federal aid for remedial students. Those who make assignments to "track" classes are frequently unaware of course content, and misassign students for this reason. In short, tracking does not appear to be the result or cause of racism or systematic underestimation of the ability of black students.[10]

Some critics of tracking distinguish between hierarchical and nonhierarchical courses. Hierarchical courses require a certain level of achievement in the subject: a student should not take advanced French before taking beginning French, or solid geometry before algebra and plane geometry. Other courses, however, do not require previous courses in the same subject. English literature is said to be one example; geography, especially of specific countries, is thought to be another. In nonhierarchical courses, there is supposedly no need to group students by ability or by proficiency in the subject. This reasoning considerably weakens the antitracking argument, especially as it applies to higher grade levels. The opponents of tracking tend to have a narrow view of what subjects are hierarchical, but on any reasonable basis, much of the curriculum falls into this category.

What are the alternatives to tracking? At what point does the need to classify pupils for instruction become "tracking," with all of its negative implications? The critics of tracking do not provide any guidance on this issue. The Committee on Policy for Racial Justice recommended "staff development programs in multicultural education" as an important alternative or solution to tracking. This recommendation is hardly a practical solution to the problems of assigning pupils to programs and courses.

Another frequently suggested alternative is "cooperative learning."

This alternative calls for dividing classes into groups of students who can teach and learn from one another. Although cooperative learning may be a useful pedagogical device, it cannot possibly resolve the most important tracking controversies.

Finally, it seems indisputable that the antitracking rationale has received widespread but highly uncritical academic and media support.[11] In view of my earlier discussion of the media and I.Q. issues, this is not very surprising, but it underscores a critical point. Racial conflict in education often is fostered by inaccurate media interpretations of educational research. In such cases the conflict is all the more intractable because all the parties believe that "educational research" supports their position.

By and large, teachers are ambivalent about tracking or support it, albeit reluctantly in many cases.[12] Interestingly enough, the Council on Exceptional Children, an organization whose 57,000 members specialize in teaching handicapped and gifted pupils, supports tracking. Tracking is one of many instances in which the disadvantaged minorities support policies that encounter strong albeit not unanimous opposition from professional sources.

Bilingual Education

Bilingual education is a major exception to the usual alignment of forces on tracking issues. As we have just seen, the black and Hispanic civil rights organizations oppose tracking. In the case of bilingual education, however, the separation of disadvantaged minorities in school activities is not merely tolerated; it is regarded as a civil right deserving legal protection. This development illustrates how the phrase "civil rights" is applied to rights that were not even discussed when the civil rights statutes were enacted.

Since the Bilingual Education Act of 1968, the federal government has supported programs of bilingual education. Although bilingual education had been available previously for immigrant children in a few communities, it was established nationally by this act. The immediate stimulus to the act was the fact that the dropout rate for Hispanic pupils was even higher than that for black pupils. The civil rights rationale for bilingual education was initially set forth in federal guidelines interpreting the Civil Rights Act of 1964. The guidelines took the position that a non-English-speaking child who could not understand classroom instruction was suffering from discrimination on the basis of national origin. Paradoxically, this guideline was upheld by the Supreme Court in 1974 in a case involving Chinese pupils who did not understand English; the Supreme Court decision not only established bilingual education as a right under the 1964 Civil Rights Act but also had the effect of expanding the number of recipients entitled to it.[13] In 1974 only twenty-three language groups were receiving bilingual instruction of one kind or another; by 1990 the number had risen to 145.[14]

Pupils of Hispanic origin are by far the largest group receiving bilingual education. Significantly, the rationale for bilingual education advanced by Hispanic organizations differed from that espoused previously by other groups.[15] The non-Hispanic groups sought bilingual education for the limited purpose of facilitating proficiency in English. Separation from other students was viewed as a temporary arrangement, to be phased out as soon as the students became reasonably proficient in English. Hispanic organizations, in contrast, contended that self-esteem and pride for Hispanic pupils required instruction in Spanish and Hispanic culture. According to this rationale, even Hispanic children who were fluent in English were entitled to bilingual education. The 1974 amendments to the Bilingual Education Act of 1968 explicitly endorsed the cultural rationale for bilingual education; in effect, they "encouraged Hispanic children to view themselves as a group apart—permanently culturally distinct."[16] And by eliminating the 1968 restriction to low-income children, they greatly increased the number of children who could participate in federal programs of bilingual education.

Thus in six years bilingual education was transformed from a transitional program to help low-income children learn English to a longer-term program to give all children from non-English-speaking backgrounds instruction in their native languages and cultures. Although students are supposed to be assigned to bilingual programs until they are proficient in English, the programs may actually prevent such proficiency; Hispanic students in bilingual programs are frequently taught primarily in Spanish. Furthermore, their instruction often emphasizes Hispanic instead of U.S. culture, thus emphasizing their separateness from American society.

On its merits, the case for bilingual education is extremely weak. This is true even for the limited objective of helping children learn English; one comprehensive review concluded that 71 percent of the studies of transitional bilingual education showed it to be ineffective or counter-productive as a means of achieving this objective. One recent incident illustrates the ineffectiveness of bilingual programs. Con Edison is the major utility company serving New York City. In 1988 it tested 7,000 applicants, primarily from New York City, for entry-level positions. Passing an aptitude test in English was required for employment. Of the 4,000 applicants who passed, not one had been educated in the city's bilingual education program.[17]

The example helps to explain why some large corporations are spending substantial sums to teach their employees English. Such spending is certain to erode support for public education. Public schools have been viewed as our primary means of helping non-English-speaking youth become proficient in English. In the past, knowledge of their native language and cultural heritage was viewed as primarily the responsibility of families and religious or ethnic organizations. Public schools cannot effectively exercise this responsibility and simultaneously function as an integrative institution. The two objectives pose policy and practical dilemmas that public schools cannot resolve.

It is instructive to compare contemporary views to those that prevailed almost a century ago. In 1908 the Russell Sage Foundation published the results of its "Backward Children Investigation." The study was conducted by a distinguished educator with the cooperation of the New York City public schools. At the time, the schools enrolled large numbers of non-English-speaking pupils being raised in immigrant households. The dropout rates for these children were extremely high by contemporary standards. Nevertheless, the report, entitled *Laggards in Our Schools,* asserted that "Everywhere that investigations have been made it has been conclusively shown that ignorance of the English language is a handicap that is quickly and easily overcome and has little influence on retardation."[18]

Politically, bilingual programs are supported by organizations, primarily Hispanic, that represent non-English-speaking populations. Proponents of bilingual education point out that many immigrant groups have retained their ethnic and cultural heritage, including proficiency in their native language, without weakening commitment to democratic institutions. This argument overlooks at least one critical difference. The non-Hispanic groups that maintained their ethnic and cultural heritage were a very small proportion of the larger society. There was no danger that proficiency in their native language would be regarded as a substitute for proficiency in English. In contrast, Hispanics constitute 8 percent of the population, and the proportion is likely to increase. In some large states, such as California, Texas, and Florida, they are already a major political force, and often seek to modify political processes to accommodate non-English-speaking populations.

To understand why bilingual education flourishes despite its educational ineffectiveness, it is essential to understand its political dynamics. The teacher unions include many teachers whose positions depend on bilingual programs. Understandably, union leadership supports their demands for public financial support; it would be suicidal for a union leader to oppose important constituencies within the union on the basis of long-run educational considerations. Similarly, school administrators and would-be administrators seldom challenge the bilingual lobby; to do so would jeopardize their position or chances of getting a position in any district or government agency with a significant Hispanic constituency.

Fundamentally, bilingual education is based on ethnic politics. Hispanic political leaders view bilingual education as a source of patronage and jobs for their constituents. Lip service is paid to integration and proficiency in English; failure to achieve these objectives is allegedly due to failure to fund bilingual education adequately. In economic terms, bilingual education is a prime example of the subordination of consumer to producer interests.

As bilingual education becomes institutionalized, reducing it becomes increasingly difficult. Its costs continue to increase despite its educational ineffectiveness.[19] In short, bilingual education cannot fulfill its avowed objectives, but cannot be dropped for political reasons that are not laid on the table. Beyond any doubt, its direct and indirect costs exacerbate the problem of justifying our huge investment in public education.

Standardized Testing

Racial conflicts over educational testing raise intractable political and educational problems for public education. To appreciate this, it is first necessary to understand the concept of "disparate impact." Disparate impact was established as a legal doctrine in *Griggs v. Duke Power Co.*, a case decided by the U.S. Supreme Court in 1971.[20] The plaintiffs were thirteen black employees in a power plant. Prior to 1965 the company had restricted black employees to the labor department; the highest-paid job in this department paid less than the lowest-paying jobs in the four all-white operating departments. In 1955 the company had required a high school diploma for initial employment in any department except the labor department and one of the four all-white departments, and for transfers to the other three white departments.

The Civil Rights Act of 1964 became effective on July 2, 1964. Title VII of the act prohibited racial discrimination in employment. On July 2, 1964, the company ended its policy of restricting blacks to the labor department. Transfers to the higher-paying job categories, however, required a high school diploma. White employees in these categories hired before 1955 were exempt from the diploma requirement. The company also required that except for the labor department, all new employees had to achieve acceptable scores on two widely used aptitude tests.

The black plaintiffs sued the company, alleging that its new policies were racially discriminatory. Their argument was that although racially neutral on their face, the company's policies had a disparate impact on black employees. It was further contended that the policies could not be justified on business grounds.

At the trial, the company conceded that the aptitude tests did not measure the ability to perform in the positions for which passing the tests was a prerequisite. The company's defense was that Section 703(h) of the Civil Rights Act of 1964 allowed the use of ability tests, provided they were not intended as a means of racial discrimination.

In his decision upholding the plaintiffs' argument, Chief Justice Warren Burger asserted that "if an employment practice which operates to exclude Negroes cannot be shown to be related to job performance, the practice is prohibited." Burger's opinion went on to state that employers must show "business necessity" for utilizing tests that had a disparate impact on black employment.

The *Griggs* decision was a landmark change in civil rights litigation. The reason is that intent to discriminate was no longer essential to support a claim of discrimination. In effect, the *Griggs* decision shifted the burden of proof from the employee to show discrimination to the employer to show there was none. This shift had far-reaching implications because virtually any racially neutral criteria used by employers would disqualify a higher proportion of blacks than whites. Whether the employer used years of formal education, test scores, arrest and conviction records, drug use, health conditions, or any other nonracial criteria, the effect would be to screen out a higher proportion of blacks.

Whether the differences should be considered "disparate impact" is a matter of judgment that was not clarified in the *Griggs* decision. In subsequent cases, "business necessity" was interpreted stringently; arrest and conviction records, past work history, and wage garnishments were held not to be job-related criteria for employment.[21]

Prior to the *Griggs* decision, plaintiffs alleging racial discrimination in employment had to demonstrate disparate treatment at some point in the employment process. After *Griggs*, plaintiffs could prevail by showing disparate impact instead of disparate treatment. Thus tests used as a basis for certifying teachers were vulnerable if the test results had a disparate impact on blacks taking the test. Within a short time, any racially neutral criteria were suspect if their use had a disparate impact among racial groups. As Epstein points out, the sponsors of the Civil Rights Act of 1964 explicitly denied that the act was intended to function this way; it could not have been enacted otherwise. But, in the vernacular, that was then and *Griggs* is now.[22]

The *Griggs* decision was a unanimous one. For several years, legal scholars generally ignored it. In recent years, however, several have criticized the decision for (1) dropping the need to show intentional discrimination, (2) imposing an overly restrictive standard of job relatedness or business necessity, (3) failing to consider the number of qualified black employees in the job market, and (4) being vague concerning the market area to be used as the basis for estimating disparate impact. Insofar as these matters are vague, employers tend to protect themselves from litigation by utilizing quotas and acting on the basis of worst-case scenarios.

Griggs involved a private-sector employer, but the decision was subsequently applied to the public sector in 1972.[23] Consequently, the disparate-impact doctrine applies to public education. Furthermore, the doctrine has not been limited to employment. Whenever the application of a racially neutral criterion has a disparate impact on disadvantaged minorities, legal challenge to it becomes a distinct possibility. To illustrate, if suspension from school for three unexcused absences has a disparate impact on disadvantaged minorities, the policy is likely to be challenged as racially discriminatory. Understandably, conflict and litigation over disparate impact is a growth industry.

The disparate-impact doctrine underlies black opposition to standardized tests. Such opposition has been directed against several different types of tests: intelligence, aptitude, and achievement tests have all been

targets from time to time. Also, black plaintiffs have frequently challenged testing of teachers as racially discriminatory.

Statements by the Committee on Policy for Racial Justice illustrate the
rationale for opposition to testing:

> Intelligence testing became a popular tool to reinforce notions of
> white genetic intellectual superiority . . . The new fad of mental
> testing accelerated this push for segregation by reinforcing preju-
> dices and by confusing native intelligence with disparities in envi-
> ronmental conditions.

> Overall, then, serious questions must be raised about the validity
> of standardized testing and its effects not only upon black and
> minority children but upon quality education for all.

> Student performance on time-restricted, multiple-choice, standard-
> ized tests does not show innate aptitude, nor does it indicate
> whether the test-taker is capable of writing an essay or crafting a
> poem. Indeed, testing becomes a dangerous instrument of social
> oppression when test results are seen as revealing native abilities
> uninfluenced by environmental conditions. Furthermore, over-
> reliance on standardized testing distorts the educational process,
> determining what is taught in the curriculum rather than assessing
> student acquisition of an independently determined knowledge
> base.[24]

A follow-up statement asserts that "we do not call for the abandon-
ment of standardized testing in the schools," but in view of the committee's sweeping criticisms and its failure to identify any acceptable standardized tests, its disclaimer has no practical significance. As a matter of
fact, several black and Hispanic organizations endorsed a 1990 "Statement to Urge a Ban on Standardized Testing of Young Children"; the
NAACP Legal Defense and Education Fund was one of the forty endorsing organizations. Several nonethnic educational organizations also endorsed the statement, which proposed a ban through the second grade
except for "mandated bilingual testing."[25]

The civil rights organizations serving disadvantaged minorities also
support the ban against standardized testing urged by the National
Center for Fair and Open Testing (FairTest) and the New York Public
Interest Research Center (NYPIRC). Their joint publication *Standardized
Tests and Our Children* introduces various topics by such headings as:

Many Tests Are Biased
Standardized Tests Penalize Imagination and Critical Thinking
Standardized Tests Damage School Quality
Testing Damages Accountability
Is There Anything Good About Standardized Tests? Not Much.

The publication advises readers on how to introduce "authentic evaluation in all grades" "to replace standardized multiple-choice testing." Throughout, it emphasizes the argument that standardized testing is unfairly biased against disadvantaged minorities.[26]

Racial controversies over testing have several important educational consequences. Because the controversies involve a large number of tests and complex technical matters, I shall not try to present a comprehensive analysis of the issues. Instead, I shall only summarize my views briefly, and try to relate them to the broader topic of racial conflict in education.

In general, I do not agree that standardized tests unfairly discriminate against disadvantaged minorities. Test items are reviewed carefully to screen out items that are objectionable on these grounds, and on other grounds as well. It is very unlikely that any standardized test in general use unfairly discriminates against disadvantaged minorities.

In considering recommendations to ban standardized testing, we should not overlook its origins. In the early years of public education, before standardized tests, oral examinations were commonly used to evaluate students. Their variability and the fact that the results were not available to others stimulated reliance on written examinations. Consequently, essay examinations became the most common basis for evaluating student achievement. In the early 1900s, however, research on teacher assessment of essay examinations severely weakened professional and public confidence in such assessment. In the most influential study of this kind, the researchers sent the same examination papers to about two hundred schools and asked the teachers to grade the papers according to the standards used in their school. The results indicated that the teachers relied on different standards, weighed various factors differently, and were not consistent in grading essays of similar quality. Efforts to improve both oral and written essay examinations continued, but reliance on them never recovered fully from the criticisms of them in the early 1900s.[27]

The mobility of the population added to the pressure to use more consistent ways of assessing aptitude and achievement. For example, as college admissions became regional and national instead of merely local, standardized tests replaced or supplemented teacher assessments, which fluctuated widely even when identical achievement was involved. Educational literature is replete with evidence that other means of assessment—including those now advocated by critics of standardized testing—are characterized by subjectivity, racial, gender, and socioeconomic bias, and a host of other factors that undermine reliability.[28]

On the face of it, an assessment instrument that is publicly available, open to professional and lay criticism, prepared with extensive technical assistance, and widely monitored is less likely to be characterized by racial bias than assessments that are practically impossible to monitor for objectivity and consistency. All too often, the critics of standardized testing compare an imperfect existing mechanism (standardized tests) with an ideal mechanism whose superiority has yet to be demonstrated. To illustrate, FairTest and NYPIRC suggest the following alternative to standardized tests: "Students could do historical research, write up their findings (a product), and explain and answer questions about it (a performance). The end result can be scored, perhaps by a team of educators, students, parents and other community members. Each student can get feedback about his or her work during the process and at the end. This already happens with projects for science fairs."[29]

Significantly, the suggestion says nothing about who will organize the team, how much staff time it will take, whether team members will be paid, or whether volunteers will be available if they are not. It does not tell us whether black students and parents will evaluate the work of white students or vice versa and what safeguards will prevent racial discrimination where the parties are from different racial, religious, or socioeconomic groups. Nor does it explain why third parties should have confidence in team judgments, when standardized testing emerged in part because of the absence of validity and reliability when student achievement was assessed this way.[30]

Of course, family background and social capital affect achievement, but that is not a deficiency in achievement tests. The tests reveal the fact of unequal achievement; abolishing the mechanism that reveals it makes no sense whatever. Different family environments affect children's health in different ways, but nobody urges the prohibition of medical tests for this reason. The contention that since everyone lives in a culture, tests cannot be culture free, and hence should be banned or deemphasized, is likewise unpersuasive. Airline pilots are recruited from different racial groups and cultures, yet no one proposes to abolish standardized tests for becoming an airline pilot.

Finally, the predictive accuracy of standardized achievement tests appropriately used does not vary from one racial group to another. Of course, a valid argument for standardized achievement testing does not necessarily justify other types of standardized tests, such as intelligence and aptitude tests. This point, however, is consistently disregarded by critics. Because their criticisms are of standardized tests per se, it appears that they are not motivated by objections that apply only to certain kinds of tests. Essentially, the civil rights critics of standardized testing would ban the use of the helpful information provided by tests because it is not complete or perfect information. This is simply indefensible. Most of our information is helpful, not complete or perfect.[31]

The foregoing comments notwithstanding, opposition to the use of standardized testing sometimes has merit even when opposition to the test per se does not. Legislation requiring teachers to pass a state test or be fired is a case in point. Some teachers have been teaching and receiving favorable evaluations for twenty years or more. They have acquired tenure, that is, a property interest that cannot be taken from them without due process of law. Under these circumstances requiring the teacher to pass a statewide test or lose certification (and therefore employment) is a highly dubious policy. I support more teacher testing and higher standards for some teaching positions, but the procedures adopted to implement these objectives are also important. School boards as employers also have rights and responsibilities in these matters, and inflexible state mandates may conflict with school board autonomy. One can support higher standards for teacher certification but oppose the dismissal of veteran teachers who do not pass a state test. The fair and sensible way to introduce the higher standards is to apply them to future teachers, not to veteran teachers.

How does racial conflict over testing affect the future of public education? Opposition to student testing is critical in this regard. As a result of the attacks on testing, public schools tend to avoid assessment of student achievement by objective measures. Instead, greater reliance is being placed on such subjective measures as teacher judgments. As this happens, citizens lose confidence in the credibility of public schools. Within the schools, the absence of objective standards weakens student incentives to study and to learn. Insofar as comparative levels of achievement no longer come into play, students lack meaningful comparisons with one another, hence incentives to improve are weakened. Opposition to testing for other purposes, such as teacher licensing, also weakens confidence in school quality. Even when tests are used for this purpose, their low standards for passing may weaken public support as much as the absence of testing.

As early as 1978, Paul Copperman warned that the elimination of standardized testing was leading to educational decline.[32] He identified the disadvantaged minorities and the public education establishment as the major opponents of standardized testing; as he analyzed the situation, their success would render it impossible to hold educators accountable or to assess educational innovations. In the years since Copperman published his prescient analysis, conflict over testing has emerged in every state and at every level of government. No matter how it turns out, politically important constituencies are dissatisfied and try to change the outcome. In this conflict, the evidence relating to testing plays only a minor role. That is one reason the conflict will continue and will continue to erode support for public education.

Quotas and Affirmative Action

In and out of education, affirmative action and ethnic quotas have become highly controversial issues. It is even difficult to define these terms in a way that is widely accepted; as so often happens, the interested parties try to define them in a way that predetermines the policy issues. In this discussion I shall define a quota as any policy that is based on a specified or required racial proportion of personnel. Policies that 10 percent of teachers be black or that 5 percent of admissions to graduate school be from Asian ethnic groups are examples of quotas.

Several reasons underlie opposition to quotas. First, quotas are contrary to the principle of treating individuals according to their merits. Suppose a quota requires that 10 percent of the teachers employed be from disadvantaged minorities. To meet the quota, it will normally be necessary to employ teachers from disadvantaged minorities who are less qualified than some teachers not protected by quotas. Otherwise there would be no need for the quota. Under the quota system, however, some white teachers who are not responsible for past discrimination against blacks, and who are better qualified than some beneficiaries of the quota, will not be employed for racial reasons. Furthermore, the beneficiaries of quotas do not have to show that they are actually victims of discrimination. If they could show that they are, they would not need quotas to get redress. If they cannot show that they are victims of past discrimination, they should have no claim to be beneficiaries of a quota.

Another objection is that quotas are a threat to economic efficiency. Any enterprise will suffer if less qualified personnel are employed. In addition, quotas present intractable legal and administrative problems. Who is to be considered "black" or "Hispanic" if there are quotas for these groups? In some cases, applicants for employment have deliberately changed their ethnic classification to "black" or "Hispanic" to increase their prospects for employment. The prospect of having the U.S. Supreme Court decide who is black or Hispanic and who is not dismays many citizens.

The arguments for quotas essentially assert that they are an expeditious way of mitigating ethnic conflict and achieving an ethnic balance that will foster social cohesion. Also, it is contended that the victims of "reverse discrimination" do not experience the stigma and loss of opportunity associated with racial discrimination.[33] In effect, the pro-quota forces view quotas as a convenient way to achieve equality of outcomes, an objective that goes far beyond redress for past discrimination.

Ostensibly, the antiquota forces seem to have the upper hand. I say "ostensibly" because there is disagreement over whether certain policies constitute quotas. On this issue, it is irrelevant whether the term "quota" is explicitly included in the policy. The basic issue is whether a policy would coerce employers to adopt or accept quotas, even if not characterized as such. A clear majority opposes explicit quotas, but there is no clear majority on what forms of affirmative action would be quotas or lead to them. These issues require some discussion of affirmative action.

Like quotas, affirmative action may apply to virtually any educational activity in which the proportion of persons from different racial groups is or may be an issue. Affirmative action is especially difficult to define because it has taken on so many different forms and meanings. According to some, it consists of a vigorous effort to identify qualified minority candidates. Others define it as a policy of employing disadvantaged minority candidates if their qualifications are substantially equal to those of nonminority candidates. In still another version, affirmative action is the adoption of numerical goals and specified procedures for employment or recruitment of disadvantaged minorities. That is, in some situations affirmative action is a quota system, in effect.[34] I define affirmative

action as any policy that is consciously intended to increase the proportion of disadvantaged minorities, absent any specific proportion that
must be reached.

Generally speaking, affirmative action commands much more support
than quotas. Opposition to affirmative action is based partly on the view
that it leads to quotas, or that certain versions of it are really quotas
under a more palatable label. This was evident from the congressional
debate over civil rights legislation in 1990 and 1991. The Democratic
majority in Congress supported the proposed legislation as "affirmative
action"; President Bush initially opposed it on the grounds that it would
lead to quotas, even though the legislation included an explicit disclaimer of their legitimacy.

Education is one of the major areas in which issues pertaining to
affirmative action are debated and litigated. In fact, the most important
single legal case on the subject involved a lawsuit to gain admission to
the medical school at the University of California, Davis.[35] One of the
issues in this case was whether the university could admit minority applicants instead of Alan Bakke, a white candidate who was the plaintiff in
the case. The resolution of the case depended in part on whether, or to
what extent, the university could rely on race as one of the criteria to be
applied in admissions to medical school.

The university had initiated a program intended to recruit more non-
Asian minority students. Those students were placed in a special pool of
applicants. Indisputably, admissions from this group had average test
scores substantially below those of the other students admitted. Although
Bakke was admitted in a 5–4 decision by the U.S. Supreme Court, even
the five justices who voted to admit him disagreed on the reasons for
their decision. Subsequent judicial decisions and legislation have not
resolved the uncertain constitutional status of "affirmative action" and
of preferential treatment of persons from disadvantaged minorities.[36]

Whatever the constitutional status of affirmative action, every major
public school organization supports it. I shall not try to state how each
defines or practices the concept; it appears, however, that public school
organizations are more receptive to quotas and preferential treatment
for disadvantaged minorities than public opinion generally. In fact, the
NEA's constitution and bylaws embrace quotas extensively. Some of the
relevant provisions are as follows:

All appointive bodies of the Association except the Review Board
shall be designated by the term *committee*. There shall be a minimum

of twenty (20) percent ethnic-minority representation on each committee.

If after any period of eleven (11) consecutive membership years a member of an ethnic-minority group has not served as President, the Association shall take steps as may be legally permissible to elect a member of an ethnic-minority group.

Members from ethnic minorities shall comprise at least twenty (20) percent of the Board. The Representative Assembly shall elect additional directors as appropriate to assure such ethnic-minority representation on the Board . . .

Members from ethnic minorities shall comprise at last twenty (20) percent of the Executive Committee. The Representative Assembly shall elect additional Executive Committee members as appropriate to assure such ethnic-minority representation.

Affiliates of the Association shall take all reasonable and legally permissible steps to achieve on their elective and appointive bodies ethnic-minority representation that is at least proportional to the ethnic-minority membership of the affiliate.

Each affiliate shall apply the one-person-one-vote principle for representation on its governing bodies except that the affiliate shall take such steps as are legally permissible to achieve ethnic-minority representation at least proportionate to its ethnic-minority membership.

The Association shall, as vacancies arise, employ at all levels of service at least the same ratio of any ethnic minority as is that ethnic minority to the total population of the United States;

Ethnic minority shall mean those persons designated as ethnic minority by statistics published by the United States Bureau of the Census. This designation shall specifically include Black, Mexican-American (Chicano), other Spanish-speaking groups, Asian-American, and Indian.[37]

Few, if any, other major organizations in the United States are so thoroughly committed to quotas. To appreciate the significance of this commitment, we must relate it to the changing environment in civil rights and ethnic politics. Despite the constitutional and statutory prohibitions against discrimination, the economic and educational progress of disadvantaged minorities has fallen far short of the expectations of the 1960s. As the slow pace of improvement persisted, the ethnic and civil rights organizations representing disadvantaged minorities changed their strategy and objectives. These changes include:

1. "Racism" instead of deliberate racial discrimination and racial segregation is viewed as responsible for the lag in educational achievement levels by disadvantaged minorities. "Racism" is seldom defined, but it usually turns out to be nonracial policies that allegedly prevent disadvantaged minorities from achieving economic or educational equality.
2. "Racial balance" or "diversity" or other vague objectives have replaced the elimination of government-imposed segregation and of racial discrimination in the public and private sectors as policy objectives.
3. Organizations with large constituencies of disadvantaged minorities have begun to move away from an emphasis on individual rights to be free from discrimination to an emphasis on policies based on membership in a disadvantaged group. Quotas and preferential treatment for disadvantaged minorities are the two leading policies in this category, although a strong argument has been made that it includes all forms of affirmative action.[38]

As the NEA's adoption of quotas illustrates, these changes are not confined to civil rights or ethnic organizations: they emerge in organizations in which the disadvantaged minorities play an important role. In either case, the changes are likely to lead to intractable conflict. (The absence of controversy over racial quotas in the NEA since their adoption in 1976 is remarkable, but I doubt that it will continue indefinitely.) By and large, a broad consensus approved the end of government-imposed racial segregation and the prohibitions against intentional racial discrimination in private employment. The change from opposing racial discrimination to supporting quotas and preferential treatment, however, presents a drastically different situation.

To avoid any misunderstanding, let me make it clear that I do not take the position that quotas were never justified. From 1962 to 1969 I was employed as an expert witness and consultant for the NAACP Legal Defense and Education Fund on school integration cases. During that time, quotas were sometimes proposed as a remedy for massive refusals by recalcitrant employers to adhere to nondiscrimination policies. In these situations, some sort of group remedy was required, not only to redress large-scale discrimination in the past but to enjoin it in the future. Regardless of whether quotas were justified in these cases (I thought they were), these situations differ sharply from those to which quotas are applied today. For example, the beneficiaries of the NEA's quota provisions do not and need not claim that the NEA, or anyone else, has discriminated against them, or that the NEA is determined to practice racial discrimination in the future.

Like political and membership organizations generally, the ethnic civil rights organizations are under pressure to provide immediate benefits to their constituents. As the overall position of disadvantaged minorities failed to meet expectations, the organizations representing them espoused quotas and preferential treatment more openly than they had in the past. Unfortunately, the knowledge, skills, habits, and attitudes required to take advantage of the absence of discrimination cannot be achieved within a short time; they often require years of study and hard work. Preferential treatment and quotas cannot substitute for these requirements and may even be antithetical to them. Realistically, "no preferential treatment or quotas" is the only position that might be supported by a broad consensus in American society. Thus insofar as public policy fosters preferential treatment or quotas, or is perceived as doing so, intentionally or not, we can expect racial conflict to intensify.

Conclusion

The preceding discussion has not presented a comprehensive summary of racial conflict in public education. A more complete list would include conflict over the following:

1. The desirability of "Afro-centered" curricula.
2. The portrayal of minorities in instructional materials.
3. Procedures to identify retarded students or students requiring other kinds of special treatment.
4. Disciplinary procedures that have a disparate impact on minorities.
5. Racial conflict over administrative positions.
6. Teacher employment and assignments. When Hispanic organizations promote bilingual education, they are promoting

teaching positions for Hispanics; "black studies" and "Afro-centered" curricula provide more jobs for black teachers; and so on. Media treatment of curriculum issues typically ignores patronage or employment aspects and conveys the erroneous impression that the parties to the conflict simply differ on what is best for children.

7. The appropriate allocation of resources to schools and programs serving racially different student bodies.

8. The research issues selected for study, the issues avoided, the conclusions reached, and research funding. All of these have been profoundly affected by racial conflict.

Racial conflict in education is likely to continue. First, the ethnic civil rights organizations are constantly probing hitherto neglected areas for evidence of discrimination. Second, government agencies, school districts, and institutions of higher education have established a host of full-time positions devoted to affirmative action and/or other racially oriented issues. Significantly, this bureaucracy has expanded during a period when deliberate racial discrimination has declined. We have no reason to expect this particular bureaucracy to be the first to declare that its mission has been completed and that it should go out of business. Instead, it will discover new evidence and new forms of racial discrimination in education. To put it bluntly, we have institutionalized racial conflict.

Although racial conflict sometimes has beneficial consequences, it must be viewed as a major obstacle to educational reform. Teachers and school administrators are highly sensitive to racial disparities in achievement. Superintendents are frequently hired for ability to deal with these disparities—or fired for alleged inability to do so. Unquestionably, the disparities are a sensitive issue at all grade levels. In general, the higher the standards, the greater the disparity between disadvantaged minorities and other students. Consequently, the way to avoid or minimize the disparities is to lower the standards. This solution reduces any disparate impact on the minority students. It also enables teachers and administrators to avoid racial controversy and administrative hassling likely to result from applying higher standards.

In my opinion, this lowering of standards is occurring daily in thousands of classrooms; its negative effects may pose a more serious problem than the effects of controversies that are widely publicized. I am not asserting that every teacher in every classroom follows this pattern. Un-doubtedly, many do not. Regardless of what happens in classrooms, however, public education faces a dilemma that it cannot resolve. On the one hand, it is unable to reduce substantial ethnic disparities in educational achievement. On the other hand, it cannot face the fact openly. The only alternative is to obscure the fact, but this can be done only by obscuring the educational achievement of all students.

In part, the public schools' dilemma is of their own making. Public education, like the media generally and higher education, has uncriti-cally accepted the conclusion that ethnic differences in educational achievement must be due to "racism" or "poverty." This conclusion is based on the fear that concessions to any other explanation would be intolerable. This fear did not dominate civil rights policies in the mid-1900s. In its first case dealing with quotas, the national staff of the NAACP was careful not to support them. One staff attorney was "very disturbed" about the efforts of a local affiliate to pressure a grocery chain into proportional employment, "since it appears to condone a quota system . . . and would be, of course, disastrous."[39] Another attorney who partici-pated in NAACP litigation characterized proportional employment as "unsound" and urged that the NAACP "base our demands . . . on the democratic principle that we are entitled to equal opportunity based upon merit and ability to compete in the labor market without being pre-judged on account of race or color."[40]

As a matter of fact, Thurgood Marshall, the NAACP's leading attorney in the school segregation cases and later a Supreme Court Justice, was explicitly critical of any ethnic group claims for preferential treatment. In his oral argument before the Supreme Court in the school segregation cases, Marshall said:

What we want is the striking down of race . . . They give tests to grade children so what do we think is the solution? Simple. Put the dumb colored children in with the dumb white children, and put the smart colored children with the smart white children—that is no problem.

There are geniuses in both groups and there are lower ones in both groups, and it has no bearing. No right of an individual can be conditioned as to any average of other people in his racial group or any other group.[41]

And in February 1956 an interviewer interpreted Marshall this way: "at the very core of his concern was not the Negro but the individual human being." Improving conditions for blacks "was a worthy cause, but it wasn't his cause." Instead, his cause was "a society whose law and government were based on a fundamental belief in individual worth, individual opportunity, and individual responsibility."[42] Subsequent statements and judicial opinions by Marshall are less adamant in upholding individualism, but the statements quoted reflect the dominant view of the civil rights movement in the mid-1900s. In fact, long before then, black educators had protested against certification standards that were lower for black than for white teachers.[43] Their demand was for equal treatment, not preferential or less rigorous treatment.

Membership in a group is irrelevant if one is being judged as an individual. Regrettably, in their efforts to achieve benefits for their members, ethnic and racial interest groups foster treatment of people as group members, not as individuals. Conflict that weakens public education is certain to increase as long as disadvantaged minorities emphasize preferential policies and treat emphasis on personal responsibility as "racism" or "blaming the victim." As matters stand, public education cannot stem the rising tide of race-oriented demands or respond to them in ways that do not alienate its middle-class support.

Because of ethnic divisions, government benefits in the United States are often viewed in an ethnic perspective. The prime example is welfare, which is widely perceived as going to unmarried black women who bear children as a means of support. Since black mothers constitute about half of all single-parent families, the perception is not completely groundless. Regardless, such disparities and perceptions often lead to hostility to government services. The popular perception is that "they," not "we," are receiving the benefits. It is much easier for homogeneous populations, such as the Japanese, to accept benefits that are viewed in a racial frame of reference in the United States.

Race-conscious policies arouse highly emotional reactions, and their growing prominence bodes ill for public education. In the past the disadvantaged minorities sought the same educational environment provided the white majority. Today there is a growing emphasis on their right to a different educational environment. Of course, there are and will continue to be differences of opinion among blacks and Hispanics on this issue, but we are witnessing an ethnically driven movement for educational separatism and differentiation. Unlike movements that inadvertently weaken public education, this one may explicitly support alternatives to it. As Linda F. Perkins comments:

> The nation's public school systems have not served blacks well, throughout the nineteenth and twentieth centuries . . . private schooling has accounted for a substantial portion of black education. As working conditions within predominantly black schools continue to be poor and achievement levels and attendance rates of black students remain low, it may be that blacks will return to private schools as an alternative to the unsuccessful efforts of the public schools.[44]

Perkins urges blacks to emphasize private schools more than in the past. If a sizable proportion of black parents and leaders do so, the political base of public education will erode very quickly.

9

≈ Equality of Educational Opportunity Reconsidered

Racial conflict is only one aspect of equality of educational opportunity. This chapter continues the discussion of that aspect but also seeks to clarify the nonracial aspects. My major objective is to compare equality of educational opportunity under public education with its probable development under a market system.

Despite the attention paid to equal opportunity issues, their emotional intensity is seldom fully appreciated. If you have enjoyed equal opportunity but do not achieve or earn a high income, you are responsible for your failure to do so. If "society" or some other external factor has denied you equal opportunity, your self-esteem is not as vulnerable. Also, society is more willing to help the disadvantaged who are seen as not personally responsible for their plight. Thus there will always be conflicting views on how to define equal opportunity and what must be done to establish it. Ethnic differences in income and achievement exacerbate this problem, but it would exist regardless; the tendency to blame the umpire is not confined to athletic contests. And just as low achievers will tend to underestimate the extent of equal opportunity, persons who are high achievers or have high incomes will tend to overestimate it.

An analogy may help to clarify the meaning of "equality of educational opportunity." Suppose the intent is to provide equality of opportunity to win a one-mile race. Suppose also that I was born with only one leg. It might seem impossible to equalize my chances of winning the race, but it could be done. Government might amputate one leg of everyone else who entered the race, assuming anyone did enter after this means of equalizing opportunity was announced.

Needless to say, this is not what people have in mind in referring to equality of opportunity. They do not think of it as weakening the strongest competitors but as providing additional support for the weaker ones. As the hypothetical race illustrates, however, how equality is achieved is of the utmost importance; is it achieved by restricting those deemed to have advantages, or by empowering those deemed to be disadvantaged? Another critical point is that two different meanings of "equality of educational opportunity" are involved. One meaning is fair and open competition for scarce rewards: scholarships, grades, admission to higher levels of education, and so on. Another meaning is that everyone has a mathematically equal chance to succeed. When I refer to equality of educational opportunity, I mean opportunities to succeed in fair and open competition. "Fair and open competition," however, leaves many questions unanswered.

Most discussions of equality of educational opportunity assume that whatever the level of equality, raising it would be even better. If there is equality of opportunity for secondary education, we should expand it to cover a college education. If there is equality of educational opportunity for undergraduate education, we should expand it to graduate school. Although popular, this point of view fails to come to grips with some basic issues.

One is the conflict between equality of educational opportunity and liberty. Another is the relationship between equality of educational opportunity and productivity. A third is the extent to which government should seek to eliminate inequalities arising from nonschool factors, such as socioeconomic status. As we shall see, these issues are closely interrelated.

The Conflict between Equality and Liberty

Educational opportunity depends on several factors. Many of them, such as family interest in education and family resources, are not controlled by schools. Theoretically, our educational system might eliminate or neutralize the effects of these nonschool factors. As was proposed by Plato, we might take children from their families and raise them from birth in state institutions. Even this would probably not lead to equality of educational opportunity; the children of the more powerful government leaders would receive better opportunities than others. This happens wherever government completely controls education. In the United

States, no one proposes such a drastic approach, partly because it would require destruction of other social institutions, such as families and religious organizations. Inasmuch as there is no support for a Platonic approach, several nonschool factors affect equality of educational opportunity in the real world.

Let us consider the matter as it typically arises. Children begin school at age 5. Government pays for their education through high school. (For present purposes, I shall ignore the costs of education below the college level borne by families.) Conceptually, government could expand equality of educational opportunity in several ways. It could pay for additional grade levels, such as preschool or college. Or it could subsidize certain educational services for disadvantaged students, such as remedial reading or enrichment programs. Note, however, that whatever government does along this line, additional costs are involved. These costs must be paid from tax revenues. As taxes go up, there is a corresponding restriction on taxpayers' freedom to spend their money as they see fit.

Although often overlooked, there is a basic conflict between liberty and government efforts to foster equality of educational opportunity. The resolution of this conflict depends partly on our answer to this question: To what extent should government eliminate or reduce inequalities of educational opportunity resulting from parental interests, family resources, geographical location, cultural influences, and other nonschool factors affecting educational achievement?

Our answers to this question differ widely. One reason is uncertainty or conflict over the educational influence of nonschool factors. Some analysts minimize the importance of family stability and family structure; they charge that public schools are citing these things merely to excuse their failure to educate certain groups effectively. Others contend that spending more for public education would be futile as long as family life is in such disarray.

Developments in health care illustrate the fiscal consequences of equality in public services. In 1972 the Social Security Act was amended to cover 80 percent of the costs of kidney treatment. Every year, about 50,000 Americans suffer from kidney failure. Renal dialysis is an appropriate treatment for a large number of these patients. The costs of renal dialysis varied from $10,000 to $30,000 when the federal government began to defray 80 percent of the costs.

Prior to this time, there were more machines than patients. Afterward, it was impossible to accommodate all the patients seeking dialysis. Although the wealthy could ordinarily buy treatment, life and death choices had to be made among others. Federal reimbursement, however, led to greatly expanded production of dialysis machines; within a short period of time, machines were widely available to all who requested renal dialysis.

As often happens, the resolution of one problem led to some new ones. One federal report alleged that doctors were excessively providing renal dialysis for patients; clearly, it was in their financial interests to do so. Furthermore, the criteria for deciding who would receive renal dialysis varied widely; for example, some doctors applied age standards that were not applied by others. While all of this was going on, the total costs of renal dialysis grew dramatically. In 1974, the first year for which federal payments were made, federal expenditures for dialysis treatment were $229 million; by 1990, expenditures were $3.56 billion.[1] Obviously, this meant that less was available for other social needs, such as better education, or for other medical problems. Inevitably, the question arose: Why should the federal government be spending so much for kidney patients when many more patients die from cancer or circulatory ailments?

Needless to say, patients suffering from kidney failure are not likely to assess the costs and benefits of renal dialysis objectively. Neither should we expect the providers of renal dialysis to do so. Is the case any different in education? Should we expect the student or parent beneficiaries, or the providers of education, to be objective about the costs and benefits of education subsidies? I do not think so. And just as equalizing health care may entail indefensible costs, so may some efforts to "equalize" educational opportunity. Inasmuch as the producers generate most of the pro-equalization rhetoric, we have good reason to be wary.

Who Pays for Equalization?

Whatever way we equalize educational opportunity, government typically pays the additional costs. Question: Who pays government to cover the increased costs? To answer this question, we must ask another: What level of government would absorb the cost? The budgetary problems of the federal government (which arise partly from efforts to equalize other services and benefits) preclude any substantial federal absorption of the equalization costs. Local school districts might pick up more of the costs, but the large urban districts where most of the disadvantaged live simply cannot do so. Since higher tax rates would induce companies and families to relocate, it is difficult to raise local taxes to equalize educational opportunity. For several reasons, therefore, state governments have to take the hit when we expand equality of educational opportunity. In 1920 state governments provided only 16.5 percent of school revenues, whereas the local and federal shares were 83.2 and 0.3 percent respectively. In 1990–91 state governments provided 49.3 percent of school revenues and the local and federal shares were 44.5 and 6.2 percent respectively.[2] In large part these changes resulted from efforts to equalize equality of educational opportunity by equalizing expenditures per pupil within each state.

For most of our history, school revenues were based on property taxes. Over time, school districts differed widely in the amount of taxable property per pupil. Some districts included a great deal of taxable property but relatively few pupils. These districts were able to spend more per pupil despite a much lower tax rate than districts that included less taxable property but higher numbers of students. Poor districts with high tax rates for education still could not raise as much revenue per pupil as wealthy districts with low tax rates.

Since 1968, lawsuits in at least thirty-two states have alleged that the state system of financing public education fails to provide equality of educational opportunity.[3] Legally speaking, school boards are agencies of the state governments. Thus the legal argument was that the states were not providing equal treatment by allowing education funding to depend on where pupils resided. The funding system was alleged to be unfair to both taxpayers and pupils in poor districts.

In 1973 the U.S. Supreme Court held that these funding inequities were not a violation of the Fourteenth Amendment.[4] The court's reasoning was that education was not a fundamental interest subject to judicial scrutiny under the Fourteenth Amendment; states did not have to provide public education at all. The court concluded that the issue was one for the states to resolve. Since 1973, efforts to equalize school funding have focused on state judicial and legislative action. As of 1989, seven state supreme courts had declared their state funding of education to be unconstitutional, whereas ten had upheld their school funding legislation. No consensus on the underlying issues is evident, and many cases are still being litigated and new ones initiated.[5]

The issue in these cases is not whether inequities exist. It is whether the inequities violate state law or state constitutions. The most common state response has been to increase state aid to education and reduce the proportion of school revenues from local property taxes. What is often overlooked, however, is that sales and other regressive taxes are the major source of state revenues. The more school revenues come from the states, the larger the share paid by lower-income groups. Thus it is highly doubtful whether the efforts to achieve equity in school funding have been successful. Wide differences in per-pupil expenditures may have been reduced somewhat, but lower-income groups are probably paying a larger share of the total costs of public education.

As pointed out in Chapter 6, affluent taxpayers are likely to deduct state and local taxes on their federal tax returns, but most taxpayers take the standard deduction. This situation has important educational implications. Popular attention is focused on federal legislation like Head Start that provides assistance to disadvantaged children. Meanwhile, affluent taxpayers receive much larger education subsidies from the federal government through the deductibility of state and local taxes. Understandably, proposals to eliminate their deductibility are fiercely resisted by states with high proportions of affluent taxpayers.

As with so many issues, a double standard is operative. Public school organizations allege that tuition tax credits for the expenses of private schooling would be a subsidy to the affluent. Actually, existing tax policies subsidize the affluent who enroll their children in expensive public schools. To do so, the parents must first have enough capital to buy homes in affluent neighborhoods: Shaker Heights, Beverly Hills, Edina, Scarsdale, Chevy Chase, and so on. It requires more resources than poor people have to do so. Every year, however, the taxpayers in these districts benefit from the deductibility of their school taxes. The increasing reliance on state aid instead of local property taxes to finance public education does not remedy the problem. State revenues are based primarily on regressive taxes, such as sales taxes. Insofar as they are derived from state income taxes, they reduce but do not eliminate the inequities resulting from deductibility on federal tax returns. In short, the emphasis on appropriations for disadvantaged children is like a shell game; while attention is focused on them, the indirect subsidies to affluent parents for the education of their children in public schools are much larger.

Interestingly enough, research on who pays for public education in England also challenges the assumption that it benefits low-income families. E. G. West has shown that the expansion of public education there was accompanied by large increases in taxes on consumption items, such as tobacco products. Taking into account all the taxes paid for education, most families would have been better off if government had simply subsidized those unable to pay instead of providing the service for everyone.[6]

Who Benefits from Equalization?

A much higher proportion of students from middle- and upper-income families than of those from poor or low-income families graduate from high school and college. Thus poor and low-income families are doubly hurt by state support for education: they pay out a higher proportion of their income in taxes for education, but a much lower proportion of students from within their own ranks benefit from it. Table 9.1 shows the percentage of the 17-year-old population that graduated from public high school by ten-year intervals from 1870 to 1989. In interpreting the table, bear in mind that until the 1940s public high schools were predominantly college preparatory institutions and their graduates were preponderantly from the middle and upper middle classes.

In the light of the figures in Table 9.1, whose interests were best served by maintaining high schools at public expense? Why would poor parents want to support high schools at public expense when so few of their

Table 9.1. Size of 17-year-old population and percentage graduating from public high schools, 1870–1989

Year	Number of 17-year-olds (in thousands)	High school graduates (%)[a]
1870	815	2.0[b]
1880	946	2.5[b]
1890	1,259	1.8
1900	1,489	4.2
1910	1,786	6.2
1920	1,855	12.4
1930	2,296	25.8
1940	2,403	47.7
1950	2,034	52.3
1960	2,672	60.9
1970	3,757	68.9
1980	4,262	64.5
1989[c]	3,761	66.4

a. Includes graduates of regular day school programs. Excludes graduates of other programs, when separately reported, and recipients of high school equivalency certificates.
b. Includes graduates of private high schools.
c. Estimated.
Sources: Current Population Reports, ser. P–25; National Center for Education Statistics, Digest of Education Statistics, 1990 (Washington: Government Printing Office, 1991), 108.

children attended them? Realistically, the shift from private to public education was of greatest benefit to upper-middle-class families with large numbers of children, a common family pattern in the 19th and early 20th centuries. Contrary to popular opinion, public education is still characterized by severe inequities, higher education even more so.

As pointed out in Chapter 2, the demographic base of public education has been eroding. The erosion has led to an all-out producer effort to keep everyone in school as long as possible. Although couched in the rhetoric of equal opportunity, keeping everyone in school as long as the traffic will bear is even more inequitable than a system of public education serving primarily an upper-middle-class clientele. Let us see why this is so.

Minimum wage and compulsory education laws require youth to attend school until their upper teens. These laws raise the income of workers who are already above minimum but decrease the earnings of workers who cannot find employment at the minimum wage; such unemployed workers lose valuable training and experience in addition to cash wages. The disequalizing effects of minimum wage and compulsory education laws are evident if we consider lifetime earnings. Those who do not benefit from additional formal education could narrow and sometimes erase the gap in lifetime earnings if allowed to work full time at an earlier age. Instead, they are forced to choose between idleness and unwanted and unneeded formal education. (We have already seen that there are no civic benefits to extended formal education.) Indeed, the disequalizing effects are further exacerbated when persons who cannot find employment at the minimum wage seek employment that is not covered by the minimum wage laws; wages in uncovered employment are depressed because more persons are forced to seek employment in that sector.[7]

Political Barriers to Equity

As a higher proportion of school revenues comes from the states, responsiveness to local preferences becomes less important. Ability to function effectively in legislative and political processes becomes more important. This adds to the disadvantages of the minorities who are disproportionately poor. For instance, compared to whites, blacks are less likely to vote or belong to political parties, contribute less to parties and candidates, sign fewer petitions, attend fewer political rallies, are less active in voter registration, and see government as less responsive to their needs.[8]

These indications of black disadvantage in the political process are by no means exhaustive. Voter attitudes on public opinion polls have consistently understated white opposition to black candidates. Although such opposition is not necessarily or always based on race, it is sometimes. If racial prejudice exists equally among blacks and whites, black candidates are more disadvantaged because there are more white than black voters. Under these circumstances, why should blacks, or the disadvantaged generally, rely on the political system to improve their educational situation? Why especially should they rely on state legislative action when so much that happens in state legislatures depends on political processes well hidden from public view? Even in the absence of discrimination in the political process, reliance on it to improve education is an uphill struggle.

An obvious answer is that there is no alternative to reliance on the political process. There is just enough plausibility in this response to conceal its falsity. If the disadvantaged voters joined with others who support a market system, the shift to it would come promptly. True, it would be necessary to rely on political processes to effectuate such a change, but it would be just as easy to change to a market system as to enact the less drastic reforms that already evoke the united opposition of the public school establishment.

At the present time, "institutional racism" is often alleged to be a major obstacle to black and Hispanic progress. The phrase refers to public policies that are racially neutral on their face but nevertheless function to the disadvantage of minorities. The change from electing city councils by wards to electing them at large in municipal elections is often cited as an example; the change is allegedly made to prevent black neighborhoods from electing black council members. Personally, I do not agree that public policies that have a disparate impact on blacks are necessarily racist, but let us accept the idea for the moment. In that case, the more one detects institutional racism in the political process, the stronger the argument for a market system of education.

Equalitarian Dilemmas

It is often overlooked that efforts to achieve group equality conflict with equal opportunity between individuals. This point was evident in the

Bakke case discussed in Chapter 8. As we have seen, Bakke's application to medical school was not accepted although his qualifications were superior to those of minority applicants who were accepted; to increase the proportion of minority students, the medical school had reserved 16 of 100 openings for blacks, Asians, native Americans, and Chicanos. Clearly the effort to achieve group equality was in direct conflict with equality between individuals.

The conflict is inherent in all efforts to promote group equality. All such efforts require deviation from the principle that equality should be a relationship between individuals. Unfortunately, the advocates of equality often advocate both kinds of equality, unaware that they are advocating contradictory objectives.

Such contradictions are inevitable even if only one disadvantaged group is involved. In practice, the conflicts between group and individual equality often involve several groups. Indeed, perhaps 75 percent of the population are members of groups specifically protected against discrimination. Consequently, affirmative action for women may conflict with affirmative action for blacks and Hispanics, or vice versa. As we add additional groups, we add to the discrimination against groups and individuals who supposedly most need protection against it. White men are not the only group who may suffer from efforts to achieve group equality.

Equal Prospects or Equal Means?

Government provision of equal means for students of unequal talent will result in unequal outcomes. For this reason, some analysts contend that equality of educational opportunity exists when two individuals of equal talent and interest have the same probability of achieving a certain educational goal. At first glance, this approach makes good sense. If a disadvantaged high school student has the ability and interest to perform well in college, we want such a student to have the same prospect of doing so as an affluent student of equal ability and talent.

Despite its obvious appeal, this definition of equality of educational opportunity encounters difficult practical problems. First, if our objective is equal prospects for success, we must adopt unequal means. Given the multitude of factors that affect the prospects for success in any field, the distribution of means (whether in cash or services) poses extremely difficult information and political problems. We would have to know what factors impede success and to what degree. We would also have to know what means would overcome the obstacles to success. All of these matters are highly controversial, to say the least.

Chapter 2 pointed out the importance of social capital for educational development. One school of thought is that increased government appropriations can overcome the handicaps resulting from a lack of social capital, but this position is no longer so widely held. Unless we agree on the obstacles to success, the distribution of means to achieve it will not command widespread support. Of course, this is not justification for taking no action at all to increase equal educational opportunity.

If equal educational opportunity meant equal chances to be successful, we might use a lottery to decide who would receive higher levels of education. This would achieve equality at a heavy price. If luck instead of hard work decided the outcome, students' incentives to study would be weakened considerably. In short, this way of equalizing opportunity would involve unacceptable costs.

The most troublesome problem with equality as equal prospects is that there is no agreed-upon way to apply it to students of diverse talents and interests. Consider the students in a seventh-grade homeroom. A has the talent and interest to be a nuclear scientist. B wants to be a beautician. C and D have average academic ability but no strong interests at this time. E wants to become a plumber. F plans to work in a family clothing store. And so on. With due regard for the unpredictability of talents and interests, what is required to equalize educational opportunities among these different students?

Public schools usually try to provide equality of means with some exceptions to equalize prospects. For instance, we spend more to educate handicapped students or students who are not proficient in English, or students who need remedial services. In these cases, we deviate from equal means on the basis of need. Most people are comfortable with the underlying idea, which often arises outside of education as well. Suppose as a result of a threat on your life, a police officer is assigned to guard your home. The police provide unequal means because unequal means are necessary to provide equal protection.

Ostensibly, more funds are spent for disadvantaged students. This is a common impression since they are the beneficiaries of highly publicized appropriations targeted to their needs. As we have seen, the public school establishment claims that public school costs are higher than private school costs because public school student populations include higher proportions of disadvantaged students. The claim that more is spent on disadvantaged students is not necessarily valid, however; in many districts, it clearly is not.

Generally speaking, teachers prefer to teach upper-middle-class pupils in upper-middle-class schools. To the extent that seniority prevails in transfers to open positions, the most senior teachers end up teaching in such schools. Inasmuch as teacher salaries are based largely on seniority, the per-pupil cost of educating upper-middle-class children often exceeds the average per-pupil costs in inner-city schools in the same district.[9] Even when the costs of special services in inner-city schools are taken into account, school districts often spend substantially more per pupil on their upper-middle-class students. The disadvantaged pupils receiving special services costing $5,000 per classroom may be taught by a teacher receiving $25,000 annually; meanwhile pupils not receiving $5,000 in special services may be taught by a teacher paid $40,000 annually. There is no doubt that this situation is a common one. In some districts, such as Philadelphia, teachers have gone on strike to block efforts to assign the most experienced teachers to inner-city schools.

Although most people accept some exceptions to equal means, the exceptions raise several difficult problems. Most exceptions are justified on the basis of special need. If exceptions are allowed, however, various groups seek an exception in their own behalf; it is easy to think of reasons why your group deserves special help. Rural areas claim unequal means because they have to spend more for transportation. Urban districts claim unequal means because urban areas are characterized by severe family and neighborhood breakdowns. The argument is made that gifted students are being neglected, so we now have organizations devoted to making sure gifted students have special courses and programs. There is no commonly accepted way to measure these claims; the outcome usually depends on political considerations, not on the merits of the exceptions.

Some people are willing to be taxed much more than others to foster equality of educational opportunity. Some are reluctant to be taxed very much because they doubt the efficacy of equalization policies. Some are willing to support expanding equal access to health care but not education, or vice versa. A critical point is that the choice between equality of educational opportunity and liberty is not an irrevocable once-and-for-all decision; the conflict arises in a host of decisions and the same individual may be on different sides, depending on the specifics of each decision. For example, an individual may support expanding Head Start in the elementary grades but be opposed to race-exclusive scholarships in higher education.

Once we recognize that absolute equality in any service is impossible to attain, our approach to issues of equality takes on a different character. Knowing that we cannot fully equalize access to health care, shelter, and education, who should decide what is most important to buy? Given a choice, many parents would choose health care or shelter over educational opportunity. In other words, the presumed beneficiaries of equality of educational opportunity would often assign a higher priority to improving other services. This is a strong argument on equity grounds for leaving the decisions to consumers instead of mandating the levels of equality in various services.

Equality of Opportunity in the Classroom

Most discussion of equality of educational opportunity ignores equality issues relating to classroom procedure. One exception is the possibility that teachers perceive disadvantaged minority students as less able and thereby set in motion a self-fulfilling prophecy that is harmful to them. The fact is, however, that issues of equal educational opportunity are present every day in classrooms regardless of their ethnic composition. Quite possibly, the way teachers resolve these classroom issues is even more important than the aspects of equal opportunity that are widely publicized. Regardless, the resolution of equal opportunity issues within classrooms provides some helpful clues to the way such issues are resolved at the school, district, state, and federal levels.

Christopher Jencks, a professor of sociology at Northwestern University, has discussed these issues thoughtfully and I shall follow his analysis of them. Jencks visualizes an elementary teacher (Ms. Higgins) who believes that equity and excellence are important. Ms. Higgins's class enrolls a heterogeneous group of twenty-five pupils. Jencks does not assume any particular grade level, but let us assume Ms. Higgins teaches fourth grade. In that case, some of her pupils may read at the eighth- or ninth-grade level, even higher; others, however, will still be reading at a first-grade level. The pupils will vary in other ways as well: interest in school work, parental support, resources at home, and so on.

From the standpoint of equality of educational opportunity, how should Ms. Higgins allocate her time among these pupils? Jencks suggests at least five different ways, all based on principles that deserve serious consideration. Following his terminology, they are as follows:

1. *Moralistic justice.* Ms. Higgins devotes more time to students who try harder. Since ascertaining level of effort is often difficult, she may tend to equate effort with achievement, even though superior achievement by A may require less effort than average achievement by B.

2. *Humane justice.* Ms. Higgins allocates more time to pupils who are most disadvantaged.

3. *Myopic utilitarianism.* The students who want Ms. Higgins's time the most get it.

4. *Enlightened utilitarianism.* Ms. Higgins tries to maximize social welfare in the long run. This requires taking into account the benefits to others and avoiding of time allocations based on immediate benefits or satisfactions.

5. *Democratic equality.* Every student gets equal time, regardless of effort or short- or long-range benefits to students or to anyone else.[10]

As Jencks points out, each principle leads to a different distribution of Ms. Higgins's time. Of course, teachers may act on different principles from one situation to the next, but that only underscores the problem. As Jencks asks, is there any value in the principle of equality of educational opportunity if it embraces or is perceived to be consistent with so many conflicting patterns of teacher conduct?

Before attempting to answer this question, let me raise another one that Jencks does not discuss. Is there any consistency between the ways teachers resolve educational opportunity issues in classrooms, and the policies or philosophies of the schools in which they teach? For instance, the school philosophy may be "humane justice," that is, that the school should try to compensate for students' disadvantages as best it can. Yet even if this is official policy, teachers may often deviate from it in day-to-day classroom activities. For example, they may allocate more time to students who try harder, even if they are not the most disadvantaged students in the class. My guess is that inconsistency prevails, not only among teachers but among schools and school districts as well. Schools rarely if ever adopt policies on teacher time that give teachers any practical guidance on equal opportunity issues. In addition, teachers are not asked their views on the subject when they are interviewed, and equality issues in the classroom are treated peripherally in most programs of teacher education.

What, then, should we conclude about equality of educational opportunity? Is it merely a rhetorical device? Inasmuch as it is used to support contradictory policies, is the phrase really meaningless? At least one eminent scholar, James S. Coleman, has concluded that it is, because achieving complete equality of educational opportunity is impossible.[11] In my view, however, Coleman's conclusion is not justified for two reasons. First, the practical impossibility of achieving complete equality of educational opportunity does not render the concept meaningless. We may not be able to establish a colony in a distant galaxy, but that fact renders the concept impossible of fulfillment, not meaningless. Second, the concept of equality of educational opportunity may not tell us what to do in certain situations, but it can still be useful in telling us what not to do. As Jencks points out, circumstances often justify deviations from equal time to students regardless of need, advantage, or benefit. The concept of equality of educational opportunity requires justification for such deviations; it does not or should not necessarily prohibit them.

The Conflict between Equality and Productivity

Everyone wants both equity and excellence. What if, however, measures to equalize opportunity jeopardize the *average* level of educational achievement? This possibility is not mere speculation. International comparisons indicate that the educational systems with the highest average levels of educational achievement are also those with the most extensive tracking.[12] Although the evidence to this effect is not conclusive, it is too substantial to be dismissed out of hand. Furthermore, there is at least one good reason to anticipate this outcome. Education is not equally valuable to everyone; some students will benefit from it far more than others with equal opportunities to learn. Understandably, our society as a whole may conclude that differential investment in education pays a higher social dividend than a strict egalitarian approach to it.

Let me concede that the identification of talent is frequently difficult and uncertain, should always be regarded cautiously, and should be subject to change with new evidence. Nevertheless, we cannot continue as talent agnostics forever. At some point, decisions have to be made: Should society invest more of its resources in educating this person? If it should, in what educational endeavor? Educational rhetoric often refers to developing everyone's talents to the limit; this is the sort of fuzzy rhetoric that gets us into trouble. It is impossible for society to develop every one of everyone's talents; it probably cannot develop all the talents of one person. The question is, who should decide how much to invest in different talents?

The Rawls Solution

In recent years, one particular effort to reconcile equality of opportunity and productivity has dominated policy analysis. As propounded by John Rawls, the solution is that "the higher expectations of those better situated . . . work as part of a scheme which improves the expectations of the least advantaged members of society."[13] This position asserts that inequalities may be justified only if they lead to betterment of "the least advantaged members of society." Strictly speaking, it does not consider inequalities justified if they better most members of society; the Rawlsian requirement is that they benefit "the least advantaged members."

Although the principle seems clear, its application to specific circumstances may not be. How can we tell whether an inequality will benefit the "least advantaged" members of society? Who are "the least advantaged" and on what criteria? If an inequality benefits most people, including the disadvantaged but not the least advantaged, most people will probably feel the inequality should be permitted if not encouraged. Furthermore, the Rawls proposal might allow much greater inequality than now exists; an inequality might benefit everyone, but benefit the top socioeconomic strata more than the lowest.

One can challenge Rawls's proposal in many ways, but it does suggest a guide to resolution of some equality issues. The critical point is that not all inequalities are undesirable. If they contribute to the welfare of the disadvantaged, or are essential to it, they may be justified.

How does this relate to equality of educational opportunity? Investing in the education of the more talented may result in more benefits for everyone than investment in the education of the less talented. Of course, we cannot equate "more talented" with "most favored" in socioeconomic terms, or "least talented" with "the disadvantaged." However, unless we are prepared to select future mathematicians, doctors, engineers, scientists, and so on by lot, we have to rely on the admittedly imperfect ways of identifying talent that we have. We can and should search for better ways, but we cannot wait for a procedure that is unerringly accurate; no such procedure is likely to emerge.

Undeniably, the most widely used measures of talent indicate that it is not proportionately distributed throughout all social classes. Even if it is, however, equality of educational opportunity can be pushed to a point of diminishing returns. Practically speaking, we must scrutinize appeals to equality for their impact on the level of equality. Also, we must consider who benefits from and who pays for policies ostensibly intended to help the disadvantaged. This scrutiny casts serious doubt on public education as the vehicle of equality of educational opportunity.

The Distribution Dilemma

A belief on the part of the disadvantaged that they have been accorded a fair opportunity to succeed is an important social benefit that may not show up in conventional cost accounting. Unfortunately, using the rhetoric of equal opportunity as a fig leaf to cover subsidies to the middle class has little effect on this belief. Furthermore, additional help will seldom be enough to persuade its beneficiaries that they are being treated fairly. "Fairness" is a moving target that is impossible to reach.

Recognizing the self-serving nature of most rhetoric on equality is essential, but it does not tell us when additional equalization would be counter-productive. A thousand dollars spent by a millionaire for a bottle of rare wine could do more good if spent to educate a disadvantaged child. Fair enough. But what about the producing side? Do we treat nonproducers the same as producers? Are there any ethical as well as economic considerations in how much we take from producers to distribute to nonproducers, or less productive producers? Of course, we have a political system that resolves such questions, but politics does not resolve the ethical or economic issues. Legislators may vote to redistribute, or not to redistribute, because that is what their constituents want, but on what basis should the constituents decide what should be done?

In my view, the ethics and economics of distribution should be related to the ethics and economics of production. The issue here is not only how we determine who is most likely to be productive. It is how should we distribute the gains from increased productivity. Unless the poor stand to benefit from increased productivity, they have no stake in the policies that would foster it.

The distributional arrangements must avoid weakening producer incentives while providing adequate incentives for the disadvantaged to "have faith in the system." Achieving such a balance through our political system is an immensely difficult task. First, there is no unified social control over investment in education and the distribution of the returns. Second, the informational problems are more difficult. Who benefits, by how much? Third, the link between effort or sacrifice and return is much more difficult to ascertain. Fourth, the problem of achieving agreement on the extent and distribution of increased productivity becomes more complicated as the number of parties involved increases; when tens of millions are involved, we are bound to overinvest or underinvest on a large scale. And so on.

Race complicates the problem, perhaps to the point of rendering it insoluble on a widely accepted basis. It is essential to have widespread popular support for our economic and educational system. Some redistribution is necessary to achieve this objective. A major danger is that socioeconomic differences will also be, or be perceived as, racial differences as well. When this happens, a ''We-They'' attitude undermines both willingness to redistribute and acceptance of the importance of productivity. Public education tends to emphasize redistribution without regard to its effects on productivity. Efforts to call attention to the latter are characterized as racist, motivated by greed or selfishness, lacking in compassion, or some other pejorative phrase. As long as this situation prevails, public education cannot reach a sensible accommodation between productivity and equality of educational opportunity. No matter what government does to equalize educational opportunity, it will not be enough to satisfy our professional equalitarians. In their pursuit of equality without regard to productivity, many are just as self-serving as the opponents of policies intended to achieve greater equality are supposed to be.

Public Education and the Mythology of Equal Opportunity

As Chapter 1 pointed out, public schools were not established to provide equality of educational opportunity. On the contrary, in view of the fact that the majority of children did not even attend high school until the 1930s, public education was an extremely inegalitarian institution.

From 1890 to 1940, high school retention rates increased dramatically. Several factors contributed to this development. Compulsory education laws raised the age of school leaving. In most states, child labor laws, aggressively supported by the labor movement under the guise of helping children, made it difficult or impossible for urban children to enter the labor market.

Typically, students had to stay in school until they were eligible to work full time as an adult. Along with the labor movement, the public school establishment vigorously supported the expansion of public education. In the period 1930–1960, public education was swept up in the movement widely known as "life adjustment education." Great stress was placed on "meeting the needs and interests" of students—in brief, on instituting curricular and extracurricular changes that would supposedly appeal to the rising hordes of secondary school students who would have dropped out in an earlier era. Courses such as home economics, typing, business mathematics, driver education, consumer education, and the like were introduced in states and school districts everywhere. A few voices of protest were raised, but they had no appreciable impact on the course of events in public schools.

Efforts to persuade students to stay in school in the first half of the twentieth century differed in at least one fundamental way from current efforts. In earlier times, it was assumed that most students were not able to perform rigorous college preparatory work: trigonometry, physics, chemistry, and so on.[14] The assumption was not based on racial considerations. Today, however, it is politically and often educationally impossible to challenge publicly the view that most students can successfully complete rigorous college preparatory programs. Paradoxically, although the need for vocational or commercial or general tracks was initially based on white perceptions of differential abilities among white students, the existence of such tracks has come to be challenged by black leaders as "racist."

It is understandable why contemporary opinion should fail to appreciate the enormous inequality in public education generations ago. What is much less understandable is the widespread failure to appreciate how public education, especially public higher education, continues to favor middle- and upper-class families. At one time, most college students were enrolled in private institutions. After World War II the market share of public institutions increased, to the point where they enrolled an estimated 77.8 percent of the college population in 1991.[15] Government funding that enabled public institutions to keep tuition charges extremely low was the main reason for this expansion. Furthermore, even the private institutions have been subsidized by government in various ways: research grants, scholarships, student loans at less than cost, and so on.

These enormous middle- and upper-class subsidies allegedly enable qualified poor students to go to college. With each increase in public assistance, professorial salaries rise while the higher education lobby warns that if the government does not provide more assistance, it will fail to provide "equal opportunity" to economically disadvantaged students. Meanwhile, despite frantic efforts to recruit disadvantaged students from minorities, there is only a negligible increase in their number, especially in critical scientific and technical fields.[16] The same inequalities that characterize secondary education are still operative, except at even higher and more expensive grade levels.

In a market system, those who can afford higher quality pay for it; that is how our economic system is supposed to work. Government provides food, health care, and shelter for those who cannot afford these things. It does not, however, provide equality of gastronomic opportunity, health care, or shelter. Instead, it provides a certain level of support below which no one is supposed to fall. The levels of government assistance may go up or down, depending on the state of the economy and other factors, but the goods and services provided this way are not intended to be equal to those purchased from personal funds.

Why is equality of educational opportunity a major issue, but not equality of shelter or of food? Perhaps we should be more concerned about the level of these other benefits for the poor, but that is not the issue here. Even if we improved these benefits, the rationale would not be equality but the adequacy of government assistance. Food and shelter are just as important as formal education for the long-range welfare of children; in some respects, they are much more important. Nevertheless, equality with respect to these benefits is not a major political issue. The reason is that the producers of food and shelter do not regard equalization as an objective; their interests are served by adequacy, not equality of consumption.

The case is otherwise in education. The educational producers use "equality of educational opportunity" to maximize their own welfare in several ways. The higher the level at which we institutionalize the concept, the more benefits for the educational producers. In an earlier era, government provided elementary education for everyone; today, full government support through high school is virtually universal. The argument is now being made that government should absorb the costs of higher education as well. Many justifications are given for this proposal, but "equal educational opportunity" is the most persuasive. The producers are well aware that it is much easier to demonstrate "inequalities" than "inadequacies."

Equality of Opportunity under a Market System

There are several reasons to believe that a market system would be more conducive than public education to equality of educational opportunity. First of all, our preoccupation with government as the focus of equalization efforts is contrary to our experience. That experience demonstrates that a market system equalizes access to services more effectively than government provision of them. At one time, only royalty had access to the arts. The masses could not afford to enjoy the work of musicians, painters, dancers, and other artists. Today, the arts are available to virtually everyone through radio, television, records, and tapes. What was formerly a privilege of the few is now available to the masses—surely, a major step toward equality. Similarly, foods that once were available only to royalty—and then on a limited basis—are available to everyone, even buyers using food stamps. Breezes that formerly required servants or slaves are now available to everyone by means of electric fans. During the Middle Ages, the nobility resented efforts by others to imitate their clothes. Laws were passed to prevent this, and to ensure that dress reflected social status. Eventually, such efforts to maintain inequality of dress were swept away by the rise of capitalism and mass production. These equalizing developments, and thousands like them, were not the result of benevolent government. They were the outcome of an economic process, not a political one.

In a market economy, producers constantly seek larger markets. Their incentive is that larger markets bring them larger financial rewards, but their actions benefit others as well by enlarging the scope of equality. For instance, the poor today have access to worldwide systems of communication that were not available to even the wealthiest citizens in earlier times. Producers achieve larger markets by increasing quality and reducing cost. In effect, the process tends to expand equality of consumption. Vaccines equalize access to health care, telephones to communication, and so on.

As a matter of fact, market processes have even affected the definition of "poor" or "disadvantaged." Most "poor" people in the United States today have better shelter, eat better, and own more property than did the average U.S. citizen for most of this century. According to the Bureau of the Census:

22,000 poor households own swimming pools or Jacuzzis
38 percent of the poor own their own homes
62 percent of poor households own a car
14 percent of poor households own two cars
31 percent of poor households have microwave ovens
almost half of poor households have air conditioning.

According to one recent analysis, after adjusting for inflation, the per capita expenditures of the lowest fifth of U.S. households in income in 1988 exceeded the per capita income of the median American household in 1955. The average "poor" American lives in a larger house or apartment than does the average Western European. Poor Americans eat far more meat, are more likely to own cars and dishwashers, and are more likely to have basic modern amenities such as indoor toilets, than is the general Western European population.[17]

In short, the "poor" are a moving target. We must distinguish between the absolute poor—those who lack food, shelter, or resources—and those who are poor only in the sense of having less than most of their fellow citizens. No one doubts the existence of the poor in the absolute sense. It appears, however, that their number is much less than might be supposed from media treatment of the subject.

The distinction between absolute and relative poverty is relevant to our analysis of equality of educational opportunity. People tend to be more willing to alleviate absolute than relative poverty. Willingness to pay higher taxes to equalize opportunity will depend partly on the amount of the tax bite; it will also depend partly on the nature of the inequality being eliminated or reduced. Appeals to help the poor cite the absolute poor as examples; lumping them with the relative poor may jeopardize assistance for the absolute poor.

Under the circumstances that prevail in education, market systems are likely to reduce discrimination, whether against blacks or any other minority. Inasmuch as racial discrimination is prohibited by law, the objections to a market system based on predictions that schools would discriminate in enrollment or employment are weak to begin with. Let us suppose, however, that there is a gray area in which schools can discriminate without violating the law. First, consider the matter from a management perspective. Suppose two schools are competing. One welcomes black students; the other does not. Other things being equal, the former will attract more students than its discriminating competitor. It is contended that other things will not be equal because the school that discriminates will gain more students (students who prefer such a school) than it will lose from its discriminatory policies. I shall consider this possibility shortly; first, let us consider the matter from a teacher perspective. The school that avoids black teachers will narrow its pool of applicants and therefore may have to pay higher wages to satisfy its prejudices. The school that does not discriminate in employment can take advantage of the entire pool of qualified teachers. Let us not overlook the fact that unions of white employees in the United States supported racial discrimination to avoid competition from black workers. White unions in South Africa were among the leading proponents of apartheid for precisely this reason.

Actually, segregation per se was only one way that governments discriminated against blacks in public education. Black teachers were often paid much less than white ones. Black schools had less equipment, fewer books, less adequate facilities. They had fewer educational options and fewer services. In view of the appalling level of government discrimination against blacks, not just in education but in other public services as well, it is somewhat anomalous that blacks should regard government provision of service as most likely to provide equal treatment.

In part, black attitudes are based on U.S. Supreme Court decisions holding government-imposed racial segregation to be unconstitutional, the enactment of the Civil Rights Act of 1964, and the establishment of several federal agencies to remedy alleged instances of racial discrimination. What is widely overlooked is that the 1954 U.S. Supreme Court decisions struck down racial segregation imposed by governments, local, state, and federal. The decisions might have some bearing on which level of government provides the most protection for civil rights, but they are irrelevant to whether markets result in more racial discrimination than government delivery of the same service. Integrated private schools existed in many states that racially segregated their public schools. Furthermore, government compliance with the Civil Rights Act has been less forthright than private-sector compliance. In public education, litigation over compliance has dragged out for decades; in 1990 the U.S. Supreme Court resolved school assignment cases that had been litigated for nearly twenty years.

In some situations, market forces have reduced racial discrimination sanctioned by government. Price V. Fishback has described an interesting example in West Virginia in the early 1900s. At that time, the coal companies had to recruit coal miners because of tight labor markets. Many mines were in isolated areas lacking an adequate labor supply. To recruit miners, the coal companies brought in European immigrants and blacks from nearby states. The wages of black and white miners were substantially equal. In addition, the coal companies actively sought to reduce unequal treatment for blacks in the public schools. The reason was fundamental: equal educational opportunity for miners' children was helpful in recruiting black coal miners. School expenditures for white and black children were substantially equal in West Virginia at a time when per-pupil costs in nearby states were two to seven times higher for white than for black children.[18]

In 1896 the U.S. Supreme Court upheld the "separate but equal" doctrine in *Plessy v. Ferguson*. Nevertheless, southern states and school districts flagrantly ignored the "equal" dimension of the decision; about 1910, for example, southern school expenditures per black student were only 40 percent of expenditures per white student. Indeed, in a well-known study published in 1944, the Swedish sociologist Gunnar Myrdal expressed surprise that public education for blacks had not been abolished completely in the South during the period when they were being disenfranchised by various means.[19]

Robert A. Margot points out that economic competition preserved what little support black schools received. Blacks migrated to areas where educational opportunities were better. As a result, southern farmers and industrialists were forced to support education for blacks in their own self-interest. As Margot puts it, "the ability of Southern blacks to 'vote with their feet' placed limits on local government discrimination."[20]

Notwithstanding such examples, Cass R. Sunstein argues that market forces cannot eliminate or even reduce discrimination in certain types of situations. Sunstein concedes that market forces have reduced racial discrimination in some situations; nevertheless, in his view, market forces, if not regulated by government, will intensify rather than reduce discrimination.[21] To illustrate Sunstein's argument, suppose a grocery store would gain white customers if it excluded black customers. If the store would gain more white customers than the black customers it would lose, discrimination against blacks would be a rational economic policy for the store to follow.

Conceptually, Sunstein's argument may be valid. In practice, civil rights legislation would prohibit discrimination by schools in a market system. This suggests that government action may be essential to reduce discrimination, but it does not follow that government provision of service is superior to private delivery on this criterion.

At the present time at least, participation in any sort of discriminatory enterprise carries a stigma. Politically ambitious individuals avoid any such activity. Notwithstanding popular opinion to the contrary, David Duke's 1991 campaign for governor of Louisiana illustrates this point. In becoming a candidate, Duke dropped his ties to racist organizations. His campaign posture was opposition to preferential treatment, not discrimination against blacks. Although he may have gained some support because of his racist past, he clearly was on the defensive about it during the campaign. Similarly, companies seeking minority customers, that is, just about every large company in the United States, avoid any appearance of racism. As a matter of fact, political and business leaders go out of their way to identify with minorities in a host of ways.

In an educational market, schools would compete to enroll minorities, not to exclude them. As Chapter 10 will demonstrate, institutions of higher education, including the most prestigious ones, are making strenuous efforts to enroll disadvantaged minorities. Granted, this was not always the case, but a reversion to the era of discriminatory practices is highly improbable. With Harvard, Yale, Stanford, and other prestigious institutions of higher education aggressively recruiting students from disadvantaged minorities, the argument that under a market system prestigious elementary and secondary schools would exclude them stretches credulity, even apart from the legal considerations involved.

Conclusion

Equality of educational opportunity plays a crucial role in discussions of a market system of education. Perhaps the one point of agreement is that it is a complex topic. One recent effort to analyze "equality" identified 108 distinctive meanings, with the possibility of thousands more if secondary distinctions were introduced.[22] Needless to say, the discussion in this chapter was not comprehensive; its purpose was to raise some neglected issues.

One such issue is whether a market system would ameliorate or exacerbate inequality in American society. Both arguments agree that education is an investment in human capital. The antimarket argument is that if the level of such investment is resolved by market forces, the affluent will invest more and receive more from their investment than the poor. This would exacerbate inequality in American society. This objection overlooks several important considerations. One is the extent to which public education has always favored its upper-middle-class clientele. Because of its monopoly status, however, public education can no longer avoid responsibility for the education of the disadvantaged. Its recent efforts to address the problem have not emerged from concern about the education of the disadvantaged; instead, they have emerged from concern over the political consequences of continued failure to address it.

A second neglected issue is that equality of educational opportunity should not be considered in isolation from equality and adequacy of other services, such as health care and shelter. Many children would be better served by greater investment in these areas. Inasmuch as we cannot equalize all services, or even any one of them, public policy should provide an adequate minimum level of service while leaving broad areas of discretion to individuals. Under the existing system, the issues are resolved on the basis of producer political clout, not discretion exercised by consumers as circumstances warrant.

Third, we must not ignore the relationships between investment in human capital and productivity. Beyond a certain level, equal investment in human capital, or in the educational dimensions of it, is not always or necessarily in the interests of the disadvantaged. This is especially evident in arguments for more spending for "education." Such arguments lead to subsidies for the unproductive as well as the productive dimensions of education. Academics will continue to disseminate arguments for "equality," but even the disadvantaged will eventually recognize their self-serving nature.

The conventional criticism of voucher plans is that affluent families would be their main beneficiaries; surprising as it may seem, however, a market system based on educational vouchers might be more helpful to poor than to affluent families. Upper-middle-class parents can consider public school quality in their residential decisions or choose private schools. The poor are less able and less likely to do so. Thus upper-middle-class parents may be less interested in shifting schools if educational vouchers are enacted. This may explain why lower-income parents show more interest than upper-middle-class parents in school choice proposals. After all, families who need government assistance for shelter are more interested in housing vouchers than families who are living comfortably in their own residences.

Minority dissatisfaction with public education is intensified by our political rhetoric, which asserts that all students can achieve at high levels. This is simply not true, however politically expedient it may be to assert it. The unpalatable truth is that equality of educational opportunity is more likely to intensify than to reduce inequality of educational achievement. One reason is that the factors holding back high achievers are more amenable to school control than the factors holding back low achievers. To illustrate, students who can learn calculus in college can ordinarily do so in high school. A market system is likely to provide increased opportunities for them to do so. Thus the achievement gap will widen unless low achievers improve commensurably. They are unlikely to do so on any scale comparable to the acceleration of high achievers. Thus as some students learn calculus at age 15 instead of 19, the achievement gap at the secondary level will widen. I see no practical way to avoid this, especially since several factors depressing achievement are beyond school control. To avoid inequality by limiting choices or levels of achievement is senseless, even if there is a constituency for doing just that. The size of this constituency is not to be underestimated; Aaron Wildavsky, one of our most astute policy analysts, has argued that it is already a major threat to our political and economic strength.[23]

Whenever a large bureaucracy owes its existence to a problem, the problem never goes away. If experience is any guide, the problem gets worse, and so it has in education. The civil rights bureaucracies have been forced to change their objectives; the tragedy is that they have adopted redistribution and equal outcomes instead of self-help as their new objectives. Perhaps an even greater tragedy is that a muddled majority seems unable to cope with the problem. It may be too early to draw this conclusion, but it is not too early to be concerned about it. To observe the current discussions of equality, one would never suspect the extent to which government policies create inequalities, or are based on ignorance of the full range of their consequences, or exaggerate the power of government to equalize services without harm to other objectives.[24]

In the meantime, public education is undergoing the most far-reaching change in its political base since it was established 150 years ago. For most of that time, the middle and upper classes in American society strongly supported it. Its leaders were prestigious public officials. The small number of parents who opted for independent schools never really threatened public education and its authority was widely respected. The expansion of secondary and then higher education has led to a decline in the prestige of both. Whether this decline could have been avoided is debatable, but it is no longer reversible. Public education's favorable political and educational environment has been eroding, gradually but unmistakably. The outcome will not be limited to increased support for private education. It will also include a major reorientation of entry into the labor force. At the present time, media treatment of education is dominated by college preparation and college admissions; relatively little attention is devoted to school failure to prepare young people for the world of work. The massive costs of this failure cannot be sustained indefinitely. Inevitably, business will replace secondary education as the primary education and training agency for many students currently forced to invest their time unproductively in public schools. The public school lobby, aided and abetted by its allies in higher education, will resist the change as "exploiting" children, but the self-serving nature of their resistance will be manifest.

10

≈ The Impact of
Higher Education on
the Public Schools

By virtually any standard, the United States has by far the largest system of higher education in the world. In 1989–90 institutions of higher education:

enrolled 13.2 million students
employed 762,000 faculty members
awarded 448,000 associate, 1 million bachelor's, 301,000 master's, and 34,400 doctoral degrees
spent $126.8 billion.[1]

No other nation enrolls such a high proportion of its population in higher education, employs as many faculty members, or spends as much on higher education. What is this mammoth enterprise supposed to achieve? First, the conservation and transmittal of our intellectual and cultural heritage, broadly conceived. Second, higher education is supposed to carry out various research functions. It does not simply transmit our intellectual and cultural heritage; it is supposed to add to it in various ways. Finally, higher education is a service enterprise; for example, professors are usually expected to be active in professional or civic organizations, or to use their expertise to assist communities and governments. These functions are widely accepted; nothing I have to say is based on a unique point of view about the functions of higher education.

The effectiveness of higher education in fulfilling its functions is highly debatable. I regard higher education as a disaster area, even more than public education, but the following analysis does not depend on this assessment. My purpose is not to critique higher education but to point out how it will affect the future of public education.

230

At the outset, a few points about higher education need to be emphasized. First, the higher education lobby is a well-organized, generously funded, highly articulate, and politically influential interest group. This important fact is often overlooked because there are so many subgroups within higher education, and they sometimes are in conflict with one another. There are organizations of state universities and land grant colleges, of research universities, of community colleges, of denominational institutions, of liberal arts colleges, and of institutions that are not research oriented. Three major faculty unions (AFT, NEA, and AAUP) represent professors, and boards of trustees have their own national organization. Scores, if not hundreds, of organizations such as the American History Association and the American Physical Society enroll faculty members in different fields. In addition, virtually every profession has a national organization to look after its interests in higher education: the Association of American Law Schools and the American Association of Colleges for Teacher Education are illustrative.

These organizations often disagree on specific issues. For instance, in the allocation of federal funds, research universities differ from community colleges, state-supported institutions from private ones, and urban institutions from nonurban. These differences underscore two critical points. One is that institutions of higher education act in terms of their own interests. The other point is that we should not underestimate their collective influence because of conflicts within their ranks. Unions and management often have conflicts at the bargaining table but combine forces to exclude foreign competition from the U.S. market. In this respect, higher education is a highly sophisticated interest group. More effectively than most, it has learned how to manage internal conflict for the welfare of the larger group. Needless to say, however, the higher education lobby always characterizes its proposals as in the public interest. No doubt some are, but all somehow turn out to be in the interest of higher education.

The Dynamic Relationships between Colleges and Public Schools

College Admission Requirements and Public Education

Most professors, especially at the undergraduate level, think of public education in terms of preparation for college. They are highly critical of public schools, which they blame for the poor preparation of college freshmen. "If the public schools would do their job properly, we could do ours"—such is the thought process in academe. There is some validity to it, but essentially those who think this way are confusing cause and effect. The causal relationships run mostly in the other direction; that is, higher education has a much larger influence on public education than vice versa.

The nationwide adoption of Carnegie units illustrates this point. In the early 1900s the Carnegie Foundation for the Advancement of Teaching decided to set up a pension plan for retired professors. To do this, the foundation had to distinguish colleges from high schools; at the time, the dividing line was not clear. Eventually colleges were defined as institutions that required sixteen units for admission: four in English, three in science, three in mathematics, and six in history and social studies. A unit was defined as attendance for fifty to sixty minutes a day, for 140 days.

Within a short period of time, colleges everywhere began to require sixteen "Carnegie units" for admission. Although the mix has changed, many still require a certain number. In any case, the high schools acted promptly to conform to these college admission requirements: the high school curriculum since the early 1900s has been based on a policy intended to establish a pension plan for professors.[2] One could hardly ask for more persuasive evidence that higher education has been a basic influence on secondary education.

College admissions requirements have changed, especially since the mid-1960s. Between 1965 and 1970 ten states required all state public institutions of higher education to admit all graduates of public high schools within the state; by 1990 twenty states had this requirement.[3] It was taken for granted that open admissions would present colleges with large numbers of less-qualified students; hence remedial and counseling bureaucracies expanded dramatically.

The fundamental point here is the impact on high schools. Suppose students know that to be admitted to college they must pass a certain number of courses (units) in science, mathematics, English, and history. Students who plan to go on to college obviously have a strong incentive to study diligently. This incentive disappears when students are admitted to college regardless of subjects taken or level of performance. In effect, high school graduation is no longer a terminal point at which a student with no significant educational achievement must withdraw from formal education. High school is more like elementary school, with little or no differentiation on the basis of achievement.

Over time, declining academic standards in high schools contributed to their decline in elementary schools. One of the nation's leading scholars on the effects of education has emphasized that "reduced demands and greater flexibility in high school have a strong impact in reducing the achievement demanded in elementary school. Or, more generally, when one educational level modifies the demands it makes either for admission or in its own curriculum, these modifications reverberate downward to the next level, causing it in turn to modify its demands."[4]

Earlier Enrollment Options

One way for colleges to counteract declining enrollments is to recruit high school students who can perform college work. The number of such students is undoubtedly very large. Many college courses merely add to or repeat high school courses, but do not require higher levels of academic achievement. A good high school student is usually able to pass most college-level courses during the time now spent in high school.

Colleges are already tapping into this source of customers in two ways. In one, illustrated by the Advanced Placement (AP) Program of the College Board, college-level courses are taught in the high schools by high school teachers. In this program, the students receive college credit when they enroll in college. Credit for AP courses is based on scores on tests administered by the Educational Testing Service (ETS). In 1991 about 351,000 high school students took AP examinations, and about two-thirds qualified for college credit or placement. This was an increase of almost 50 percent over the number who took the examinations in 1981.[5]

In another pattern, the high school students enroll in college courses taught by college instructors, courses usually taken by college freshmen and sophomores. To illustrate, a Minnesota law enacted in 1989 allows public high school students to enroll in institutions of higher education. The state aid that would normally go to the local school district is paid to the college on a pro rata basis: if half of a student's program is in college courses, half the student's state aid goes to the college. In 1990–91 about 6,700 students took advantage of the program.[6] The number appears likely to increase, and other states are adopting or showing interest in the idea.

As colleges seek to maintain their enrollments, they will probably rely more heavily on programs like Minnesota's. The AP program benefits the students but does not provide any direct financial benefit for the participating colleges. Participation in a Minnesota-type program enables colleges to attract cash customers immediately. At the same time, however, school district income from state aid is correspondingly reduced. Some high schools are already threatening to guide students away from colleges that recruit students this way, but they are fighting a losing battle. There is no way public high schools will be able to prevent more talented students from leaving earlier than in the past.

At the present time, earlier withdrawal from high school does not help students who wish to enter the labor force; they are prevented from doing so by archaic child labor laws, enacted and maintained by the collusion of organized labor and the public education lobby. In the past, private-sector employers did not object strenuously to restrictions on teenage employment because there was a plentiful labor supply. In the 1990s, however, we can anticipate more employer support for earlier work options. To the extent that this change in policy comes about, it will accelerate the decline in high school enrollments.

Intercollegiate Athletics

The relationships between intercollegiate and high school athletics also illustrate the negative effects of higher education on secondary education. The advent of television led to much larger revenues for college football and basketball events. Competition for outstanding high school athletes led colleges to recruit athletes who could not have been admitted under the standards applied to other students. On many campuses, new courses were created to sustain the fiction that these athletes were really students. These developments resulted in several highly publicized incidents. In 1989 Dexter Manley, a nationally known professional football player, testified that he had been functionally illiterate while playing for Oklahoma State University from 1977 to 1980. Kevin Ross, who played basketball for four years at Creighton University, subsequently enrolled in a Chicago elementary school to learn to read. Seven members of the basketball team at California State University–Los Angeles filed suit against the university for academic fraud. The university eventually settled the case for $1,000 in damages, educational benefits, and a public apology.[7]

A survey by ETS showed that of 1977 college freshmen who played football or basketball in college, only 20 percent of the black players had graduated six years later; also that the majority who received degrees had majored in physical education, sports administration, or "communications."[8] In 1983, a group of college presidents led the effort to establish standards for freshman athletes known as Proposition 48: in order to be eligible to play during their freshman year, athletes had to maintain a C average in eleven core-curriculum courses in high school and score a minimum of 700 on the combined verbal and mathematics sections of the Scholastic Aptitude Test (SAT) or 15 on the American College Testing program. These required test scores are equivalent to the average test score for ninth-grade students, yet there was considerable opposition to the requirement when the National Collegiate Athletic Association adopted it in 1983.

According to a recent study of intercollegiate athletics, "some secondary school programs now emulate the worst features of too many collegiate programs."[9] High school athletes have delayed graduation to extend their athletic eligibility; students in the eighth grade have withdrawn from school for a year in order to be physically more mature during their period of eligibility for high school athletics. Grades and transcripts have been altered to render high school athletes eligible to enter college. High school athletic teams often devote a staggering amount of time to athletic practice instead of schoolwork. This is happening despite the fact that only one high school athlete in ten thousand receives an athletic scholarship to a major university. A 1986 study showed that although almost 1.5 million high school students participated in football and basketball, only 240 athletes entered the ranks of the National Football League and the National Basketball Association that year.[10] Of course, the situation raises serious questions about high schools as well as colleges. What is the value of high school counseling programs if thousands of students are neglecting their education for a one-in-ten-thousand chance to earn a brief living as a professional athlete? But the main point here is that lower standards in higher education have led to lower standards throughout public education.

Grade Inflation

Chapter 4 pointed out the discrepancies between report cards and achievement levels in the public schools. Such discrepancies only follow the lead of higher education, where grade inflation first emerged as a serious problem. It did so because the lower college admission standards inevitably led to lower standards for passing courses and for graduation. For example, a study of fifty public and private research universities showed that from the early 1960s to the mid-1970s the percentage of "A" grades went from 16 to 34, of "C" from 37 to 21. During these years, indices of student ability, such as SAT and ACT scores, were declining.[11]

In the 1960s and 1970s many institutions of higher education adopted Pass/Fail grading. This system weakens incentives to achieve and conveys less information than letter grades: a student who barely passes receives the same grade as a student who performs brilliantly. Grade inflation also received a major impetus from faculty members seeking to help male students to stay in school to avoid the draft. According to the peculiar logic of higher education, it was unfair to apply less rigorous standards only to male students; the upshot was a weakening of standards for female students as well. Student evaluation of teachers also contributed to grade inflation. Thus while universities enrolled much larger numbers of unqualified students, and while their curricula were being watered down to avoid failing grades on a large scale, grade point averages rose dramatically. In some institutions, half or more of the courses required for graduation were P/F courses. One study showed that 59 percent of institutions of higher education allowed students a P/F option; the larger the institution, the more likely that it would do so.[12] Not surprisingly, the use of P/F grades below the college level also increased. Teachers welcomed a practice that let them avoid distinguishing different levels of work and risking negative reactions from low achievers. The appeal of the process is very similar at all grade levels, but higher education led the way in catering to it.

Educational reformers typically urge public schools to establish and maintain higher standards of educational achievement. Such recommendations are futile while grade inflation prevails in higher education. Sad to say, it is practically impossible to eliminate or substantially reduce it there. Too many academic departments would be devastated by any such action. They easily command enough power, internally and externally, to block realistic reporting of student achievement.

Financing Higher Education

Who should bear the costs of higher education? The higher education establishment urges that government do so. Government should make higher education available to every qualified student, supposedly because the returns to society are worth the investment. The way to do this is to have government absorb most of the costs of higher education. In addition, grants and loans should be available on favorable terms, especially to students from disadvantaged minorities. As a result of widespread support of these policies, approximately 78 percent of the students enrolled in institutions of higher education are in public institutions. On the average, they pay much less than students in private institutions. In 1988–89 the average annual rate for tuition, room, and board in private institutions was $11,189; in public institutions, it was only $4,274.[13]

An alternative would be to require everyone to pay from personal resources if reasonably able to do so. This policy would enable government to provide assistance to more poor students, and/or more assistance to each such student. Higher education organizations oppose means-tested approaches to student aid. As the higher education lobby sees it, aid to students should be universal, not means-tested; if this is unavoidable, the means test should be as liberal as possible, so that the highest possible number of students should be eligible. Despite the criticisms of universal benefits discussed in Chapter 9, higher education has been very successful in enacting its positions on financing higher education. Government expenditures for higher education have increased enormously. Nevertheless, enrollments of students from disadvantaged minorities have lagged far behind. The benefits of increased government expenditures for higher education have not gone to the poor; they have gone to middle- and upper-class students and professors. Despite its self-serving rhetoric, the higher education establishment espouses policies that are against the interests of lower-income groups.

On the one hand, institutions of higher education foster the idea that higher education is essential for success. They work cooperatively with various occupational organizations to establish college degrees as a legal or practical requirement for entering certain occupations. This process adds enormously to the costs of training and of employing persons who have the training. It also forces employers to pay higher salaries to compensate for the earnings foregone while in training.

Simultaneously, higher education appeals to government to make higher education available to everyone. It is so successful in this effort that millions of high school graduates who have no particular interest or need for higher education nevertheless devote years to it. Because they bear so little of the direct cost, and because going to college is a cultural norm, the low return on the investment is easily overlooked.

Higher education is allegedly priced below its real cost so that the poor can take advantage of it; actually, if government provided support only to able students who truly could not afford to pay for higher education, its expenditures on higher education would drop precipitously. This would enable government to provide larger subsidies for students with a genuine need for assistance. Such an outcome would also relieve the tax burdens on the less-affluent groups that provide considerable financial support for higher education through regressive sales taxes. It would also result in smaller academic budgets, fewer academic jobs, less generous academic salaries, and a host of other outcomes contrary to the interests of the producers of higher education.

Significantly, one of the largest items in the 1991 budget of the U.S. Department of Education was $5.4 billion to cover the cost of guaranteed student loans. This amount would have been even higher if institutions of higher education had been able to enact government loan guarantees more to their liking; as it is, they have defeated efforts to require demonstrated ability to do college-level work as a condition of eligibility for a student loan. They were quick to realize that government-guaranteed loans were an effective way to prop up the demand for higher education; understandably, they have lobbied diligently to weaken the conditions of eligibility for such loans. The end result is an enormous drain on the federal budget, sanctified by the claim that it is a contribution to "equality of educational opportunity."

Medical education illustrates another basic flaw in this rationale. It appears that investment in medical education is highly profitable. It is highly profitable, however, partly because of monopolistic practices by the medical profession. To this extent, it is a mistake to attribute physicians' high incomes to medical education; investing more in medical education would be unproductive despite the correlation between such education and income. Similarly, many other high incomes associated with higher education are due to monopolistic practices, not to any enhanced skill resulting from lengthy periods of higher education.

As is to be expected, the returns on investment in education vary from person to person, field to field, time to time, and place to place. Clearly, governments as well as individuals often fail to predict the decline of various occupations or the growth of new ones. This being the case, who should decide how much education, of what kind, an individual should pursue: the individual (or his parents), or the government? Mistakes will be made in either case, but they will be corrected more quickly if individuals make the decisions. This requires more individual and less government influence over educational decisions.

Existing policy requires students to choose education over work at the secondary level. At higher levels, government absorbs most of the costs of staying in school even when there is no good reason to do so. These policies work against the interests of middle- and upper-income families as well. Our most prestigious institutions of higher education frequently proclaim how competitive they are. On other occasions, they challenge the idea that competition has any role to play in higher education. For instance, in May 1991 the Ivy League colleges (Brown, Cornell, Columbia, Dartmouth, Harvard, University of Pennsylvania, Princeton, and Yale) entered into a consent agreement with the U.S. Department of Justice over a lawsuit alleging that the colleges were violating the antitrust laws by agreements that eliminated financial competition for students. Although the colleges did not concede that they had been violating the law, their position during the investigation leading up to the lawsuit was that colleges should not be subject to the antitrust laws. Commenting on the consent agreement, one college representative asserted that "Schools like ours should not be seen as competitors in the same way that toaster manufacturers are."[14]

These sentiments reflect a longstanding attitude in higher education that it should be considered exempt from antitrust regulation even when its actions are clearly anticompetitive.[15] The Massachusetts Institute of Technology (MIT), also charged with suppressing competition, elected not to participate in the consent agreement. Instead, MIT chose to defend itself in court against the charge. On September 2, 1992, a federal judge ruled that MIT had violated the antitrust law. The judge's opinion stated that "MIT's attempt to disassociate the Overlap process from the commercial aspects of higher education is pure sophistry. No reasonable person could conclude that the Ivy Overlap agreements did not suppress competition."[16] It would be astonishing if this anticompetitive attitude did not foster anticompetitive attitudes at lower levels of education.

The trend toward public absorption of the costs of higher education highlights the dominance of producer interests in educational reform. About half of our high school graduates go on to college. Directly or indirectly, government spends a great deal on them. It spends much less on students who do not go on to college, a much less affluent group. Not surprisingly, our institutions of higher education ignore this bias in their efforts to generate more public support. "If you want government help, buy what we are selling.'' This is the message from our academic equalitarians.

The lack of attention to students who are not going on to college is one of the basic weaknesses of the educational reform movement. Undoubtedly, it relates partly to the fact that most educational reformers are college graduates who think about K–12 education largely in terms of preparation for college. Whatever the reasons, the situation illustrates how academic rhetoric about equal opportunity ignores actual practice in higher education.

Teacher Education

Teachers are educated in institutions of higher education. In 1985–86, over 99 percent of classroom teachers held bachelor's degrees; over 51 percent held one or more advanced degrees. The vast majority had taken some college work for credit after the bachelor's degree. In most states, some graduate study is required for administrative positions; the proportion of school administrators holding advanced degrees or graduate credit is much higher than that of classroom teachers.

Teacher education is a huge industry. In 1988–89 public schools employed more than 2.3 million teachers. The attrition rate in 1987–88 was about 5.6 percent.[17] Replacements are not all new graduates; many are former teachers returning after pregnancies, raising a family, other employment, and so on. Even so, the number of graduates required to fill vacancies every year is obviously quite large. In addition, a large number of school administrators enroll in graduate courses and programs every year.

The situation can be best explained in terms of producer and consumer roles. The institutions of higher education are the producers. They produce graduates who are or can be certified to teach. The consumers are students—prospective teachers. They want to be certified to teach at the lowest cost, in the easiest way. Eventually, school districts will want to employ them—at which point the former consumers become producers. The prospective teachers have an interest in good preparation, but it hardly matters whether one institution has a better program of teacher education than others. The students expect to be certified and get a job regardless of where they received their teacher training.

University departments of education are not the sole producers of teachers. Most of the coursework taken by prospective teachers is outside the departments of education. Usually elementary teachers take more education courses than secondary teachers, but both groups take most of their courses outside the field of education. The significance of this point is not to be underestimated. Many academic departments, even entire institutions, often depend on prospective teachers to sustain their enrollments. Imposing high standards for teacher education programs would lower their enrollments and threaten their survival. Their incentive to keep standards low is very strong indeed.

Two widely neglected facts underscore this point. One is that faculties as a whole usually have a dominant voice in setting admission and degree requirements. There are very few faculties that could not adopt higher standards for admission to and graduation from programs of teacher education if they were determined to do so. This point applies to grade point averages, aptitude test scores, course prerequisites, or any other way to implement high standards.

The second fact also reveals the faculty stake in low standards. Although there is much controversy over testing, we can test knowledge of a subject. Whether we can accurately test a person's ability to teach it is controversial, but ability to test knowledge of the subject is not. After all, at the end of each course, professors usually give a final examination. It would be ridiculous to argue that we cannot use tests to ascertain whether or not prospective teachers know their subject.

Currently, to be certified to teach a subject, prospective teachers ordinarily must take a certain number of credit hours in the subject. The amount of credit required varies widely from state to state. Courses with the same title often have different subject matter; courses with dissimilar titles may offer essentially the same subject matter. Grading standards also vary widely. The upshot is that state requirements relating to credit hours in a subject are not very meaningful.

Such problems could be conveniently resolved by state examinations. Instead of prescribing a certain number of credits, states could institute examinations in the subjects to be taught. This does not happen because most institutions of higher education are opposed to it. Most cannot risk having their graduates perform poorly on the state examinations, especially after receiving good grades in several courses in the subject. The higher education interest in obscuring the value added by higher education outweighs any consumer interest.

On college campuses, one frequently encounters allegations of poor quality directed at teacher education. This theme is frequently expressed in charges that teacher education overemphasizes methods of teaching and devotes insufficient attention to courses in the subjects to be taught.[18] It is difficult to get a handle on this issue, and I shall not try to do so here. It should be noted, however, that the critics of education courses are not necessarily disinterested observers: many are academics who propose replacing education courses with their own. Significantly, the critics rarely advocate state examinations to ascertain the subject-matter competence of prospective teachers. Their failure to do so suggests that their major objective is a larger piece of the academic pie, not improvement in the preparation of teachers.

John Stuart Mill seems to have recognized the dangers of certification as early as 1859:

> It would be giving too dangerous a power to governments, were they allowed to exclude any one from professions, even from the profession of teacher, for alleged deficiency of qualifications; and I think . . . that degrees, or other public certificates of scientific or professional acquirements, should be given to all who present themselves for examination, and stand the test, but that such certificates should confer no advantage over competitors other than the weight which may be attached to their testimony by public opinion.[19]

Even if most institutions of higher education did not have a stake in low standards for prospective teachers, uniformly high standards to enter the teaching profession are out of the question. Of course, public schools employ many highly talented individuals, but consider the numbers. There are approximately ten times as many public school teachers as physicians in the United States. It would be impossible for medical schools to maintain high standards for admission if the number of physicians increased tenfold.

Popular and academic perceptions on this issue appear to be based on the SAT scores of high school juniors who say they would consider careers in education. Some data indicate that prospective teachers rank near the bottom of student groups planning to enter various occupations. However, several large-scale studies present a more favorable picture. One such study indicates that the typical preservice elementary teacher graduated in the top third of his or her high school class, and that this group averaged 898 on the SAT, close to the national average of 906 for all college freshmen. In fact, the average for preservice secondary teachers was 955, significantly higher than the average for all college fresh-men.[20]

Whatever the actual talent level of education majors, there is no realistic prospect of any sizable upward change for a long time to come. Future teachers are composed of many subgroups: preschool, elementary, secondary, special education, and so on. Secondary teachers include teachers of many different subjects. The talent level among teachers is not distributed equally among all these subgroups. Future teachers of mathematics, physics, and/or chemistry have much higher academic aptitude and achievement levels than future teachers of physical education. Not surprisingly, the talent shortages in education are most evident in the specializations that command higher salaries in other fields. For example, individuals who can teach mathematics successfully tend to be persons who can earn more in noneducational positions requiring mathematical aptitude. Inasmuch as institutions of higher education cannot recruit enough prospective teachers in the fields requiring scarce talents, increasing the academic requirements for them is out of the question.

Perhaps nothing better illustrates the naïveté of educational reform rhetoric than the suggestions to raise the level of talent in teaching. The usual way to obtain a higher level of talent is to pay for it. As a practical matter, this cannot be done in education. School districts cannot raise teacher salaries now in order to attract more talented teachers four, six, or ten years in the future. Furthermore, all or most districts in a state or region would have to raise salaries; there is no feasible way to make this happen, except perhaps in a few small states like Hawaii or Rhode Island.

The overwhelming majority of teachers are paid according to their degrees and credits and their years of teaching service; teaching field or grade level taught or teaching effectiveness has nothing to do with salary. A teacher with a bachelor's degree in physics is paid the same as a teacher with a bachelor's degree in physical education or history or elementary education. As long as this policy prevails, the only way to raise salaries for teachers in fields of scarcity is to raise them for all teachers, regardless of subject or talent level required. It is unrealistic to expect 15,000 school boards to do this; with over 80 percent of the nation's teachers employed pursuant to collective bargaining contracts that prohibit salary differentials by teaching field or grade level, it isn't going to happen.

Suppose our nation were to raise the salary level of teachers by 5 percent—not a huge increase and certainly not enough to achieve a major inflow of highly talented persons in fields of shortage. Yet even this modest an increase would require at least 10 billion dollars, and most of it would go to teachers in fields where the supply of qualified teachers is already larger than the demand.

The reality is that the level of talent of teachers is more likely to deteriorate than to go up. Education is predominantly a female occupation: in 1990, 71 percent of all public school teachers and 78 percent of new teachers hired since 1985 were women. At the same time more and more women are entering other professional, technical, and managerial fields. Thus although more women are choosing careers outside the home, noneducational fields are becoming more attractive to highly talented women.

Teacher education is also subject to racial pressures to lower or not to raise its standards. The larger the institution, the more likely it is to be vulnerable to pressure from disadvantaged groups. They add to the pressure to recruit more black and Hispanic teachers even though the pool of qualified minority students cannot possibly meet the demand for them. State departments of education are also subject to this pressure. In 1990 five states reported scholarships or fellowships to recruit future teachers from minorities. Twelve states had some type of loan program for this group and 20 states had some type of special recruitment effort to recruit minorities into teaching.[21] If not halted judicially, this type of legislation is likely to become more widespread. Even if the disadvantaged minorities were not as opposed to testing (of both students and teachers) as they are, the pressure to lower standards would be overwhelming. Inasmuch as the colleges have a large stake in maintaining a supply of students, the conflict between increasing the number of minority teachers and raising standards in teacher education will be resolved in favor of the former. Widespread denials that there is any such conflict are to be expected, but the reality is inescapable.

The sheer number of teachers renders it virtually impossible to raise their levels of compensation. Many reform proposals emphasize the importance of raising the prestige of teachers; in view of the close relationship between compensation and prestige in American society, this will be very difficult. In addition to compensation levels, the prestige of teaching is closely related to its place in the university structure. This in turn depends partly on the role of secondary education in the overall system of education. In European nations, secondary education is viewed as preparation for college. Secondary schools are selective, and they require fewer but more highly qualified teachers. The training of secondary teachers is more likely to be accepted as an appropriate university function.

In contrast, teacher education has little if any prestige in U.S. universities. Some of the most prestigious universities shun it altogether. Most public school teachers are trained in the state colleges, which have less prestige than the public universities. As Burton R. Clark points out: "Among the public universities, a general rule prevails: the higher the status of the university, the less involvement it is likely to have in teacher education," and "The bias against teacher education in U.S. higher education is durable and deeply rooted. No wonder that upper secondary education in the U.S. is in serious trouble."[22]

To summarize, institutions of higher education have their own agendas and their own interests. Other things being equal, they would naturally prefer to have better-qualified students enroll in teacher education programs. Unfortunately, no institution acting on its own can do very much to achieve this result—which will be a long time in coming no matter who is able to achieve it. In the meantime, any significant reduction in the number of students preparing to be teachers would be an immediate disaster. Faced with a choice between policies leading to an immediate disaster and policies that avoid immediate pain, institutions of higher education will choose the latter, regardless of their negative effects on education below the college level.

Antimarket Bias in Higher Education

Higher education is a major obstacle to objective consideration of a K–12 market system of education. One reason is that the governance structure of higher education is based squarely on producer control, and we cannot expect producers to be favorably disposed to systems that challenge that control, if only by suggestion or juxtaposition. A related reason is that the culture of higher education is pervasively hostile to competition in the marketplace. Let me comment first on the implications of the governance structure of higher education for education below the college level.

In general, professors control, and believe that they should control, such matters as standards for admission and graduation; grading policies; personnel selection, promotion, tenure, and dismissal; and most if not all other important policy and personnel issues. The extent of professorial control varies from institution to institution. Even when the faculty does not legally or formally control certain matters, custom or tradition or administrators' fear of faculty dissatisfaction may result in de facto faculty control. Such control, whether de facto or de jure, helps to ensure that professorial interests will take precedence over improving education below the college level.

The critical point is that the dynamics of faculty self-government are similar to the dynamics of any legislative process. If a change, such as the elimination of certain courses, would disadvantage some faculty members, they will actively oppose it. Because the potential losers will participate in future decisions affecting their colleagues, support for policies that would cause pain to other faculty members is a risky business. This is not to say that every faculty member makes every recommendation on the basis of self-interest. That would be as ridiculous as contending that self-interest plays no role whatsoever in faculty self-government. The ideology of higher education assumes that disinterested scholars resolve issues on the basis of the welfare of students, their institution, their profession, and society. The fact that college and university faculty have interests of their own that often affect their recommendations is not so much denied as ignored. Unfortunately, since most of the changes needed in higher education to improve K–12 education would adversely affect many academicians, the changes are extremely difficult to make.[23]

The same dynamics operate at the leadership level. When a university is searching for a new president, faculty search committees ordinarily interview candidates. Every faculty interest group is alert to ensure that the new president supports its interests. Knowing this, candidates avoid positions that could threaten any academic interest group. By the time most candidates reach the top of the greasy pole, they have lost their freedom to act contrary to the wishes of the faculty. Thus absent any strong external pressures it is highly improbable that higher education will change the policies that contribute to the debacle in K–12 education.

A number of distinguished scholars have alleged that an antimarket bias pervades higher education generally. Bertrand de Jouvenal has suggested an interesting explanation of it.[24] According to de Jouvenal, success in a market system depends on responding successfully to what consumers want. Professors, however, are in the business of telling consumers or voters what they should want. The market for advice on what we should want is not a robust one. Most professors in public policy and cultural fields would not make out as well if their services were evaluated by market criteria. Consequently, professors rely on nonmarket criteria for allocating prestige and income. Resentment of market criteria is a matter of course among those whose services are not highly valued on the basis of such criteria.

Notwithstanding de Jouvenal's analysis, institutions of higher education claim to be highly competitive. In certain contexts, such as fundraising, perhaps they are. Still, earlier in this chapter, we saw that our most prestigious institutions of higher education have been forced to discontinue several anticompetitive practices relating to student fees. Unfortunately, the anticompetitive aspects of higher education are not limited to its approach to student fees.

Another anticompetitive aspect is higher education's elaborate credentialing system, with its emphasis on degrees and courses. Still another is the departmental structure in most universities: the idea is that if you are not a member of a certain department, what you say must be irrelevant to its subject matter. To cover up the arrogance of this point of view, much is made of "interdisciplinary" programs—as if combining cartels results in a competitive system.[25]

Note also the inconsistency between intellectual freedom in the real marketplace and in higher education. In the former, if you think of a better product or better way to make one, you prosper and your competition suffers as a result. As noted in Chapter 3, economic progress would be impossible if all producers were protected. Does the nature of higher education justify its status as an exception to the general rule? Should the producers of knowledge be exempt from the rules that govern the producers of widgets or automobiles? Academics argue that they should be an exception, but just about every group of producers tries to protect itself by such claims.

From the standpoint of K–12 education, the way higher education is organized is not the most harmful manifestation of its antimarket bias. Higher education's degradation of work experience and of jobs that do not require a college education is even more destructive. Thus academics are quick to put down "flipping hamburgers" as the kind of low-wage, unskilled, dead-end work that will be the fate of youth who lack a college education. Yet as Ben Wildavsky and others have shown, McDonald's, which hires one of every fifteen first-time job searchers in the United States, operates a large-scale training and employment program that has provided a tremendous number of managerial positions for young people shunted aside by academic institutions.[26]

Notwithstanding its prestige and its resources, I doubt whether higher education can avoid an agonizing reappraisal by the American people. As one observer comments:

> The market for ideas is the market in which the intellectual conducts his trade . . . Self-esteem leads the intellectuals to magnify the importance of their own market. That others should be regulated seems natural, particularly as many of the intellectuals see themselves as doing the regulating. But self-interest combines with self-esteem to ensure that while others are regulated, that regulation should not apply to themselves . . . It may not be a nice explanation but I can think of no other for this strange situation.[27]

Thus far, higher education has managed to avoid accountability for the K–12 debacle it has done so much to create. Still, as John Dewey sagely observed, once people start thinking, it is impossible to predict where they will stop.

11
≈ Educational Research
   and Development

Research and development in education differ profoundly from research and development in the private sector. Because advocates of R&D in education typically cite its productive role in the private sector, let me begin with a brief summary of the process in that sector. There is no single pattern, but the process typically includes the following elements:

1. *Basic research* that expands opportunities for either process or product innovation.
2. *Invention,* which can be regarded as the discovery of technological advances and the development of working models.
3. *Innovation,* which includes the establishment of facilities for large-scale production. Innovation is usually the most costly phase of R&D, amounting to approximately 65 percent of R&D investments in the private sector from 1960 to 1985.[1]
4. *Diffusion,* which is the process of adoption by users.

All of these stages are interactive; for example, the diffusion stage often leads to new inventions. We should also recognize that most "restructuring" of private enterprise results from the technological changes emerging from R&D. For instance, without computer technology, air travel would be a very different industry: the technology affects airplane performance, safety, schedules, routes, ticket prices, maintenance, and every other phase of the industry.

During the period when public education was being widely established, no attention was paid to educational R&D. As a matter of fact, the leading history of U.S. education does not even mention the subject.[2] Today, however, interest groups based largely in higher education advocate increased federal appropriations for educational R&D. One recent development underscores their success in this regard.

Institutions of higher education frequently receive grants or enter into contracts to conduct research. In general, the funds received for this purpose are divided into direct and indirect costs. The direct costs are the costs incurred specifically for a research project. The indirect costs are overhead costs that are charged to the project but not incurred solely by it. For example, a research project adds to the work load of the university's business office, research is conducted in buildings that depreciate, and campus security costs may increase.

All such indirect costs are usually covered by adding an overhead rate to the direct costs. If the direct costs are $1 million and the overhead rate is 50 percent, the university receives a contract for $1.5 million. Understandably, universities set their overhead rates as high as the traffic will bear. A striking example of this received national publicity in 1991 as a result of a federal investigation of Stanford University. Stanford's overhead rate of 74 percent was among the highest in the nation. Federal audits revealed that Stanford had been fully or partially reimbursed for the following expenses:

$707,737	expense of operating a shopping mall for profit
$218,230	operating expenses, chancellor's home, 1986–1990 (chancellor had died in 1985)
$184,286	depreciation on yacht used for recreation by students and faculty (Stanford had paid $100,000 for the yacht)
$45,250	retreat for board of trustees at Lake Tahoe
$24,000	fresh flowers $2,000 per month
$1,300	upkeep of tomb of Leland Stanford, wife, and son
$1,200	antique commode.

These items are just a sample of the expenses for which Stanford had been partially reimbursed from federal funds for "research." In 1990 Stanford had received approximately $240 million in research funds from the federal government. As a result of the investigation, its overhead rate was reduced to 55.5 percent. After all, since a university, not a defense contractor, was involved, any overcharging must have been "inadvertent error," not criminal fraud. Meanwhile, several of the nation's other elite universities suddenly discovered that they were overcharging the federal government for indirect costs, and acted "voluntarily" to lower their overhead charges. Clearly, universities have received billions in indefensible research charges over the years.[3]

In any event, academics who assert the importance of research are not necessarily disinterested parties. On the contrary, many are dependent on research grants and contracts for a comfortable if not lavish level of support. In their eyes, the policy problem is always how to persuade others to spend more for "research."

Overcharging for indirect costs is strong evidence of producer domination; under a truly competitive system, such overcharging could not have continued for so long on such a large scale. The underlying problem is a clear conflict of interest. On the one hand, universities are supposed to be centers of research. On the other hand, research is needed on how well universities are performing this function. As is illustrated by the overcharging for indirect costs, universities and public schools share a common characteristic. Both are very unlikely to inform their consumers about their deficiencies as producers.

In education as in other fields, the outcome of R&D may be either a process innovation or a product innovation. Process innovations are changes in the way factors of production transform inputs into outputs; product innovations are new goods. In the following discussion, however, I shall use the phrases "policy research" and "educational technology" instead of "process innovation" and "product innovation." Although not precisely equivalent, the terms to be used are widely accepted in education and used in the relevant educational literature.

As used here, policy research is a very broad category. It includes program evaluation, research on teaching methods, evaluation of policies such as the age limit for compulsory education, surveys, legislative analysis, and research on school governance, to cite just a few examples. As long as education is provided by public schools, virtually every aspect of it is a public policy. This being the case, policy research is an extremely broad field, with no obvious limit on claims for public financial support.

In practice, technological innovation and policy research may be closely related, even interdependent. An instructional technology, such as computer assisted instruction (CAI), may be cost-effective if policies requiring the presence of teachers in classrooms can be changed. Policies governing the legal liabilities of school boards or insurance coverage may also have to be changed. Similarly, the use of new security technology may require new policies on school security. A great deal of policy research, however, has no direct bearing on technology.

Funding for Policy Research

In the private sector, R&D is based on the anticipation that companies will eventually profit from it. This incentive is lacking in public education; school districts have no reason to fund R&D when the benefits would go largely to pupils outside the district. This is especially true when the district contribution does not affect the viability of the project. In short, school districts tend to be "free riders" when it comes to educational R&D.

The free rider problem is not the only obstacle to school district investment in R&D. Politicians (including school board members) prefer immediate benefits whose costs are paid by future generations—that is, after the politicians who enacted the benefits have left public office. Legislation that inflicts immediate pain for long-deferred benefits is politically unattractive. The controversies over reducing the federal deficit illustrate this point. So does the fact that school districts, like government agencies generally, underfund maintenance of facilities and equipment.[4] When teachers threaten to strike unless the district raises salaries, it is difficult for school officials to adopt a long-range view of spending priorities. Obviously, if districts underfund maintenance of existing facilities, they are even more likely to underfund educational R&D. With the latter, there is no assurance of a return on investment, and any such return, in whatever form it takes, will not materialize for several years, if indeed it ever does. To expect parents and teachers to accept such expenditures while immediate needs, as they perceive them, are not met is to expect the politically impossible. We should also note that district budgets are usually insufficient to fund R&D that would be useful elsewhere.

Finally, even in the unlikely event that a school district did invest in R&D, and did develop an innovation that could be utilized by other districts, the dissemination problems would be formidable. In the private sector, companies have sales and marketing divisions to sell the products and services resulting from R&D. School districts do not have sales managers or marketing divisions. A few school districts sell instructional materials developed from district funding, but such materials constitute an insignificant share of the market for instructional materials. If school districts had a larger market share, private publishers would undoubtedly protest the unfair competition from government.

All of these considerations also inhibit investment in educational R&D by state governments. With over half of school district revenues coming from state aid, it would be more logical for state governments than local school districts to invest in educational R&D. Nevertheless, each state would recognize that the productivity of educational R&D would not be materially affected by its own contribution. This being the case, the rational course of state action is to be a free rider. In addition, all the other reasons not to invest in educational R&D apply to state governments: they also are under severe pressure to spend for immediate tangible benefits, not uncertain long-range ones.

This brings us to the argument for increased federal spending for educational R&D. Except for possible use of U.S. innovations by other nations, federal support for educational R&D avoids the free rider problem. It also substantially reduces the political problems inherent in state and local expenditures for long-range benefits. Federal expenditures for educational R&D are only a minuscule proportion of the federal budget, and thus are less vulnerable politically. In addition, the federal government funds R&D in several fields, so funding for educational R&D is consistent with federal practice generally. A few hundred million dollars in the federal budget is hardly noticeable, whereas much smaller amounts are visible and vulnerable targets in state and local budgets.

These factors help to explain why educational policy research found a home in the federal government. In the 1960s and 1970s, federal agencies initiated several programs to improve education. Congress and the executive branch sought feedback on the efficacy of these programs. Understandably, evaluation of them required a national approach; a program such as Head Start might be effective in one area but not in another. Since then, most federally funded research has been related to federal legislation, actual or contemplated. It is highly debatable, however, whether the research issues that receive federal support are the issues that deserve priority from an educational standpoint.

It comes as no surprise that educational organizations support increased federal funding for educational R&D. The American Educational Research Association (AERA), the professional organization of educational researchers, is especially active in this regard. In 1990 AERA enrolled over 16,000 members, most of them college professors of education. In testimony on the president's 1991 budget request, Gerald E. Sroufe, AERA's Director of Governmental and Professional Liaison, asserted that "there is too little research because there is too little funding."[5] This point of view is widely accepted within the field of education, as it is in every field of research. Notwithstanding this acceptance, it is a highly questionable position.

Generally speaking, the advocates of increased federal spending for educational R&D avoid the subject of total spending for it. The impression they convey is that if not for federal funding, educational R&D would be starved for lack of funds. Educational researchers also avoid the role of commercialization, which is the most effective means of translating R&D into benefits for consumers. In fact what we already spend for educational research is grossly underestimated, and its benefits are grossly exaggerated.[6]

In my opinion, the "more funds are needed" approach is egregiously misleading. For one thing, a staggering amount is spent for educational research by institutions of higher education. These institutions employ approximately 35,000 professors of education, the overwhelming majority of whom claim to be devoting at least some of their professional time to educational research. According to recent surveys, 10 to 20 percent of faculty time in departments of education is allocated to research; for purposes of discussion, I shall assume that education faculty members devote 14 percent of their time to educational R&D.[7] This would be a reasonable if not conservative estimate for the institutions in which I have been employed: Emory University, University of Illinois, Oklahoma University, Yeshiva University, Hofstra University, Rhode Island College, University of Hawaii, City University of New York, University of Southern California, Ohio University, and University of Pennsylvania. University policies and surveys on work load at these institutions usually allocated more professorial time to research.

True, some professors of education conduct research on the problems of higher education or on other issues outside of K–12 education. This group, however, is probably exceeded by the number of professors in other fields whose research pertains to K–12 education. For example, the most outstanding research on equality of educational opportunity and on comparisons of public to private schools was conducted by James S. Coleman, a professor of sociology.[8] Studies of the economics of education have been conducted by prominent professors of economics; similarly, scholars in psychology, child development, law, nutrition, public administration, and school finance often focus on educational problems.

As a rough estimate, the dollar value of education faculty time spent on research in 1988 was about $375 million.[9] Faculty time is not the only resource devoted to educational research in institutions of higher education. Doctoral dissertations are supposed to be based on research. Time spent working on doctoral dissertations must also be included in estimates of the resources devoted to educational research. From 1971 to 1988, institutions of higher education awarded an average of 7,300 doctoral degrees in education annually.[10] The recipients of these degrees are mainly public school teachers and administrators or faculty members teaching education courses in institutions of higher education.

Generally speaking, a doctoral dissertation is supposed to require one year of full-time work. There are reasons to rely on higher or lower estimates, but one year's work is a reasonable estimate. Let us assume that the value of the time spent per degree recipient averaged $45,000 per year.[11] On this basis, the value of graduate student time devoted to educational research exceeds $328 million annually. Granted, some student time is outside the scope of elementary and secondary education, even broadly conceived; but the estimate does not include the value of the time spent on educational research by graduate students in psychology, child development, social work, economics, and other fields related to public education.

In addition to the research conducted in institutions of higher education, considerable amounts are spent for this purpose by nonprofit organizations outside academia. The philanthropic foundations appropriate substantial amounts every year for educational R&D. These funds are allocated to a wide range of educational organizations, state departments of education, institutions of higher education, nonprofit organizations, school districts, and individuals. It is not always clear whether a particular grant or contract should be categorized as educational R&D, but the ones that should probably amount to hundreds of millions annually.[12] Some of it goes to institutions of higher education, where it pays for professorial time that might otherwise be used for duties other than research.

To illustrate, the most highly publicized study of school effectiveness in recent years was sponsored by the Brookings Institution.[13] This study was funded by federal as well as foundation funds, but Brookings provided most of its support. The principal investigators were a full-time employee of Brookings and a Stanford professor of political science. Similarly, the Educational Testing Service (ETS) is a nonprofit organization that spends millions annually for educational R&D.[14] In addition, many persons who work in educational R&D are employed by school districts, state departments of education, or nonprofit organizations with research interests. The dollar value of their time devoted to educational R&D is undoubtedly substantial.

Educational research is also conducted in other countries. Of course, a great deal of this research, even if of high quality, would not be useful in the United States, but some of it would be. Such research is often disseminated internationally by means of books and journals. There are also expenditures for educational R&D by companies that sell instructional materials and other products and services to the education market; these will be discussed when I take up technological innovation.

This discussion strongly suggests that lack of funding is not the main obstacle, or even a major obstacle, to productive educational R&D. To be sure, funding may not be available for scores of worthwhile projects. Still, we must face the fact that billions have been spent on educational R&D, especially in the past thirty-five years, but that we have relatively little to show for it.

Despite this dismal track record, some prominent business leaders also recommend larger federal appropriations for educational R&D. For example, David F. Kearns, a former CEO of Xerox Corporation who was appointed under-secretary of education in June 1991, expressed such support in 1968:

> The federal government's role in education is limited, and should continue to be so. but within that limited role, the federal government should do more than it does . . .
>
> Public education is a $150-billion-dollar-a-year business, but the federal government spends only $100 million on research to support it. At least three times that amount should be appropriated for research on school and classroom organization, learning theories, and instructional techniques and emerging educational technologies.[15]

Kearns greatly underestimated federal appropriations for educational R&D, perhaps because he failed to include expenditures outside the Department of Education. More important, he ignored nonfederal spending for educational R&D when he urged increased federal spending for it. The question that needs to be addressed is not how to generate higher federal appropriations for educational research and development. It is why is there so little return from the huge investment already being made by the federal government, institutions of higher education, philanthropic foundations, and other organizations and agencies trying to improve public education. Let me defer my answer to this question until we have also considered R&D on technological innovation.

Research on Educational Technology

Technology is a wild card in our educational situation. Although the following discussion will focus on educational technology, technology of a more general nature could also have major implications for education. Chapter 2 pointed out that since the Industrial Revolution most men work away from home and that more and more women have begun to do so in recent years. Today, however, current and anticipated technology are making it possible for more adults to work at home. If large numbers of adults should do so, we could experience significant increases in home schooling and/or in children's social capital.

Some analysts believe that educational technology will revolutionize education. Others contend that technology will be helpful but not the basis for restructuring education. The skeptics point to educational television to illustrate a long list of innovations that turned out to be much less "revolutionary" than their advocates predicted.

My belief is that educational technology, or technology that applies to education, will have major effects on all the issues discussed in this book, but I do not anticipate these effects until early in the twenty-first century. It is part of my argument that we cannot take full advantage of educational technology under public education; while technology has the potential to improve education, public education is not conducive to its utilization. It is nonetheless possible that developments in educational technology could greatly accelerate the change to a market system of education.

My point of departure is an analysis of educational R&D by Lewis J. Perelman.[16] Perelman is one of the few analysts who regard the absence of technological innovation in education as a major problem. This conclusion is based on the labor intensive nature of education. A study by the Office of Technology Assessment (OTA), an agency established by Congress, found education and social work to be our most labor-intensive industries: their labor costs amounted to 93 percent of output value, compared to 54 percent for all private business.[17] Perelman points out that education's productivity not only is low but is declining. From 1950 to 1989, the dollar cost of education, adjusted for inflation, quadrupled, while at best, quality of output did not improve and enrollments were stationary or declining.

As Perelman sees it, the low productivity is due to the lack of investment in technology. As evidence, he cites the OTA study's conclusion that capital investment per employee is only $1,000 per employee in education, whereas it is about $50,000 for the U.S. economy as a whole and runs as high as $300,000 or more in some high-tech industries. Even other labor-intensive industries show capital investment of $7,000 to $20,000 per employee.

As bad as this situation appears to be, Perelman argues that the data grossly understate our underinvestment in educational technology. The reason is that *"Education is the only business in which the consumer does the essential work."*[18] That is, the activity of students ultimately determines the productivity of education. If students are counted as workers, the situation becomes drastically worse: capital investment in education should be counted as $100–$200 instead of $1,000 per worker.

Perelman then turns to the R&D gap that allegedly underlies the lack of investment in educational technology. Depending on what is counted as research, the U.S. Department of Education spent between $136 million and $388 million for research in FY 1989. Only about $1 million of this was spent to develop advanced instructional technology. In contrast, the Department of Defense spent about $200 million for instructional technology, and the National Science Foundation spent about $15 million just for research on teaching science and mathematics.[19]

According to the OTA assessment, the education sector invests less than 1.0 percent of its total revenues in R&D. Nationally, expenditures for R&D are 2.5 percent of GNP; the figure for the average firm is 2 percent of sales. In the high-tech information-based industries, the investment in R&D is much higher. For example, *Business Week* found that the five leading firms in computer software and services spent 16–29 percent of their revenues on R&D. Whereas education spent less than $50 per employee on R&D, these five companies spent $30,000 to $42,000 per employee.[20] Inasmuch as spending for R&D per employee appears to be a reliable predictor of business success, this gap between education and the rest of the economy raises some basic issues. Perelman concludes that: "In essence, the public school is America's collective farm. Innovation and productivity are lacking in American education for basically the same reasons they are scarce in Soviet agriculture: absence of competitive, market forces."[21]

If Perelman's conclusion is valid, and I believe it is, educational R&D presents a paradoxical situation. On the one hand, it includes a heavily overfunded sector devoted to policy research serving producers. On the other hand, it includes an extremely underfunded sector devoted to educational technology. In my opinion, both of these conclusions are accurate and both result from the same cause, to wit, the fact that education is funded, provided, and regulated by public agencies. A brief analysis of the structural problems of policy research, and of R&D on educational technology, will help to clarify this point.

The Role of Incentives

Essentially, expenditures for R&D in education are isolated from the environment that justifies such expenditures in the private sector. In the latter, producers have entrepreneurial incentives to develop productive innovations. These incentives are largely absent from educational R&D. In their absence, it can be argued plausibly that we are overspending on educational R&D.

A recent book by James S. Coleman helps to explain the critical role of incentives in policy research. As Coleman points out, the academic leaders in his own field, sociology, emphasized research on urban groups and urban problems. They assumed that if their research exposed deplorable conditions, various policymakers would remedy these conditions. This did not happen. The reason is that research is used by policymakers primarily to legitimize what they are doing. When research indicates the desirability of changing policies, it is used primarily by those who want to change the policies. Policy research is also used when policymakers are divided on the relevant issues, or when policymakers want to persuade public and legislative opinion that policy changes are needed. In such situations, policy research may be a source of support. On the other hand, policy research is ignored by policymakers who feel no pressure to legitimize their policies. Research also tends to be ignored, unfunded, or even defunded if it points in politically unpopular directions.[22]

Coleman's analysis explains why a great deal of university research is never utilized. It contrasts sharply with the academic perception that users just aren't aware of all the useful research that exists. In line with this view, the U.S. Department of Education established the Educational Research Information Center (ERIC). Under the ERIC system, interested parties can feed their research into the system, or access the system to locate research on topics of interest. Essentially, it is an electronic retrieval system.

The main users of ERIC are professors and graduate students, not school district personnel seeking answers to practical questions. The system does not function like a practitioner-oriented medical information system, in which doctors feed in certain symptoms and get back a menu of tests and possibilities. Very few teachers use the ERIC system this way, and even school administrators are not heavy users of the system. As in most other fields, professional journals appear to be the main source of information for teachers and administrators.

Differences in incentive systems explain the differences in use of the ERIC system. Professorial promotions, salaries, and tenure depend partly on research and publication. These activities require cognizance of prior research on whatever a professor may be investigating. In contrast, teachers and administrators lack incentives to access the ERIC system. The possibility that research could be helpful on a pedagogical problem is insufficient incentive for most public school personnel to use the ERIC system.

Another weakness of educational research is the absence of continuous interaction between its producers and consumers. Market research in the for-profit sector avoids this weakness. As production and consumption in the United States became oriented to national instead of local markets, producers needed new kinds of information. The communications industries, advertisers, and producers needed to answer new kinds of questions. The audiences they were trying to reach were national, hence the questions were national in scope. How many people listened to radio programs at certain times? What were their demographic and cultural characteristics? How did they react to various advertising approaches? And so on.

Market research emerged in order to answer these kinds of questions. It is a research industry outside of higher education. Its research is producer oriented; producers pay for it and use it extensively. In contrast, as Coleman points out, the early policy research that was acclaimed among academicians did not have a major impact on policy. Coleman concludes that its ineffectiveness was due to its isolation from the parties who would have to use the research. The assumption that good policy research would somehow come to the attention of policymakers and be used by them was simply unrealistic.

Similarly, the incentives to develop the ERIC system in education did not emanate primarily from teachers and school districts. They emanated primarily from professors, that is, other producers of information. Research in education is used, but primarily by other researchers; it does not inform and guide practitioners. In the private sector, researchers put corporate funds (hence their own jobs) at risk. In contrast, professorial research places only taxpayer and/or donor funds at risk. As we might expect, corporate-sponsored research is more focused and more subject to scrutiny by potential users. Ultimately, such research has to improve the corporation's bottom line. Professorial research is usually evaluated by other professors who have no significant stake in the outcome; understandably, it tends to lack the rigor and focus of research in the for-profit sector.

In the field of education, as in the social sciences generally, each individual professor decides what topics to investigate. Under these circumstances, it is extremely difficult to apply a critical mass of research talent to a major issue. In the private sector, companies can direct a large number of experts to focus on the same research problem. Thus the private sector has the advantages of scale as well as of focus and accountability.

In certain fields, such as biomedicine and agriculture, university research funded by government does seem to be productive. In such cases, however, factors that do not prevail in education are important. In biomedicine, pharmaceutical companies have commercial incentives to convert basic research into viable products. These incentives are lacking in public education. In agriculture, farmer-owners welcome research and labor-saving technology, since it enhances their producer benefits. In education, in contrast, the teacher unions not only oppose the introduction of any such technology; they are adamantly opposed to R&D that might lead to it. Also, research on human behavior seems to be less productive generally than research on physical processes. One can debate how the lines are drawn and point to exceptions, but research on topics of interest to educators, such as student incentives, has not been especially productive. This point also applies to research outside the school setting; for example, employee motivations and incentives have been studied extensively, but managers do not know much more about these matters than they did generations ago.

Earlier I estimated the annual value of graduate student time devoted to educational research as about $328 million. The output contributes very little that is or should be of interest to policymakers. A brief look at the dynamics of doctoral dissertations helps to explain this waste of resources.

Among professors and institutions of higher education, the ability to attract doctoral students is important from several standpoints. One is economic; institutions may benefit financially from professors and programs that enroll large numbers of doctoral students. To compete with other institutions, universities arrange the process of earning a doctoral degree to be as convenient as possible for students; the institution's academic reputation and financial situation usually affect the dissertation requirements.

Typically, advising doctoral candidates or serving on dissertation committees is part of professional work loads. From the student's standpoint, the doctoral degree—the piece of paper, as it were—is far more important than any skill or knowledge it supposedly represents. They need the degree to be eligible for many middle- or upper-level positions in education. To students, the requirement is simply a hurdle to be overcome; they naturally prefer the dissertation topic most likely to be completed and approved in the shortest possible time. Whether the topic is substantively important is of secondary interest, or of no interest at all. Indeed, this is often true about the professorial perspective as well; increasing university income is usually much more important than the production of useful research. Anyone who doubts this should check the titles and use of dissertations from institutions that award large numbers of doctoral degrees.

Professors usually have wide latitude in deciding what dissertation topics are acceptable. They can easily arrange research topics that contribute to their courses, or their business or consulting interests, or whatever interests them at the moment. For example, many professors moonlight as arbitrators or mediators in labor disputes. Consequently, their doctoral students frequently end up writing dissertations about these processes but rarely select dissertation topics that would challenge the desirability of collective bargaining. After all, professors who evince doubts about its desirability are not likely to be selected as arbitrators. Meanwhile, taxpayers who supposedly benefit from research do not have the vaguest idea of what is happening to their tax dollars.

In addition, policy research suffers from political pressures that are not to be underestimated. In the private sector, R&D priorities are set by market forces and market opportunities. In contrast, political factors often play a dominant role in research funded by government. This applies to technical and scientific as well as policy research. For years, Congress has been earmarking research funds in the field of health care. As this happens, political clout, not technical expertise, becomes the dominant factor in awarding federal R&D contracts and grants. The same process is operative in education. Unfortunately, the astute researchers, in health care, education, or any other field, are not necessarily constituents of the most powerful Congressmen.

Political considerations often determine the issues selected for research and even the research outcomes. Of the $60 million appropriated for R&D by the U.S. Department of Education in FY 1990, $50 million was for studies mandated by Congress. Naturally, the congressional sponsors of legislation are gratified by a favorable evaluation of it. Individuals and organizations seeking research funds are well aware of this, as are Department of Education officials who contract for the research. Congressmen and Department of Education officials are not likely to promote research that discredits congressional policies and programs. The modus operandi of some companies conducting research under contract is not deliberate falsification of results but subtle accommodations that can have the same effect. Plausible but misleading questions can be asked. Research results can be reported in ways that are technically defensible but do not really explain anything. Potentially embarrassing issues may not be raised.

Coleman cites a timely example of this tendency: the research on the efficiency of job training programs for minority youth.[23] The usual way of evaluating such programs is to investigate the number of participants who were employed as the result of the program. This number is then treated as the measure of program effectiveness. Suppose, however, that the participants merely replaced other employees. In that case, the program would not have enhanced employment; it would merely have changed the identity of the employed and the unemployed. And even if job training programs achieved some additional employment, the full cost of doing so would have to be taken into account in a realistic evaluation of the program. The costs would include not only the dollars appropriated for the program but the effects of higher taxes on employment and productivity. Upon being informed that 90 percent of the participants in a job training program were subsequently employed, most people would conclude that the program was successful; actually, it might not be successful even if every participant were subsequently employed.

The Prospects for Improving Policy Research

The foregoing analysis strongly suggests that research on educational policy is largely a waste of resources. The prospects for improvement are dim. The research arrangements governing professors of education cannot be changed in isolation from those governing research in other academic fields, and no change in these arrangements is in sight. Similarly, we cannot exclude political considerations from publicly funded educational research while such considerations play a dominant role in other fields. Finally, the argument for more funding of educational policy research rests upon some dubious assumptions about research personnel. The argument assumes a cadre of competent personnel, stymied in their research due to a lack of funds. Even if this assumption is valid (which is doubtful), some questions remain. In view of the tremendous waste of research funds, how can we be confident that increased appropriations would go to the researchers who would use the funds productively? Why is there so little effort to use existing funds more effectively? Let us not forget that in 1969, the National Academy of Education issued a report calling for increased funding of educational research. Its call was granted, but the results have fallen far short of the expectations. No doubt some qualified researchers could use additional funding, but this is always true in every field.

In short, it is questionable whether additional federal funding would generate more useful policy research. What we can do, however, is to convert the public policy questions into market issues. Let me use class size as an example of how to do this. Class size has been the subject of thousands of books, articles, dissertations, term papers, school district memoranda, organizational resolutions, and reform reports. Next to the level of teacher salaries, it is the most important factor affecting school costs. Differences in class size are cited to demonstrate inequality of educational opportunity, and limits on class size are a major objective of teacher unions at the bargaining table. Federal funds for disadvantaged children are sometimes used to reduce their class size, and other important dimensions could be cited.

The research on class size indicates that within broad limits, reducing class size does not result in significant gains in pupil achievement. To achieve even modest gains, classes would have to be smaller, and the costs would be prohibitive. Furthermore, as class size is reduced, more teachers are needed, exacerbating the problem of maintaining teacher quality. Generally speaking, therefore, smaller classes benefit teachers, not pupils.

When a U.S. Department of Education report drew this conclusion in 1988, the presidents of the NEA and the AFT charged that educational research was being politicized. In fact, both prior and subsequent researchers who could not reasonably be regarded as politically motivated reached the same conclusion. Of course, restrictions on class size can sometimes be justified on grounds of teacher welfare, but the teacher unions virtually always characterize smaller classes as a pupil benefit. Parenthetically, smaller classes appear to benefit disadvantaged pupils the most, but smaller classes for the disadvantaged would be inconsistent with the opposition to tracking.

How would class size be resolved in a market system? Let us assume that school X and school Y are competing for students. School Y tries to take advantage of its larger class size by charging lower tuition. Parents will now have a choice.

School X	School Y
Tuition: $3,500	Tuition: $2,500
Class size: 20	Class size: 25

School Y will claim that its lower tuition does not lead to any impairment of educational achievement. School X will no doubt challenge Y's claim. Over time, Y will have to produce the evidence or lose enrollments. If Y can substantiate its claim, X will be forced to increase its class size to compete. The issue is resolved through market, not political, processes.

Meanwhile, what will happen to the professors who conduct research on class size? There is no need for them to do so at public expense. If they conduct such research, it will be as employees of educational companies. They may be employed to find out what mix of price and class size and anticipated educational achievement would increase the company's market share. Their research may be more useful than it was in the past, but it will not be conducted on the public payroll.

The same process would apply to most other policy issues that are debated among academics. Initially, schools would operate according to the various positions in these debates. Over time, market forces would resolve either the merits or parent preferences concerning these various positions. School boards and state officials would no longer impose their views on everyone on the basis of research by academics who do not suffer the consequences of their errors.

Perhaps nothing better demonstrates the fatuousness of "educational reform" than the widespread attention to "restructuring." With professional help at hand, school districts everywhere are "restructuring." In practice, "restructuring" consists of applying a new label to conventional changes. My favorite example is from the Los Angeles Unified School District, where the superintendent disseminated a list of actions being taken to "restructure" school district operations. One such action was that schools could buy postage directly from the post office instead of by requisition from the district purchasing office![24]

In for-profit enterprises, restructuring is usually the result of technological change. In public education, however, teachers, school administrators, and academics equate restructuring with administrative or managerial changes totally unrelated to technological change. An effort to "restructure" public education in the 1950s failed for precisely this reason. During those years, there was considerable attention to "team teaching." Educational experts pointed out a critical difference between teachers and physicians. The latter are supported by a wide range of medical occupations—nurses, pharmacists, X-ray technicians, nutritionists, laboratory technicians, and so on. In contrast, teachers do it all—supposedly with the result that "professional" teachers end up doing work that should be performed by sub-professionals. Generously supported by foundation grants, especially from the Ford Foundation, several school districts plunged into "team teaching" and "differentiated staffing."

Predictably, the entire effort was a fiasco. The reason we have X-ray technicians is that there are X-ray machines; without the technology, the occupations based on it would not exist. This may seem obvious, but one would never know it from the educational scene. School districts are "restructuring" simply by applying the label to every managerial or administrative change, regardless of the directions they take.

More than seventy years ago William Hurrell Mallock pointed out several instances in which governments refused to support R&D that eventually turned out to be enormously productive.[25] In some cases, governments actually blocked the necessary R&D, either because of failure to appreciate its possibilities or because of pressure from interest groups. Of course, companies for profit have sometimes turned down opportunities to develop immensely successful innovations; for example, several major corporations failed to take advantage of opportunities to develop the technology that led to Xerox and other copying technology. The difference is that mistakes are more likely to be recognized and corrected promptly in a market system. The paucity of inventions and patents from nations without market economies provides impressive confirmation of this point. More to the point, so does educational R&D in the United States.

Reference has already been made to James S. Coleman's landmark study of equality of educational opportunity. Once it became clear that the study's conclusions challenged instead of supported government policies, the government agencies that sponsored the research tried to bury it. First they tried to distort it; as Coleman tells it, "We had many . . . battles to fight with agency officials who did not like the results we had achieved, many problems in merely maintaining the integrity of the research report in the face of attempts to rewrite it."[26]

Inasmuch as education is a highly labor-intensive industry, it might be expected that educational research would focus on ways of reducing this dependence. This is the normal pattern of R&D in other labor-intensive industries. Such research could take a variety of forms in education. For instance, to what extent does the presence of a certified teacher affect educational achievement? If research revealed that some of the work done by $40,000-a-year teachers could be performed as effectively by $15,000-a-year paraprofessionals, the savings could be enormous. Nevertheless, very little research is conducted on any such ways of increasing efficiency.

This neglect clearly has a political basis. In the 1970s teacher unions adamantly opposed federally funded experiments on contracting out instruction. The unions forced the research projects to adopt restrictions that crippled them educationally and destroyed their viability as experiments about anything.[27] Subsequently, federal R&D projects in education have avoided labor-saving issues. Educational research funded by the U.S. Department of Education is caught in a insoluble dilemma. On the one hand, the labor-intensive nature of education suggests the desirability of R&D devoted to reducing its labor intensity. On the other hand, the NEA and the AFT are the major political supporters of research funding—and are adamantly opposed to research that has the potential to reduce the required quantity or skill level of educational workers. It's as if the automobile industry depended on the United Auto Workers for research on labor-saving technology in the automobile industry. There is no explicit Faustian bargain, but there is no need for one. The educational research community avoids issues that might displease the teacher unions, and the latter support educational research insofar as it does not threaten union influence in any way.

Government funding cannot consistently overcome the political obstacles to R&D that threatens powerful interest groups. The exceptions do not justify reliance on a system so vulnerable to political considerations. In any event, it is futile to adopt private-sector levels of investment in R&D isolated from the profitmaking context in which they are effective. Anyone who doubts this need only compare the advances in services provided by the private sector with those in services provided by public school teachers. Transportation, food service, data processing, communications—in all of these cases and countless others, the improvements in services provided privately are clearly visible. In instruction, however, schools operate much as they did fifty years ago. In many cases, schools have even failed to adopt instructional technology that is widely used in the private sector; the incentives to do so are lacking.

In education, the fact that research is not proprietary is viewed in a positive light. After all, who would be so selfish as to deprive children of a better way to read in order to make a profit? And because most professors work for government or nonprofit institutions, neither they nor their institutions have an entrepreneurial stake in the research they do. This is changing in some scientific and technical fields but not in education.

The contrast in outcomes is remarkable. Researchers in for-profit companies tend to publish their research when their company manufactures and markets a product based on the research, if they publish it at all. To publish the results before then would alert the competition and give it a free ride on the research conducted to date. When research is finally published, however, it is scrutinized by government agencies and competing companies. In many fields, such as pharmaceuticals and auto safety, mistakes and deliberate deception are costly—sometimes very costly. For these reasons, research in the for-profit sector is more likely to be accurate and thorough. Of course there are instances to the contrary, but we are considering central tendencies.

In academe, the pressure is to publish as often and as soon as possible. Salaries, promotions, and tenure often depend on the frequency of publication. There is no proprietary interest in the research, and there are strong personal incentives to publish it. Often poor research gets as much credit as good research, sometimes more. Academics like to refer to higher education as "a marketplace of ideas." This confuses support among professors, who have their own agendas and seldom suffer the consequences of their errors, with support from consumers who pay cash for their decisions.

Producer Bias in Educational Research

As Coleman points out, policy research generally serves producer rather than consumer interests. For example, as college admissions expanded and colleges received admission requests from a national instead of a local base, the colleges needed better mechanisms to evaluate applications. This led to the establishment of the Scholastic Aptitude Test, now administered by ETS to millions of high school students every year. In effect, a relatively small number of colleges with a permanent interest in the SAT generated the R&D needed to establish it.

The decision of which college to attend is much more important to the students than to the colleges that accept or reject them. Why is there not research that would enable students to evaluate colleges? One reason is that it is much easier for a small number of colleges to act cooperatively in their own interests than for millions of students to do so. True, several handbooks purport to rate colleges. Aside from the fact that most of their information is provided by the colleges themselves, the college guides are not based on R&D remotely comparable in funding or quality to the R&D that underlies the SAT. Similarly, there is little if any research on how parents can evaluate teachers and schools and educational services.[28]

In the private sector, consumer feedback plays a critically important role in shaping R&D. When a new product is introduced (often after considerable market research and field testing), the producers may be unaware of certain problems or of opportunities to improve it. Competition for consumers helps to address these problems, but it is absent from public education. Parental complaints are difficult to present, especially in large school districts. Collective bargaining contracts severely limit the time parents can talk to teachers. Grades and report cards conceal more than they inform. Political processes, such as school board elections and meetings, are a poor substitute for the interaction and feedback that characterizes R&D in the private sector. Sales data, customer surveys, warranties, and customer hotlines are some of the ways market systems generate information that is used to benefit consumers. In education, private schools are much more active than public schools in conducting this kind of research.

A 1991 report entitled *Research and the Renewal of Education,* sponsored by the National Academy of Education (NAE), unwittingly confirms the producer bias in educational research. NAE characterizes its seventy-five members as "renowned educational leaders or researchers." At least twenty of the members are on the faculty at Harvard, Stanford, the University of Chicago, or Teachers College, Columbia University. A codirector of the report, Diane Ravitch, was appointed assistant secretary of education for educational research and improvement shortly after the report was released. Because of its sponsorship, the NAE report can be regarded as an authoritative expression of mainstream educational thinking about educational research. The following analysis consists of my reactions to various aspects of the report.

1. On funding and support, the report "recommends that overall research funding for education be increased from current expenditures. Today education receives only about one half a percent of the total aggregate $300 billion spent on U.S. educational institutions at all levels (about $150 billion)."[29] As Chapter 6 and this chapter make clear, the figures cited are appalling understatements of the amounts spent for education at all levels and for educational research. These figures undermine the credibility of the entire report.
2. Although the report recognizes that several federal agencies fund educational research, it does not list them or provide dollar estimates for any except the Department of Education.[30] The omissions have the effect of understating federal expenditures for educational R&D.
3. Despite the fact that several NAE members are employed by institutions that have been forced to return excessive overhead charges, the report ignores the issue. One might expect a report on new directions for federally sponsored research to acknowledge that some reforms are needed on the recipient side.
4. We are told of a need to restructure schools, but not a single sentence in the report suggests that interest-group opposition to it or the absence of technology is a problem. The report is oriented almost entirely to what professors do.[31]
5. The NAE survey of twenty-eight large foundations showed that in 1989 their total grants amounted to $1.1 billion. Of this amount, $272 million went for education, including $36.7 million for educational research. The report cites this as evidence that "Foundations devote only a small portion of their funds for education and a minuscule amount for educa-

tion research.''[32] For the sake of discussion, let us assume that the foundations not included in the NAE survey did not contribute very much to educational R&D. The fact remains that the NAE figure covers only ''research,'' not ''research and development.'' For this reason alone, it underestimates the amount spent for educational R&D.

6. The report urges ''new incentives to draw talented young people into the field of education research, including scholars from disadvantaged and minority groups.''[33] No evidence is presented on why this is needed. Since the educational research community does include minority members, the implication seems to be quotas or proportional representation.

7. The report cites equity in school funding as strong evidence of the efficacy of educational research.[34] As pointed out in Chapter 7, developments in this field could just as easily be cited to illustrate its ineffectiveness and political bias.

8. The report compares spending for educational R&D to spending for R&D in the for-profit sector (said to be 4 to 6 percent) but does not mention the absence of competition and profit incentives in educational R&D or their role in the for-profit sector.

9. The report acknowledges that pork-barrel politics and political concerns play a significant role in allocations of federal research funds. Its solution is ''further study'' of the viability and value of a National Panel of Reviewers to ''advise the federal R&D effort, proposing consensus on what is known and recommending new studies to close gaps in the research base.''[35] The self-serving nature of recommendation is obvious.

Somewhat inadvertently but no less unmistakably, the NAE report reveals the mind-set of educational researchers in our universities. That mind-set runs as follows: Government provides public education. To improve it, government must experiment with different policies and programs under carefully controlled conditions. Research is needed to ensure that the conditions are properly controlled and the results useful for evaluating policies and programs. Government has to find out ''what works,'' and the way to find out is through research, funded largely by government.

In my view, as long as these attitudes are dominant, educational

R&D will continue to be a hopeless quest for educational improvement. Producer domination forestalls even the improvements that could be achieved independently of any move to a market system of education. Significantly, other nations with higher levels of educational achievement than the United States spend less per pupil for educational R&D. If these nations know more about how to educate (though spending much less for R&D) why do we not learn from them? If their superior achievement is due to noneducational factors, such as greater family stability, perhaps we should foster these other factors instead of spending more for educational R&D. As matters stand, the educational research community advocates more spending on educational R&D so that we can catch up educationally with nations that spend much less for it than we do.

12

≈ The Educational Agenda
and Its Problems

B
y now the reader may be persuaded that public education as we know it will not survive. What will replace it is not so clear. We are in a period of transition—but transition to what?

Clues to what should and will happen can be found in the reasons why public education is a lost cause. Among these, economic reasons are paramount. My reference is to the crushing economic costs of disincentives to study, of compulsory education beyond sensible limits, of excessive credentialing and licensing, of labor intensiveness and technological poverty, of massive waste in R&D—in short, to the costs of producer control and of an industry geared to political action instead of better service as the way to enhance producer benefits. As these costs become widely recognized, the pressure to change will be overwhelming.

The demise of the opposition to lending money for interest is an appropriate analogy. Until the Middle Ages, Christian dogma forbade the charging of interest. Eventually, however, the prohibition could no longer be sustained, even as a fiction. The religious changes that made charging interest legitimate were simply a recognition of the fact that its prohibition was blocking productive activities on a massive scale.

Similarly, public education is blocking productivity on a scale that is no longer acceptable. The other reasons to adopt a different system will also play a role, but the economic ones will be decisive. To be consistent with the economic reasons, however, the changes will have to incorporate market approaches to basic educational problems. The massive inefficiencies cannot be remedied by nonmarket approaches.

Beyond this, our crystal ball becomes cloudy for three reasons: (1) market systems can be introduced in a variety of ways; (2) market structures, as distinct from market processes, are inherently unstable; and (3) variations in the political, economic, educational, and demographic circumstances of the states will affect the outcomes. There is also a time problem. For instance, the best system might be one in which government paid only for the education of children whose families could not afford it. Such a system might be possible fifty years from now. An emphasis on it here would only divert attention from essential changes that can be effected within a much shorter period of time.

With these caveats in mind, let me outline the educational agenda called for by our autopsy.

1. To move toward competition and away from producer control or veto power, children should be provided with vouchers redeemable in public or private schools, nonprofit or for profit, denominational or nondenominational.
2. In general, educational restrictions should not apply to schools for profit unless they also apply to nonprofit or public schools.
3. Except for pupils whose families are unable to pay, vouchers should not cover all of the costs of education. Although the amount of the voucher will be somewhat arbitrary, one half the per-pupil cost of public schools would be a reasonable point of departure; however, these costs should be estimated more realistically than they are at the present time.
4. Private schools should not be required to accept all students who apply, but legislation might provide incentives for them to do so.
5. Starting no later than the senior high school level, parents should be required to pay at least 10 percent of the costs from their own pockets.
6. Compulsory education should end at age 14: students who have attained that age should have the option of full-time employment or continuation of formal schooling.
7. Students should have opportunities and incentives to complete their education within a shorter period of time. If a student can finish high school in three years instead of four, some of the savings should accrue to the student, perhaps in the form of a subsidy for advanced education or training.

8. Ethnic disparities in educational achievement may be a matter of government concern, but they must not be regarded as prima facie evidence of racial discrimination. Reliance on such nebulous objectives as "racial balance" or "diversity" as camouflage for preferential treatment of disadvantaged minorities should be terminated immediately.

9. Efforts to convert schools into melting pots should be abandoned, along with the fallacious assumption that students in melting-pot schools will be more devoted to democracy or more tolerant of racial, religious, and socioeconomic differences.

10. The PTA should eliminate teacher participation in its governance structure. The organization of parents that emerges should represent students and parents, not serve as an obedient affiliate of the public school producers. An organization responsive to parental interests will regard public education as a means, not as an end that must be protected against competition at all costs.

11. Although a federally mandated curriculum is out of the question, a nationally accepted one, especially in mathematics and science, is not only possible but desirable. A national curriculum can be consistent with state and local options.

12. The groups that demand transmittal of their ethnic or cultural heritage, through courses such as Afro-American or Holocaust studies, should carry the financial burden of transmitting it.

13. Curricula intended to solve pressing social problems should be eliminated and new ones strongly resisted; however, such curricula could be private school options.

14. School districts should not be allowed to increase their revenues by designating pupils as "learning disabled." Such decisions should be made by independent agencies that are responsible for containing costs as well as for providing any special assistance to which students are entitled. This would be a conflict of interest, but it is one that must be faced somewhere in the system.

15. Custodial services must be distinguished from educational ones, and the differences should be reflected in the expenditures and anticipated outcomes. Whenever appropriations are made for any subgroup of students (retarded, blind,

emotionally disturbed, and so on) the legislation should spell out the standards for evaluating the effectiveness of the appropriations. The educational producers in recipient states and school districts should be evaluated independently with respect to these standards.

16. Insofar as they are intended to restrict competition, legislative barriers to contracting out instructional or support services should be eliminated. Union proposals to restrict school district rights to contract out services should be a prohibited subject of bargaining.

17. Teachers should be required to take state examinations in the subjects they are employed to teach. Teacher scores on such examinations should be available to school employers, but states should not be allowed to deny certification or employment on the basis of such scores; if school boards or schools wish to employ teachers who don't know their subject, they should be allowed to do so and face political accountability for their policies.

18. Federal statistics on school costs should include all the costs incident to the provision of services, whether or not carried on school budgets. Where reliable data are not available, the reports should highlight this point, not bury it in small print. States that refuse to provide the required data on school costs should lose some federal funding.

19. Deliberate falsification of student achievement or attendance should be a criminal offense, leading minimally to exclusion from educational employment.

20. School districts should be required to show the anticipated short- and long-term costs of each fringe benefit, on both per-teacher and aggregated bases. The format should make it possible for citizens to assess the accuracy of these estimates. States and school districts should also be required to show the present value, including district and state contributions, of teacher pension benefits. All data on teacher compensation should be available on citizen demand, without regard to the purpose thereof.

21. In addition to or in lieu of school vouchers, vouchers for separate subjects, such as remedial instruction in basic skills, should be made available. At the high school level, subject vouchers might replace school vouchers entirely.

22. States should mandate report cards that provide objective, usable information about pupil achievement and conduct. Such information should be provided in both criterion-referenced and normative modes. Districts and schools should also be required to provide summaries of student evaluations that unambiguously indicate the extent of low achievement among students.

23. Home schooling should be permitted, perhaps even subsidized as long as the pupils demonstrate reasonable progress on whatever criteria are used to assess student achievement in the state or school district.

24. School boards should be abolished or appointed by mayors, not elected in "nonpartisan" elections in which the organized producers have more influence than the unorganized consumers.

25. School boards should be allowed to contract out the management of the school district, just as hospitals are able to contract out hospital management.

26. The primary focus of education must be on what students know and are able to do. "Able to do" includes the personal habits and attitudes essential to competent performance in occupational and civic roles. Civil rights legislation and policy must not be enacted or interpreted to be in conflict with this emphasis. Diplomas, degrees, and certificates must be abandoned as either goals of education or criteria of educational achievement, in favor of goals such as higher proportions of students who can perform at specified levels.

If this agenda were implemented, how would various interest groups be affected? In the vernacular, who would be the winners and who would be the losers? Because most parties would be winners in some ways and losers in others, the answer to this question is not a simple matter. In my opinion, the long-range benefits would far exceed the losses for the overwhelming majority of students and citizens, even of groups that oppose the changes. The short-term answer, however, might differ from the long-range one. The proposals call for students and their families to absorb a larger share of the costs of formal education, from high school on. Therefore, students who utilize formal education to the hilt would be short-range losers. Conversely, students who do not go on to college or who prefer to accept full-time employment sooner would be immediate winners. Their lifetime earnings would increase and they would be taxed less to pay for the education of upper- and middle-class students. They would also benefit from the increased productivity of the economy generally. And although I am emphasizing economic outcomes at this point, I believe that students who do not go on to college would be much better off with respect to noneconomic outcomes as well.

As noted in Chapter 9, implementation of the agenda would probably lead to higher overall incomes but also to increased inequalities in income. In other words, if the standard of winning or losing is income equality, the disadvantaged would be losers; if the standard is their absolute level of achievement or income, they would be winners. Of course, implementation of the proposed agenda could give priority to increased productivity while noneducational policies simultaneously fostered increased equality. Although the conflict will not necessarily be resolved consistently, its resolution in education is likely to be affected by its resolution elsewhere. My sense of the matter is that "equality" is losing ground to productivity very slowly as a primary social objective. With many reservations and much trepidation, I believe this trend is in the right direction, but distributional concerns should not be ignored.

Although the proposals can be considered individually, some should be considered jointly for various reasons. For instance, parents will oppose charges for educational services that have hitherto been provided free of charge. Such charges might be acceptable, however, as part of a package that includes accelerated opportunities to finish school or to enter full-time employment.

Conceptually, not all of the recommendations are essential to a market system. For example, the proposals on teacher and student testing could be adopted independently of any move toward such a system. Nevertheless, as long as education is a public monopoly, there is less chance that the testing changes will be adopted. In other words, even desirable nonmarket reforms may not be achievable in the absence of a market system.

Considered in isolation, a market system would probably require a much smaller education bureaucracy than exists under public education; however, a three-sector education industry might combine more of the deficiencies than the positive features of each sector. Although I do not believe this outcome is likely, some experience with a three-sector education industry will be necessary to understand how each sector is affected by the presence of the others.

The Transition Problem

A common mistake in previous efforts to enact a voucher system has been the demonstration fallacy, to wit, the assumption that if policy A is demonstrated to be better than policy B, A will be adopted. In the real world, the superiority of a policy is no guarantee of its adoption. Even in the private sector, the most efficient system is not always adopted. One reason is that the transition costs may be prohibitive.

Suppose I own a car that gets thirty miles per gallon of gas. Suppose also that I can buy another car, identical in all respects except that it gets thirty-one miles per gallon. Suppose also that the second car would cost $10,000 more than the trade-in value of the car I already have. On these facts, I would not change to the more efficient car. The transition costs would outweigh the benefits. Analogously, the costs of a transition to a market system of education might outweigh the benefits reasonably to be expected from the transition.

According to my analysis, however, the benefits of a market system would greatly exceed the costs. If this is the case, why doesn't our nation move to a market system of education? The answer is that the supporters of a market system have been unable to overcome objections to the transition costs. In toto, these costs are far outweighed by the benefits; the transition problem lies in the distribution of costs and benefits. Some groups would absorb the costs; others would reap the benefits. Unfortunately, the groups that would suffer the losses are able to block the change. The transition problem is how to redistribute the costs and benefits to make the change possible.

Transition costs often block the introduction of more efficient systems in the private sector. In that sector, decisions on the introduction of more efficient systems, including technology, are based on economic considerations. A company estimates the costs of changing its system of production. The costs might include new equipment, training, temporary shutdowns, and so on. These estimates are compared with estimates of the anticipated gains in productivity. If the total gains appear to exceed the total losses, the company tries to effect the change.

Employee Perspectives on Transition Costs

It often happens, however, that the employees oppose changes to a more efficient system. The change might mean that certain types of employees would no longer be needed. Or employees might have to learn to perform different tasks. In any event, employees do not ordinarily consider system change primarily in terms of company efficiency. Their major concern is the impact of the change on their own interests. For this reason, employees often oppose change to a more efficient system because they believe they would be worse off if the change were made. Such opposition is a transition cost. In many situations, it has forced companies to forgo the change.

If a company is in a competitive field, its inability to adopt a more efficient system will lead to its decline. If the company enjoys a monopoly, it may continue to use the inefficient system, even though its profits will be less than if the change were made. Of course, if it is a monopoly, the workers may have no other source of employment. This may intensify their opposition to the change.

The size of the gains made possible by a change is crucial. Eventually, the potential gains may be so large that it becomes possible to buy out the opposition. It has been estimated that the resistance to labor saving technology breaks down when an investment equivalent to the lifetime wages of one worker enables a company to replace at least five workers.[1] At that point, it becomes possible to overcome the opposition by negotiating a distribution of the gains from increased efficiency.

The foregoing account is oversimplified in several ways. Unemployment does not necessarily result from increased efficiency. Often, employment increases because demand for the product or service grows as producers become more efficient. Also, many improvements in efficiency simply enable workers to perform certain functions more effectively. The point is that regardless of the overall merits of a change, opposition from people who feel threatened by it is a formidable obstacle to overcome.

It is instructive to consider transition costs in industries that have experienced tremendous increases in productivity. Agriculture is one such industry. In 1820 about 70 percent of the U.S. labor force was employed in agriculture. Today less than 3 percent is so employed; and yet the industry not only feeds the U.S. population but also produces huge surpluses that are sold abroad. This phenomenal increase in productivity was made possible by a highly receptive attitude toward more efficient technology. This receptivity was due to the fact that farmers were owners as well as operators. For this reason, conflict between owners (management) and employees over new technology was seldom a problem in agriculture.

Significantly, such conflict has emerged in recent years where agricultural workers are not owners. In California, the United Farm Workers (UFW) has tried to prohibit research on agricultural technology and its introduction into the workplace. Such efforts have not been successful, but they illustrate the critical point. Attitudes toward educational technology are greatly affected by the extent to which workers have a direct stake in its development and utilization. Under public education, however, neither teachers nor administrators nor support employees benefit directly from the introduction of more efficient technology. Under private ownership of schools, they often would have such a stake. Thus even in a three-sector industry, the for-profit sector would be more likely to develop educational technology and to utilize it effectively.

The fact that the transition costs may precede the benefits by several years is another major obstacle. Although a shift to a market system would have some immediate benefits, many others would not be demonstrable for at least a few years. Market processes take time to develop. As the nations of Eastern Europe are finding out, recognition that a market system is better does not ensure a painless transition to it.

In education, habits, attitudes, and institutional structures will have to change. Time must be allowed for new organizations and new arrangements to emerge. Time is also required for the changes to affect the day-to-day activities of pupils, teachers, administrators, and parents. The public school establishment, ever alert to point out that there are no quick fixes, will nevertheless ignore the fact that it takes time for market processes to take hold.

Political Costs and Benefits

The transition from public education to a market system will involve political as well as economic costs. For present purposes, political costs can be viewed as losses in voter support, political contributions, and campaign workers. Many elected officials depend upon teacher unions for all of these things.[2]

If teacher unions were seriously weakened, as they would be under a market system, many of the elected officials who depend on them for support would be voted out of office; their opponents would reap the political benefits of the transition to a market system. The situation would not be one in which elected officials would lose one constituency but gain others. That would happen, but only in a few cases. In terms of existing political alignments, the Democrats would ordinarily lose and the Republicans would ordinarily gain; the public employee unions are a major Democratic constituency.

This is problem enough, but more is to come. The potential conflict between political winners and political losers exists at three levels of government: local, state, and federal. Resolving the problem at only one or even two levels may not be sufficient. For example, local school boards may be unable to contract out instructional services because of the state licensing or collective bargaining laws. States that wish to adopt a market system may be stymied by federal legislation that discriminates against schools for profit. No matter how much support for a change exists at one level of government, it may be impossible to implement it without changes at other levels.

The difficulty of enacting appropriate legislation at three levels of government is greatly exacerbated by the fact that the levels have different constituencies. An urban school board with a heavy minority population may respond differently from its state electorate as a whole. The state electorate may respond differently from the nation as a whole as represented in Congress. These variations provide opportunities to block action at one level that may be essential at all levels of government.

The Free Rider Problem

For the sake of discussion, let us assume that a shift to a market system would bring about widespread improvement in education. A prior question arises. Whose interests would be served by exercising the leadership to bring about the change? I am not asking who would benefit from the change itself. My question is who would benefit from devoting the time and resources to make it happen.[3]

Clearly, it would not be in the interests of parents to devote their time and resources to achieving a market system of education. Parents may believe in the superiority of a market system, but that is not likely to motivate them to work toward this objective. The effort to achieve a market system will be a lengthy, expensive process with no assurance of success. Even if it is successful, the benefits will go mainly to families that do not contribute anything to the effort. Inasmuch as the efforts of any particular parent are not likely to affect the outcome, parents will tend to be free riders on the issue.

Obviously, we cannot expect the public school establishment to support changes toward a market system. For that matter, we cannot even expect most private schools to do so. Most private schools are denominational schools. These denominations include public school parents, teachers, administrators, and board members. Denominational leaders must avoid offending their public school constituents, hence their support for a market system is highly problematic.[4] Although many denominational school leaders claim to support a market system, their underlying interest is in support for their own schools.

The independent private schools do not support a market system for different reasons. First, the most prestigious independent schools attract a full complement of students under the status quo. Second, independent private schools generally are reluctant to exercise leadership on market issues. They fear that their activities will be perceived as efforts by the affluent to aid the affluent. Most private schools have no interest in expanding beyond their present facilities. Rhetorically, they may support market terminology, but their actions do not reflect any understanding of, or commitment to, a market system of education. Support for private schools, or for parents who wish to send their children to private schools, is not necessarily support for a market system of education.

In some respects, it is becoming more difficult to create a constituency that might lead the fight for a market system. Schools for profit are not yet a major constituency in the politics of education. In the meantime, the absence of a strong promarket constituency enables the antimarket forces to strengthen their monopoly position.

The Transition Balance Sheet

In the private sector, the transition to a more efficient system is primarily if not entirely an economic decision. A company estimates the costs of the transition. The company also estimates the gains over time from the transition. If these exceed the costs by a sufficient amount, the decision is made to implement the change. Of course, companies sometimes underestimate costs and/or overestimate savings, but at least their estimates appear on a single balance sheet.

This is not the situation in public education. In the first place, there is no consensus on how to measure the output of education. High school graduation rates are sometimes used, but states with lower graduation rates may have higher standards. Test scores are another possibility, but what tests should be used, and how should the pupil mix be factored in?

Also, reliance on test scores is often said to neglect important outcomes not subject to testing. Other measures of output encounter difficulties of their own. In any event, as long as there is widespread disagreement about what is or should be produced, there will probably be widespread disagreement about how to measure the gains from any change in the system.

The cost side presents a different set of problems. Nationally, in 1990–91, 49.3 percent of school revenues came from the states, 44.5 percent from local governments, and 6.2 percent from the federal government. The mix varied widely from state to state. The state share varied from 7.3 percent in New Hampshire to 91.2 percent in Hawaii; the local share from 0.1 percent in Hawaii to 90.8 in New Hampshire; and the federal share from 2.4 percent in New Hampshire to 15.5 percent in Mississippi.[5] Obviously, the economic and political implications of a shift to a market system will vary widely from state to state and by level of government. That is, the transition costs and the distribution of the gains may vary so much that what is possible in one state or school district may not be in another.

As we have seen, many costs of public education are not carried on school budgets. Some costs, such as those carried on the budgets of institutions of higher education, might be reduced in a market system but would not show up as an efficiency gain under existing school accounting procedures. Unlike the situation in a private company that can consolidate costs and benefits in a single balance sheet, the costs of public education are scattered among different levels of government and different agencies within the same level. This renders it difficult to assess overall gains in efficiency. For instance, suppose that in some subjects teachers with less formal training are as effective as teachers with college degrees, and suppose that it becomes widespread practice to hire teachers without degrees to teach these subjects. At least in the short run, only part of the saving would show up on school budgets. The change would justify a significant drop in expenditures for higher education, but this gain would not be apparent in school accounting. The difficulty of gathering and presenting all the costs and benefits on a single balance sheet constitutes an enormous strategic advantage for the public school lobby. The losers in a shift to a market system would be immediately visible; the beneficiaries frequently would not be, especially since many important benefits would require years to materialize. In Adam Smith's famous phrase, some benefits would result from an "invisible hand"— but invisible hands are not potent political slogans.

Attitudes toward taxes illustrate the strategic importance of visibility in the political process. Taxes are more visible in the United States than in several nations with higher tax rates. The greater awareness of the tax bite leads to greater opposition to tax increases. In education, the obvious identity of those who would lose and the difficulty of identifying the long-range beneficiaries add up to a major political obstacle to support for a market system of education.

The Bias against Market Systems

As the discussion of taxes illustrates, the reception accorded policy proposals depends partly on preexisting attitudes. As we might expect, proposals to shift to a market system of education are affected by popular attitudes toward market systems. These attitudes can be changed, but they are very important, especially in the short run. Chapter 10 discussed the antimarket bias in higher education; its prevalence among professors of education, public school teachers, and the public at large should also be noted.

Professors of education share the antimarket attitudes that prevail in higher education generally. In addition, many have reasons of self-interest for opposing a market system of education. The reason is that most policy issues would be resolved through market, not political processes. For instance, if parents preferred smaller classes enough to pay for them, schools would offer smaller classes. Controversies over how to teach reading, or school discipline, or dress codes would be resolved in the same way. Some professorial expertise in education would be useful in a market system; a great deal would not be.

As matters stand, the schools of education train teachers and administrators to function in the existing system. Their focus is on performance within the system, not on critical analysis of that system. Students, too, choose programs that will help them do a better job in the existing system. They will not be interested in market delivery of educational services unless they perceive a market system to be imminent. Students seek jobs in the existing system; school boards and administrators are not likely to be favorably impressed by degrees from institutions with a reputation for challenging the rationale for public education. In short, the institutional stake in the existing system is a deterrent to critical analysis of it.

Furthermore, professors of education frequently serve as consultants to school districts, public school organizations, and state and federal

agencies. Logic and experience suggest that challenges to public education are not conducive to such employment. For these and other reasons,
the intellectual resources for a shift to a market system will be found
mainly outside the schools of education, perhaps outside higher education generally.

Individuals and groups that enjoy monopoly status are seldom critical
of the justification for it. Understandably, public school teachers do not
criticize the system in which they work. Their organizations, publications,
conferences, and shop talk reinforce rather than challenge that system.
Of course, there is much talk about the importance of "changing the
system." Such rhetoric, however, does not refer to a change to a market
system. "Changing the system" simply means making changes within the
present framework of public education.

Widespread failure to understand market processes also contributes
to the bias against them among public school personnel. For instance,
many believe that in a market system morals and concern for others are
subordinate to profits. From this perspective, it is easy to visualize a list
of horribles: schools would hire cheaper, unqualified teachers; school
cafeterias would serve lower-quality food; out-of-date textbooks would
not be replaced. At every point, there would be a conflict between profit
and educational need. Who can doubt that profit would prevail?

In discussing such views, we must bear in mind that markets differ.
In some, buyers and sellers face serious problems of compliance and
enforcement; in others, they do not. What would school markets be like?
Schools cost a lot to build (or rent or buy); they cannot pack up and
move overnight. Most school buildings are not readily convertible to
other uses, except at considerable loss. Schools depend heavily on repeat
players; few could survive if they had to enroll a new student body every
year. Also, when schools compete for students, their reputations will be
extremely important. Schools will suffer if they develop a reputation for
incompetence or fraud. As economists have pointed out, market systems
function most effectively in environments characterized by trust and the
avoidance of predatory behavior.[6]

In the educational situation, the best protection that parents could
possibly get would be perfect competition among schools. To see why,
suppose competition forces schools to offer similar services at similar
prices. Let us say there are five schools, competing intensively for students. If one gets a reputation for shady dealing, it loses out completely.
Why would any parents enroll their child in such a school, knowing that

its services and prices were no better than those of four other available schools? Competition that involves repeat players is an excellent consumer safeguard. The danger would not be competition but the absence of it.

Even if some schools fulfilled the most negative stereotypes of market behavior, genuine competition would minimize the problem within a relatively short time.

In general, organizations of public school personnel assume that public services are egalitarian and market processes are not. They conveniently overlook the fact that public high schools, during most of the years of their existence, were overwhelmingly college preparatory institutions serving an upper-middle-class clientele. This author can remember when newspaper society pages informed readers about the college decisions of local high school graduates. Meanwhile, on-the-job training and for-profit trade schools served many students who did not go on to college.

No consideration is given to the fact that a significant number of schools for profit specialize in the education of the disabled or the difficult to educate. At the same time, many public schools, such as the specialized high schools in New York City, screen applicants on the basis of academic criteria. Here again, the critics of a market system rely on a double standard of judgment.

The fact is that virtually every aspect of education is characterized by an antimarket bias, perhaps all the more insidious because it is seldom recognized. School finance is oriented to the redistribution of wealth, not the generation of it. Rhetorically, the importance of a productive economy is often acknowledged, but it is assumed that "more education" contributes to this objective. The culture of education treats teachers as dedicated but underpaid "professionals." The outcome is a diffuse resentment against the system that supposedly fails to appreciate their efforts. The fact that public school salaries are substantially understated and are much higher than the teacher salaries in the private sector counts for nothing in this culture. While the basest motives are attributed to private-sector producers, the pursuit of teacher welfare is treated as a concern for pupil welfare. The social benefits of market systems are ignored, as are the negative effects of services provided by government. The blind faith in government regulation and the total neglect of competition as consumer safeguards also illustrate the antimarket bias in public education.

Within the field of education, competition is often blamed for developments that result from other causes. The low quality of courses taken by teachers for salary credit illustrates this point. Most teachers are paid on the basis of their years of experience and academic credits (courses and degrees). Nevertheless, few if any school districts insist on any performance levels for the courses or degrees. The result is that teachers are paid billions every year for worthless courses and degrees. Institutions of higher education compete for students by dropping residence and academic requirements, lowering course standards, eliminating dissertation or term paper requirements, giving open book examinations, and/or inflating student grades. These developments supposedly illustrate the evils of competition. In fact, however, they illustrate the dangers of paying for credentials instead of for demonstrated achievement.

If students need high school diplomas to qualify for withdrawal from school, drivers' licenses, or employment, competition between schools will follow the same pattern. Students will shop for the easiest way to receive a diploma; schools that award diplomas for mediocre achievement will attract students away from schools that impose high standards. Suppose, however, that in order to qualify for a driver's license, applicants had to read and write at specified levels that were not tested by the schools but by external independent agencies. Surely, in that case, the competition between schools would be to teach students to read and write as soon as possible. As long as our society values credentials that do not require genuine achievement, competition among schools will have negative outcomes. The remedy is not to eliminate competition; it is to eliminate the emphasis on credentials instead of performance.

Cooperation versus Competition

Market systems require competition. Many people, however, believe that children should grow up in a cooperative, not a competitive environment. On this view, it appears logical to reject a market system of education. I say "appears" because there is no reason the educational environment of schools in a market system must itself be competitive. Many parents enroll their children in private schools that emphasize cooperation, multicultural and multi-ethnic student bodies, and so on. In a market system, schools might even compete on the basis of which school environment was least competitive. There would be no contradiction involved in such competition.

In the real world, cooperation and trust are essential to the existence of a market system. If buyers and sellers could not rely on promises made, market transactions would not occur, or would not occur as often for mutual benefit. This is often overlooked because critics think of markets in terms of one-shot transactions. Of course, companies for profit, like government officials, may make mistakes, lie, cheat, or fail to fulfill their obligations. One of the overriding virtues of a market system is that it is self-correcting in ways government cannot emulate; after all, it is usually much easier to change producers than to change elected officials and/ or entrenched bureaucracies.

Competitive enterprise also enhances cooperation among employees. Nobody doubts that Japanese automobile companies (1) are highly competitive, and (2) are characterized by a high degree of cooperation and team spirit. Buyers and sellers, too, must cooperate to accomplish an exchange. In short, the notion that market systems are antithetical to cooperation is nonsense; cooperation is an integral part of such systems.

Markets and Social Conflict

When Milton Friedman proposed a voucher system in 1962, one of his reasons was the need to reduce social conflict over education. In the ensuing years, relatively little attention has been paid to this reason. This neglect is unfortunate because social conflict and its deleterious effects on education are even greater today than in 1962.

Public opinion often fails to recognize that market systems foster cooperation and interaction between persons who disagree on basic values. This is extremely important in a heterogeneous society such as ours. The United States is becoming "the first Universal Society"—that is, a society not dominated by any particular ethnic or religious or economic group. As heterogeneity increases, so does the cost of efforts to impose majoritarian solutions on the population as a whole. These costs should not be underestimated. According to some political theories, the capacity of market systems to avoid or diminish these costs is their most important feature. We are no closer today than in the past to commonly accepted goals of education. Even among groups and individuals who agree on the goals, basic disagreement remains on how to achieve them. The question is whether the costs of majoritarian determination of educational issues are worth the benefits; as heterogeneity increases, the answer is less likely to be in the affirmative.

The importance of this point is not limited to issues arising out of ideological or cultural differences. A market system would avoid a great deal of conflict that arises over other types of issues as well. Suppose citizens A and B agree completely on the goals of education and also on the means: teachers, curriculum, schedule, and so on. Still, they may disagree on how teachers should be paid. Citizen A may believe that teachers should be paid for services rendered, as they are now. Citizen B may believe that teachers should be paid on the basis of results, as is sometimes the practice in employment. In a market system, this issue will not have to be resolved by government, and the resolution will not have to be imposed on all schools. Instead, the parties will be able to resolve the issues between themselves, that is, by their contractual arrangements. If citizen A is willing to pay for educational services rendered and take his chances on the outcomes, he should be permitted to do so. If citizen B insists on results and is willing to pay a producer who will guarantee them, presumably at a higher rate, he should be able to enter into such contractual arrangements.

In a market system, the relationships between producers and consumers are governed by contract. For this reason, a market system provides the flexibility required to resolve issues of accountability and risk. Lawyers sometimes provide services on a contingent fee basis; unless their services are successful, they are not paid, or are not paid as much. Similarly, salespersons are often paid on a commission basis instead of receiving salaries not tied to the amount of their sales. Public schools cannot provide comparable flexibility. Aside from its thrust for "equality," which is opposed to differentiations among students and teachers, the public school system cannot accommodate different contractual arrangements among the parties. Even if parents want to pay more for guaranteed results, divisive political controversy over who will assess the results, the criteria and frequency of assessment, the payment schedule, and so on will preclude such an approach. While educational reformers are preoccupied with issues like accountability and merit pay, the fact that a market system would obviate most of them is simply ignored.

Totalitarian and Racist Schools

Popular failure to understand how market systems function also underlies the fear that schools devoted to totalitarian and racist ideologies would thrive in a market system. Obviously, public schools have not been completely successful in eliminating such ideologies; if they had been, there would be no problem. It is highly doubtful, however, that such schools would be a problem under a market system. First, it is very unlikely that they could acquire the facilities and staff and attract enough students to stay in business. The regulatory obstacles would also be formidable. Furthermore, antidemocratic schools are likely to be highly inefficient and noncompetitive with other schools. One reason is that they would face major problems of scale, both in staffing and in student enrollment. For instance, suppose such a school were to advertise:

TEACHERS WANTED

New KKK school recruiting teachers
Adherence to white supremacy required
Openings at all grade levels
Salary and benefits negotiable.

I doubt that there would be many applicants. A school that would employ only teachers with this ideology would be at a severe disadvantage in recruiting staff. Again it must be emphasized that prejudicial attitudes have costs. If a school recruits only teachers with racist views, it will have to spend more to recruit teachers and the teachers will not be as competent as teachers in schools without such restrictive criteria. It is also unlikely that such schools could attract enough students to be viable. How many students would want to attend a high school that no other school would accept as an opponent in sports? Or that colleges and employers would shun?

Paradoxically, the Ku Klux Klan has been a strong supporter of public education. As a matter of fact, the Klan was the major political sponsor of an Oregon initiative that required everyone aged 8–16 to attend public schools. The state constitutional provision that resulted was eventually held to be unconstitutional by the U.S. Supreme Court in the celebrated 1925 case of *Pierce v. Society of the Sisters of Jesus and Mary*.[7] The belief that public schools were more hospitable to KKK ideology than private schools received some recent support when David Duke ran for governor of Louisiana in 1990. Duke had been active in the KKK and had espoused racially oriented policies until a short time before running for governor. Virtually every national civil rights organization had denounced him as a racist. Nevertheless, he received 55 percent of the white vote in the runoff election.[8]

The question that must be raised is whether Duke received 55 percent of the white vote despite his KKK/racist background or because of it. To argue that it was because of his racist background is to demolish the argument that public education is some sort of bulwark against racist ideologies. On this issue, the public school lobby should not be permitted to cite large numbers of voters supporting racist ideologies while avoiding the implications of where those voters received their education.

Regardless of the weight one gives to Duke's Nazi activities as a teen-ager, they were evident during his student years at a New Orleans public high school. I do not allege that public schools were responsible for David Duke's teenage support for Nazism; what is incontestable is that public schools were unable or unwilling to prevent it. By the same token, private schools are not necessarily responsible for the antidemocratic views of their graduates, but I do not expect public school organizations to show any restraint on this issue.

Undoubtedly a market system would bring about increased differentia-tion of educational services. Such increased differentiation would not necessarily lead to increased emphasis on narrow indoctrination, that is, private goods that conflict with public ones. For example, parents might choose a particular private school for its effectiveness in teaching basic skills. Summer camps and for-profit learning centers provide some evi-dence on the nature of consumer choice in education. More and more summer camps specialize in computer education, science, foreign lan-guages, treatment of obesity, proficiency in various sports, or educational travel. I do not believe these specializations are antidemocratic or conflict with any public benefit. The same phenomenon is emerging in for-profit companies that provide instructional services in regular school subjects. Most of these companies provide instruction in basic skills; in recent years they have begun to offer instruction in a wider variety of subjects, hoping to capture the enrichment market as well as the remedial market. These camps and learning centers provide impressive evidence that the kind of specialized schools parents want present no danger to democratic institutions. Interestingly enough, one type that has failed to emerge is the school or service devoted to antidemocratic indoctrination.

Paradoxically, some people support public school choice as a way to weaken the movement to create a market system of education.[9] Perhaps nothing better illustrates the hypocrisy of their argument that a market system of education would pose a threat to democracy. Increased choice within public schools could weaken parental support for private schools only on the assumption that the choices parents want could be provided by public as well as private schools. It is hypocritical to argue that private school choice is a threat to democracy but public schools that provide the same options are not. The hypocrisy suggests that the danger of antidemocratic schools is being conjured up for propaganda purposes.

Educational Fraud

Another argument raised against a market system of education is that it would lead to educational fraud on a large scale. Proponents of this argument cite evidence such as the high rates of default on student loans by students from proprietary colleges. U.S. Department of Education figures on the Guaranteed Student Loan (GSL) program show, for example, that in FY 1987 the default rate for students from proprietary institutions was 33 percent, much higher than the rate for any other type of institution (the rate for all types of institutions taken together was 17 percent).[10] This kind of evidence is cited to show that schools for profit are more likely to exaggerate their benefits or enroll unqualified students in order to make a fast buck.[11]

When government encourages an activity by protecting investors against loss, the outcome naturally is imprudent investment. The savings and loan fiasco is the showcase example. If government had not insured the deposits in the savings and loan companies, both the depositors and the savings and loan institutions themselves would have been more prudent. The same principle applies to the GSL program. Guaranteed loans reduce the risk to students, thereby encouraging imprudent use of their time. Furthermore, the guarantees protect educational institutions against loss in enrolling students unlikely to benefit from the additional education or to repay the loans. Not surprisingly, the GSL program is an extremely wasteful one. In 1990 the cumulative value of defaulted student loans (for which the federal government is ultimately responsible) reached $7.8 billion; in FY 1990 alone the default costs reached approximately $2 billion.[12]

The significance of the higher default rate among proprietary institutions is a matter of considerable controversy. A strong argument has been made that the regulations governing student loans ensure that propriety institutions will enroll a high proportion of high-risk students. This is interesting apart from the controversy over default rates. Quite possibly, many students in the program pose a risk of default that should not be accepted, but the principle is not applied evenly across sectors. The high dropout rates in some public high schools are not attributed to the fact that the schools are public. Instead, they are attributed to the fact that the public schools enroll a higher proportion of high-risk students. It is seldom contended, however, that the public schools should not enroll them because their risk of failure is so high. The loan defaults expose the costs of investment in high-risk students, but they do not establish the conclusion that producers in schools for profit are more self-serving than those in public schools. Significantly, the Department of Education concluded that "The default program is not simply a proprietary school problem; it exists for all institutions."[13]

On this issue, there is a tendency to emphasize form over substance. Public education has experienced widespread fraud of several types: bribes for textbook adoptions, bogus credit for advancement on the teacher salary schedule, rigging of bids for supplies, nepotism, kickbacks on contracts. Nor are fraudulent practices confined to the business side of public education. As we have seen, excessive claims of educational achievement are a common practice. Fraud in reporting attendance is also very pervasive, as are high school diplomas that are worthless from an educational standpoint.

To summarize, fraudulent conduct will emerge from time to time in all sectors: public, nonprofit, and for profit. Would a market system of education result in a higher incidence of educational fraud? Perhaps, but it is very much an open question. It should not be overlooked that fraud is more likely to be recognized and exposed in a competitive than a monopolistic environment. The competitors of fraudulent schools have an interest in detecting and exposing fraud, whereas this safeguard does not exist in a monopolistic environment. In other words, competition may be a better safeguard than regulation.[14]

Inasmuch as we do not have a competitive market system, the existing levels of fraud are not indicative of the patterns that would emerge under such a system. Furthermore, the issue is not only whether there is "more" fraud in the private sector but how much more (if any) and what would happen under a market system. What does not make sense is to regard one isolated dimension of fraud as dispositive of a very complex issue.

Conclusion: Obstacles to a Market System

The public school forces contend that the American people support the public school monopoly because public schools educate young people effectively. In my view, an opposite conclusion is called for. As pointed out in Chapter 7, the American people support public education partly because they have little understanding of how market systems function. Not that support would always follow understanding; interest groups threatened by a market system are not going to support it. Nor do I mean to suggest that only selfish interests oppose a shift to a market system. Even so, the widespread failure to understand how market systems function is a major obstacle to their acceptance. Because of the tremendous variety of markets, people are often confused about the essential features of market systems. This confusion is especially evident when one-shot "let the buyer beware" markets are not distinguished from markets with long-term repeat players and heavy emphasis on producer reputations. The paradoxical outcome is that public education survives partly because it fails to educate students about market systems.

Another obstacle to a market system is the uncritical support for voucher plans that include several anticompetitive provisions. The Milwaukee voucher plan discussed in Chapter 1 is an example. Parents' choices as consumers are limited by restrictions on producers. An analogy may help to clarify this crucial issue. Assuming that we have the resources, we can buy any kind of car we want. Suppose, however, that government dictated the number of seats, the weight, the colors, mileage efficiency, the type of brakes, storage capacity, and so on that automakers could produce—all while we enjoyed the formal freedom to buy the car of our choice. In this situation, the restrictions on the producers would be de facto restrictions on consumers as well.

The same problem arises under voucher plans that include private schools. The restrictions on producers, which vary from state to state, include the number of days of school, the length of the school day, teacher certification, state approval of instructional materials for reimbursement, courses that must be offered, and various regulations and mandates related to school facilities. Where these restrictions are extensive, it is understandable that "choice" has little appeal to parents. Its opponents attribute parental indifference to the concept of choice itself, not to the legal environment that renders it ineffective.[15]

It should be clear by now that the obstacles to a market system are much broader and more complex than has been generally realized. A minimal list must include the following obstacles:

1. The fact that millions of public school teachers, administrators, support-service employees, and their organizations are

threatened by the change and will do everything they can to prevent it.

2. Haphazard and misleading media treatment of educational issues, based largely on "facts" provided by producers.

3. A political process that renders it extremely difficult to achieve long-range benefits that require short-range losses.

4. The pervasive underestimation of the actual costs of public education and of the negative outcomes associated with universal benefits.

5. The formidable opposition of professors and academic organizations.

6. The trauma associated with writing off a huge cultural and psychological investment in public education.

7. A lack of unity among the denominational groups that would presumably benefit from strengthening parental choice of private schools.

8. A low level of popular understanding of market systems that leaves public opinion vulnerable to irrational and dishonest objections to such a system.

9. The diffuse nature of public education, which renders it extremely difficult to compare its costs and benefits to the costs and benefits of an alternative system.

10. The heavy hand of inertia, one of the most underrated of all factors in social relationships.

To date, the forces favoring a market system of education have failed to overcome or neutralize these obstacles. Sooner or later, however, their ritualistic denunciations of the public school opposition will be replaced by more effective strategies and tactics. When that happens, the pro-market forces will overcome the transition problems outlined in this chapter.

13
≈ The Transition Solution

revious efforts to establish a market system of education have been overwhelmingly defeated by the organized forces of public education. Have those forces succeeded because their position is persuasive? Or have they succeeded because the promarket forces have not adopted the most effective strategy and tactics? To answer these questions, we need to take a critical look at past attempts to establish a market system of education. Since the efforts to establish a voucher system have failed for the same reasons as the efforts to establish a market system, I shall include voucher supporters as supporters of a market system even though the inclusion is not always accurate.

Lessons from the Past

Political conservatives and libertarians are the main sources of support for a market approach to education. For editorial simplicity, and despite greater libertarian awareness of the importance of schools for profit in a market system of education, I shall use the term "conservative" to apply to both. Thus the term includes but is not limited to the following groups, organizations, and publications:

1. The Reagan and Bush administrations.
2. Conservative foundations and policy organizations such as the Heritage Foundation.
3. Conservative membership groups, such as the Eagle Forum and Citizens for a Sound Economy.

4. Academic centers deemed to have a promarket orientation.
5. Conservative (and neoconservative) media, such as *National Review, Public Interest, Commentary,* and *An American Spectator.*
6. Some business leaders (although there is no consensus on the issue in the business community).

It is obviously impractical to summarize and evaluate the positions of each of these on educational matters. I believe, however, that the following examples fairly represent conservative strategy and tactics regarding a market system of education. In view of the prestige of the parties involved, the examples clearly demonstrate mainstream conservative thinking on the issues. My assertion is that none of the entities listed has challenged this thinking.[1]

The Oregon Voucher Initiative

In 1990 a group of Oregon citizens succeeded in getting an educational voucher initiative on the ballot for the November elections. The initiative was the first to combine public and private school choice. It also provided that the state could not add new regulations governing private schools for a period of three years after the effective date of the proposed voucher system.

The sponsors of the initiative met with the leaders of the Oregon Education Association (OEA) in an effort to gain OEA support. They sought to persuade the OEA that the initiative would improve education and raise the professional status of teachers: If the initiative passed, children would no longer be a captive audience; teachers would be serving clients who had chosen them. Good teachers could be paid their just deserts. And so on. As we might expect, the OEA was adamantly hostile to the initiative. The sponsors came to regard public school teachers and their unions as the focal point of the opposition, as indeed they were. In the election, the initiative lost by a margin of more than two to one.

Let us contrast the strategy followed in Oregon with the strategy employed in similar situations by the Thatcher government in England. On several occasions, that government sought to privatize various industries that had been owned and operated by the government. As in Oregon, the employees and their unions in these industries were strongly opposed to privatization. To neutralize this opposition, and even to convert it into support, the government sold stock in the private companies that would take over the denationalized industries. This stock was offered at deep discounts to employees in those industries. The discounts ensured a favorable financial result for these employees if privatization was successful.

Note how the British approach differs from the strategy in Oregon. In Oregon the appeal was to parents as consumers; the producers of education were treated as the opposition. No effort was made to give a substantial number of teachers any financial incentive to support instead of oppose the voucher initiative.

Of course, the specific solution adopted by the Thatcher government could not have been adopted in Oregon; the Oregon initiative did not involve the transfer of public schools to a for-profit corporation. Nevertheless, supporters of the Oregon initiative might have adopted a similar strategy. For example, the initiative might have included generous retirement benefits for teachers who retired within a specified number of years after its passage. It might have reduced the number of years before pensions were vested, provided additional years of pension credit, replaced the teacher contributions by state contributions, or a mix of these and other sweeteners. Nothing along this line was even considered.

The Oregon initiative was endorsed by the *Wall Street Journal* and a host of conservative media. It was also featured at conferences sponsored by the Heritage Foundation, the Free Congress Foundation, and the American Legislative Exchange Council. Vice-President Quayle made a campaign appearance in Oregon to support it. At no time, however, were questions raised about the failure of the initiative to include any concrete benefits for teachers.

Perhaps the initiative would not have passed even if its supporters had mounted a sophisticated effort to neutralize teacher opposition. Regardless, the failure in Oregon and elsewhere even to consider financial incentives for teachers was ineptitude, pure and simple. However one characterizes the oversight, it was shared by an impressive array of conservative experts on education and political strategy.

Public School Choice

In January 1989 President Reagan and President-elect Bush addressed a White House conference on educational choice. Both lavished praise on public school choice as a major educational reform; the President-elect stated that enabling parents to choose the public school attended by their children would be the leading educational priority of his administration.[2] In addition, other high-ranking officials in both the outgoing and the incoming administrations declared their support for the concept. Within days, conservative columnists enthusiastically praised public school choice, characterizing it as the introduction of market processes and competition into public education. Later in 1989 the Bush administration sponsored five regional conferences to promote public school choice. It also published and distributed free of charge *Choosing a School for Your Child,* a booklet intended to help parents choose public schools wisely.[3] In addition, a host of conservative organizations, publications, and leaders endorsed public school choice as a major reform.

Indisputably, the conservative supporters of public school choice envisaged it as similar to competitive market processes in the private sector.[4] This is astonishing, especially from sources that are supposed to be knowledgeable about market systems. In Chapter 1, I noted five conditions that are essential to the existence of competitive markets. Not one of these conditions exists under public school choice. Most could not, even potentially. For instance, in a competitive market inefficient producers must improve or go out of business. How will school authorities decide that a school is inefficient? On the basis of a decline in enrollment? Suppose the teachers counter that students are transferring out because the school adheres to high standards. If students need a diploma to qualify for employment and can get one more easily at a school with lower standards, transferring will be a rational action for them regardless of school efficiency. Thus it is impossible to assume inefficiency or poor teaching merely because enrollments decline.

In any case, public school choice bears only a superficial resemblance to competition in the marketplace. Although public school choice receives support for other reasons, the analogy to a competitive market process has been decisive in generating widespread conservative support for it.[5]

In view of its flawed rationale, the trivial nature of public school choice as a reform should come as no surprise. The evidence from Minnesota, the state widely acknowledged to be most active in providing public school choice, is instructive. In 1989–90 Minnesota's public schools enrolled 735,000 students. Of these, 3,218, or less than one-half of one percent, officially transferred to a public school out of their district. About 20 percent of those who transferred said they did so for academic reasons. About 40 percent cited what were predominantly reasons of convenience, such as the fact that the school was closer to their place of employment or was closer to home despite being in another district.

Realistically, 3,218 is an exaggeration of the number of transfers due to open enrollment. Before open enrollment was instituted, several thousand students changed schools every year through voluntary interdistrict transfers, which required the approval of both the sending and receiving districts. Unquestionably, many transfers that took place under open enrollment would have taken place anyway under the voluntary program. If the number of transfers under open enrollment is reduced by the number that would have occurred in its absence and further reduced by the transfers for nonacademic reasons, the number remaining is minuscule indeed. And since we have no evidence that this minuscule number did better at the new schools, or did not transfer back in the following years, the cosmetic nature of this nationally acclaimed "reform" is evident. Furthermore, the proportion of transfers by every disadvantaged minority was lower than their proportion of the total student population in the state, a striking refutation of the claim that public school choice would be especially helpful to disadvantaged minorities.[6]

What are we to make of the fact that the president of the United States unambiguously adopted public school choice as his top educational priority, and that with very few exceptions such as Milton Friedman, the entire conservative establishment embraced choices offered by a public monopoly as a significant market-oriented reform? This was bad enough, but subsequent events were even more revealing. More than two years after he announced that public school choice was his top educational priority, President Bush appointed David F. Kearns, the CEO of Xerox Corporation, to be Deputy Secretary of Education. Kearns's major statement on educational policy was a book entitled *Winning the Brain Race*,[7] which outlined a "bold new plan" to reform American education, thereby restoring competitive capability to the U.S. economy. Sad to say, the bold new plan turned out to be public school choice. Parenthetically, public school choice was not a new idea; a book advocating it had been published in 1973.[8]

To avoid any misunderstanding, let me emphasize that I do not oppose public school choice. What I oppose is the idea that it ever had the potential to be a significant reform. This negative view is not the result of hindsight; it had been articulated it long before the fatuous predictions and claims made for public school choice by the conservative establishment.[9] These predictions and claims reveal an astonishing intellectual deficiency in conservative positions regarding market systems as well as public education.

Contracting Out

Lack of attention to contracting out is still another example of ineptitude among conservative supporters of a market system of education. Unquestionably, a worldwide trend toward privatization emerged in the 1980s. In this context, "privatization" refers to using private contractors instead of public employees to deliver services. In the United States state and local governments have contracted with private companies for many kinds of services:

hospital management	waste removal
prison management	water purification
data processing	fleet maintenance
security	meter collection
labor negotiations	homeless shelters
asset management	legal services
custodial and maintenance services	printing.

This list is only suggestive; hundreds of public services are contracted out at various levels of government.

In education, pupil transportation and food service are often contracted out, as are other services from time to time. Except in unusual circumstances, however, instruction is not contracted out, and neither is school management. Examples of contracting out school management are so rare that such contracts in Miami (1990) and Duluth (1992) received nationwide publicity.

Several questions can be raised about this state of affairs. Is managing a hospital easier than managing a school? If not, why should contracting out hospital management be fairly common while contracting out school management is virtually unheard of? Why do school districts frequently contract out pupil transportation but not instruction? Is there a sound public policy explanation or is this simply a historical accident? If the latter (as I believe), why does the situation continue?

Actually, in the 1980s, while the worldwide trend was toward privatization, it became more, not less difficult for school districts to utilize

contracting out. The teacher unions began to organize support personnel: bus drivers, cafeteria workers, custodial and maintenance employees,
and so on. Because many of these employees were concerned about
contracting out, the teacher unions had to address the issue; they did so
by pledging to prohibit or weaken contracting out. In other words,
opposition to contracting out was an effective organizing strategy. Inevitably, the teacher unions proposed restrictions on contracting out that
applied to teaching as well as support services.

I am not contending that contracting out is always good and opposition to it always bad.[10] School districts should use it much more than they
do, but that is not my point here. Instead, I am trying to invite attention
to the myopic range of conservative attention in the field of education.
That conservatives have overlooked contracting out in education is
hardly to be disputed. Not a single R&D project funded by the U.S.
Department of Education since Reagan took office in 1981 deals with
contracting out by school districts. This is especially noteworthy because
the department itself contracts out most of its research and services.
Likewise, it appears that none of the foundations that support conservative causes has funded any R&D in this area. Whatever the reason, it
cannot be a lack of funds; as pointed out in Chapter 6, foundations
spend millions every week on educational reform.

New Directions in Transition Strategy and Tactics

Proponents of social change must frequently choose between alternative
strategies. For instance, the tax limitation movement seeks to minimize
government spending across the board. Citizens who believe that government is spending too much on formal education must decide whether
to devote their resources to the tax limitation movement or to focus
on spending for education. Although both alternatives would reduce
spending on education, they differ in several important ways.

The possibility that proposals that would affect government generally
may lead to a market system of education cannot be dismissed out of
hand. Nevertheless, the following discussion is limited to efforts explicitly
intended to establish such a system. Any effort here to probe broader
efforts to change government policies would take us too far afield.

Public education is primarily a state and local responsibility. Understandably, education receives less attention in Washington than foreign
relations, the economy, or national politics, the main topics that preoc-

cupy our nation's capital. Clearly, the conservative organizations based in the capital reflect its preoccupation with noneducational topics. Finding someone in Washington who has read a teacher union contract proposal, handled a teacher grievance, or prepared a school budget is not easy; despite frequent contact with the U.S. Department of Education and Washington-based conservative organizations, I have met only one person affiliated with them who (I think) has done any one of these things. That is the bad news. The good news is that the past failures to move toward a market system of education are not necessarily indicative of the outcome under knowledgeable leadership. Efforts to establish a market system of education may not succeed even with such leadership, but we are a long way from having to draw that conclusion.

One of the lessons to be learned from the unsuccessful efforts of the past is that abstract appeals to entrepreneurial opportunities for teachers will not persuade a significant number of teachers to support a market system of education. Like most people, most teachers are not entrepreneurially oriented. For this reason, most teachers will not be impressed by the opportunities that would become available in a market system. To be sure, there are entrepreneurially oriented teachers. For instance, some public school teachers own or operate for-profit summer camps, and more might welcome opportunities to do so. Perhaps a market system could be initiated by vouchers for summer school instruction, available to schools for profit. Such vouchers could tap into the interest in a longer school year while avoiding the objection that "more of the same" would not be productive.

This is only one possible way that a market system could develop outside of public schools, with public school teachers playing a role in both systems. There are some interesting precedents for this in other public services. For example, bus companies sometimes need large numbers of drivers at peak hours. Rather than hiring more regular drivers or paying heavy overtime, they sometimes contract with their regular drivers to work extra hours as independent contractors rather than as employees working overtime. Analogously, teachers teaching summer school might do so as independent contractors, not as school district employees working an extended school year. Interestingly enough, teachers in Japan often function as independent contractors outside of their regular school day. In the United States, the teacher unions will try to block such arrangements, but they could be vulnerable to internal pressures from members who like the idea.

Needless to say, the teacher unions will characterize any financial incentives for teachers as bribes. Bribes are secret inducements to act contrary to law; the strategy suggested would be neither secret nor violative of law. Instead, it would be based on the distinction between union interests and teacher interests. Despite union rhetoric to the contrary, these interests are not always identical. To be sure, the proposed strategy would not eliminate union opposition, but it could render such opposition ineffective. In doing so, it would avoid a major weakness in prior efforts to establish a market system of education.

Opposition Research

Generally speaking, the promarket forces are severely handicapped by their lack of sophistication about public education. For instance, the NEA negotiates separate contracts for professional staff working in Washington and staff working in various regional offices. Interestingly enough, the contracts are not reprinted in NEA publications going to its membership. One reason is that it would be difficult to ask teachers to accept a dues increase so that many of their employees could earn three or four times as much as they do, including fringe benefits that would surprise teachers in the boondocks. What the natives don't know is unlikely to make them restless.

Another reason for the obscurity of the contracts is that they include provisions that would embarrass the NEA and its affiliates if widely disseminated. For instance, the contracts specifically provide for the NEA's right to contract out work.[11] As previously noted, the NEA is opposed to contracting out by school districts. Needless to say, an NEA representative member trying to negotiate a school district prohibition against contracting out could be highly embarrassed by the fact that the NEA contract explicitly allows it.

In years of observing conservative strategy and tactics, attending conservative conferences, listening to conservative speeches, and reading conservative publications—all dealing with public education—I have yet to encounter one individual who had read the contracts between the NEA and its staff unions. Even the few who were vaguely aware of them had never obtained and analyzed the contracts for whatever insights they might provide. The promarket forces cannot afford to ignore such potentially useful evidence that the unions do not practice what they preach.

As noted in Chapter 8, the NEA and its state affiliates support a wide range of policies that are anathema to many groups in our society: for example, the NEA has adopted racial quotas more extensively than any other major organization in the nation, and the teacher organizations can be fairly described as radical feminist organizations. The promarket forces have not taken advantage of the unions' vulnerability on such issues, partly because of their lack of information about the unions.

Agency Shop Fees

Promarket forces also overlook opportunities to weaken the financial base of union influence. For example, they would benefit from publicizing the "service fees" that the unions charge nonmembers. Typically, a union represents all the employees in a "bargaining unit," whether or not they all are members of the union. To avoid the possibility that some employees will benefit from union representation but refuse to pay for it, unions negotiate clauses that require nonmembers to pay service fees as a condition of employment. The U.S. Supreme Court has held that such clauses per se, also referred to as "agency shop" or "fair share" clauses, do not violate the constitutional rights of employees who refuse to join the union.

Initially, the service fees were set at the same amount as union dues. This practice was successfully challenged on the grounds that a portion of union dues was spend for nonbargaining purposes, especially political ones. Forcing employees to contribute to political activities was held to violate their constitutional rights. As a result, the service fees that can be charged to nonmembers are limited to the costs of bargaining and closely related activities. The federal courts have become heavily involved in litigation over which union expenditures are for "bargaining" and which are for "political" activities.[12]

It should now be apparent why the issue is so important. If the Supreme Court adopts an expansive view of "bargaining services," the unions can negotiate for larger payments to the union by nonmembers. Judicial decisions that adopt a more restrictive view will reduce the amounts that unions can raise by such fees. True, school boards have to agree to the union proposals, but most boards end up doing so. Because the service fees are extremely important to the unions, school boards can get important concessions in return. The costs of the concessions, however, are paid by nonmembers of the union, not by the school boards.

In my view, the distinction between bargaining and political costs is a distinction without a difference in public education. Teacher salary schedules are public policies. Labeling them "terms and conditions of employment" does not change that fact. As I see it, spending service fees to negotiate school board policies is no more and no less a political activity than spending the fees to achieve the same result by state legislation. Either both activities should be regarded as political or neither should be. Fortunately for the unions, however, my view of the matter is not the law and is not likely to be the law for quite some time to come.

At the present time, the outcome of the extensive litigation over service fees is not clear. Its practical effects will depend not only on the legal outcomes but on how many teachers pay the service fees, the amounts they have to pay, and the counter-measures the unions can take against narrow interpretations of "bargaining activities."

Until recently, the promarket forces have been unaware of the strategic opportunities presented by this issue. The overwhelming majority of teachers do not know their rights in this matter. It would not be difficult to inform all teachers of their right to challenge service fees, the procedures for doing so, how service fees are calculated, and where to get assistance in challenging union policies. A major effort along these lines is long overdue regardless of one's views about a market system of education. The question is not whether such challenges will weaken the unions; it is how much they will do so.

The Labor Constituency for a Market System

Typically, supporters of voucher campaigns assume that parents are their primary constituency. It seems plausible to do so—after all, parents are directly affected and prefer having a choice to not having a choice. Plausible as it seems, however, this strategy is inadequate. First, parents of school-age children constitute a shrinking percentage of the voting population. Second, a substantial proportion of parents are satisfied with their public schools. Third, parents as such are extremely difficult to organize; effective parent organizations are usually composed of parents who face severe household problems in educating their children. Parental support is highly desirable, but it is far from a sufficient condition to pass a market initiative.

In order for a market initiative to succeed, it must also attract support from noneducational constituencies for noneducational reasons. Workers in competitive industries might be one such constituency. As previously noted, public school teachers are amply protected against risk. Although some private-sector employees enjoy various job protections, public school teachers enjoy much stronger protection than most workers in our society. From an equity standpoint, why should private-sector workers but not teachers face the threat of competition? Inasmuch as a system based on competition is the general rule, the burden of proof should be on the exceptions to it. Furthermore, if protection from competition is justified, employment that incurs the risk of competition should pay more than employment that does not. The underlying issue here has important strategic as well as policy dimensions.

International competition is weakening private-sector unions in both the United States and Western Europe. Meanwhile, public services have expanded, and so has public-sector unionism. Membership in the AFL-CIO reflects these sectoral changes in union membership.[13] Unionization in the public sector, however, is heavily dependent on the monopoly status of public services; in its absence, public-sector unions would decline rapidly.

A consequence is that the public- and private-sector unions have divergent interests. The public-sector unions will favor the expansion of public services, which will require higher taxes and, in some cases at least, risks to the competitive position of American industry. The private-sector unions will be more oriented to low taxes and a stronger competitive position for industries that have to compete internationally. The promarket strategy of the 1990s should capitalize on this conflict of interest between the teachers and the competitive sectors of the U.S. economy.

Unity as a Coalition Imperative

The public education establishment enjoys a strategic advantage in its access to, and influence in, noneducational organizations. When such organizations consider educational issues, they naturally invite leaders of public school organizations to express their views. Whether the leaders represent school boards, school administrators, or teacher unions, their message is clear and consistent: "Protect public education. Do not support a market approach to education."

In contrast, no individual or organization represents a consensus among the promarket forces. When critics of public education address

noneducational organizations, they cannot speak for a unified movement. Even if they represent an organization or an interest group, their
views may differ widely from those of other promarket forces. In other
words, while the public education establishment sends a clear and consistent message, its critics do not. As a result, the public school forces enjoy
a strategic advantage that is widely overlooked.

To offset this public school advantage, the promarket forces must
develop a more unified position on the basic issues. The position need
not be applicable to every state, but it must maintain the unity of the
promarket forces while achieving two objectives: (1) refutation of the
case for the public school monopoly; and (2) presentation of a viable
proposal for a market approach. "Viable" means that all the major
interest groups supporting a market approach will support the proposal.

The history of voucher proposals shows why this step is essential.
Conservatives frequently cite public opinion polls showing that a majority
of citizens support vouchers. Such polls are misleading because certain
features of the voucher plans are omitted. For example, denominational
groups differ sharply on the extent of regulation they would accept
under a voucher plan. The "majority" that supports a voucher plan
shrinks quickly and dramatically when a proposed plan includes regulatory features that are acceptable to some but not all voucher supporters.
This shrinkage of support may emerge over the amount of the voucher,
eligibility requirements, or any of several other issues.

For this reason, the assault on Fort Public Education must be preceded
by an agreement on its objectives and its strategy and tactics. That is, the
leaders of a promarket coalition must know what kind of concessions they
can and cannot make on such matters as state regulation, certification of
teachers in private schools, mandatory curricula, and religious practices.
These issues cannot be avoided; it is imperative that they be resolved
earlier rather than later. Otherwise the promarket coalition will be ineffective at the public opinion level and highly vulnerable to breakup at
the legislative level. Achieving the needed unity does not necessarily
require establishing a new organization, but it does require that coalition
members agree on certain basic issues at the outset.

The availability of funds to develop such unity and to act upon it
effectively is a problem, but a manageable problem. Every day, conservative sources spend large sums on such ratholes as public school choice,
school site management, merit pay, parental involvement, stay-in-school
projects, school-business partnerships, cooperative learning, and career

ladders. The list is endless, and the amounts are staggering, not even counting the enormous amounts contributed for endowed chairs to advocate conservative dogma. If spent intelligently, a small proportion of these funds should be sufficient to achieve a market system of education.

Denominational Schools in a Promarket Coalition

In my opinion, we cannot move to a market system of education without the strong support of denominational schools. Inasmuch as denominational support is contingent on the inclusion of denominational schools in the benefits made available to private schools, it is necessary to examine this issue briefly.

It has long been argued that compulsory education in the absence of government support for private schools is a violation of the religious freedom guaranteed by the First Amendment. Public schools teach certain views that are contrary to the religious views of some parents. If education is compulsory, and acceptable private schools are not available, religious freedom is violated in two ways. Tax funds are used to finance views some parents deem antireligious, and children are forced to attend schools that are hostile to their religious views. The legal freedom to attend nonpublic schools does not remedy either problem. There may not be an acceptable private school in the area, or the parents may not be able to afford it. In either of these cases, their children will be educated in an antireligious environment from the parental point of view.

The main counter-argument is that there is no government obligation to fund private services for citizens dissatisfied with public services. Government is not obligated to support your membership in a tennis club because the public courts are not satisfactory to you. Likewise, it is not required to produce bottled water if you reject publicly supplied water, nor is it required to buy your transportation if you object to travel on a public carrier. Of course, the rebuttal is that you do not have a constitutional right to a water supply as you do to freedom of religion.

Public schools could avoid conflict with religious freedom in various ways: for example, a public school system could be limited to the teaching of basic skills. Religious freedom becomes an issue primarily as the result of school activities that antagonize religious groups but are not essential to any legitimate educational objective. Controversies over making condoms available in the schools illustrate this point. The idea that giving condoms to students free of charge and without parental consent is essential to the legitimate objectives of public education is simply indefensible. The public school forces may win many of these battles, but each victory brings them closer to losing the war.

In the past, several major Protestant denominations opposed assistance to parents who wanted their children educated in denominational schools. This position reflected the Protestant orientation of public schools: "separation of church and state" was initially a fig leaf to cover Protestant domination of public education.[14] In recent years, however, evangelical Protestant groups have become highly critical of public education. Sex education, restrictions on prayer, neglect or denigration of creationism, and the absence of support for marriage and traditional family values have contributed to this trend. For these reasons, denominations opposed to educational vouchers in the past are becoming strongly supportive of them.

While we cannot move to a market system without the support of denominational schools, neither can we do so primarily for denominational reasons. Our society is becoming increasingly secular. If religious organizations were unable to enact a voucher system when their influence was much greater than it is today, reasons of religious freedom will not suffice to achieve either a voucher or a market system. The fact that evangelical Protestants and orthodox Jews have become very active supporters of private schooling does not invalidate this conclusion.

In the past, church-and-state issues have dominated the debate over educational vouchers. Although understandable, this domination has had unfortunate side effects. For one thing, it has obscured the efficiency issues. It is necessary to recognize that the religious freedom argument for a market system of education rests on different and potentially conflicting grounds from the efficiency argument. In the future, it will be essential to avoid treating the religious rationale for vouchers as a market rationale for them. To do so runs the risk that practical and legal arguments against vouchers redeemable in denominational schools will bring down more general voucher plans. I believe, however, that it is possible to mobilize denominational support without prejudice to the broader arguments for allowing market forces to work in education.

In the long run, under a market system, schools for profit may gain market share at the expense of denominational as well as public schools. As we have seen, many parents of pupils in denominational schools are interested primarily in better education, not religious guidance. Experience in health care also suggests that a voucher system open to schools for profit might ultimately weaken enrollments in denominational schools or lead to changes in their character. In health care, an overwhelming proportion of fees are paid by government or by third-party insurers. Over time, the nonprofit hospitals have become remarkably similar to for-profit ones. Even the amount of medical care provided free of charge in nonprofit hospitals does not differ markedly from that in for-profit hospitals.[15] It would be premature to predict the same outcome in education, but some factors clearly point in this direction.

Who Will Lead?

Democratic political candidates tend to oppose any move toward a market system of education. The public employee unions, especially the NEA and the AFT, are heavily represented in Democratic Party primaries and party conventions; of the 4,928 delegates to the 1992 Democratic national convention, 512 were NEA or AFT members—the largest interest-group contingent among the delegates.[16] Also, as long as black political leaders regard government as the main source of black progress, Democratic candidates are not likely to support market-oriented changes; to do so would antagonize too many key constituencies in the Democratic party.

Republican candidates for public office are less likely to oppose a market system. Their tendency will be to avoid the issue, especially in close elections. A Republican candidate who can achieve a substantial minority among teachers is not likely to endanger it by embracing a market system of education. By and large, therefore, political leaders in both major parties will be opponents or followers, not leaders, of public opinion on a market system of education. Such a system is likely to emerge first in states that allow voter initiatives. In such states, nongovernmental organizations have a chance to enact legislation by direct vote of the electorate. The procedure has many drawbacks, but it does provide a way to overcome the legislative obstacles to a market system.

Who will provide the leadership that is essential to the transition? Although leadership can come from anywhere, the business community is the most likely source; however, it is essential to avoid any illusions on the subject. One sometimes encounters the fantasy that big business controls public education. In the real world, most businessmen have little interest in public education and would be only too happy to ignore it if they could. The business leaders who do get involved in educational reform are divided on what should be done and why. Furthermore, some focus on efforts to protect their own companies, whereas others participate in broader efforts from which their companies would benefit; success at the company level may weaken incentives to work for system changes. In addition, many business leaders are easily co-opted by the public school establishment. Many who are not would expose their companies to unacceptable risks by advocating a market system of education. Finally, it is easy to overestimate business leaders' sophistication about, and commitment to, free enterprise; many business leaders owe their success to, and devote much of their time to seeking, government assistance to stifle competition.

In view of these realities, what reason is there to anticipate business leadership of the transition to a market system of education? First of all, the consequences of inadequate education fall directly and heavily on business, and do so at all levels of employment. At the high tech levels, the growing shortages of scientists and engineers are creating severe manpower problems. At entry levels, the problems are just as serious. More and more companies are unable to recruit employees who can read safety signs, or compute discounts plus sales taxes, or write simple reports. U.S. companies are under a severe competitive disadvantage that can no longer be ignored.

A crucially important consideration is that business leaders have the leverage to implement a transition. Not that they can do so by themselves, but they can establish the coalitions that are essential for this purpose. The conventional view is that aroused parents must "take charge" of schools; the reality is that a handful of business leaders can do more than thousands of unorganized parents. Unlike the parental interest, the business interest is permanent, hence it cannot be stonewalled until the reformers give up. Much as it might wish to do so, business cannot withdraw from the effort. Of course, some multinationals can move their operations overseas, but most U.S. companies cannot adopt this solution.

Business leaders might also lead the way toward a market system of education by entering the education market directly. As pointed out in Chapter 1, it is not easy to compete against a free service, but some companies may find market niches that demonstrate the educational potential of the for-profit sector. The growth of privatization in such major industries as health care and prisons has stimulated corporate interest in education for profit, hence increased activity along this line is a real possibility. Such activity has the potential to bypass the political efforts to move to a market system.

The philanthropic foundations oriented to market solutions to social problems are another potential source of leadership. Whether or not the individuals who will lead the transition come from these foundations, it is imperative that the foundations change their approach to educational policy. As matters stand, producers enjoy overwhelming domination of educational research and of access to media and political forums. This domination cannot be challenged by isolated individuals in organizations scattered around the country; it is essential to establish a market-oriented educational organization capable of conducting its own research and challenging producers in the media and in political settings. The establishment of such an organization will require basic changes in the market-oriented foundations themselves. It will be interesting to see whether their officials, who never tire of emphasizing the need for change in others, can change their own strategy on educational improvement.

Conclusion

Historically, conservatives in the United States have defined freedom as the absence of legal restraints. You are free to purchase X if you are not legally restricted from purchasing X. Liberals in the United States have tended to define freedom as the power to do something. You are free to purchase X if you have enough money to buy X. The liberal definition leads to a more activist role for government; it has to provide the means if citizens are to be free, that is, empowered to do things.

In controversies over educational vouchers, the liberal and conservative approaches to freedom are reversed. The conservatives, generally in favor of vouchers, argue that freedom is the power to do, hence government must provide the means for attending schools of choice. Meanwhile, liberals typically argue that freedom in education is the legal freedom to attend schools of choice. Accordingly, they oppose government vouchers that would enable parents to enroll their children in schools of choice. At the same time, conservatives would be horrified by widespread acceptance of the power-to-do concept of freedom; liberals would be just as shocked by widespread acceptance of the idea that freedom should be interpreted as the absence of legal restraints on a given action. One could hardly ask for a more striking example of the inconsistencies that characterize voucher controversies.

In this book I have tried to avoid various fallacies shared by both supporters and opponents of vouchers. Perhaps the most important is that a voucher system is tantamount to a market system. On the contrary, the voucher plans embodied in state or federal legislation, enacted or proposed, rarely incorporate the basic elements of a market system. The proposals may be justified on other grounds, but most of them are not even interim steps toward a market system. For example, choice proposals that help parents of students in denominational schools, who thereupon lose interest in a market system of education, are a step away from, not toward, a market system.

Interim steps may very well be necessary; it is unreasonable to anticipate the emergence of a fully developed market system in one stroke. Incremental improvements should not be rejected because of utopian expectations. Nevertheless, willingness to accept any sort of voucher plan as a beginning step has often lead to noncompetitive voucher proposals, such as the one adopted in Milwaukee. When such plans fail to bring about widespread improvement, they are deemed failures of a market system, even when they are the antithesis of such a system.

This outcome is virtually certain when schools for profit are not allowed to compete with public and nonprofit schools. Nonprofit schools are not likely to protest the restrictions on schools for profit: if they can get assistance without competition, so much the better. In the past, schools for profit have been much less influential politically than public and nonprofit schools, hence it has not been difficult to restrict their growth statutorily. As will be discussed shortly, this situation may be changing as a result of recent developments.

It should not be assumed however, that progress toward a market system will necessarily be incremental; a rapid transition should not be dismissed as out of the question. The promarket forces will have one ineradicable advantage in the years ahead. That advantage is the inherent futility of conventional school reform. The direction of change in public opinion is not in doubt: the emergence of a market system is a question of when, not if. Furthermore, once a market system begins to emerge, its supporters may be able to avoid crippling restrictions or protracted delays. One major breakthrough will more than compensate for ninety-nine major defeats. There are precedents for rapid change in education: for example, it took less than ten years to go from the first teacher collective bargaining contract to having more than 50 percent of the nation's teachers working under such contracts. This is more than incremental change, both in terms of how policy is made and in the proportion of school employees affected by the change. Regardless of its merits, a market system of education could emerge just as rapidly.

How much improvement of what outcomes would occur under a market system? We must bear in mind that in education students perform most of the work, and that some of the most important student variables are not controlled by school systems. Others can be controlled but only at a prohibitive cost. The fact of the matter is that very little is known, or at least agreed upon, about the relative importance of various factors affecting educational outcomes. Even for the same student, variations in age, grade level, subject, classmates, and personal circumstances may result in variations in achievement. The helter-skelter nature of educational research is due partly to this fact; one can make a plausible argument for the importance of scores of factors. An additional complication is the duration of the change: the results ten years after the establishment of a market system could be drastically different from the results after one year. And, of course, as various states set up market systems of education, there will be important differences among the market systems themselves.

Despite these caveats, I believe that a market system will demonstrate its superiority promptly, especially if costs as well as outcomes are considered. As we have seen, cost comparisons have problems of their own, but overall they are more defensible than comparisons of outcomes. A rigorous comparison of costs would also add to the pressure to clarify outcomes, a development that is long overdue. Nevertheless, a market system is not likely to emerge simply as a less expensive way to achieve a given level of educational output. Although this is a valid reason to make the change, the change is not likely to be made primarily for this reason.

The change to a market system of education will come about because the conditions that gave rise to public education no longer exist and its rationale is no longer viable. Here, we have a choice. On the producer side, we have a system in which 4.5 million school district employees advance their interests by political action. The policy alternative is a system in which their interests are served by providing better service at a lower price. On the consumer side, we have a system in which consumers lack information, lack incentives to get information, and must try to achieve their educational objectives through political processes in which the cards are stacked against them. The policy alternative is a system in which consumers can act individually with reasonable prospects for success if their views are shared by even a relatively small number of others. Granted, this way of formulating the alternatives is an oversimplification. Nevertheless, from a systems point of view, it is not a misleading one. Surely, the choice between these alternatives is clear, even if the details are not.

≈ Epilogue

Several recent developments may have important ramifications for the transition to a market system of education. Because it was not feasible to discuss them in previous chapters, I shall do so here. First, however, I would like to point out a caveat that applies to my entire analysis.

In recommending policy changes, there is a temptation to exaggerate the benefits and minimize the negatives of the changes. This temptation is exacerbated by media tendencies to pay more attention to extremes than to positions that try to balance both positive and negative considerations. The definition of sociology as the study of unintended consequences is a striking recognition of the gap between the intentions and predictions asserted to support policies and the policies' actual consequences in practice.

To avoid any such gap, let me emphasize that the advent of a market system of education will not be the end of educational history. In addition to the problems already discussed, several others will or may arise under a market system. I cannot refrain, therefore, from adding a cautionary note to the argument of this book.

For the sake of discussion, let us assume that a declining birth rate has greatly reduced the size of the K–12 market. Public, nonprofit, and for-profit schools find themselves competing for a declining number of students. At some point, they will be forced to consider the benefits of collusion instead of competition. To achieve a survival level of K–12 funding, schools in all sectors may have to compromise their differences.

317

As a matter of fact, this frequently happens. Monopoly sometimes results from the breakdown of competition, and competition sometimes results from the breakdown of monopoly. Under certain circumstances, monopoly and competition can be viewed as complementary ways of retaining market share or even of staying in business. Thus, down the road, competition in the education industry may lead to a two- or even a three-sector monopoly, arranged to prevent new entrants into any of the sectors. This is not a reason to break up the public school monopoly. It is only a reason to avoid the assumption that once established a market system would necessarily continue unabated.

The Edison Project

On May 16, 1991, Christopher Whittle, CEO of Whittle Communications, announced the Edison Project, a plan to establish a national chain of profitmaking schools. The plan called for the first group of schools to open in 1996, and an enrollment of 2 million students in 1,000 schools by 2010. A second press conference in February 1992 identified the seven-member design team for the project; a third, in May 1992, featured the appointment of Benno Schmidt, the president of Yale University, as CEO of the Edison Project.

Prior to the announcement of the Edison Project, Whittle Communications had been active in television, book and magazine publishing, advertising, and other activities involving the media. In education, it had created Channel One, a twelve-minute news program that includes two minutes of commercial advertising. In exchange for requiring pupils to watch Channel One, schools receive television equipment and auxiliary services free of charge; Whittle Communications' revenues come from the advertisers on the program. Despite a great deal of controversy over requiring children to watch advertising, Channel One is a commercially successful program that reaches about 40 percent of all secondary school students in the United States.

The appointment of Schmidt was a major worldwide news item. For example, it was the lead article in the *Financial Times,* which is published in New York, London, Paris, Frankfurt, and Tokyo.[1] It was featured in all major print and electronic media, and the editorializing and analyzing have been nonstop since it was announced. Generally speaking, however, the media and professional reactions have missed the significance of the appointment. Typically, they have speculated on whether Whittle can

bring about basic change in American education. Fundamentally, however, he has already done that, regardless of the fate of the Edison
Project.

The significance of the appointment of Benno Schmidt was this: As a
result of it, serious discussion of educational reform can no longer ignore
the role of schools for profit. Prior to the appointment, not a single
major report on educational reform, governmental or private, paid any
attention to them. All envisaged public schools as the locus of reform. A
few recommended voucher plans that included nonprofit schools; to my
knowledge, however, none specifically identified schools for profit as
major players, even potentially. In effect, the Schmidt appointment raises
the possibility that education will become a three-sector industry by the
year 2000.

Indisputably, the Edison Project constitutes a dramatic change in the
approach to educational R&D. The project has budgeted $60 million for
the design phase; in addition, Whittle is seeking $750 million for the
development phase. As far as I know, no one has challenged these
amounts. This is not to say that Whittle will necessarily raise the amount
for the development phase, but the figures are being taken seriously by
all concerned. As pointed out in Chapter 11, the National Academy of
Education report on educational research, released in July 1991, asserts
that educational R&D is underfunded but does not mention the possibility that the underfunding might be resolved or ameliorated by schools
for profit.[2] It would be difficult to find a more glaring example of
educational neglect of market alternatives.

For that matter, the Edison Project is virtually certain to generate
more useful reforms than the New American Schools Development Corporation (NASDC), the Bush administration's plan to establish a "break
the mold" school in every congressional district.[3] During the next few
years, the nation will have an unparalleled opportunity to compare
educational R&D under government and nonprofit auspices with educational R&D in the for-profit sector. The comparison is likely to illustrate
the superiority of R&D in the for profit sector. The NASDC funds are
charitable contributions, mainly from business foundations. If NASDC
projects fail to develop worthwhile innovations, the contributors (and
the researchers) will not suffer as a result; the funds were written off
when contributed. In fact, it is doubtful whether NASDC itself will survive
very long since it was publicized from its beginnings as a Bush administration initiative. In contrast, the Edison Project funds are investments; the

Edison Project must prove its worth in the marketplace or the investors lose their equity.

Another important difference lies in dissemination. If a NASDC project produces a worthwhile innovation, there is no assurance whatsoever that school districts will adopt it. The Edison Project, however, begins with the assurance of widespread adoption by several schools. This is only one example of the fact that the Edison Project can rely on economies of scale, but NASDC projects cannot.

The Edison Project is also shattering the conventional wisdom on educational compensation. Among educators, there is widespread curiosity over Schmidt's compensation as CEO of the Edison Project. The widespread perception is that it must have been astronomical to entice him from the presidency of Yale University. Accurate or not, the perception helps to demonstrate that large rewards that only the private sector can offer are essential to attract top-flight talent into education.

All this is not to say that the Edison Project necessarily will be a business success. For one thing, it faces all-out opposition from the education establishment, especially the teacher unions. As pointed out in Chapter 3, the unions are cognizant of the fact that competition would weaken them in several ways. Undoubtedly, they will do everything they can to prevent it. They will pressure elected and appointed public officials to interpret and apply the statutes and regulations on teacher certification, building codes, zoning, pupil transportation, class size, corporation taxes, child labor, whatever, in the most obstructive ways possible. If the Edison Project must absorb heavy costs in opposing these efforts, it may go down in flames regardless of its educational merits.

Efforts to cripple the project this way face problems of their own. Private schools in the United States are largely unregulated. The reason is that most are (or were until very recently) denominational schools. Consequently, close regulation of them raised the danger of conflict between public officials and religious organizations. Most public officials are eager to avoid this kind of conflict.

Generally speaking, state statutes and regulations governing private schools do not distinguish nonprofit from proprietary schools. Consequently, new regulatory burdens that apply to private schools will be opposed by existing private schools and their parent religious organizations. Efforts to impose new regulatory burdens solely on proprietary schools will appear to be a obstructionist tactic directed at Edison Schools. After all, schools for profit already exist, albeit in minuscule numbers. A rush to regulate them under the circumstances will be difficult to defend. We can expect such efforts to be made, but Edison Project strategy assumes that they will not be successful.

Successful or not, we can expect a major effort to portray profits as an evil objective that can be achieved only by taking advantage of children. This is already a dominant theme as evidenced by Jonathan Kozol's criticism of Schmidt for joining the Edison Project: "If it is idealism which motivates him, I don't understand why he has to commercialize his intelligence. Why not set up a nonprofit foundation and not give deference to the almighty dollar?"[4] The Russian people are fortunate that Kozol is not leading the effort to restructure a society devastated by the notion that seeking profits is morally inferior to governmental or nonprofit activity.

Edison Project strategy assumes that parents are not likely to transfer their children out of schools that are satisfactory. Its plan is to enroll pupils at the preschool level, and to rely on positive preschool experiences to convince parents to keep their children in Whittle Schools. There is, however, a great deal more regulation of for-profit preschool programs and day care than of private schools. For this reason, regulatory obstacles may be a critical problem at the outset. On the positive side, Edison Schools will not be competing with a free service during the preschool years. Their prospects at higher grade levels will be much more promising if they can meet parental expectations at the preschool level.

The project timetable calls for 150,000 students in the fall of 1996, but the students will be "probably aged 1 through 6." The plan is to add a grade a year.[5] Thus Edison Schools may not enroll students in the first grade until 2000 or close to it, and K–12 Edison Schools may not emerge until 2010. The goal of 2 million students by 2010 is an audacious one, but conceivably most of this enrollment may be at the preschool level. In any case, Edison Schools may avoid direct competition with public or private schools for several years at least. Indeed, the Edison Project can argue that it will be helping achieve the Education 2000 goal of having all children in the first grade ready for school by the year 2000.

From the Edison Project standpoint, the critical issue is how many parents will be willing to pay the tuition that will be charged. Obviously, price and quality will affect the answer, but so will other factors. Suppose the children of President X or Governor Y or Mayor Z or Michael Jordan were to enroll in Edison Schools. Enrollments might rise dramatically regardless of other considerations. I have no idea of what kind of market analysis or approach undergirds the Edison Project game plan, but cost and quality will certainly not be the only factors affecting parental decisions. After all, they are not now, in either public or private education.

According to its news releases, Edison Schools will not charge more than the average cost per student in public schools. Those who doubt that this is feasible overlook two critical points. One is that the official statistics on per-pupil costs in public schools understate the real costs, perhaps by as much as 50 percent. Indeed, one of the important side effects of the Edison Project is likely to be public awareness of the real costs of public education. If it cites the real instead of the official costs, the Edison Project will easily be able to fulfill its commitment to charge less than the average per-pupil costs of public schools. Of course, if the average cost per pupil in public schools is $8,000 instead of $5,000, the Edison Project's larger margin of safety may not be very helpful; fewer parents will be willing to spend $8,000 instead of $5,000 for their children's education. In any event, Edison Schools should be able to provide much better education for substantially less than the real per-pupil costs of public education.

In practice, pupils in Edison Schools may achieve as well as public school pupils at only half the cost of public education or less. This would be an enormous achievement but would not necessarily help the Edison Project. If Edison Schools cannot stimulate greater achievement than the public schools, parents will have no incentive to enroll their children in them. Compared to Edison Schools, the public schools may be grossly inefficient, but their inefficiencies are absorbed by public, not parental funds. For this reason, Edison Schools could be much more efficient than public schools but nevertheless fail as a business venture.

The second critical point widely overlooked in assessments of the viability of the Edison Project is its potential for using school facilities for multiple commercial purposes. In my opinion, potential revenues from such uses could be just as important to the project's survival as student tuition. Schools have many types of facilities that could be made available, for a fee, for other activities outside (and in some cases even within) school hours:

   meeting rooms
   auditoriums
   food service facilities

parking space
work spaces
educational equipment, such as audiovisual recorders
recreational facilities, such as tennis courts, swimming pools,
    playgrounds
computers.

These facilities are often used in a very limited way. The food service facilities may be used only to provide lunch; they may be idle the rest of the day and all the time when school is not in session. In short, public schools typically do not utilize their facilities efficiently for nonschool purposes.

This underutilization is inherent in public ownership of schools. School management has no incentive to achieve full utilization; it would not share in the savings or "profits." Indeed, school management has disincentives to utilize its resources fully. If, for example, the school cafeteria were leased to a private entrepreneur for use after school, any income received by the school would merely replace other funds made available to it, food service companies not using school facilities would object, and so on. To be sure, the "community school" concept incorporates multi-use of school facilities and has been around a long time. Nevertheless, multiple use available only to public services under public control is very different from multiple use that can take advantage of commercial possibilities under commercial control.

The Edison Project changes the economics and politics of the situation by changing the ownership of the school. The responsibility for full utilization of school facilities is exercised by a private-sector owner, not a board of education. Obviously, a private-sector owner does have financial incentives to use facilities in the most efficient way. With this in mind, let us consider briefly some of the multiple-use possibilities of private ownership of school facilities:

1. In the nation there are almost a thousand franchised for-profit learning centers that serve pupils attending regular school but outside the regular school day. Typically, they are open from 3:00 to 9:00 P.M. Monday through Thursday, on Saturdays, and during the summer. The facilities are purchased or leased from private funds. It should be possible to use Edison Project facilities for this purpose.
2. Schools have auditoriums, meeting rooms, parking spaces,

and meal facilities. They can be rented for a fee, with meal services as an add-on.

3. In many situations, college courses or other training programs could be conducted in Edison Schools. Such use need not be confined to education courses.

4. Where schools could not be open for sit-down meals, they might be used for catering and takeout services after regular school hours. A private company might operate the school lunch program under contract and also a variety of other programs, such as "meals on wheels."

5. Professionals rendering services to children could pay for locating in Edison facilities, where they could serve children before, during, and after the regular school day.

It remains to be seen whether the Edison Project will pursue these possibilities, but any significant success in doing so would invalidate conventional analysis of school costs and revenues. The project is also likely to emphasize acceleration as a student benefit. Unquestionably, if it can reduce the number of years of schooling with no loss of achievement, the Edison Project will be able to demonstrate extremely large student benefits, not to mention benefits to the government in reducing the costs of education and adding to economic output. The potential of acceleration appears to be greater at secondary levels, but it is likely to play a prominent role in whatever plans are eventually adopted. The Edison Project also plans to enter the school management field, but its plans in this regard were not available for analysis.

Let me now address some problems instead of advantages that are not fully appreciated at this early stage of development. One is that the sources of capital for the Edison Project may dry up for reasons not related to its economic or educational feasibility. Another is that the project will have to select a large number of sites and negotiate their availability under conditions of great uncertainty; site acquisition and development could be a more difficult problem than the development of a better educational system at a reasonable cost to parents. Clearly, the widespread assumption that the fate of the Edison Project depends on its educational program is highly simplistic from an entrepreneurial point of view.

The most frequent criticism of the Edison Project is that it will foster inequality of educational opportunity. According to its critics, the parents who enroll their children in Edison Schools will be from the upper middle class. Their enrollment will weaken the parent pool devoted to improving public education; public schools will increasingly serve disadvantaged minorities and will lose an important political constituency.

For the time being, the objection is moot. Whittle has pledged to provide scholarships for 20 percent of the students to ensure that Edison Schools provide opportunities for disadvantaged students. Although his reasons are understandable, I question whether the 20 percent policy can or should survive in the long run.

For the sake of discussion, let us assume that the Edison Project ushers in a competitive market system of education. Suppose a competing school company is able to offer comparable service at a much lower price because its tuition fees do not cover the costs of scholarships for the disadvantaged. What then? Is the Edison Project morally obligated to adhere to the 20 percent rule at the risk of losing market share or going bankrupt? I don't think so.

The costs of educating the disadvantaged should be shared by everyone, not just the parents who enroll their children in Edison Schools. I am not criticizing the Edison Project for its plan to have tuition subsidize 20 percent of its student body. If the project can succeed regardless, more power to it. My contention is that the project should not be obligated as a matter of public policy or morality to provide scholarships to the disadvantaged. We do not require buyers of other goods and services to subsidize indigent consumers this way. Significantly, efforts to require doctors and lawyers to provide some service to the indigent on a pro bono basis are widely regarded as inequitable from both producer and consumer points of view. Any such policy or requirement in education will be a major obstacle to reducing the cost and/or raising the quality of the service.

Instead of requiring parents to subsidize disadvantaged pupils, the Edison Project might support scholarship funds to which nonparents, especially corporations, could contribute. This would spread the cost and help to avoid the possibility that the subsidy in the tuition fees could threaten the viability of Edison Schools. In fact, corporation-sponsored scholarship funds for K–12 students are increasing rapidly and may become a major source of private school tuition for disadvantaged pupils, regardless of the Edison Project.

Initially, the Edison Project was committed to accepting all students who applied, up to school capacity. Perhaps because the commitment might have been impossible to fulfill, it appears to have been modified so that it may not include students so severely disabled that they could not benefit from attending Edison Schools.[6] School services for some disabled students require $100,000 or more annually. Obviously, Edison Schools cannot enroll many such students at the average per-pupil cost in public schools, whether based on real or official costs; adherence to the policy of accepting all applicants could lead to an economic or public relations disaster, or both.

At the political level, the Edison Project could trigger the formation of a business coalition that has the resources to achieve significant progress toward a market system of education. This outcome is more likely if several large companies participate in the project. Here we come to a fundamental change that the Edison Project may have initiated in U.S. education.

Conservative efforts to reform education have been a fiasco partly because of overemphasis on parents as the primary constituency for reform. As previously noted, however, most parents are satisfied with their children's public schools. This is especially true of parents in the affluent suburbs. Regardless, even dissatisfied parents seldom constitute an effective lobby for basic change. In contrast, business has the resources and the incentives to take effective political action. If several large corporations participate in the Edison Project, we may see the emergence of a coalition that will pose a real political threat to the public school establishment.

To avoid a premature collision with the public school establishment, Whittle has repeatedly asserted that his objective is to create models for public school reform. I am skeptical. Does Toyota introduce innovations in the hope that General Motors will learn from them? In any case, public school leaders are not buying Whittle's benevolent explanation. More important, public schools probably will be unable to follow the lead of Edison Schools even if they wish to do so. Public schools are subject to different laws, regulations, incentive structures, economic and political dynamics, cultures, and policymaking criteria. The supposition that they can promptly adopt private school innovations is wishful thinking. If the Edison Project achieves a beachhead, a massive invasion of schools for profit will probably follow. Knowing this, the public school lobby will do everything it can to prevent the establishment of the beachhead.

In the immediate future, the Edison Project will have to resolve the nitty-gritty problems of school location, organization, curriculum, educational technology, food service, transportation, and maintenance, to cite just a few. At this point, what will emerge is anybody's guess; the project is a leap of faith, not a product of number crunching. The first news release on the Edison Project includes this statement:

> Private profit making schools . . . will be the most effective way to achieve significant improvement in elementary and secondary education. It might turn out that one top executive in one of our largest corporations could do more to bring about meaningful reform than the combined efforts of the public education establishment—paradoxically, not by trying to achieve educational reform but by trying to conduct a profitable business.

I know this statement well; it is a quotation from *Beyond Public Education,* a book of mine published in 1986.[7] Will Whittle be the business executive who fulfills the prophecy? Perhaps, perhaps not. If the Edison Project is not successful after all the publicity it has evoked, its failure will be publicized to discourage all such efforts thereafter. Needless to say, if it does fail, its opponents will not be scrupulous about identifying the reasons.

The California Educational Choice Initiative

On October 25, 1991, a group of California citizens known as the Excellence Through Choice in Education League (EXCEL) filed an initiative petition with the California attorney general. In August 1992, after several legal controversies, the California secretary of state announced that the initiative qualified for submission to the electorate.[8] Should the initiative be approved, it would probably be the most significant step toward a market system of education in the history of U.S. education. Because of its significance I shall quote the initiative in its entirety before discussing it.

The Parental Choice in Education Amendment

The following section, the "Parental Choice in Education Amendment," is hereby added to Article IX of the California Constitution:

Section 17. Purpose. The people of California, desiring to improve the quality of education available to all children, adopt this Section to: (1) enable parents to determine which schools best meet their children's needs; (2) empower parents to send their children to such schools; (3) establish academic accountability based on national standards; (4) reduce bureaucracy so that more educational dollars reach the classroom; (5) provide greater opportunities for teachers; and (6) mobilize the private sector to help accommodate our burgeoning school-age population.

Therefore: All parents are hereby empowered to choose any school, public or private, for the education of their children, as provided in this Section.

(a) *Empowerment of Parents; Granting of Scholarships.* The state shall annually provide a scholarship to every resident school-age child. Scholarships may be redeemed by the child's parents at any scholarship-redeeming school.

(1) The scholarship value for each child shall be at least fifty percent of the total amount of state and local government spending per student for education in kindergarten and grades one through twelve during the preceding fiscal year, calculated on a statewide basis, including every cost to the state, school districts, and county offices of education of maintaining kindergarten and elementary and secondary education, but excluding expenditures on scholarships granted pursuant to this Section and excluding any unfunded pension liability associated with the public school system.

(2) Scholarship value shall be equal for every child in any given grade. In the case of student transfer during the school year, the scholarship shall be prorated. The Legislature may award supplemental funds for reasonable transportation needs for low-income children and special needs attributable to physical impairment or learning disability. Nothing in this Section shall prevent the use in any school of supplemental assistance from any source, public or private.

(3) If the scholarship amount exceeds the charges imposed by a scholarship-redeeming school for any year in which the student is in attendance, the surplus shall become a credit held in trust by the State for the student for later application toward charges at any scholarship-redeeming school or any institution of higher education in California, public or private, which meets the requirements imposed on scholarship-redeeming schools in Section 17(b)(1),

(2), (3), and (5). Any surplus remaining on the student's twenty-sixth birthday shall revert to the state treasury.

(4) Scholarships provided hereunder are grants of aid to children through their parents and not to the schools in which the children are enrolled. Such scholarships shall not constitute taxable income. The parents shall be free to choose any scholarship-redeeming school, and such selection shall not constitute a decision or act of the State or any of its subdivisions. No other provision of this Constitution shall prevent the implementation of this Section.

(5) Children enrolled in private schools on October 1, 1991, shall receive scholarships, if otherwise eligible, beginning with the 1995–96 school year. All other children shall receive scholarships beginning with the 1993–94 school year.

(6) The State Board of Education may require each public school and each scholarship-redeeming school to choose and administer tests reflecting national standards for the purpose of measuring individual academic improvement. Such tests shall be scored by independent parties. Each school's composite results for each grade level shall be released to the public. Individual results shall be released only to the school and the child's parent.

(7) Governing boards of school districts shall establish a mechanism consistent with federal law to allocate enrollment capacity based primarily on parental choice. Any public school which chooses not to redeem scholarships shall, after district enrollment assignments are complete, open its remaining enrollment capacity to children regardless of residence. Children shall be deemed residents of the school district in which they are enrolled for fiscal purposes.

(8) No child shall receive any scholarship under this Section or any credit under Section 17(a)(3) for any year in which the child enrolls in a non-scholarship-redeeming school, unless the Legislature provides otherwise.

(b) *Empowerment of Private Schools; Redemption of Scholarships.* A private school may become a scholarship-redeeming school by filing with the State Board of Education a statement indicating satisfaction of the legal requirements which applied to private schools on October 1, 1991, and the requirements of this Section.

(1) No school which discriminates on the basis of race, ethnicity, color, or national origin shall redeem scholarships.

(2) To the extent permitted by this Constitution and the Consti-

tution of the United States, the State shall prevent from redeeming scholarships any school which advocates unlawful behavior; teaches hatred of any person or group on the basis of race, ethnicity, color, national origin, religion, or gender; or deliberately provides false and misleading information respecting the school.

(3) No school with fewer than 20 students may redeem scholarships, unless the Legislature provides otherwise.

(4) Private schools shall be accorded maximum flexibility to educate their students and shall be free from unnecessary, burdensome, or onerous regulation. No regulation of private schools, scholarship-redeeming or not, beyond that required by this Section and that which applied to private schools on October 1, 1991, shall be issued or enacted, unless approved by a three-fourths vote of the Legislature or, alternatively, as to any regulation pertaining to health, safety or land use imposed by any county, city, district, or subdivision of the State, a majority vote of qualified electors within the affected jurisdiction. In any legal proceeding challenging such a regulation as inconsistent with this section, the governmental body issuing or enacting it shall have the burden of establishing that the regulation: (A) is essential to assure the health, safety, or education of students; (B) does not unduly burden private schools or the parents of students therein; and (C) will not harass, impede, injure, or suppress private schools.

(5) Notwithstanding Section 17(b)(4), the Legislature may enact civil and criminal penalties for schools and persons who engage in fraudulent conduct in connection with the solicitation of students or redemption of scholarships.

(6) Each school may establish a code of conduct and discipline and enforce it with sanctions, including dismissal. A student who is deriving no substantial academic benefit or is responsible for serious or habitual misconduct related to the school may be dismissed.

(7) After the parent designates the enrolling school, the State shall disburse the student's scholarship funds, excepting funds held in trust pursuant to Section 17 (a)(3), in equal amounts monthly, directly to the school for credit to the parent's account. Monthly disbursals shall occur within 30 days of receipt of the school's statement of current enrollment.

(8) Expenditures for scholarships issued under this Section and savings resulting from the implementation of this Section shall

count toward the minimum funding requirements for education established by Section 8 and 8.5 of Article XVI.

(c) Empowerment of Teachers; Conversion of Schools. Within one year after the people adopt this Section, the Legislature shall establish an expeditious process by which public schools may become independent scholarship-redeeming schools. Such schools shall be common schools under this Article, and Section 6 of this Article shall not limit their formation.

(1) Except as otherwise required by this Constitution and the Constitution of the United States, such schools shall operate under laws and regulation no more restrictive than those applicable to private schools under Section 17(b).

(2) Employees of such schools shall be permitted to continue their state-funded pension and health care programs on the same terms as other similarly situated participants so long as they remain in the employ of the school.

(3) Such schools shall receive State educational appropriations, other than those authorized in Section 17(a)(2) and Section 17(c)(2), only through scholarship redemption.

(d) Definitions.

(1) "Charges" include tuition, fees, books, supplies, transportation, room and board, and other educational costs.

(2) A "child" is an individual eligible to attend kindergarten or grades one through twelve in the public school system.

(3) A "parent" is any person having legal or effective custody of the child.

(4) "Qualified electors" are persons registered to vote, whether or not they vote in any particular election.

(5) The Legislature may establish reasonable standards for determining the "residency" of the children.

(6) "Savings" from the implementation of this Section shall include, but not be limited to, net savings resulting from the transfer of students from public schools to scholarship-redeeming schools, lower interest expense and reduced bonded indebtedness than would otherwise be incurred for construction, acquisition, leasing, or other creation of new public school capacity to accommodate increases in the number of school-age children beginning with the 1993–94 school year, and amounts reverting to the State under Section 17 (a)(3).

(7) A "scholarship-redeeming school" is any school, public or

private, located within California, which meets the requirements of this Section. No school shall be compelled to become a scholarship-redeeming school. No school which meets the requirements of this Section shall be prevented from becoming a scholarship-redeeming school.

(8) A "student" is a child attending school.

(9) "Total state and local government spending" in Section 17 (a)(1) includes, but is not limited to, spending funded from all revenue sources, including the General Fund, federal funds, local property taxes, lottery funds, and local miscellaneous income such as developer fees, but excluding bond proceeds and charitable donations.

(e) *Implementation*. The Legislature shall implement this Section through legislation consistent with the purposes and provisions of this Section.

(f) *Limitation of Actions*. Any action or proceeding contesting the validity of the adoption of this Section or the validity of any provision thereof shall be commenced within six months from the date of the election at which this Section is approved; otherwise this Section and all of its provisions shall be held valid, legal, and incontestable.

(g) *Severability*. If any provision of this Section or the application thereof to any person or circumstance is held invalid, the remaining provisions or applications shall remain in force. To this end the provisions of this Section are severable.

Conflicts in the Development of the Initiative

I was present as an observer at a 1991 meeting in Los Angeles between EXCEL leaders and Bill Honig, the California state superintendent of public instruction. At the meeting, Honig offered to support public school choice if EXCEL would drop its efforts to sponsor an initiative providing support for private as well as public school choice. Honig explicitly asserted that "We have $10 million to beat you." Nobody saw fit to ask the identity of the "We"—probably because everyone understood that the California Teachers Association (CTA) was the only organization capable of raising that amount to defeat a school choice initiative. Honig's offer was rejected a few days after the meeting. It illustrates the fact that public school choice is often advocated as a means of diverting support from choice legislation applicable to private schools.

The most interesting disagreements in the development of the initiative were among parties who support choice plans that include private schools. For example, after a one-week visit to California, Jeanne Allen, then the education analyst for the Heritage Foundation, disseminated a memorandum urging that the initiative be dropped. In its stead, she urged EXCEL to work for a pilot project to be placed on the ballot in 1994. Allen's reasons were that EXCEL lacked the time and funds to conduct the kind of voter education campaign essential for success. She also asserted that the initiative would compete for funds with the 1992 presidential and senatorial campaigns, as well as a number of key congressional races. In her view, a defeat in California would set back the movement for educational choice for five to ten years.[9]

Allen's memorandum evoked widespread anger among initiative supporters. For example, Milton Friedman, after detailing his disagreements with Allen's analysis, concluded his letter to her by expressing his strong objections to foundation involvement in California's state politics.[10]

Another disagreement concerned a substantive issue that had to be resolved before the initiative petition was submitted. In discussions leading up to the final draft of the initiative, John Coons and Stephen Sugarman, two prominent voucher advocates, proposed that the amount of the voucher be 90 percent of the average per-pupil cost for comparable pupils in public schools. The initiative figure, however, was set at 50 percent. Coons and Sugarman also urged that the voucher plan cover all costs for a certain proportion of disadvantaged students. Initially, they proposed that private schools participating in the voucher plan be required to reserve 25 percent of their new admissions for disadvantaged pupils supported entirely by vouchers. Subsequently, they were agreeable to a 15 percent quota. Coons and Sugarman also urged that either the voucher be high enough to pay all the school costs or the extra charges be scaled according to family ability to pay. Eventually, they urged that if schools charged more than the voucher, the amounts charged should be sufficient to defray the costs for students who could not pay the additional charges.

As it happened, polling conducted by the initiative indicated that any set-aside for disadvantaged students would have a negative impact on voters. For this reason, the set-asides were dropped from the initiative; because of a tight schedule, they were dropped without consultation with

Coons and Sugarman, who thereupon withdrew their support of the initiative.[11]

This sequence of events illustrates a point emphasized in Chapter 12. Unless and until voucher supporters agree on the specifics of a voucher plan, their nonspecific agreement on the desirability of vouchers may be a poor guide to their support for a specific plan. In the California situation, the set-asides were dropped because polls indicated that they would be a political liability. If the issue was only tactical, withdrawal from the coalition over it would have been an overreaction. Obviously, Coons and Sugarman regarded the set-asides as matters of principle that could not be sacrificed for political reasons. Not surprisingly, they also disagreed with the conclusion that the set-asides were political liabilities.

In the past, Coons and Sugarman (both law professors) have emphasized the need to prohibit or restrict states from adding regulations governing private schools. To avoid the possibility that a voucher plan might be emasculated by such additional regulations, they drafted initiative provisions that would have virtually precluded subsequent regulation of private schools. Nevertheless, to promote equality of educational opportunity, they proposed to require private schools to enroll a significant number of students whom the schools might not wish to accept. This willingness to interfere with private school autonomy illustrates the way some equalitarians subordinate other objectives to their version of equality of educational opportunity. Under the policies proposed by Coons and Sugarman, private schools could not raise their charges even if parents were willing to pay them, unless the parents were also willing to subsidize the additional charges for disadvantaged students. Coons at least did not regard this limitation as a major inconsistency with a market approach, which it clearly is. Suppose carmakers could not add improvements to automobiles unless buyers subsidized the improvement for disadvantaged car buyers. In that case, the kind of proposal made by Coons and Sugarman would be perceived immediately as an intolerable restriction on the liberty of buyers and sellers.

In addition, the Coons-Sugarman proposal raises several administrative problems. However "poverty" or "disadvantaged" is calculated, some parents would not necessarily be eligible every year. If parental income rises above the eligibility line, is the subsidy withdrawn? If not, it ends up going to parents who are not disadvantaged. If it is withdrawn, how would voucher plans neutralize the temptation for families to keep their earnings low enough to qualify for the subsidy? In view of the practical difficulties of implementing the proposal, its restrictions on liberty, its antimarket effects, and its tendency to force parents to absorb the costs of educating the disadvantaged, the policy argument for deleting the proposal seems even stronger than the political one; paradoxically, some EXCEL leaders who opposed the set-asides on policy grounds were nevertheless willing to accept them for political reasons. In any event, the Coons-Sugarman proposal illustrates the way voucher advocates erroneously assume that their proposals are consistent with a market system of education.

Policy Issues

The initiative raises several issues that have been discussed in previous chapters:

1. *Per-pupil costs:* The initiative sponsors were aware of the fact that per-pupil costs are systematically underestimated in government figures on the subject. Nevertheless, the initiative does not address this issue as clearly as it might have. It calls for including "every cost to the state, school districts and county offices of education of maintaining kindergarten and elementary and secondary education." Are the costs of the state teacher bargaining law to be included? The costs of state legislative committees on education? The costs of teacher training carried on higher education budgets? Many such costs are not currently counted as per-pupil costs, and litigation may be necessary to resolve whether they will be so counted pursuant to the initiative. Undoubtedly, efforts will be made to categorize several costs as "health" or "welfare," perhaps by transferring their administration from school districts to other public agencies. If successful, these efforts would reduce the amount of the scholarships to be made available to students in private schools without reducing the services made available in public schools.

2. *Earlier withdrawal from school:* In my opinion, it is unfortunate that the initiative does not include the option of withdrawing from school before age 16. A student might be better off working than continuing in school, but the initiative does not provide this option. It allows students to be dismissed if they receive "no substantial benefit" from schooling but not if they are substantially better off working instead of attending school.

3. *Teacher benefits:* The initiative does not include any benefits for teachers that might weaken their opposition. Some earlier drafts in-

cluded such benefits, but the provisions were poorly drafted and eventually deleted.

4. *Independent scholarship-redeeming schools:* The initiative provisions relating to "Empowerment of Teachers; Conversion of Schools" are not likely to have any effect, one way or another. Commanding the California legislature to establish "an expeditious process by which public schools may become independent scholarship redeeming schools" is wishful thinking, not a mandate that will be taken seriously. It would be surprising if many schools were established pursuant to Section 17(c).

5. *Regulation of private schools:* Section 17(b)(4) is intended to prevent efforts to emasculate the initiative by imposing new and onerous restrictions on private schools. Although the concern is legitimate, Section 17(4) may be a case of overkill. Private schools are subject to regulation as corporations as well as by education law. It is not clear whether the initiative precludes new restrictions on corporations applicable to private schools. Most likely, regulations adopted after October 1, 1991 that apply to all corporations or businesses will be applicable to private schools, but this remains to be seen. Again, the issue illustrates the importance of the specific language of voucher legislation and the inevitability and importance of judicial interpretation of it.

Prospects for Passage

Voucher legislation proposed to establish a market system of education often could not possibly do so. This reservation is not applicable to the California initiative. If enacted, it would provide vouchers on a scale and under conditions that would allow a three-sector education industry to emerge.

In my opinion, the initiative is subject to legitimate criticism. Nevertheless, if one agrees that a market system is essential to remedy the basic deficiencies of public education, the initiative deserves support. No other local, state, or federal legislation, actual or proposed, comes even remotely close to the initiative in fulfilling the requirements of a market system of education. Little, if anything, would be gained by waiting for a better initiative. By the same token, most of the opposition to the initiative has nothing to do with its specifics. The public school establishment and its allies would oppose the initiative even if all their criticisms of it were met in some way.

What are the chances that the initiative will be approved by the California electorate? Although several factors will affect the outcome, none appears more important than the June 7, 1994, date. This date means that the initiative will be on the ballot in a primary election. Because voter turnout in primaries is usually low, interest groups play a more influential role in them. For this reason, the date favors the public school opposition to the initiative. The CTA is the largest contributor to political campaigns in California and is widely acknowledged to be the most powerful political force in the state. Defeating the initiative will take precedence over every other union objective, just as it will for AFT affiliates and organizations of school administrators. Since most higher education faculty unions in California are affiliates of the NEA or the AFT, they will also oppose the initiative. To be successful, therefore, the initiative must overcome the opposition of an overwhelming majority of California's 400,000 public school and college employees and their families. This will be an extremely difficult task for EXCEL, a volunteer organization lacking an established base of members or financial support.

As a matter of fact, EXCEL tried strenuously to place the initiative on the ballot in the November 1992 general election. Its effort failed for highly controversial legal reasons. This is not to say the initiative would have won in 1992 but it clearly faces an uphill battle in 1993.

If the outcome is uncertain, the nature of the campaign against the initiative is not. There are two companies in California that specialize in collecting signatures for initiative petitions. In connection with EXCEL's efforts to get the initiative on the 1992 ballot, the president of one such firm submitted a sworn statement to a California court asserting that he had been offered $400,000 to refrain from gathering signatures for an initiative. The offer was made by the signature-gathering firm employed by the CTA.[12] In a statement disseminated at the 1992 NEA convention, CTA president D. A. Weber explained the union's efforts to dissuade voters from signing the EXCEL petition as follows:

And you and I, the California Teachers Association, decided to do something very dramatic, something nobody had ever tried in the nine decades that the initiative has existed in this state. We decided to create an organized campaign to block an initiative from getting enough signatures to qualify for the ballot.

We realized that we would be accused of acting in an "undemocratic" manner. What was wrong, after all, with letting the people vote on an issue?

Our answer was firm: There are some proposals that are so evil that they should never even be presented to the voters. We do not believe, for example, that we should hold an election on "empowering" the Ku Klux Klan. And we would not think it's "undemocratic" to oppose voting on legalizing child prostitution.

Destroying public education, in our view, belongs in that category.[13]

The Italian sociologist Vilfredo Pareto once observed that men find it easy to convert their interests into principles. Perhaps he should have added that they also find it easy to convert their opponents into the forces of evil. Although "some proposals . . . are so evil that they should never even be presented to the voters," readers are invited to draw their own conclusions on whether the school choice initiative is such a proposal.

The November 1992 Elections

In the November 1992 national elections, the NEA and the AFT overwhelmingly supported the Clinton/Gore ticket. Only a Pollyanna would assert that the election outcome will not have any adverse effects on the pace of change toward a market system of education. Even on the most pessimistic view, however, the election outcome (including the overwhelming defeat of a voucher initiative in Colorado) does not portend a revival of faith in public education. Although the rationale for public education has reached the terminal stage, I have taken the continued existence of public education for granted. Its monopoly status will decline, but in irregular fashion. It must be remembered that the election was not a referendum on public education; for that matter, President Bush and Ross Perot, the candidates opposed by the public school forces, received a majority of the popular vote. Furthermore, the election results did not affect the underlying social and demographic factors that are weakening public education: low birth rates, aging of the population, the decline in children's social capital, increasing social conflict over educational issues, inefficiencies in government operation, insoluble informational problems, and so on.

While in office, the Bush administration could have used federal resources to publicize the futility of conventional school reform. It might have publicized the real costs of public education, its exaggerated outcomes, its anti-entrepreneurial culture, its inadequate information system, its domination by producers, and a host of other deficiencies that are inherent in public education. It might have, but it did not. Furthermore, the Reagan and Bush administrations never fully appreciated the possibility that school choice plans might turn out badly precisely because they did not incorporate the essentials of a market system. As a result, they uncritically endorsed every choice plan, including public school choice, as a step toward a market system. In doing so, the Bush administration especially may have done more to discredit than to promote a market system of education. Its uncritical assumption that school choice is tantamount to a market system achieved the all-out opposition of the teacher unions, confused the substantive issues, and set the stage for a backlash against future efforts to establish a market system of education.

The election of the Clinton/Gore ticket is a lost opportunity to inform the American people about the terminal condition of public education. Realistically, however, that opportunity would probably have been wasted even had the Bush/Quayle ticket been reelected. My argument was never predicated on support or leadership from the Bush administration; on the contrary, one of my objectives in this book has always been to point out its ineptitude concerning educational reform. However, I did not assume that the promarket forces would encounter all-out opposition at the federal level. As a result of the 1992 election, such opposition is probable. The election, therefore, is a negative development from the standpoint of a market system of education. It does not, however, rule out the possibility of a major breakthrough in the next four years or invalidate the basic argument of this book. The future of a market system of education depends much more on the actions of its supporters than on those of its opponents.

≈ Notes

1. Why an Autopsy?

1. Milton Friedman, *Capitalism and Freedom* (Chicago: University of Chicago Press, 1962), 85–107; Robert B. Everhart, ed., *The Public School Monopoly* (San Francisco: Pacific Institute for Public Policy Research, 1981); and Paul E. Peterson, "Monopoly and Competition in American Education," in William H. Clune and John F. Witte, eds., *Choice and Control in American Education* (New York: Falmer Press, 1990), 47–78. For a contrary view, see David B. Tyack, "The Public Schools: A Monopoly or a Contested Public Domain?" in Clune and Witte, *Choice and Control.*
2. On May 16, 1991, Christopher Whittle, CEO of Whittle Communications, held a news conference to announce the Edison Project, a plan to raise $2.5 billion to open 200 K–12 schools for profit by the fall of 1996 (see Epilogue). Another for-profit company with national plans is Education Alternatives, Inc., based in Minneapolis, which already operates a few public schools under contract.
3. See Myron Lieberman, *Privatization and Educational Choice* (New York: St. Martin's Press, 1989), esp. chaps. 1–4, for a discussion of school districts as buyers of services.
4. See the quotation from D. A. Weber in the Epilogue, at note 13.
5. For a strong argument for using changes in the tax code to promote a market system of education, see Thomas W. Vitullo-Martin, "The Impact of Taxation Policy on Public and Private Schools," in Robert B. Everhart, ed., *The Public School Monopoly* (San Francisco: Pacific Research Institute for Public Policy, 1982), 423–429.
6. E. G. West, *Education and the State,* 2d ed. (London: Institute of Economic Affairs, 1970), 127.

7. Alan J. DeYoung, *Economics and American Education* (New York: Longman, 1989), 31–32; Jack High and Jerome Ellig, "The Private Supply of Education: Some Historical Evidence," in Tyler Cowen, ed., *The Theory of Market Failure* (Fairfax, Va.: George Mason University Press, 1988), 361–382. For a remarkable discussion of the origins of public education in England, see West, *Education and the State.*

8. Lloyd P. Jorgenson, *The State and the Non-Public School, 1825–1925* (Columbia: University of Missouri Press, 1987); Gerard V. Bradley, *Church-State Relations in America* (Westport, Conn.: Greenwood Press, 1987); Everhart, *Public School Monopoly;* David Tyack, Thomas James, and Aaron Benavoit, *The Law and the Shaping of Public Education, 1785–1954* (Madison: University of Wisconsin Press, 1987); Otto F. Kraushaar, *Private Schools from the Puritans to the Present* (Bloomington, Ind.: Phi Delta Kappa, 1976); and Rockne M. McCarthy, James Skillen, and William A. Harper, *Disestablishment a Second Time* (Grand Rapids, Mich.: Eerdman's Publishing, 1982).

9. Jorgenson, *The State and the Nonpublic School,* 69–70.

10. See the references in notes 6 and 8.

2. The Future Context of Public Education

1. Ben J. Wattenberg, *The Birth Dearth* (New York: Pharos Books, 1987).

2. Bureau of the Census, U.S. Department of Commerce, *Statistical Abstract of the United States, 1990* (Washington: Government Printing Office, 1990), 16.

3. Barry A. Kosmin et al., *National Jewish Population Survey* (New York: Council of Jewish Federations, 1991).

4. Bruce S. Cooper and Grace Dondero, "Survival, Change, and Demands on America's Private Schools," *Educational Foundations* 5 (Winter 1991), 51–73, esp. 63–67.

5. Ibid.

6. The Postsecondary Enrollment Options program is one of four options offered by the state of Minnesota. Another is the Enrollment Options Program, widely referred to as open enrollment.

7. Myron Lieberman, "The Future of the Custodial School," *Phi Delta Kappan* 58 (Sept. 1976), 122–125.

8. The adverse effects of minimum wage laws on disadvantaged minority youth are discussed in Richard E. Wagner, *To Promote the General Welfare* (San Francisco: Pacific Research Institute for Public Policy, 1989). See also David Forrest and S. R. Dennison, *Low Pay or No Pay?* (London: Institute of Economic Affairs, 1984), 24–25.

9. Wattenberg, *The Birth Dearth,* 11.

10. "Birth Dearth Bears Worries for Japan," *Washington Post,* Oct. 29, 1990, A20.

11. Christine L. Day, *What Older Americans Think: Interest Groups and Aging Policy* (Princeton, N.J.: Princeton University Press, 1990). My discussion of issues pertaining to the elderly relies heavily on Day's book, which includes an extensive bibliography.

12. Ibid.; and see Myron Lieberman, *Privatization and Educational Choice* (New York: St. Martin's Press, 1989), 299–302.

13. Richard D. Lamm, "Again, Age Beats Youth," *New York Times,* Dec. 2, 1990, 19.

14. Wagner, *To Promote the General Welfare,* 180–190; Michael J. Boskin, ed., *The Crisis in Social Security: Problems and Prospects* (San Francisco: Institute for Contemporary Studies, 1978); Peter J. Ferrara, *Social Security: The Inherent Contradiction* (Washington: Cato Institute, 1989), and *Social Security: Prospects for Real Reform* (Washington: Cato Institute, 1985); Robert I. Lerman and Hillard Pouncy, "The Compelling Case for Youth Apprenticeships," *Public Interest* (Fall 1990), 62–77; Jackson Toby, "Of Dropouts and Stay-Ins: The Gershwin Approach," *Public Interest* (Spring 1989), 3–13.

15. This discussion of social capital is based primarily on James S. Coleman, *Foundations of Social Theory* (Cambridge, Mass.: Harvard University Press, 1990). Coleman is largely responsible for the widespread acceptance of the concept and the terminology among academics and policymakers.

16. Office of Educational Research and Improvement, U.S. Department of Education, *Youth Indicators, 1991: Trends in the Well-Being of American Youth* (Washington: Government Printing Office, 1991), 42–43.

17. Ibid., 44–45. The figures include both full- and part-time employment. See also Nicholas Zill and Carolyn C. Rogers, "Recent Trends in the Well-Being of Children in the United States and Their Implications for Public Policy," in Andrew J. Cherlin, ed., *The Changing American Family and Public Policy* (Washington: Urban Institute Press, 1988).

18. Coleman, *Foundations of Social Theory,* 579, 609.

19. *Youth Indicators 1991,* 48–49.

20. John H. Langbein, "The Inheritance Revolution," *Public Interest* (Winter 1991), 15–31.

21. *Youth Indicators, 1991,* 16–19.

22. Janet Finch and Jennifer Mason, "Divorce, Remarriage and Family Obligations," *Sociological Review* 38 (1990), 231–234.

23. Coleman, *Foundations of Social Theory,* 600–603; Christopher Jencks, *Rethinking Social Policy* (Cambridge, Mass.: Harvard University Press, 1992), 196–198.

24. John C. Sommerville, *The Rise and Fall of Childhood* (New York: Random House, 1990), 9.

344 ≈ Notes to Pages 30–42

25. Coleman, *Foundations of Social Theory*, 608–609. See also Elaine Ciulia Kamarck and William R. Galston, *Putting Children First* (Washington: Progressive Policy Institute, 1990).
26. Gloria Gallardo and Margaret M. Kirchman, "Age-Integrated or Age-Segregated Living for Semi-Independent Elderly People," *Physical and Occupational Therapy in Geriatrics* 6, no. 1, (1987), 71–80.
27. James S. Coleman, "The Rational Reconstruction of Society," *American Sociological Review,* in press.
28. "Proposed Day-Care Rules in Maryland Require Holding and Talking to Infants," *Education Week,* Sept. 5, 1990, 18.
29. Michael Levin, *Feminism and Freedom* (New Brunswick, N.J.: Transaction Books, 1987), 16–54.
30. See Carmel Shalev, *Birth Power* (New Haven, Conn.: Yale University Press, 1989), for a discussion of the implications of reproductive technology.
31. List of speakers provided by New York City Board of Education. Some speakers may have been categorized in more than one way, and the actual number undoubtedly differed from the list made available to me.
32. "New Challenge of Youth: Growing Up in a Gay Home," *New York Times,* Feb. 11, 1991, A-12.
33. Nathan Glazer, "The Future under Tuition Tax Credits," in Thomas James and Henry Levin, eds., *Public Dollars for Private Schools: The Case of Tuition Tax Credits* (Philadelphia: Temple University Press, 1983), 100.
34. "Seeds of Murder Epidemic: Teen-Age Boys with Guns," *New York Times,* Oct. 19, 1992, A8.
35. *Youth Indicators, 1991,* 128–131; "FBI Finds Major Increase in Juvenile Violence in Past Decade," *Washington Post,* Aug. 30, 1992, A13.
36. Office of Juvenile Justice and Delinquency Prevention, *Federal Juvenile Delinquency Programs, 1988* (Washington: Department of Justice, n.d.), p. 55.
37. James S. Coleman, Thomas Hoffer, and Sally Kilgore, *High School Achievement* (New York: Basic Books, 1982), 99, 186–197.
38. Richard M. Cyert and David C. Mowery, eds., *Technology and Employment,* Report of the Panel on Technology and Employment, Committee on Science, Engineering, and Public Policy (Washington: National Academy Press, 1987), 169.
39. "Trade Talks with Japan Facing a Stormy Reopening on Thursday," *New York Times,* Jan. 13, 1991, 5.
40. Myron Lieberman, *Public School Choice* (Lancaster, Pa.: Technomic Publishing, 1990).

41. Frank Levy and Richard C. Michel, *The Economic Future of American Families* (Washington: Urban Institute Press, 1991).

3. Producer-Consumer Conflict

1. Aaron Wildavsky, *Searching for Safety* (New Brunswick, N.J.: Transaction Publishers, 1988).
2. Under California's teacher bargaining law, teacher union initial proposals must be presented at a meeting of the school board and become part of the public record. The proposal quoted was part of the public record in scores of California school districts.
3. The NEA has supported various measures to assist California farm workers. *NEA Handbook, 1990–91* (Washington: NEA, 1990), 239, 288, 302. The AFT has adopted similar policies, both on its own and as an affiliate of the AFL-CIO.
4. *West's Annotated California Code, Reorganized,* secs. 41375, 41376.
5. Ibid., sec. 41372.
6. See Myron Lieberman, *Privatization and Educational Choice* (New York: St. Martin's Press, 1989).
7. For references and a cogent analysis of the issues, see Richard E. Wagner, *To Promote the General Welfare* (San Francisco: Pacific Research Institute for Public Policy, 1989), esp. 112–116.
8. *NEA Handbook, 1991–92* (Washington: NEA, 1991), 234, 298, 309. AFT policy positions are not published in a single document, but it is hardly necessary to document AFT support for the policies under discussion.
9. Jackson Toby, "Of Dropouts and Stay-ins: The Gershwin Approach," *Public Interest* (Spring 1989), 3–13; and David J. Armor, "Carrots or Sticks for High School Dropouts?" *Public Interest* (Winter 1992), 76–90.
10. Allen E. Buchanan and Dan W. Brock, *Deciding for Others: The Ethics of Surrogate Decision Making* (New York: Cambridge University Press, 1989).
11. *NEA Handbook, 1991–92,* 239, 298; "Child Labor Deterrence Act of 1991," *Child Labor Monitor* 2 (Summer 1992), 6–7.
12. NEA and AFT opposition to such assistance is expressed in scores of their publications and policy statements. For the quotation, see Epilogue, at note 13.
13. *NEA Handbook, 1990–91,* 217, 243, 257, 289.
14. For a more comprehensive discussion of the issues pertaining to merit pay, see Myron Lieberman, "Are Teachers Underpaid?" *Public Interest* (Summer 1986), 12–28.
15. Myron Lieberman, *Education as a Profession* (Englewood Cliffs, N.J.: Prentice Hall, 1956).
16. See Myron Lieberman, *The Future of Public Education* (Chicago: Univer-

sity of Chicago Press, 1960), 259–270; "A Foundation Approach to Merit Pay," *Phi Delta Kappan*, 41 (Dec. 1959), 118–122; "Shanker Backs Teacher Merit Pay Based on Standard National Test," *New York Times*, July 12, 1985, I1; and "Take the $25 Million and Run," *Government Union Review* (Winter 1990), i, 1–23.

17. Kenneth J. Meier, *Regulation* (New York: St. Martin's Press, 1985).
18. NEA and AFT organizing materials are replete with commitments to block the contracting out of support services.
19. See *Privatization Report*, published annually by the Reason Foundation, Santa Monica, Calif.

4. The Information System of Public Education

1. Polling data provided by fax from *Washington Post*, Sept. 16, 1992.
2. Estimates based on telephone calls to legislative representatives of state school associations in California, Ohio, and New York, March 1991.
3. For an insightful commentary on direct democracy initiatives, see Julian N. Eule, "Judicial Review of Direct Democracy," *Yale Law Journal* 99 (May 1990), 1503–1588.
4. The reference is to "Proposition 13," a California initiative that was widely regarded as the forerunner of a "taxpayers' revolt."
5. Eule, "Judicial Review of Direct Democracy."
6. James S. Coleman, *Foundations of Social Theory* (Cambridge, Mass.: Harvard University Press, 1990), 600–603, 632–634.
7. Newspaper Advertising Bureau, *Newspapers in American News Habits: A Comparative Assessment* (New York: Newspaper Advertising Bureau, July 1985); *Summary Report, American Public Opinion Poll* (Washington: Education Writers Association, 1977); Shanto Iyengar and Donald R. Kinder, *News That Matters* (Chicago: University of Chicago Press, 1987), 112–133.
8. J. R. Dominick, "Education as Portrayed in Network TV Newscasts," *Educational Horizons* 62 (Spring 1984), 86–89. See also M. J. Robinson, "How the Networks Cover Education: Schools Are Not the Media's Pet," *American Educator* 8 (Spring 1984), 18–21.
9. NEA news release, July 1, 1987.
10. M. J. Finkelstein, *The American Academic Profession* (Columbus: Ohio State University Press, 1984); R. H. Linnell, ed., *Dollars and Scholars* (Los Angeles: University of Southern California Press, 1982).
11. Linnell, *Dollars and Scholars*.
12. Jeffrey A. Raffel and Lance R. Groff, "Shedding Light on the Dark Side of Teacher Moonlighting," *Educational Evaluation and Policy Analysis* 12 (Winter 1990), 404–414.

13. Myron Lieberman, "Are Teachers Underpaid?" *Public Interest* (Summer 1986), 12–28.

14. Amy Stuart Wells, "A Study of Education Reporting in American Newspapers" (M.S. thesis, College of Communications, Boston University, 1986), 1, 26–27.

15. Ibid., 2.

16. Ibid., 6–13.

17. This statement is based on discussions with publishers, reporters, and/or editors from the *New York Times* and the *Washington Post.*

18. Wells, "Education Reporting in American Newspapers," 23.

19. Ibid., 14–19, 33.

20. National Commission on Excellence in Education, *A Nation at Risk* (Washington: Government Printing Office, 1983).

21. U.S. Department of Education, *Back to School Forecast, 1990,* Aug. 23, 1990.

22. "Average Salaries of Teachers Up: Dollar Gap among States Widens," *NEA News,* press release regarding *Estimates of School Statistics, 1989–90,* April 30, 1990.

23. See David J. Wynne and Charles W. Watters, "Teacher Compensation: How It Compares with the Private Sector," *Government Union Review* (Summer 1991), 31–43; also Lieberman, "Are Teachers Underpaid?"

24. The estimates for the NEA and the AFT are based on data provided by these unions in their Labor Organization Annual Report, Form LM-2, covering the period Sept. 1, 1989–Aug. 31, 1990. The estimate for their state and local affiliates is my own, based on a variety of factors; it is probably a low estimate.

25. Mark Snyderman and Stanley Rothman, *The I.Q. Controversy* (New Brunswick, N.J.: Transaction Publishers, 1988).

26. Ibid.

27. Ibid., 212–213.

28. National Center for Education Statistics, *The State of Mathematics Achievement* (Washington: Government Printing Office, 1991), 380.

29. John Jacob Cannell, *Nationally Normed Elementary Achievement Testing in America's Public Schools: How All Fifty States Are above the National Average* (Daniels, W.Va.: Friends for Education, 1987), 1–2. For a good discussion of the Cannell report, see Chester E. Finn, Jr., *We Must Take Charge* (New York: Free Press, 1991), 100–104.

30. The terminology here follows the usage in Glen E. Robinson and James M. Craver, *Assessing and Grading Student Achievement* (Arlington, Va.: Educational Research Service, 1989). Unless otherwise indicated this publication is also the source for the data cited in the discussion of grades and report cards.

31. 1971 Policy Resolution, Board of Directors, National Council of Teachers of English. Technically at least, the resolution is still NCTE policy.
32. Paul Copperman, *The Literacy Hoax* (New York: William Morrow, 1982), 105.
33. *Peter W. v. San Francisco Unified School District,* 60 Cal. App. 3d 814, 131 Cal. Rptr., 854 (1976).
34. Marie McDonald, *Teachers' Messages for Report Cards* (Belmont, Calif.: David S. Lake, 1971).
35. Article IV(E), Teacher Rights, Evaluation of Students, in *NJEA Sample Agreement,* Model Contract Proposal of the New Jersey Education Association (Trenton: New Jersey School Boards Association, 1983), 13.
36. Contract between the Boston Teacher Union, Local 66, American Federation of Teachers (AFL-CIO), and School Committee of the City of Boston, Sept. 1, 1989, to Aug. 31, 1992, 85.
37. *An Assessment of American Education* (New York: Committee for Economic Development, 1991), 12.
38. John E. Chubb and Terry M. Moe, *Politics, Markets, and America's Schools* (Washington: Brookings Institution, 1990), 224–225.

5. Educational Information under a Market System

1. Abigail Thernstrom, *School Choice in Massachusetts* (Boston: Pioneer Institute for Public Policy Research, 1991); and Myron Lieberman, *Public School Choice* (Lancaster, Pa.: Technomic Publishing, 1990).
2. *New York Times,* July 19, 1991, 1.
3. Arthur Seldon, *Capitalism* (Cambridge, Mass.: Basil Blackwell, 1990), 169.
4. "School Ads that Urge 'Go Public'," *New York Times,* Sept. 6, 1984, D17.
5. Michael S. Dukakis, *New York Times,* April 22, 1991, I23.
6. Information provided by the project director. See also Lieberman, *Public School Choice,* 129–131.
7. Thernstrom, *School Choice in Massachusetts,* is an excellent study of the reasons. See also Lieberman, *Public School Choice,* for a more comprehensive analysis.
8. James S. Coleman and Thomas Hoffer, *Public and Private High Schools* (New York: Basic Books, 1987), 115.
9. Janet A. Weiss and Edith E. Gruber, "The Managed Irrelevance of Federal Education Statistics," in William Alonso and Paul Starr, eds., *The Politics of Numbers* (New York: Russell Sage Foundation, 1981).
10. Patrick S. Attiyah, *The Rise and Fall of Freedom of Contract* (New York: Oxford University Press, 1985).

11. Anthony Downs, *An Economic Theory of Democracy* (New York: Harper, 1957).
12. Ibid., 239.
13. James L. Payne, "The Congressional Brainwashing Machine," *Public Interest* (Summer 1990), 4–6. See also James L. Payne, *The Culture of Spending: Why Congress Lives beyond Our Means* (San Francisco: ICS Press, 1991).
14. Fax transmittal from Committee for Education Funding, July 31, 1992.
15. Correspondence from Arnold Fege, Washington office of the National PTA. The National Citizens Committee for Education (NCCE), based in Columbia, Md., is a parent-oriented organization devoted to improving public education. NCCE is not systematically involved in congressional activities and would usually be supportive of CEF positions if it were.
16. William H. Riker, *Liberalism against Populism* (San Francisco: W. H. Freeman, 1982).
17. Catholic schools generally allow students to withdraw with tuition pro-rated without penalty. Informal discussion with Catholic school officials.

6. The Real Costs of Public Education

1. For a more detailed analysis of efficiency, equity, and liberty in the educational context, see David H. Monk, *School Finance* (New York: McGraw-Hill, 1990).
2. See U.S. Department of Commerce, Bureau of the Census, 1990, *Government Finances: Finances of Public School Systems,* Ser. GC87 (4)-1 (Washington: Government Printing Office, Jan. 1990).
3. Research Division, NEA, *Estimates of School Statistics, 1991–92* (Washington: NEA, 1991), 44.
4. Henry M. Levin, "Education as a Public and Private Good," in Neal E. Devins, ed., *Public Values, Private Schools* (New York: Falmer Press, 1989), 221–222.
5. Virginia Roach, "Special Education: New Questions in an Era of Reform," *Issues in Brief* 11 (Oct. 1991), 1.
6. See note 25 to Chapter 7 (p. 353).
7. James S. Coleman, Thomas Hoffer, and Sally Kilgore, *High School Achievement* (New York: Basic Books, 1982), 79.
8. The amounts are rough estimates by Department of Education officials. See Department fact sheet, "Congressional Action on Fiscal Year 1991 President's Budget."
9. Office of Juvenile Justice and Delinquency Prevention, *Federal Juvenile Delinquency Programs, 1988* (Washington: Department of Justice, 1988).

10. National Center for Education Statistics, *College-Level Remediation in the Fall of 1989* (Washington: Government Printing Office, 1991). See also Ansley A. Abraham, Jr., "Remedial Education in College: How Widespread Is It?" *Issues in Higher Education,* no. 24 (Atlanta: Southern Regional Education Board, 1988).

11. Information from fact sheets and brochures made available by the NCEOA.

12. "C Stands for Company, Turned into Classroom," *Wall Street Journal,* March 1, 1990, B1. Corporations in some European nations pay an education tax, but the funds are used for vocational training. Although data are not available, it seems unlikely that much if any is spent for remedial programs for basic skills.

13. Marvin Cetron and Margaret Gayle, *Educational Renaissance* (New York: St. Martin's Press, 1991), 83.

14. Emily Feistritzer, *Profile of Teachers in the U.S., 1990* (Washington: National Center for Education Information, 1990), 17–37.

15. This conclusion assumes that the only factor affecting the costs of teacher training is its duration. Although the assumption is obviously not valid, consideration of the other factors would probably strengthen the conclusion.

16. Data based on telephone calls to PERB officials, April 1991.

17. William J. Fowler, Jr., "Comparisons of State Expenditures Using a Common Reporting Standard," paper presented to the American Education Finance Association, Williamsburg, Va., March 14, 1991.

18. Research Division, NEA, *Instruction Booklet* for revising and completing reporting forms used in reporting data for *Estimates of School Statistics, 1990–91* and *Ranking of the States, 1991* (Washington: NEA, n.d.), 7.

19. Telephone discussions with William J. Fowler, Jr., OERI Senior Associate, NCES, April 26, 29, 1991; Dec. 11, 1992.

20. See Myron Lieberman, *Privatization and Educational Choice* (New York: St. Martin's Press, 1989), 71–73.

21. Fowler, "Comparisons of State Expenditures," 6.

22. Frederick H. Brigham, Jr., *United States Catholic Elementary and Secondary Schools, 1989–90* (Washington: National Catholic Education Association, 1990), 21–22; Michael J. Guerra and Michael J. Donahue, *Catholic High Schools and Their Finances* (Washington: National Catholic Education Association, 1990), 8. Although the latter study covers only high school teachers, the figure is probably applicable to elementary teachers as well.

23. Suppose the 96,000 board members devote an average of 240 hours annually to their school board responsibilities. This is the equivalent of six full forty-hour work weeks. Although such time would not be re-

quired under a market system, its value should be included in assessments of public school efficiency.

In twenty-five states school board members are not paid. In five states they receive from $25 to $60 per board meeting, nothing otherwise. Several other states prescribe annual amounts that are comparable on a per-meeting basis to the $25 to $60 range.

Setting an average hourly rate for school board time is obviously speculative. If $25 an hour is the rate, the value of board members' donated time is as follows: 96,000 school board members × 240 hours = $23,040,000 total hours donated. At $25 per hour, the value of this donated time is $576,000,000. This sum divided by 40,196,000, the number of students in public schools in 1987–88, yields a value of $14 per pupil.

24. Guerra and Donahue, *Catholic High Schools and Their Finances,* 23, and discussions with NCEA staff.

25. Ibid., 17, 18; Robert J. Kealey, *United States Catholic Elementary Schools and Their Finances* (Washington: National Catholic Education Association, 1989), 12; National Center for Education Statistics, *A Profile of Parents of Eighth Graders* (Washington: Government Printing Office, 1988), 52.

26. Project Head Start, *Statistical Fact Sheet* (Washington: Administration for Children, Youth and Families, Department of Health and Human Services, Jan. 1989), 2.

27. "Chicago Receives $40 Million to Make Schools More Public," *New York Times,* Oct. 12, 1990, A15. The grant was to be made over a ten-year period.

28. National Academy of Education, *Research and the Renewal of Education* (Stanford, Calif.: National Academy of Education, Stanford University, 1991), 18–19.

29. Carnegie Corporation of New York, *Grants and Appropriations, 1990* (New York, 1990), 8–9, 18.

30. Foundation Center, *National Guide to Funding for Elementary and Secondary Education* (New York, 1991). See also Loren Renz, *Foundations Today* (New York: Foundation Center, 1990), 30; and Nathan Weber, ed., *Giving USA: The Annual Report on Philanthropy for the Year 1989* (New York: AAFRC Trust for Philanthropy, 1990), 83–85, 103–106.

31. "Catholics Giving Less to Church, Report Says," *New York Times,* June 10, 1987, B12.

32. *The Local Education Fund: A Handbook* (Washington: Public Education Fund Network, n.d.), and copies of PEForum provided by PEFNet. It has been estimated that these foundations are raising amounts close to 2 percent of district budgets. "In Budget Crunch, California Foundations Supporting Basics," *Education Week,* April 24, 1991, 16.

33. Policy Studies Associates, *A Review of Programs Involving College Students as Tutors or Mentors in Grades K–12,* contract no. LC 89089001 (Washington: Office of Planning, Budget and Evaluation, U.S. Department of Education, 1990), 10.

34. Marsha Levine, ed., *The Private Sector in the Public School: Can It Improve Education?* (Washington: American Enterprise Institute, 1985).

35. Paul O'Neill, quoted in Press Briefing by Secretary of Education Lamar Alexander, Mr. Paul O'Neill, Governor of Colorado Roy Romer, and Governor of South Carolina Carroll Campbell (Washington: Office of the Press Secretary, White House, April 18, 1991), 3.

36. Michael Krashinsky, "Why Educational Vouchers May Be Bad Economics," *Teachers College Record* 88 (Winter 1986), 139–151; response by Edwin G. West and rejoinder by Krashinsky, ibid., 152–167.

37. Henry M. Levin, "The Theory of Choice Applied to Education," in William H. Clune and John F. Witte, eds., *Choice and Control in American Education,* vol. 1 (New York: Falmer Press, 1990), 278–279.

38. Ibid.

39. David K. Cohen, "Governance and Instruction: The Promise of Decentralization and Choice," in Clune and Witte, *Choice and Control in American Education,* 341.

7. Educational Outcomes as an Efficiency Issue

1. David H. Monk, *Educational Finance* (New York: McGraw-Hill, 1990), 323.

2. Office of Educational Research and Improvement, U.S. Department of Education, *Youth Indicators, 1991: Trends in the Well-Being of American Youth* (Washington: Government Printing Office, 1991), 75.

3. Ibid., 76.

4. Ibid., 66–67.

5. Diane Ravitch and Chester E. Finn, Jr., *What Do Our 17-Year-Olds Know?* (New York: Harper and Row, 1987), 43–84.

6. James S. Coleman, Thomas Hoffer, and Sally Kilgore, *High School Achievement* (New York: Basic Books, 1982), 188. See also James S. Coleman and Thomas Hoffer, *Public and Private High Schools* (New York: Basic Books, 1987); James S. Coleman, *Foundations of Social Theory* (Cambridge, Mass.: Harvard University Press, 1990); Daniel J. Singal, "The Other Crisis in Education," *Atlantic Monthly* (Nov. 1991), 59–74; and Charles Murray and R. J. Herrnstein, "What's Really Behind the SAT-Score Decline?" *Public Interest* (Winter 1992), 32–56.

7. Kathryn R. Wenzel, "Social Competence at School: Relation between Social Responsibility and Academic Achievement," *Review of Educational Research* 61 (Spring 1991), 1–24.

8. Ibid., 17.
9. I have used increased pregnancies and abortions as proxies for "increased sexual activity" to bring out the consequences of the latter. The direct evidence on "sexual activity" per se fully supports the analysis.
10. *Youth Indicators, 1991,* 112–113.
11. Ibid., 116.
12. Coleman, Hoffer, and Kilgore, *High School Achievement,* 188.
13. For examples see Henry M. Levin, "Education as a Public and Private Good," in Neal E. Devins, ed., *Public Values, Private Schools* (New York: Falmer Press, 1989), 215–234; and Gerald W. Bracey, "S.A.T. Scores: Miserable or Miraculous?" *Education Week,* Nov. 21, 1990, 36.
14. Coleman, Hoffer, and Kilgore, *High School Achievement,* 187.
15. Lloyd P. Jorgenson, *The Founding of Public Education in Wisconsin* (Madison: State Historical Society of Wisconsin, 1956), 114; E. G. West, *Education and the State* (London: Institute of Economic Affairs, 1970), 32–36.
16. John R. Lott, Jr., "Juvenile Delinquency and Education: A Comparison of Public and Private Provision," *International Review of Law and Economics* 7 (1987), 163–175.
17. Michael Krashinsky, "Why Educational Vouchers May Be Bad Economics," *Teachers College Record* 88 (Winter 1986), 139–151; response by Edwin G. West and rejoinder by Krashinsky, ibid., 152–167.
18. Henry M. Levin, "Education as a Public and Private Good," 220.
19. Ibid., 226.
20. Andrew M. Greeley and Peter Rossi, *The Education of Catholic Americans* (Chicago: Aldine, 1966). Greeley, a highly respected sociologist who is also a Catholic priest, concluded that certain kinds of religious education had no religious benefits and should be discontinued. His analysis engendered considerable dismay in church circles; pressure (unsuccessful) was brought to bear on him to weaken or withhold it. It would hardly appear, therefore, that the study was flawed by any pro-Catholic bias.
21. John R. Lott, Jr., "An Explanation for Public Provision of Schooling: The Importance of Indoctrination," *Journal of Law and Economics* 33 (April 1990), 199–231; and "Why Is Education Publicly Provided?" *Cato Journal* 7 (Fall 1987), 475–501.
22. Frederick H. Brigham, Jr., *United States Catholic Elementary and Secondary Schools, 1989–90* (Washington: National Catholic Education Association, 1990), 19.
23. Coleman and Hoffer, *Public and Private High Schools,* 118–148.
24. Alexander T. Smith, *Time and Public Policy* (Knoxville: University of Tennessee Press, 1989).
25. The $13,600 figure has no official source or sponsorship, but I regard it to be a reasonable estimate for the purpose at hand.

26. "At Union's Convention, 'Paradoxes' of Free Speech," *Education Week,* Aug. 31, 1991, 15.
27. New Business Item F, adopted by NEA's Representative Assembly, July 6, 1992.
28. *Choices: A Unit on Nuclear War* (Washington: NEA, 1983); Thomas Toch, *In the Name of Excellence* (New York: Oxford University Press, 1991), 153.
29. Carl Golden, *Organized Labor: Source Materials for the Study of Labor in America* (New York: United Federation of Teachers, 1991), 77.
30. *Steele v. Louisville & Nashville R.R.,* 323 U.S. 192 (1944).
31. Golden, *Organized Labor,* 77, 167.
32. Levin, "Education as a Public and Private Good," 252.
33. Robert J. Shiller, Maxim Boycko, and Vladimir Korobov, "Popular Attitudes towards Free Markets: The Soviet Union and the United States Compared," *American Economic Review* 81 (June 1991), 385–400.
34. Mancur Olson, "Comment," in Richard B. McKenzie, ed., *Constitutional Economics* (Lexington, Mass.: Lexington Books, 1984), 39.
35. Eric R. A. N. Smith, *The Unchanging American Voter* (Berkeley: University of California Press, 1989), 177–190.
36. Data from U.S. Bureau of the Census, Current Population Studies, *American National Election Studies,* 1956–1980.
37. Smith, *Unchanging American Voter,* 177–190, 214–215.
38. Nathan Glazer, *The Limits of Social Policy* (Cambridge, Mass.: Harvard University Press, 1989); Neal Gilbert, *Capitalism and the Welfare State* (New Haven, Conn.: Yale University Press, 1983); *America's Crisis at Home,* special ed. of *Policy Review* (Summer 1992).
39. Donald A. Erickson, "Disturbing Evidence about the 'One Best System,'" in Robert B. Everhart, ed., *The Public School Monopoly* (San Francisco: Pacific Research Institute for Public Policy, 1981), 393–422; and "Choice and Private Schools: Dynamics of Supply and Demand," in Daniel C. Levy, ed., *Private Education: Studies in Choice and Public Policy* (New York: Oxford University Press, 1986), 82–112. The Erickson study suggests that vouchers reduce parents' participation in their children's education. This outcome seems reasonable in the case of parents who provide all the support for private schooling prior to the vouchers; it probably does not apply to parents who provide none of it prior to voucher availability.
40. Lawrence M. Mead, "The New Politics of Poverty," *Public Interest* 103 (Spring 1991), 3–20.
41. Hans N. Weiler, "Comparative Perspectives on Educational Decentralization: An Exercise in Contradiction?" *Educational Evaluation and Policy Analysis* 12 (Winter 1990), 433–448.
42. John E. Chubb and Terry M. Moe, *Politics, Markets, and America's Schools* (Washington: Brookings Institution, 1990).

43. Building on the work of the economist Knut Wicksell, David H. Monk has proposed a complex solution to this problem within the framework of public education. For several good reasons, the proposal is very unlikely to be implemented. See Monk, *Educational Finance*, 119–121.

44. Education Writers Association, *Wolves at the Schoolhouse Door* (Washington: Education Writers Association, 1989).

45. Monk, *Educational Finance*, 24.

46. Leland B. Yeager, "Is There a Bias toward Overregulation?" in Tibor R. Machan and M. Bruce Johnson, eds., *Rights and Regulation* (San Francisco: Pacific Research Institute for Public Policy, 1983), 125.

47. Albert Shanker, "Where We Stand," advertisement, *New York Times*, Sept. 8, 1991, E7.

8. The Educational Consequences of Racial Conflict

1. Richard A. Epstein, *Forbidden Grounds* (Cambridge, Mass: Harvard University Press, 1992), 499–500. This book is a devastating critique of government intervention in employment under the guise of advancing "civil rights."

2. Abraham H. Foxman, National Director, ADL, "Statement on Race-Exclusive Scholarships," Dec. 19, 1990.

3. Hugh Davis Graham, *The Civil Rights Era: Origins and Development of National Policy* (New York: Oxford University Press, 1990).

4. *Green v. County School Board of New Kent County, Virginia*, 391 U.S. 430, 88 S.Ct. 1689 (1968).

5. Paul E. Peterson, *Are Big City Schools Holding Their Own?* (Cambridge, Mass.: Department of Government, Harvard University, 1991), 50.

6. "Where S.A.T. Scores Go," *Education Week*, May 8, 1991, 3.

7. Research Department, Minnesota House of Representatives, *Open Enrollment Study, Student and District Participation, 1989–90* (St. Paul, Feb. 1990); Abigail Thernstrom, *School Choice in Massachusetts* (Boston: Pioneer Institute for Public Policy Research, 1991); Ernest Boyer, *School Choice* (Princeton, N.J.: Carnegie Foundation for the Advancement of Teaching, 1992); and Myron Lieberman, *Public School Choice* (Lancaster, Pa.: Technomic Publishing, 1990), esp. 24–27.

8. Committee on Policy for Racial Justice, *Visions of a Better Way: A Black Appraisal of Public Schooling* (Washington: Joint Center for Political Studies, 1989), 36.

9. "Draft O.C.R. Memo Outlines Grounds for Probing Ability-Grouping Practices," *Education Week*, Feb. 20, 1991, 20–21.

10. Carolyn Riehl, Gary Natriello, and Aaron M. Pallas, "Losing Track: The Dynamics of Student Assignment Processes in High School," paper

presented at the 87th Annual Meeting of the American Sociological Association, Pittsburgh, Aug. 1992.

11. The most widely publicized academic study on the issue is Jeanne Oakes, *Keeping Track: How Schools Structure Inequality* (New Haven, Conn.: Yale University Press, 1985). According to Oakes, "What we can be quite sure of, in fact, is that the ability to learn is normally distributed, among and within social groups." This assertion is highly dubious and undermines the arguments against tracking insofar as they depend on its validity. See R. J. Herrnstein, "Still an American Dilemma," *Public Interest* 98 (Winter 1990), 3–17; Robert M. Hauser et al., "Understanding Black-White Differences," *Public Interest* 99 (Spring 1990), 110–119; and R. J. Herrnstein, "On Responsible Scholarship: A Rejoinder," ibid., 120–127. See also Samuel S. Wineburg, "The Self-Fulfillment of the Self-Fulfilling Prophecy," *Educational Researcher* (Dec. 1987), 28–37; Robert Rosenthal, "Pygmalion Effects: Existence, Magnitude, and Social Importance," ibid., 37–41; Ray C. Rist, "Do Teachers Count in the Lives of Children?" ibid., 41–42; and Samuel S. Wineburg, "Does Research Count in the Lives of Behavioral Scientists?" ibid., 42–44.

12. Daniel Gursky, "On the Wrong Track?" *Teacher Magazine* (May 1990), 47.

13. *Lau v. United States*, 414 U.S. 563 (1974).

14. Abigail Thernstrom, "Bilingual Miseducation," *Commentary* 89 (Feb. 1990), 46.

15. Ibid.; and Rosalie Pedalino Porter, *Forked Tongue: The Politics of Bilingual Education* (New York: Basic Books, 1990).

16. Ibid., p. 46.

17. Thernstrom, "Bilingual Education," 47.

18. Leonard P. Ayres, *Laggards in Our Schools* (New York: Russell Sage Foundation, 1908), 6.

19. Thernstrom, "Bilingual Education," 44–48; and Porter, *Forked Tongue*, discuss the evidence in detail. For a persuasive argument that bilingual education has negative effects on the self-esteem of Hispanic students, see Keith Baker and Susan Alexander, "Some Ethical Issues in Applied Social Psychology: The Case of Bilingual Education and Self-Esteem," paper presented at the 86th Annual Meeting of the American Sociological Association, Cincinnati, Aug. 1991. For a discussion of the politics of bilingual education, see Eleanor Chelimsky and Frederick Mulhauser, "Helping Congress to Sort out Conflicting Claims about the Research Evidence on Bilingual Education," in Steven S. Goldberg, ed., *Readings on Equal Education*, vol. 10 (New York: AMS Press, 1990), 247–267.

20. *Griggs v. Duke Power Company*, 401 U.S. 430 (1971). The most complete analysis of *Griggs* is to be found in Herman Belz, *Equality Transformed*

(New Brunswick, N.J.: Transaction Publishers, 1991), esp. 51–68; and Epstein, *Forbidden Grounds,* 159–241.

21. Belz, *Equality Transformed,* 59–68.
22. Epstein, *Forbidden Grounds,* 159–241.
23. Title VIII Amendments (Equal Employment Opportunity Act of 1972) extended Title VII of the Civil Rights Act of 1964 to state and local government and to educational institutions.
24. Committee on Policy for Racial Justice, *Visions of a Better Way,* 9, 35.
25. "Groups Aim to Block 'Stampede' to National Tests," *Education Week,* April 3, 1991, 5. The groups included the NAACP, the Mexican-American Legal Defense and Education Fund, the AASA, the NEA, FairTest, the National PTA, the National Association for the Education of Young Children, and the National Association of Elementary School Principals.
26. FairTest and New York Public Interest Research Center, *Standardized Tests and Our Children* (Cambridge, Mass.: National Center for Fair and Open Testing, 1990).
27. Willard S. Elsbree, H. R. Halsey, and Elizabeth S. Elsbree, *The Teacher's Handbook* (New York: Teachers College, Columbia University, 1929); Samuel S. Brooks, *Improving Schools by Standardized Tests* (Boston: Houghton Mifflin, 1922); Belz, *Equality Transformed,* 111–133.
28. See Elsbree, Halsey, and Elsbree, *Teacher's Handbook,* and Brooks, *Improving Schools.*
29. *Standardized Tests and Our Children,* 21.
30. See Elsbree, Halsey, and Elsbree, *Teacher's Handbook,* and Brooks, *Improving Schools.*
31. Epstein makes this point repeatedly; see *Forbidden Grounds,* 236–241.
32. Paul Copperman, *The Literacy Hoax* (New York: William Morrow, 1978).
33. A strong argument for affirmative action is to be found in Cass R. Sunstein, "Why Markets Don't Stop Discrimination," in Ellen Frankel Paul, Fred D. Miller, Jr., and Jeffrey Paul, eds., *Reassessing Civil Rights* (Oxford: Blackwell, 1991), 22–37. Also, although Belz is highly critical of the arguments for affirmative action, he summarizes them in *Equality Transformed,* 233–265.
34. For a strong argument that affirmative action inherently leads to quotas or reverse discrimination, see Michael Levin, *Feminism and Freedom* (New Brunswick, N.J.: Transaction Books, 1987), 98–130. Theory aside, concern that certain affirmative action policies would lead to quotas underlay the Bush administration's opposition to the Civil Rights and Sex Equity Act of 1991. Belz also argues this position in *Equality Transformed.*
35. *Regents of the University of California v. Bakke,* 438 U.S. 265 (1978).
36. For a comprehensive analysis of the issues raised by the Bakke case and

affirmative action, see Belz, *Equality Transformed;* Allan P. Sindler, *Bakke, DeFunis, and Minority Admissions* (New York: Longman, 1978); and Paul, Miller, and Paul, *Reassessing Civil Rights.*

37. *NEA Handbook, 1990–91* (Washington: NEA, 1990), 160–186. Quotations from constitution and bylaws: Articles III, sec. 6; IV, sec. 4; V, sec. 1(c); VI, sec. 1(c); VII, sec. 2; Bylaws 8–11(a); 10–5(c), 12–1(g).
38. Belz, Epstein, and Levin support this point of view in the references to their publications.
39. Mark Tushnet, "Change and Continuity in the Concept of Civil Rights: Thurgood Marshall and Affirmative Action," in Paul, Miller, and Paul, *Reassessing Civil Rights,* 151.
40. Ibid., 151–152.
41. Ibid., 157.
42. Ibid.
43. Linda F. Perkins, "The History of Blacks in Teaching," in Donald Warren, ed., *American Teachers* (New York: Macmillan, 1989), 349, 365–366.
44. Ibid., 365–366.

9. Equality of Educational Opportunity Reconsidered

1. Information on the costs of renal dialysis programs provided by officials of the End Stage Renal Disease (ESRD) program, U.S. Department of Health and Human Services, Aug. 27, 1991.
2. Research Division, NEA, *Estimates of School Statistics, 1990–91* (Washington: NEA, 1991), 21; National Center for Education Statistics, *The Condition of Education,* 1: *Elementary and Secondary Education* (Washington: Government Printing Office, 1990), 80–81.
3. Michael W. La Morte, "Courts Continue to Address the Wealth Disparity Issue," *Educational Evaluation and Policy Analysis* 11 (Spring 1989), 13–15.
4. *Rodriguez v. San Antonio Independent School District,* 411 U.S. 1, 93 S. Ct. 1278, rehearing denied, 411 U.U. 959, 93 S. Ct. 1919 (1973).
5. La Morte, "Courts Continue to Address the Wealth Disparity Issue," 3–15; Stephen M. Barro, "Fund Distribution Issues in School Finance: Priorities for the Next Round of Research," *Educational Evaluation and Policy Analysis* 11 (Spring 1989), 17–30; "23 States Face Suits on School Funds," *New York Times,* Sept. 2, 1992, B7.
6. E. G. West, *Education and the State* (London: Institute of Economic Affairs, 1962), 44–45.
7. Richard E. Wagner, *To Promote the General Welfare* (San Francisco: Pacific Research Institute for Public Policy, 1989), esp. 21–44.

8. I have not reviewed the literature on these issues, but several experts on politics and elections have informally concurred with these conclusions about black participation in politics.

9. One of the earliest to point this out was Patricia C. Sexton, *Education and Income* (New York: Viking Press, 1961).

10. Christopher Jencks, "What Must Be Equal for Opportunity to Be Equal?" in Norman E. Bowie, ed., *Equal Opportunity* (Boulder, Colo.: Westview Press, 1988).

11. James S. Coleman, "Equality and Excellence in Education," in H. J. O'Gorman, ed., *Surveying Social Life* (Middletown, Conn.: Wesleyan University Press, 1988), 376–392.

12. Ibid.

13. John Rawls, *A Theory of Justice* (Cambridge, Mass.: Harvard University Press, 1971).

14. Robert L. Hampel, "Historical Perspectives on Academic Work: The Origins of Learning," paper presented at a Conference on Student Motivation, Office of Educational Research and Improvement, U.S. Department of Education, Nov. 1990.

15. National Center for Education Statistics, *Projections of Education Statistics to 2001: An Update* (Washington: Government Printing Office, 1991), 6.

16. *Women and Minorities in Science and Engineering* (Washington: National Science Foundation, Jan. 1990), 136–137, 144–145; National Center for Education Statistics, *Who Majors in Science?* (Washington: Government Printing Office, June 1990); Abigail Thernstrom, "On the Scarcity of Black Professors," *Commentary* 90 (July 1990), 22–26.

17. Robert Rector, "Poverty in U.S. Is Exaggerated by Census," *Wall Street Journal,* Sept. 25, 1990, A22.

18. Price V. Fishback, "Can Competition among Employers Reduce Governmental Discrimination? Coal Companies and Segregated Schools in West Virginia in the Early 1900s," *Journal of Law and Economics* 32 (Oct. 1989), 311–328.

19. Gunnar Myrdal, *An American Dilemma: The Negro Problem in American Education* (New York: Harper and Row, 1944), 888.

20. Robert A. Margot, "Segregated Schools and the Mobility Hypothesis: A Model of Local Government Discrimination," *Quarterly Journal of Economics* 106 (Feb. 1991), 61–73.

21. Cass R. Sunstein, "Why Markets Don't Stop Discrimination," in Ellen Frankel Paul, Fred D. Miller, Jr., and Jeffrey Paul, eds., *Reassessing Civil Rights* (Oxford: Basil Blackwell, 1991), 22–37.

22. Douglas Rae, *Equalities* (Cambridge, Mass.: Harvard University Press, 1981).

360 ≈ Notes to Pages 228–236

23. For a strong argument that efforts to equalize outcomes are leading to harmful state intervention across a broad range of public policies, see Aaron Wildavsky, "A World of Difference: The Public Philosophies and Political Behaviors of Rival American Cultures," in Anthony King, ed., *The New American Political System*, 2d ed. (Washington: AEI Press, 1990), 263–286.
24. For a penetrating analysis of these and other problems growing out of efforts to equalize services, see Wagner, *To Promote the General Welfare*.

10. The Impact of Higher Education on the Public Schools

1. National Center for Education Statistics, *Projections of Education Statistics to 2000* (Washington: Office of Educational Research and Improvement, U.S. Department of Education, Dec. 1989). The figures for 1989–90 are estimates by NCES.
2. John D. McNeill, *Curriculum: A Comprehensive Introduction*, 4th ed. (Glenview, Ill.: Scott Foresman/Little, Brown, 1990), 199–200.
3. Margaret Gourtz and Linda F. Johnson, *State Policies for Admission to Higher Education* (New York: College Entrance Examination Board, 1985), 3.
4. James S. Coleman, "Equality and Excellence in Education," in Hubert J. O'Gorman, ed., *Surveying Social Life: Essays in Honor of Herbert Hyman* (Middletown, Conn.: Wesleyan University Press, 1988), 384. See also Charles Murray and R. J. Herrnstein, "What's Really Behind the SAT-Score Decline?" *Public Interest* (Winter 1992), 32–56. For an excellent account of how U.S. institutions of higher education contributed to the deterioration in K–12 education, see Robert L. Hampel, "Historical Perspectives on Academic Work: The Origins of Learning," presented at a Conference on Student Motivation, Office of Educational Research and Improvement, U.S. Department of Education, Nov. 1990.
5. *Education Week*, Nov. 13, 1991, 9.
6. Information provided by Barbara Zahn, Minnesota State Department of Education, Aug. 27, 1991.
7. "Preview 1990," *Sports Illustrated*, 63–71.
8. ETS study cited in Richard E. Lapchick, *Pass to Play: Student Athletes and Academics* (Washington: NEA, 1989), 13.
9. "Prep Schools' Use of Transfer Players in Sports May Lead to Success, but Often Raises Eyebrows," *Education Week*, April 24, 1991, 6–7.
10. Lapchick, *Pass to Play*.
11. C. James Quann, *Grades and Grading* (Washington: American Association of Collegiate Registrars and Admission Officers, 1984). For an early

and penetrating analysis of grade inflation in both K–12 and higher education, see Paul Copperman, *The Literacy Hoax* (New York: William Morrow, 1978), esp. 103–117.

12. Quann, *Grades and Grading.*

13. National Center for Education Statistics, *Education Statistics: A Pocket Guide, 1990* (Washington: OERI, U.S. Department of Education, March 1991).

14. "Ivy League Schools Agree to Halt Collaboration on Financial Aid," *Washington Post,* May 23, 1991, A-3.

15. Myron Lieberman, *Privatization and Educational Choice* (New York: St. Martin's Press, 1989), 184–186.

16. "MIT Ruled Guilty in Antitrust Case," *New York Times,* Sept. 3, 1992, A1, B10.

17. National Center for Education Statistics, *Characteristics of Stayers, Movers, and Leavers: Results from the Teacher Follow-up Survey, 1988–89* (Washington: Government Printing Office, June 1991), 3.

18. Lynne V. Cheney, *American Memory* (Washington: Government Printing Office, 1988).

19. John Stuart Mill, *On Liberty* (1859; London: Oxford University Press, 1966), 132.

20. *RATE III: Teaching Teachers: Facts and Figures* (Washington: American Association of Colleges for Teacher Education, 1990), 39–40.

21. *Teacher Education Policy in the States* (Washington: American Association of Colleges for Teacher Education, Dec. 1990), xi.

22. Burton R. Clark, "The High School and the University," *Phi Delta Kappan* 66 (Feb. 1985), 391–397.

23. For a more extensive discussion of faculty self-government, see Myron Lieberman, "Peer Review and Faculty Self Government: A Dissenting View," in Waris Shere and Ronald Duhamel, eds., *Academic Futures* (Toronto: Ontario Institute for Educational Studies, 1987), 79–92. The inefficiencies of faculty self-government are documented in Robert E. McCormick and Roger E. Meiners, "University Governance: A Property Rights Perspective," *Journal of Law and Economics* 31 (Oct. 1988), 440.

24. Bertrand de Jouvenal, "The Treatment of Capitalism by Continental Intellectuals," in F. A. Hayek, ed., *Capitalism and the Historians* (Chicago: University of Chicago Press, 1954), 91–122.

25. William Warren Bartley III, *Unfathomed Knowledge, Unmeasured Wealth* (La Salle, Ill.: Open Court, 1990), ch. 7.

26. Ben Wildavsky, "McJobs: Inside America's Largest Youth Training Program," *Policy Review* (Summer 1989), 30–37.

27. Ronald H. Coase, "The Market for Ideas," *National Review,* Sept. 27, 1974, 1096.

11. Educational Research and Development

1. Richard M. Cyert and David C. Mowery, eds., *Technology and Employment,* Report of the Panel on Technology and Employment, Committee on Science, Engineering, and Public Policy (Washington: National Academy Press, 1987), 24–50.

2. Lawrence A. Cremin, *American Education: The National Experience* (New York: Harper and Row, 1980).

3. Martin Anderson, *Impostors in the Temple* (New York: Simon and Schuster, 1992), 168–179.

4. Education Writers Association, *Wolves at the School House Door* (Washington: Education Writers Association, 1989).

5. Gerald E. Sroufe, testimony before the House Appropriations Subcommittee on Labor, HHS and Education, May 19, 1990, 2.

6. On educational research see Myron Lieberman, "Research and the Renewal of Education: A Critical Review," *Education Week,* June 16, 1991, 44, 34. On university research generally, see James S. Coleman, *Foundations of Social Theory* (Cambridge, Mass.: Harvard University Press, 1990), 615–649; and William Warren Bartley III, *Unfathomed Knowledge, Unmeasured Wealth* (La Salle, Ill.: Open Court, 1990).

7. *RATE II: Teaching Teachers: Facts and Figures* (Washington: American Association of Colleges for Teacher Education, 1988); *RATE III: Facts and Figures* (1990).

8. James S. Coleman et al., *Equality of Educational Opportunity* (Washington: Government Printing Office, 1966).

9. The computation was as follows: 35,000 (number of professors of education) × $50,000 (average annual compensation: $40,000 salary + 25% fringe benefits) = $1,750,000,000. This amount + $875,000,000 (overhead at 50%) = $2,625,000,000. This amount × 14% (portion of faculty time devoted to research) = $374,500,000 (dollar value of faculty time devoted to educational research).

10. National Center for Education Statistics, *The Condition of Education 1990,* 2: *Postsecondary Education* (Washington: Government Printing Office, 1990), 154.

11. This figure is based on the NEA estimate of the average annual salary for instructional staff ($35,905, rounded to $36,000) plus my own estimate, based on several sources, of 25 percent for fringe benefits. I assumed that the average student working on a dissertation could command the average teacher salary. NEA Research Division, *Estimates of School Statistics, 1991–92* (Washington: NEA, 1992), 22.

12. See *Research and the Renewal of Education* (Stanford, Calif.: National Academy of Education, Stanford University, 1991), 18; and Lieberman, "Research and the Renewal of Education."

13. John E. Chubb and Terry M. Moe, *Politics, Markets, and America's Schools* (Washington: Brookings Institution, 1990).

14. *1990 Annual Report* (Princeton, N.J.: Educational Testing Service, 1990), 39–40.

15. David F. Kearns and Dennis P. Doyle, *Winning the Brain Race* (San Francisco: ICS Press, 1988), 142–143.

16. Lewis J. Perelman, *School's Out* (New York: William Morrow, 1992).

17. Henry Kelly, *Technology and the American Economic Transition: Choices for the Future* (Washington: Office of Technology Assessment, 1988).

18. Perelman, *School's Out,* 216. Italics in original.

19. Ibid., 218.

20. Ibid., 219.

21. Ibid., 225. Despite our agreement on the point of the quotation, I regard Perelman's proposals on the subject as highly unrealistic.

22. Coleman, *Foundations of Social Theory,* 615–649.

23. Ibid., 642, 645.

24. Memorandum to Members, LEARN, Office of the Superintendent, Los Angeles, USD, July 26, 1991, pointing out "moves toward reform and restructuring."

25. William Hurrell Mallock, *A Critical Examination of Socialism* (1908; New Brunswick, N.J.: Transaction Publishers, 1988), 82–85.

26. James S. Coleman, "A Quiet Threat to Academic Freedom," *National Review,* March 18, 1991, 28–34.

27. See Myron Lieberman, *Privatization and Educational Choice* (New York: St. Martin's Press, 1989), 85–105.

28. Coleman, *Foundations of Social Theory,* 647–649.

29. *Research and the Renewal of Education,* 8.

30. Ibid., 23.

31. Ibid., 5–6, 45–60.

32. Ibid., 17–19.

33. Ibid., 10.

34. Ibid., 25.

35. Ibid., 8.

12. The Educational Agenda and Its Problems

1. Max Geldens, "Toward Fuller Employment," *Economist,* July 1984, 19–22.

2. For an excellent summary of the political influence of the NEA, see Thomas Toch, *In the Name of Excellence* (New York: Oxford University Press, 1991), 152–155. See also Mario M. Cuomo, *Diaries of Mario M. Cuomo: The Race for Governor* (New York: Random House, 1983), for an example of AFT political influence.

3. The analysis here follows Mancur Olson, Jr., *The Logic of Collective Action* (Cambridge, Mass.: Harvard University Press, 1965).

4. For a summary of conflicting private school positions on voucher issues, see Charles J. O'Malley, "Diversity of Private Education: Strength or Weakness?" paper available from the author, 4301 Adrienne Drive, Alexandria, Va. 22309.

5. NEA Research Division, *Estimates of School Statistics, 1990–91* (Washington: NEA, 1991), 37.

6. For an excellent discussion of this point with voluminous references, see *Humane Studies Review* 7 (Winter 1991/92).

7. 268 U.S. 510 (1925).

8. Based on exit poll data reported in the *New York Times,* Nov. 18, 1991, B6.

9. Myron Lieberman, *Public School Choice* (Lancaster, Pa.: Technomic Publishing, 1990), 102–103.

10. Office of Planning, Budget and Evaluation, U.S. Department of Education, *Reducing Student Loan Defaults: A Plan for Action* (Washington, n.d.).

11. David W. Steward and Henry A. Spille, *Diploma Mills* (New York: Macmillan, 1988).

12. *Reducing Student Loan Defaults,* 3.

13. Ibid., 12.

14. Mark L. Mitchell and Michael T. Maloney, "Crisis in the Cockpit? The Role of Market Forces in Promoting Air Travel Safety," *Journal of Law and Economics* 32 (Oct. 1989), 329–335.

15. Myron Lieberman, "School Choice: A Tragicomedy of Errors," *Education Week,* Dec. 9, 1992, 25.

13. The Transition Solution

1. An exception to my critique of the role of conservatives is Edwin C. Banfield's *The Unheavenly City* (Boston: Little, Brown, 1970), 132–157; however, Banfield did not discuss market approaches to education.

2. "Remarks by the President to the White House Workshop on Choice in Education," Jan. 10, 1989; "Excerpts of Remarks by President-elect George Bush to the White House Workshop on Choice in Education," Jan. 10, 1989 (Washington: Office of the Press Secretary, The Vice President).

3. U.S. Department of Education, *Choosing a School for Your Child* (Washington: Government Printing Office, 1989).

4. Donald Lambro, "Political Shifts on Education's Battlefield," *Washington Times,* Sept. 27, 1990, B4. Sources that characterized public school choice as a market process include John A. Fund, "Champion of

Choice," *Reason* (Oct. 1990), 38–40; "Consumerism Comes to the Schoolyard," *Newsweek*, Sept. 19, 1988, 77. Many others who characterized public school choice as a competitive market process are cited in Myron Lieberman, *Public School Choice* (Lancaster, Pa.: Technomic Publishing, 1990).

5. Lieberman, *Public School Choice*, 9–22.

6. All the figures for Minnesota are from *Open Enrollment Study, Student and District Participation, 1989–90* (St. Paul: Research Department, Minnesota House of Representatives, Feb. 1990), and telephone discussions with Susan Urahn, Legislative Analyst, House Research Department, Aug. 27, 1991.

7. David F. Kearns and Dennis P. Doyle, *Winning the Brain Race* (San Francisco: Institute for Contemporary Studies Press, 1988).

8. Mario D. Fantini, *Public Schools of Choice* (New York: Simon and Schuster, 1973).

9. See Myron Lieberman, *Privatization and Educational Choice* (New York: St. Martin's Press, 1989), 234–242. I and several other analysts had frequently expressed this view in prior years. In fact, my astonishment that the Bush administration considered public school choice to be a major policy initiative was one of the reasons I wrote *Public School Choice*, a book that details why the policy can be only a marginal reform at best.

10. See Lieberman, *Privatization and Educational Choice*, for a discussion of the issues related to contracting out.

11. See the appropriate provisions in the collective bargaining contracts between the NEA and the NEA Staff Organization (NEASO), June 1, 1988–May 31, 1991; and June 1, 1991–May 31, 1994.

12. For an analysis of the issues with citations to the relevant cases, see Edwin Vierira, Jr., "*Communications Workers of America v. Beck:* A Victory for Nonunion Employees Already under Attack," *Government Union Review* 11 (Spring 1990), 1–29. In 1992 the National Labor Relations Board voted to conduct public hearings prior to adopting rules governing agency shop issues. Although NLRB rules will not be directly applicable to teacher unions, they are likely to affect the teacher unions indirectly and adversely.

13. Leo Troy, "Why Canadian Public Sector Unionism Is Strong," *Government Union Review* 11 (Summer 1990), 1–32. Troy points out that private-sector unionization is declining vis-a-vis public-sector unions in all Western industrial democracies. A study released by the Organisation for Economic Cooperation and Development in July 1991 found that union membership among OECD countries decreased by 5 million in the 1980s. The largest declines were in the United States, the United King-

dom, and France. Bureau of National Affairs, *Daily Labor Report,* Aug. 12, 1991, A11–12.

14. Lloyd P. Jorgenson, *The State and the Non-Public School, 1825–1925* (Columbia: University of Missouri Press, 1987).

15. Frank A. Sloan, "Property Rights in the Hospital Industry," in H. E. Frech III, ed., *Health Care in America* (San Francisco: Pacific Research Institute for Public Policy, 1988), 103–144.

16. Information provided by NEA and AFT in response to my telephone requests in Oct. 1992.

Epilogue

1. "Yale President Quits to Lead Private School Project," *Financial Times,* May 27, 1992, 1.

2. National Academy of Education, *Research and the Renewal of Education* (Stanford, Calif.: National Academy of Education, Stanford University, 1991).

3. For a comprehensive critique of NASDC, see Lewis J. Perelman, *School Is Out* (New York: William Morrow, 1992).

4. Jonathan Kozol, quoted in *Education Week,* June 3, 1992, 1.

5. *The Edison Project,* brochure disseminated by Whittle Communications, Feb. 27, 1992, 12.

6. Communication from Rodney Ferguson, The Edison Project, Dec. 1, 1992.

7. Myron Lieberman, *Beyond Public Education* (Westport, Conn.: Praeger, 1988), 236.

8. Certified notice to "All County Clerks/Registrar of Voters," from March Fong Eu, Secretary of State, State of California, Aug. 20, 1992.

9. Memorandum from Jeanne Allen, Heritage Foundation, to "Dear Colleague," July 10, 1991.

10. Letter from Milton Friedman to Jeanne Allen, Aug. 13, 1991, 3.

11. My account of the Coons/Sugarman withdrawal from EXCEL is based on telephone discussions with EXCEL leaders Joseph F. Alibrandi and Mike Ford and a presentation by John Coons at the AERA convention in San Francisco, April 23, 1992.

12. The incident is discussed in Milton Friedman, *Parental Choice: The Effective Way to Improve Schooling,* presentation to the Commonwealth Club of California, San Francisco, Aug. 7, 1992, 7–8. Friedman's presentation is also the source for my figures on the initiative petition.

13. D. A. (Del) Weber, "Triumph and Uncertainty: California Issues and the NEA," memorandum distributed by the CTA to the 1992 NEA Representative Assembly, Washington, July 1992.

≈ Index

367

College admissions, 231–236

College Board, 233

Columbia Broadcasting System (CBS), 80–81

Columbia University, 239

Commentary, 298

Committee for Economic Development (CED), 92

Committee for Education Funding (CEF), 102–105

Committee on Policy for Racial Justice, 179, 181, 188, 357

Communication Workers of America v. Beck, 365

Competition, 4–10, 40–42, 202–203, 225, 276, 286–289, 308, 317–318

Compulsory education, 26, 54–55, 209, 274

Condoms, 36–38, 95–97, 310–311. *See also* Heterogeneity; Sex education; Social conflict

Con Edison, 184

Conservatives, 297–303, 305, 309, 314–316. *See also* Bush administration; Democratic party; Politics of education; Reagan administration, Republican party

Contracting out, 63–64, 267, 276, 277, 302–303, 305. *See also* Privatization of education

Contracts for educational services, 290

Contributed services, 119, 129–135, 136

Coons, John, 333–335, 366

Cooper, Bruce S., 342

Cooperative learning, 2, 181–182

Cornell University, 239

Copperman, Paul, 192, 348, 357

Costs of education, 114–142, 276, 277, 279–288; adult education, 127; capital outlay and interest, 120–121; in Catholic schools, 116–118, 121, 124–125; and collective bargaining, 125; contributed services, 129–135; corporate provision of, 123–124; definitional problems, 122; depreciation, 121; double counting of, 127–128; educational R&D, 125; and efficiency, 114–115; faculty time,

118, 125; family-paid, 128–129; in market system, 114–115, 118; per-pupil costs, 115; professional organizations, 128; and pupil characteristics, 117; remedial education, 123–124; school security, 117–118; special education, 117, 155–157; teacher retirement, 127; teacher training, 124–125; transition costs, 279–288; transportation, 139–141; understatement of, 118–136

Council on Exceptional Children, 182

Cowen, Tyler, 342

Craver, James M., 346

Creighton University, 234

Cremin, Lawrence A., 362

Crime, juvenile, 38–40

Cuomo, Mario M., 363

Curriculum, 157–159, 164–166, 275, 292; in Catholic schools, 152–155; conflict over, 95–97, 310–311; controversial issues in, 157–159; in public and private schools, 152–155; role of teacher unions, 158–159; multicultural, 164–166, 275

Custodial services, 155–157, 275

Cyert, Richard M., 344, 362

Dartmouth University, 239

Day care, 55–56

Democratic party, 282, 312, 338–339. *See also* Politics of education

de Jouvenal, Bertrand, 246–247, 248

Demographic factors, 17–25; aging of the population, 3; birth rates, 17–21; crime, 38–40; divorce, 27–28; ethnic changes, 19; family structure, 25–27; feminism, 32–36; and social capital, 25–32; urbanization, 28

Dennison, S. R., 342

Denominational schools, 15, 310–312. *See also* Catholic schools; Private schools

Depreciation, 121

Devins, Neal A., 353

Dewey, John, 248

DeYoung, Alan J., 342

Dirksen, Everett, 122

Disparate impact, 185–192, 275